TRANSFIGURED NOT CONFORMED

T&T Clark Enquiries in Theological Ethics

Series editors

Brian Brock
Susan F. Parsons

TRANSFIGURED NOT CONFORMED

Christian Ethics in a Hermeneutic Key

Hans G. Ulrich

Edited by Brian Brock

LONDON • NEW YORK • OXFORD • NEW DELHI • SYDNEY

T&T CLARK
Bloomsbury Publishing Plc
50 Bedford Square, London, WC1B 3DP, UK
1385 Broadway, New York, NY 10018, USA
29 Earlsfort Terrace, Dublin 2, Ireland

BLOOMSBURY, T&T CLARK and the T&T Clark logo are trademarks of Bloomsbury Publishing Plc

First published in Great Britain 2022
Paperback edition published 2023

Copyright © Hans G. Ulrich and Brian Brock, 2022

Hans G. Ulrich and Brian Brock have asserted their right under the Copyright, Designs and Patents Act, 1988, to be identified as Authors of this work.

For legal purposes the Acknowledgments on pp. ix-x constitute an extension of this copyright page.

All rights reserved. No part of this publication may be reproduced or transmitted in any form or by any means, electronic or mechanical, including photocopying, recording, or any information storage or retrieval system, without prior permission in writing from the publishers.

Bloomsbury Publishing Plc does not have any control over, or responsibility for, any third-party websites referred to or in this book. All internet addresses given in this book were correct at the time of going to press. The author and publisher regret any inconvenience caused if addresses have changed or sites have ceased to exist, but can accept no responsibility for any such changes.

A catalogue record for this book is available from the British Library.

Library of Congress Cataloging-in-Publication Data
Names: Ulrich, Hans Günter, author. | Brock, Brian, 1970- editor.
Title: Transfigured not conformed : Christian ethics in a hermeneutic key / Hans G. Ulrich, Brian Brock, ed.
Description: London ; New York : Bloomsbury Academic, 2021. | Series: T&T Clark enquiries in theological ethics | Includes bibliographical references and index. |
Identifiers: LCCN 2021013489 (print) | LCCN 2021013490 (ebook) | ISBN 9780567700414 (hb) | ISBN 9780567703811 (paperback) | ISBN 9780567699992 (epdf) | ISBN 9780567699985 (epub)
Subjects: LCSH: Christian ethics. | Christian life.
Classification: LCC BJ1191 .U47 2021 (print) | LCC BJ1191 (ebook) | DDC 241–dc23
LC record available at https://lccn.loc.gov/2021013489
LC ebook record available at https://lccn.loc.gov/2021013490

ISBN: HB: 978-0-5677-0041-4
PB: 978-0-5677-0381-1
ePDF: 978-0-5676-9999-2
ePUB: 978-0-5676-9998-5

Series: T&T Clark Enquiries in Theological Ethics

Typeset by Deanta Global Publishing Services, Chennai, India

To find out more about our authors and books visit www.bloomsbury.com and sign up for our newsletters.

CONTENTS

List of Abbreviations	viii
Acknowledgments	ix
INTRODUCTION	1
Biographical Background	1
Theological Trajectories	12
Publication History	16
Outline of This Volume	19
A Reader's Guide	21

Part I
A CHRISTIAN ETHICS OF MESSIANIC PRESENCE (*ECCLESIA*)

Chapter 1
THE MESSIANIC CONTOURS OF EVANGELICAL ETHICS

THE MESSIANIC CONTOURS OF EVANGELICAL ETHICS	27
Why Freedom? The Protestant Grammar of the Christian Ethos	28
Distinguishing between Apocalyptic Event and Messianic Time	39
The Ethos of Messianic Time	42
The Witness of Broken Indeterminacy	48

Chapter 2
ETHICAL LIFE: THE FORM AND ITS FORMS ACCORDING TO BONHOEFFER

ETHICAL LIFE: THE FORM AND ITS FORMS ACCORDING TO BONHOEFFER	51
The Bonhoeffer Phenomenon and the Grammar of His Theology	51
The Forms of Ethical Life	65
The Mandates: Prefigured Forms of Human Life	72
The Secret and the Understanding	78

Chapter 3
EXPLORATIVE THEOLOGY: DISCOVERY AND DISCERNMENT

EXPLORATIVE THEOLOGY: DISCOVERY AND DISCERNMENT	82
Research: *ars inveniendi*	84
Theological Research—Explorative Theology	94

The Ways of Discernment	96
The Ways of Judgment	97
God's Acts and the Wisdom to Discern God's Acts	105

Part II
CHRISTIAN WITNESS IN THE WORLD (*POLITIA*)

Chapter 4
THE PUBLIC APPEARANCE OF RELIGION: GOD'S COMMANDMENTS AND THEIR POLITICAL PRESENCE

THE PUBLIC APPEARANCE OF RELIGION: GOD'S COMMANDMENTS AND THEIR POLITICAL PRESENCE	111
Ethics in Traditions: In Lutheran Perspective	111
The Public Presence of Religion in Society	115
Law for the People: Understanding the *Conditio Humana* in Its Political Form	122
Human Law	131
On the "Ground" of Ethics: Ruled by the Spirit	137

Chapter 5
HUMAN ECONOMIES AT THEIR LIMITS, BUT GOVERNED WITHIN THEIR LIMITS

HUMAN ECONOMIES AT THEIR LIMITS, BUT GOVERNED WITHIN THEIR LIMITS	140
Economy and Theology: Three Approaches	142
Institutional Configurations: Limits of Economy, Limits for Economy	155

Chapter 6
ADOPTION: A THEOLOGICAL ACCOUNT OF POLITICAL RESPONSIBILITY TO ENTRUSTED LIVES

ADOPTION: A THEOLOGICAL ACCOUNT OF POLITICAL RESPONSIBILITY TO ENTRUSTED LIVES	160
Children and Human Rights	164
Children: God's Heritage	167
Unfolding Creaturely Life as Encountering God's Work within His Story	174

Part III
RECEIVING GIVEN LIFE (*OECONOMIA*)

Chapter 7
GOD'S STORY AND ENGELHARDT'S BIOETHICS: CHRISTIAN WITNESS IN MODERN MEDICINE

GOD'S STORY AND ENGELHARDT'S BIOETHICS: CHRISTIAN WITNESS IN MODERN MEDICINE	179
The Inability of Reason to Engineer the Human	182
How Christian Hope Relates to the "World" Even in Modern Times	191
Witnessing Another World to the World	200

Chapter 8
A THEOLOGICAL-CRITICAL HERMENEUTICS OF LIFE: ENGAGING
    GENETIC SCIENCE   206
    Beyond Moral Questions, to Seek the Good: Exploring
        Nature's Goodness   217
    Further Topics: Changing Ethical Approaches and Questions   225

Chapter 9
GOD'S TRANSFIGURING PRESENCE: NEWLY CREATED IN THE
    PRESENCE OF DISABLED PEOPLE   230
    Translocation   235
    The Transfiguration of Bodily Existence   242
    God's Reality and Story: Embodiment   251

Ulrich Publication List   267
Bibliography   287
Index   303

ABBREVIATIONS

CD	Karl Barth. *Church Dogmatics*. Edinburgh: T&T Clark, 1956–75.
DBWE	*Dietrich Bonhoeffer Works (English)*. Minneapolis: Fortress Press, 1995–2014.
DBWE 1	*Sanctorum Communio*
DBWE 3	*Creation and Fall*
DBWE 4	*Discipleship*
DBWE 6	*Ethics*
DBWE 8	*Letters and Papers from Prison*
LW	*Luther's Works*. American edn. St. Louis: Concordia, 1955–86

ACKNOWLEDGMENTS

Hans Ulrich: This book came about through the initiative of, and intensive collaboration with, Brian Brock. This book is just as much Brian's book, and in special respects, he is its coauthor, given our theological cooperation since his study visit in Erlangen (2003–4). Brian had the idea for the title, and he realized the significance of the book for the theological understanding between languages and traditions, and thus also for the theological grammar employed in this book. In his introduction, moreover, Brian expanded on his own perspective, which shows clearly that theological work moves within a tradition that is also interwoven with history and the stories, like mine, narrated by Brian in the introduction, embedded in that tradition.

Brian developed the outline and the structure, crafting a coherent book out of the texts that were previously given as talks on various occasions. This was made possible only by Brian's linguistic and stylistic revision of all of the texts, with a great understanding of meaning and significance, to ensure theological understanding in comprehensible English. No words of gratitude could be too much. This truly is also his book.

My special thanks also go to Susan Parsons, who initiated a very stimulating discussion about the basic tenet of the book, which we then conducted, not least with regard to the question in which sense theological ethics follow a certain "humanism" or, as I believe, rather the matter of man in his life with God, which is not absorbed in any humanistic concept.

My gratitude for this book goes in equal measure to all those with whom I have exchanged theological ideas intensively over many years, with a range of theologians from the English-speaking context such as Oliver O'Donovan, Stanley Hauerwas, Mike Mawson, Philip Ziegler, and then in a special manner with my wife, Karin Ulrich-Eschemann, with Gerhard Sauter, Peter Dabrock, Urs Espeel, Eberhard Hadem, Gerard den Hertog, Stefan Heuser, Reinhard Hütter, Marco Hofheinz Johannes von Lüpke, Roland Pelikan, Johannes Rehm, Ingrid and Wolfgang Schoberth, Jochen Teuffel, Jaroslav Vokoun, and Bernd Wannenwetsch. I am particularly grateful to Walter Doerfler as an invaluable interlocutor in discussing genetics and molecular biology, a field that has become increasingly important for ethics. I must express much more than formal thanks to Robert Heimburger, who compiled the bibliography with the utmost care.

Since, as Brian Brock indicates in his introduction, this book belongs to a particular tradition of theological work, it is promisingly allowed to ask how this tradition—and with it, theological ethics—is carried forward. I thank my wife, Karin Ulrich-Eschemann, and her theological work and practical sermons, for redirecting the focus onto the tradition as it is passed on in worship in the series of witnesses. In the grounded hope that the story will continue, I dedicate this book to our children Christine Ulrich and Eva Marie Ulrich-Riedhammer, both of whom are also engaged actively with "ethics," to our children-in-law Sebastian Riedhammer and Stefan Schwarz, and to our grandchildren, Marta Noemi, Lotte Frida, Jonathan, and Benjamin. With the same hope I dedicate this book to Stephanie and Brian Brock's children, Adam, Caleb, and Agnes.

Brian Brock: Thanks to the Department of Divinity, History and Philosophy at the University of Aberdeen, first for awarding research support in the form of Dr. Kenny Laing, who undertook a first round of formatting the many raw files from which this manuscript was comprised. The further award of regular research assistance took form in Dr. Robert Heimburger, who not only conscientiously text edited the whole manuscript but assembled the index. Thanks also to Susan Parsons, who made extremely helpful suggestions on the whole draft, as did Amy J. Erickson, Jon Coutts, Arne Rasmussen, and Michael Mawson. Finally, this book has been for me an expression of gratitude to Hans Ulrich, who was unstintingly welcoming during my time studying with him in Erlangen in 2003–4. Never one to talk about himself, I am acutely aware what a gift it was for him to spend two long days with me at his home in November 2019 telling me his story and answering my barrage of clarifying questions. I am sure I am not the only one who will find the story I now can tell in the introduction riveting.

INTRODUCTION

Brian Brock

Hans Günter Ulrich is, unfortunately, not widely known in the English-speaking world. This is in part because it is only with his final major work, *Wie Geschöpfe Leben*, that English-speaking theologians have become aware of his work. *Geschöpfe* is, however, a mountain that appears to many newcomers who have heard rumor that it is worth climbing as a sheer and unclimbable wall. This volume of Ulrich's late essays can be considered foothills from which beginners can at least glimpse the summits of his major works. After outlining Ulrich's biography and intellectual influences, this introduction will briefly summarize those major works. The main content of the volume is a collection of Ulrich's late essays, chosen to put on display the main lines of Ulrich's theological approach, which can be characterized as a unique combination of critical theory and a theology of divine presence.

Biographical Background

Ulrich was born on November 5, 1942, in a busy port city in northeastern Germany, at the time the third largest city in the country. Stettin was the city's name at the time of his birth, but the catastrophe soon to arrive would see it ceded to Poland and renamed Szczecin. Hans was his mother Luise's second son. Hans's father, Johannes, was a businessman working in trade related to the port, a profession that, even to this late stage of the war, had been exempted from the draft. With the stalling of Hitler's great push to Stalingrad, however, the Wehrmacht was becoming ever more desperate for soldiers. The last draft exemptions began to be revoked, and Johannes's number came up in in 1943. Johannes was sent to the Italian front as a military policeman and given the task of hunting German deserters far behind the battle line. It was highly dangerous work, as partisans (guerrilla fighters) had become very active—and effective—in Italy. In 1944 a partisan bullet felled Johannes. In his letters home he confesses that he had never fired a shot.

Before the war, the family had been comfortably well off, but Johannes's conscription left Luise in a vulnerable position soon to become desperate. Now a widow with two small boys and pregnant with a third child, she knew she had to leave a city that was to be decimated by Allied air raids by 1944. Packing her valuables, she prepared to travel to the other end of Germany, to stay with her parents, a retired schoolteacher and his wife. Christian and Sofie Meyer lived in a small village in Franconia, at the southern edge of central Germany. More disaster struck during the move, as the family's furniture and valuables that Luise had sent ahead were lost as the ship carrying them was sunk. The large house in Stettin was also lost in the confiscation of property that accompanied the expulsion of German citizens during this time. Luise's third child, a girl, was born 1944, in Franconia, never to meet her father. The war had been disastrous for a couple who had never supported it nor joined the Nazi Party (NSDAP).

Life as a displaced person in Franconia for the newly widowed Luise was to be markedly different than the comfortably middle-class existence in Stettin. Hans's grandparents and the inhabitants of Franconia were welcoming and supportive at a time when refugees, widows, and their children were almost too numerous to count in Germany, and the government's social support system little more than a plan in the infancy of implementation. Neither did the Lutheran Church's relatively developed diaconal network have the capacity to feed the masses of destitute families displaced by the war. These would not be hungry years in the Ulrich household, since Franconia was one of Germany's most fertile agricultural regions. They were, however, years of real poverty.

Sometimes neighbor families supported Luise by taking the children for short periods. During one such visit during the 1949 school summer holiday, a friendly family took the then seven-year-old Hans on an excursion to see what was left of Nuremburg. Nuremburg had been the visual center of the Third Reich, the city in which Hitler held his annual party rallies. Hitler had chosen Nuremburg for this iconic role because the medieval castle that had been the home of the second imperial court was gloriously visible on top of the highest hill in the city. For the same reason the allies bombed the city to rubble during the war. It was an obliterated city only beginning to be laboriously cleared away by the many unemployed workers that the seven-year-old Hans first encountered. Ulrich recalls his shock when seeing for the first time the three great medieval churches of this iconic city: bombed skeletally bare, they had been stripped of their beautiful stained glass, left open to the sky.

Luise was a determined woman who insisted that even amidst all this ruin her children would not collapse into bitter brooding on a past now irretrievably lost. Ulrich remembers an incident that encapsulates her character. Once in Nuremburg Louise had taken work as a kindergarten teacher, where she found herself with many Jewish colleagues. As Hitler's anti-Semitic intentions had become clear, Luise quietly supported her Jewish colleagues as they fled. Only much later was Ulrich to discover her involvement in this dangerous collusion. Some years after the war the largest American car the young Ulrich had ever seen drove slowly into the village. Pulling up before their house, out leapt one of Luise's former colleagues. Wrapping Luise in a warm embrace, she expressed her gratitude for Luise's support and the risks she had taken, as they had made their way to safety during the dangerous years at the end of the war. Ulrich was to discover that this one refugee was not the only one. When Ulrich was a teenager, over several successive summer holidays, he and a friend cycled the more than 700-miles from southern Germany to London, where one of Luise's former colleagues allowed them to camp in their garden in Hampstead. The purpose of these trips? To look for affordable books in the famed used bookshops of London's Tottenham Court Road.

Ulrich's education began in his little village elementary school. Sensing his academic aptitude, Luise soon sent him to the *Humanistisches Gymnasium* in Kitzingen am Main. The core of the syllabus was Greek, Latin, and Hebrew. At this time church also began to play a greater role in the life of the three Ulrich children, and all three were deeply involved in their local church. It was the vibrancy of the life on display in this rural ecclesial community that first implanted the idea of studying theology in the young Ulrich. After graduating with his baccalaureate from Kitzingen, Ulrich took his first step toward studying theology by enrolling for a semester at the Lutheran Augustana *Hochschule* in Neuendettelsau, Bavaria. He intended there to improve his Hebrew and begin a preliminary study of theology.

He began his theological study officially in 1963, with his matriculation at the University of Heidelberg to study Ancient Languages (Greek and Latin) and theology. This preparation paid off handsomely, and in his second semester he passed the exam that allowed him to join a seminar on Plato's *Republic* in the original Greek. The seminar, attended by eleven other students, was taught by Hans-Georg Gadamer. Ulrich followed Gadamer's lecture courses throughout his studies. But it was the Jewish philosopher Karl Löwith who was to make the deepest impact on him. Löwith had only recently returned from exile in America and brought a combination of phenomenology and philosophical attention to history that Ulrich found gripping, as did many of Ulrich's contemporaries studying theology in Heidelberg at the time. Though a philosopher and ethnically Jewish, Löwith was also a Christian, and his teaching of philosophy focused on figures at the borderline of theology, Goethe, Hegel, Kierkegaard, and a Nietzsche presented as engaged in a life-and-death struggle with and against the Christian God.[1] It was Löwith who first impressed on Ulrich the importance of Nietzsche, who was to be the subject of his doctoral thesis.[2]

---

1. Ulrich heard Karl Löwith's lectures, published in German in 1941 and translated into English in 1964 as, *From Hegel to Nietzsche: The Revolution in Nineteenth Century Thought*, trans. David E. Green (New York: Holt, Reinhart and Winston, 1964). Löwith's most obviously theological work was written in exile and first published in English: *Meaning in History: The Theological Implications of the Philosophy of History* (Chicago: University of Chicago Press, 1949).

2. "It is indeed impossible to understand the development of Germany without this last German philosopher. His influence within the boundaries of Germany was—and still is—boundless. The Anglo-Saxon world—even Italy and France. . .—will never be able fully to comprehend it, so essentially foreign to them is what draws Germans to Nietzsche. Like Luther, he is a specifically German phenomenon—radical and fatal." Karl Löwith, *My Life in Germany Before and After 1933: A Report*, Elizabeth King trans. (London: Athalone Press, 1994), 6. On the interest of German theologians in Nietzsche during the 1930s and 1940s, and why engagement with him later and inexorable became an engagement with Heidegger,

It is almost impossible for contemporary English-language readers to fathom the turmoil of the postwar years in Germany, which was especially vociferous in the academy.³ This time of reckoning churned up every academic field, including theology, well into the 1980s. In Heidelberg, Ulrich's studies coincided a period of acute controversy over the legacy of the philosophical giant of Germany and open supporter of the Nazis: Martin Heidegger. Löwith, Gadamer, and philosopher Hans Jonas had all studied under Heidegger, and the clashes over his continuing relevance were formative for a whole generation of students. Jonas, for instance, sternly warned a lecture hall packed full of theological students not to fall for the pseudo-theological language of Heidegger.⁴ The struggles of Heidegger's students that shaped Ulrich's approach remain important today, notes Richard Wolin, because this generational cohort

> never shied away from posing the 'ultimate' questions about the meaning of human existence—questions that their contemporaries the logical positivists, following Wittgenstein's famous prescription at the end of the *Tractatus* ("about that which one cannot speak one should remain silent"), wished to banish from the realm of serious intellectual discourse. And although today the positivist legacy has been largely discredited, traces of its influence remain strong among analytical philosophers, who, following the later Wittgenstein, narrowly insist on philosophy's "therapeutic" *raison d'etre*. According to this standpoint, the idea of establishing an independent critical agenda lies beyond philosophy's purview... . Philosophy thereby surrenders—voluntarily and without a fight, as it were—its capacity for "strong evaluation": its ability to make significant distinctions in the realms of culture, morality, and truth.⁵

---

see Cyril O'Regan, "Balthasar and the Eclipse of Nietzsche," *Modern Theology* 35, no. 1 (2019): 103–21.

3. Jaimey Fisher, *Disciplining Germany: Youth, Reeducation, and Reconstruction after the Second World War* (Detroit: Wayne State University Press, 2010), 129–55; and Jürgen Habermas and John R. Blazek, "The Idea of the University: Learning Processes," *New German Critique* 41 (1987): 3–22.

4. This lecture was later published as Hans Jonas, "Heidegger and Theology," *The Review of Metaphysics* 18, no. 2 (1964): 207–33. Jonas's early academic work focuses on ancient Gnosticism and an influential appendix added later on draws out a set of crucial parallels between gnostic despair of the world and twentieth-century nihilism and existentialism. *The Gnostic Religion: The Message of the Alien God and the Beginnings of Christianity*, 2nd revised edn. (Boston: Beacon Press, 1958).

5. *Heidegger's Children: Hannah Arendt, Karl Löwith, Hans Jonas, and Herbert Marcuse* (Princeton: Princeton University Press, 2001), 234–5. That most of these figures were Jews no doubt relates to the resistance that had developed between the world wars among Jewish academics to the Marcionite tendencies in theology. See Paul Mendes-Flohr, "Gnostic Anxieties: Jewish Intellectuals and Weimar Neo-Marcionism," *Modern Theology* 35, no. 1

A Germany divided between a majority of fascists and fascist sympathizers and a smaller and diverse group of resisters and fugitives from the Zeitgeist that had dominated the 1930s and 1940s was having to somehow find new forms of collective life: a new federal constitution in West Germany, a new national identity after the enthusiasm for German ascendance that had been so destructive in the Nazi period, a new "idea of the university" and, of course, a new theology. This work had to be accomplished under trying economic conditions, with Germany divided down the middle; the West handed over to the oversight of the capitalist and technologized American empire and the East to the Asiatic, socialist Russian empire. The intellectual and political churn was so unrelenting that many intellectuals feared Germany would relapse into totalitarianism or collapse into anarchy. Though the denazification process forced many influential intellectuals of the Nazi period out of all university teaching and into a supposedly silent "internal exile," many continued to exercise influence through informal seminars for the younger generation and by corresponding with the new holders of political power who were still reeling from the catastrophe they had inherited. Many young leaders yearned for clear pronouncements about how to begin again.[6]

Precisely because so much was at stake, these were rich years to study theology in Heidelberg, where the Confessing Church struggle was still working itself out. The pro- and anti-Nazi split that had emerged in the German Protestant Church during the war rumbled on. One of the most well-known theologians of the Confessing church, Peter Brunner, taught Systematic Theology in conversation with Heinz Eduard Tödt, who taught Christian Social Ethics. But they did so alongside brown-church sympathizers (a term linking pro-Nazi theologians with the brown uniform worn by one of the very visible paramilitary wings of the Nazi Party) like Edmund Schlink, an early and later influential advocate of ecumenical theology. Among them were figures who continue to dominate their fields even today, such as Gerhard von Rad and Klaus Westermann in Old Testament.

The tensions were even more evident at the University of Göttingen, where Ulrich continued his graduate studies in 1965, finally concentrating exclusively on theology. Here the systematician and ethicist Ernst Wolf provided new impulses for Ulrich's theology. Wolf was a well-known member of the Confessing Church and a fellow traveler with the so-called dialectical theologians who aimed to recapture Luther from the orthodox Lutheranism of the National Socialist era by combining Reformed and Lutheran emphases. The systematic theologian Otto Weber, who had an ambivalent relationship to the Confessing Church, was teaching Reformed Theology alongside Walther Zimmerli in Old Testament, who was much more sympathetic. Both were also to have an enduring impact on Ulrich's theology. Overall, Ulrich found himself increasingly drawn to the group of theologians who

---

(2019): 71–80; Peter Gordon, *Rosenzweig and Heidegger: Between Judaism and German Philosophy* (Los Angeles: California University Press, 2003).

6. Jan-Werner Müller, *A Dangerous Mind: Carl Schmitt in Post-War European Thought* (New Haven: Yale University Press, 2003).

had been systematically marginalized by the National Socialists, and even sent to the front in an attempt to silence their criticisms of the national church under Hitler.

It was a febrile context in which to study theology, because even if no one spoke openly about it, everyone knew which pastor or theologian had been allied to the Confessing Church and which had been a committed or ambivalent German Christian. The complicity of the church in the attempted extermination of the Jews continued to be a suppurating wound exerting many lines of force on the theological discussion, as well as the ongoing attempts at reorientation being fitfully engaged by the nation as a whole.[7]

The refusal of many university professors to confront the past went along with the older generation's refusal to speak openly about the Nazi period more generally. Student frustration at this silence finally erupted into increasingly violent protests in West German universities beginning in 1967 and cresting in 1968. The protesters demanded nothing less than the complete purging from the universities of a longstanding patriarchal culture that now seemed no more than a mode of evasion of the work of grappling with Germany's National Socialist past. The university's continuing defense of hierarchical power structures appeared to the younger generation as a last outpost of the authoritarian attitudes that had supported the desire for a national Führer—if not a cover for open nostalgia for the imagined glories of the Third Reich. It was in this context that Ulrich's sympathies with his Confessing Church teachers crystallized as he attended one of the famous private seminars of Emanuel Hirsch, one of the systematic theologians barred from university teaching by the denazification process.[8] Though Hirsch continued to hold private seminars in his house that were to influence a wide range of influential postwar German theologians and church leaders, Ulrich sensed that the theology he offered was a seductive temptation, like the philosophy of Heidegger.

Ulrich proposed to write his doctoral dissertation on Friedrich Nietzsche after having been invited to study under Ernst Wolf. This was not an obvious move for a budding theologian, as Nietzsche was at the same time seen as the prophet of the death of God and proponent of atheism and a, if not *the*, critical source text for the supposed humanism propounded by the Nazis.[9] At the same time Nietzsche was

---

7. This aspect of the postwar wrestling with guilt and blame in Germany is incisively surveyed by Katharina von Kellenbach in *The Mark of Cain: Guilt and Denial in the Post-War Lives of Nazi Perpetrators* (Oxford: Oxford University Press, 2003). The most important document of this period is the *Die Stuttgarter Erklärung* of 1945. For the text of the Stuttgart Declaration and a discussion of the theological implications of this period of conflict, see Gerhard Besier and Gerhard Sauter, *Wie Christen ihre Schuld bekennen* (Göttingen: Vandenhoeck & Ruprecht, 1985).

8. See Gunda Schneider-Flume, *Die politische Theologie Emanuel Hirschs* (Frankfurt: Peter Lang, 1971).

9. Hermann Braun, "Nietzsche Im Theologischen Diskurs," *Theologische Rundschau* 75, no. 1 (2010): 1–44. See the four volumes of Heidegger's lectures on Nietzsche published in

also beginning to be read as a hidden theological source among the theologians with whom the maturing Ulrich had come to most strongly identify: Karl Barth, Dietrich Bonhoeffer, and Hans Joachim Iwand.[10] These theologians read Nietzsche as exposing the pretentions of liberal theologies and their self-designation as "religions" as covert worship of human self-definition. Nietzsche for them was the prophet of the death of religion—its morality and routines of self-justification— who paved the way to reorient theology on an attention to God not entrapped in human constructions.

In Göttingen Ulrich also began a lively and lifelong engagement with Gerhard Sauter, a student of Otto Weber, at this time lecturing in Systematic Theology. Ulrich sat his comprehensive exams in Göttingen to complete his undergraduate degree in 1968, immediately moving to Frankfurt to expand his knowledge of the social sciences, most memorably by taking seminars on practical philosophy with Jürgen Habermas. The young Habermas had just begun his teaching career, and had not yet gained his later reputation as the torchbearer for the recovery of Enlightenment rationality. Having recently edited a critical German edition of Nietzsche's engagement with the topic of understanding (*Erkenntnis*),[11] Habermas proved a rich interlocutor for Ulrich as he laid the groundwork for his doctoral thesis.

Ulrich followed Gerhard Sauter to the University of Mainz in 1969, where he began his doctoral work in earnest. There he also met Dietrich Ritschl, who invited

---

English as Martin Heidegger, *Nietzsche*, vols I and II, ed. and trans. David Farrell Krell (New York: HarperCollins, 1991).

10. André J. Groenewald finds Barth in his *Römerbrief* (1922) agreeing with Nietzsche that a nineteenth-century God of historical progress is dead or "Nicht-Gott," causing Barth to turn to the living God, "Interpreting the Theology of Barth in Light of Nietzsche's Dictum 'God Is Dead,'" *HTS Teologiese Studies/Theological Studies* 63, no. 4 (2007): 1430–1, 1436; see also Niklaus Peter, "Karl Barth als Leser und Interpret Nietzsches," *Zeitschrift für Neuere Theologiegeschichte/Journal for the History of Modern Theology* 1, no. 2 (1994): 251–64. Bonhoeffer's lectures on Genesis 1-3 appear to learn from Nietzsche an affirmation of life and of the human being as taken from the earth, DBWE 3, 76–7; see Peter Frick, *Understanding Bonhoeffer* (Tübingen: Mohr Siebeck, 2017), 120–1; Sabine Dramm, *Dietrich Bonhoeffer: An Introduction to His Thought*, trans. Thomas Rice (Peabody, Mass.: Hendrickson, 2007), 111. A further Nietzschean theme in Bonhoeffer's lectures is the claim that before eating the forbidden fruit, Adam lives "beyond good and evil," DBWE 3, 87; cf. "Afterword," 165-67. On Iwand and Nietzsche, see Edgar Thaidigsmann, "Das Urteil Gottes und der urteilende Mensch: Gerechtigkeit Gottes in Jesus Christus bei Hans Joachim Iwand," *Neue Zeitschrift Für Systematische Theologie Und Religionsphilosophie* 39, no. 3 (1997): 299.

11. Friedrich Nietzsche, *Erkenntnistheoretische Schriften*. Jürgen Habermas Afterword. (Frankfurt am Main: Suhrkamp, 1968). The early career of Habermas is recounted in *Habermas, Nietzsche, and Critical Theory*, ed. Babette E. Babich (Amherst, NY: Humanity Books, 2004).

Ulrich to become his academic assistant.[12] Ritschl was from the third generation of a German theological dynasty, not unlike the several generations of Torrances in Scotland only beginning to make their mark on the European theological scene at this time. Dietrich's grandfather was Albrecht Ritschl, his father Otto Ritschl, both historically oriented systematic theologians. Dietrich Ritschl thus inherited a global set of theological contacts and collaborative relationships into which Ulrich was gradually to be introduced while accompanying Ritschl on trips to many foreign countries. Ritschl taught for some years at Pittsburgh Seminary, where Ulrich first came into direct contact with the English-speaking theological world. In 1970, after his doctorate was completed, one theological ally of Ritschl's, Niels Nielsen, invited Ulrich to Rice University in Houston, Texas, where he gave his first course in English, a full term of lectures on "Nietzsche's Philosophy in its Significance for Theology." Never having formally studied English, the persistent questions of the students in his lectures and seminar discussions became his most important tutorials in spoken English. The students were well repaid for their perseverance, however, as their stock narrative of the role of Heidegger and Nietzsche in Nazi ideology was expanded by the very different narrative of German philosophy told by someone who had lived through it.

All this travel with Ritschl took place alongside Ulrich's developing dissertation on anthropology and Christian ethics in Nietzsche's philosophy, supervised by Gerhard Sauter. In 1972, Sauter was hired by the University of Bonn, and Ulrich was invited to accompany him as his academic assistant. In Bonn, Ulrich began his habilitation[13] on the theme of "Eschatology and Ethics." By taking up this theme, Ulrich entered an academic discussion that was very lively at this time. Words like "hope," "apocalyptic," and "Messianism" were once again in the air as part of a resurgent interest in eschatology among theologians, and not only in the work of his doctoral supervisor (Sauter, *Future and Promise*), but also in in the writings of Dietrich Ritschl (*Memory and Hope*), Jürgen Moltmann (*Theology of Hope*), and Walter Kreck (*Die Zukunft des Gekommenen*)—and even among philosophers, most famously, Ernst Bloch.[14]

---

12. This post combines the responsibilities of academic secretary to a senior professor with those of a junior lecturer, typically responsible for running seminars.

13. The *Habilitation* is the second dissertation, which is a prerequisite to qualify for an academic post career in Germany.

14. Gerhard Sauter, *Zukunft und Verheissung: das Problem der Zukunft in der gegenwärtigen theologischen und philosophischen Diskussion* (Zürich: Theologischer Verlag, 1965); Sauter summarizes his account of eschatology in *What Dare We Hope? Reconsidering Eschatology* (Harrisburg: Trinity Press International, 1999). Dietrich Ritschl, *Memory and Hope: An Inquiry Concerning the Presence of Christ* (New York: Macmillan, 1967); Jürgen Moltmann, *Theologie der Hoffnung: Untersuchungen zur Begründung und zu den Konsequenzen einer christlichen Eschatologie* (München: C. Kaiser, 1965); Moltmann, *Theology of Hope: On the Ground and Implications of Christian Eschatology*, trans. James W. Leitch (New York: Harper & Row, 1967); Walter Kreck, *Die Zukunft des Gekommenen:*

Bonn also saw Ulrich expanding the scope of his theological investigations into questions about the methodological status of science. His earliest research on this theme was undertaken in seminars with Niklas Luhmann, and sought points where theology might fruitfully cooperate with social science.[15] Meanwhile, Ulrich continued to intensively engage the themes of "anthropology," "biblical theology," and "biblical ethics" with Gerhard Sauter.

In Bonn Ulrich embarked on two other noteworthy ecclesial engagements. The first was his *"Vikariat"*—his curacy—undertaken in the years 1973–5. Ulrich was never ordained, despite his having completed the prerequisites for ordination, since his *Vikariat* had been completed outside his home region (*Landeskirche*). When he was hired as a university lecturer—again outside his *Landeskirche*—he was advised by his church overseer according to a common view at the time: that in a Lutheran Church, any preacher becomes ordained ad hoc if asked to preach and lead worship. This, in fact, Ulrich regularly did throughout his career, as he continues to do in academic retirement. His second ecclesial engagement was participating in a network of younger theologians across the Iron Curtain that partitioned postwar Germany. The attempt to build a collaborative network with assistants in the Theological School in East Berlin (GDR) was necessarily both ecclesial and academic, as the maintenance of church contacts was one of the few legal justifications for cross-border travel. Theologians from this group such as Wolf Krötke and Richard Schröder were later to become highly influential in East German theology.

This cross-border theology group met for many years in East Berlin, sometimes organizing formal conferences and other times meeting to worship together and engage in free theological conversation. The theological conversation was rooted in a shared Lutheran-Barthian tradition as the seminar participants had learned it from Ernst Wolf, Gerhard Gloege, and Hans Joachim Iwand in the years immediately following the war. This theology—which had grounded and oriented the resistance of the Confessing Church, not least, that of Dietrich Bonhoeffer—was insistent that the political implications of theological claims never be lost from view. Because these theologians viewed the church as a political body distinguishable from all other political or social bodies, they assumed it to be an indispensable source from which critical purchase could be gained on every empirically visible state and social grouping.

One connection from this period became particularly important for Ulrich, with the East German theologian Eberhard Jüngel, professor from 1969 in the Tübingen theological faculty. Jüngel would become a staunch political ally

---

Grundprobleme der Eschatologie (München: Chr. Kaiser, 1961); Ernst Bloch, *Das Prinzip Hoffnung*, 3 vols. (Frankfurt am Main: Suhrkamp, 1954–59); Bloch, *The Principle of Hope*, trans. Neville Plaice, Stephen Plaice, and Paul Knight, 3 vols (Cambridge: MIT Press, 1986).

15. During this period Luhmann was working on his groundbreaking two volume sociological theory of law: *Rechtssoziologie* (Reinbek: Rowohlt, 1972) translated as, *A Sociological Theory of Law* (London: Routledge, 1985).

as their careers progressed, and as editor of the monograph series *Beiträge zur evangelischen Theologie* invited publication of Ulrich's habilitation in his series, which appeared in 1988 as *Eschatologie und Ethik* (*Eschatology and Ethics*).[16] During these years in Bonn Ulrich discovered an even more important ally and inspiring theological dialogue partner in Karin Eschemann. That Karin was a Baptist and that in 1975 they married in a Baptist church displays the ecumenical spirit that suffuses both of their theologies. Ulrich-Eschemann was, like Hans, a theologian in training, and later when she started preaching in Erlangen became a formally recognized Lutheran. In due course she was appointed to the Faculty of Education at the Friedrich Alexander University Erlangen-Nuremberg.[17] During the years Ulrich was finishing his habilitation in Bonn, he and Karin welcomed two daughters into their family: Christine and Evamarie.

In 1982, immediately after the completion of his habilitation, Ulrich was offered a professorship in Christian Social Ethics at Friedrich Alexander University. The chair of Dogmatics in Erlangen at the time, Friedrich Mildenberger, also identified with the theological tradition of the Confessing Church and keenly supported of Ulrich's appointment. Mildenberger was to prove a sympathetic theological conversation partner for decades to come alongside Jürgen Roloff, Otto Merk, H. C. Schmidt, and Manfred Seitz. In 2001 Ulrich was promoted to the chair in Systematic Theology and Christian Ethics.

The theological faculty in Erlangen had been well-known as a "brown faculty" during the 1940s in their united support for the National Socialist party. The theological basis of this support was a particular interpretation of the Lutheran theology of creation orders in which nationality (and so race) were considered sites of divine revelation.[18] Unsurprisingly, the denazification process had hit the department hard, disrupting not only its collegial agreement but more fundamentally, its shared theological tradition. While Bonn had been for Ulrich

---

16. Hans G. Ulrich, *Eschatologie und Ethik: die theologische Theorie der Ethik in ihrer Beziehung auf die Rede von Gott seit Friedrich Schleiermacher*, Beiträge zur evangelischen Theologie 104 (München: Kaiser, 1988).

17. Karin Ulrich-Eschemann subsequently had a distinguished theological publication record in her own right, including, *Biblische Geschichten und ethisches Lernen: Analysen - Beispiele - Perspektiven* (Frankfurt am Main: Lang, 1996); *Vom Geborenwerden des Menschen: theologische und philosophische Erkundungen* (Münster: LIT, 2000); *Lebensgestalt Familie - miteinander werden und leben: eine phänomenologisch-theologisch-ethische Betrachtung* (Münster: LIT, 2005); *Leben, auch wenn wir sterben: Christliche Hoffnung lernen und lehren* (Göttingen: Vandenhoeck & Ruprecht, 2008); *Gerechte in der Bibel, Sünder in der Bibel: was steht geschrieben?* (Göttingen: Vandenhoeck & Ruprecht, 2008); *Gutes predigen nach dem Vorbild Jesu: Gottesdienste zu Lebensthemen* (Göttingen: Vandenhoeck & Ruprecht, 2011); *Christliche Verkündigung mit Israel: 20 Gottesdienste im Kirchenjahr* (Göttingen: Vandenhoeck & Ruprecht, 2012).

18. This period in Erlangen is recounted in Gotthard Jasper, *Paul Althaus (1888 –1966): Professor, Prediger und Patriot in seiner Zeit* (Göttingen: Vandenhoeck & Ruprecht, 2013).

an enlivening adventure in the theology of the Confessing Church, Erlangen's fraught past had left it much more intellectually fragmented, and groping toward a new shared theological tradition. In this context Ulrich pursued a theological approached that straddled academic and ecclesial worlds, not only training students who might follow his scholarly path, but also intensively engaging with, supporting, and resourcing the local church. In a theological faculty tasked with training pastors, but in a university setting tending to aspire to produce academics, Ulrich trained a large number of pastors serving to this day in Germany. In important respects these pastors are his legacy to academic theology, displaying his way of honoring the priorities of the Confessing Church that so deeply informed his theological perspective. Theology is for him a vocation that explicitly incorporates appropriate pedagogical and spiritual practices sorely missing in many theology faculties in the contemporary university.

This was to be the setting for a lifetime of wide-ranging teaching that continued even beyond Ulrich's official retirement in 2008. Ulrich's work in the philosophy of science was to flower in his work on the medical ethics committee of the University Hospital in Erlangen, which he began in 1990 and continues to the date of writing. For a decade he held a joint university lecture on the intertwining of molecular biology and ethics with the renowned epigeneticist Walter Doerfler.[19] During a different ten-year span he was a member of the university committee considering the ethics and policy around nuclear-waste technology. From 1982 onward Ulrich and Hans Julius Schneider headed up an interdisciplinary university working group investigating themes central to interdisciplinary research, such as "alterity," "temporality," intercultural hermeneutics and the philosophy of language. Ulrich has also regularly held workshops on business ethics with executives and managers of multinational corporations based in Germany, including Adidas, Puma, and Siemens.

Some of the sections of this volume were first written during Ulrich's engagements in a range of scholarly networks. From 2004 to 2009 he was President of Societas Ethica, a pan-European ecumenical society comprised of both theological and philosophical ethicists. He continues to be an active member of the "Iwand-Verein," a group devoted to elucidating the theology of Hans Joachim Iwand and preparing his collected works. For many years he was a member of the liturgical committee of the Lutheran Church of Germany working on the new prayer book for the Lutheran Church.[20] From 1989 to 1991 and again in 1996-7

---

19. The method and content of this course is described in Brian Brock, Walter Doerfler and Hans Ulrich, "Genetics, Conversation and Conversation: A Discourse at the Interface of Molecular Biology and Christian Ethics," in *Theology, Disability, and the New Genetics: Why Science Needs the Church*, ed. John Swinton and Brian Brock (London: T&T Clark, 2007), 146-60.

20. The work of this (Vereinigte Evangelisch-Lutherische Kirche Deutschlands [VELKD]) group was published as *Evangelisches Gottesdienstbuch: Agende für die Union Evangelischer Kirchen in der EKD (UEK) und für die Vereinigte Evangelisch-Lutherische*

he was a participant in the working group on "Life"[21] of the Evangelische Kirche in Deutschland (EKD), which regularly published on pressing ethical questions arising in the fields of medicine and biotechnology. During his many years in Erlangen he worked with the church office devoted to questions of work[22] teaching people in the working world in ethics and supervising the practical placement in workplaces for students in theology.[23] From 2003 to 2005 he was a contributor to the Lutheran World Federation project bringing together Lutherans from around the world with the aim of discovering what they shared as Lutheran ethicists.[24] Finally, these intensive engagements with German university, ecclesial, and public life were accompanied by Ulrich's participation from 2000 until the present in an ecumenical working group committed to finding common ground in ecumenical social ethics.[25]

Theological Trajectories

There is despair—and also promise—in the public display of desolation that is a ruined church gaping open toward the heavens. If Ulrich's earliest memories are of the ruination of the German physical landscape by war, his theological studies were no less determined by the realization that the deformations hidden in the towering theologies and philosophies of the nineteenth and early twentieth centuries had been brutally exposed. A once seemingly impregnable theological edifice that had been the envy of the (Western) theological world was in desperate need of wholesale reconstruction. Relief and exhaustion pervaded the years after the Second World War as the nations of Europe began to recover and rebuild. As Americans reveled in boom years, Germany was beginning what was to be a long and existentially fraught struggle not only to recover from the war but also to try to understand the identity and meaning of being German. No German theologian could escape such questions.

When asked to encapsulate his earliest experiences of the theological context in postwar Germany, a single word seems to Ulrich a fitting descriptor: "emptiness." It

---

Kirche Deutschlands (VELKD), (Leipzig: Luther-Verlag; Evangelische Verlagsanstalt, 2018), updated printing 2020.

21. Woche für das Leben.

22. Kirchlicher Dienst in der Arbeitswelt (KDA).

23. "Industriepraktikum." See: https://www.kwa-ekd.de/der-kirchliche-dienst-in-der-arbeitswelt-kda/

24. The "Lutheran Ethics in a Global Context" project was chaired by Karen L. Bloomquist and yielded the publication *Lutheran Ethics at the Intersections of God's One World*, ed. Karen L. Bloomquist (Genf: Lutheran World Federation, 2005). Ulrich's contribution was "On the Grammar of Lutheran Ethics," 27–48.

25. This working group is hosted by the Johann-Adam-Möhler-Institut (Paderborn) and chaired by Wolfgang Thönissen.

was abundantly clear that the early postwar years would be a period in philosophy and theology in which new beginnings would have to be made that salvaged and critically sifted the great intellectual traditions that had gone before. In this process philosophers and theologians alike found themselves with little choice but to confront the legacy of the thinker who had dominated the previous two decades, who Löwith labelled a "thinker in a destitute time": Martin Heidegger.[26]

Like Bonhoeffer before him,[27] Ulrich could see no way back to the vanished world of the village parson and respectable middle-class Christianity. Attempts by thinkers like Helmut Thielicke to recover a faithful version of the older orthodox Lutheran theology purged of its more problematic elements seemed to Ulrich stale attempts claw back the best of a German Lutheran tradition married to cultural forms irrecoverably shaken by the war and visibly melting away in the emerging new modernity. Emil Brunner, likewise, seemed too Reformed, and too Swiss, to offer the way forward to an existentially shaken German church. Nor did the resurgent popularity of the timeless universal principles of Kantian ethics seem promising as a way forward, given the utter powerlessness of this approach in limiting the wave of barbarity which it had been deployed to justify

---

26. By applying this label to Heidegger, Löwith turned Heidegger's own tools against him. Löwith (and others) had criticized Heidegger for the tendency of his late philosophy to proceed by word associations not susceptible to critical interrogation. In calling Heidegger a "Denker in dürftiger Zeit" Löwith showed the problem in his deft redeployment of the key term "dürftiger." Whereas Heidegger had used it to affirm Hölderlin's diagnosis of modernity as destitute in lacking gods, being between "the no-longer of the gods who have fled, and in the not-yet of the one to come," Löwith's application of this term as a description of Heidegger's work suggests that the thinker whose work is so fixated on time was bound to have been "meagre," "paltry," or "shallow," given his own assessment of the shallowness and inauthenticity of modernity. Karl Löwith, *Heidegger: Denker in dürftiger Zeit* (Frankfurt on Main: S. Fischer, 1953). Translated as *Martin Heidegger and European Nihilism*, ed. Richard Wolin, trans. Gary Steiner (New York: Columbia University Press, 1995). Löwith's four-chapter monograph on Heidegger is found on pages 29–134 of this volume, and the Heidegger citation in this note appears on page 39, translating a comment from Heidegger's essay, "Hölderlin und das Wesen der Dichtung." As Barth observed, "Whoever is ignorant of the shock experienced and attested by Heidegger and Sartre is surely incapable of thinking and speaking as a modern man and unable to make himself understood by his contemporaries. For we men of to-day have consciously or unconsciously sustained this shock. In our time man has encountered nothingness in such a way as to be offered an exceptional opportunity in this respect." Karl Barth, CD III.3, 345.

27. See Bonhoeffer's Letter of May 5, 1944, "Thoughts on the Day of Baptism of Dietrich Wilhelm Rüdiger Bethge": "The old village parsonage and the old middle-class ['*bürgerlich*'] house belong to a world that will have vanished by the time you grow up. But the old spirit will survive the period of its misjudgment and its actual failure, and after a time of withdrawal, renewed inner reflection, probing, and healing will create new forms for itself," DBWE 8, 385.

during the National Socialist period. Ulrich had seen firsthand how fatal it was to deploy universal moral principles without awareness of the narrative frames that inevitably supply their content. Such sensibilities were widely shared among German intellectuals in the postwar period.[28]

These wider judgments about what had and was happening in the cultural and theological landscape of postwar Germany were the backdrop against which the political-hermeneutical theology of Ernst Wolf appeared to Ulrich as a genuinely new beginning. Wolf's work continued the creative rereading of Luther characteristic of the Luther renaissance that had been so influential on theologians like Bonhoeffer.[29] Wolf's development of this theological approach acknowledged the new social dynamics just making themselves felt as Germany transitioned into the Cold War period—of urbanization, decreasingly patriarchal gender roles, heightened disputes over the relative merits of capitalism and socialism[30]—and in each of these domains also needing to forge new understandings of national identity[31] and international relations.[32] Heinz Eduard Tödt was the first German ethicist fully to develop this political-hermeneutical theology, combining the theology of Bonhoeffer with cultural Protestant currents to offer students an ethical framework that to this day remains the dominant approach among the German Evangelical Church (EKD). Wolf and Tödt began to elaborate a Christian social ethics that sought a new understanding of the commonalities between church and secular society, rejecting the insistence of Barth and Iwand that theologians must remain vigilantly aware of crucial differences between church and secular society.[33]

---

28. Thomas Mann's postwar novel *Dr. Faustus*, for instance, offers a similar critique of the failure of both Kantian ethics and middle-class morality to stem the tide of Nazi ideology, which, like the theologians, he finds an irreducibly theological question: "... alles ist und geschieht in Gott, besonders auch der Abfall von ihm . . .". Quoted in Christoph Schwöbel, *Die Religion des Zauberers: Theologisches in den großen Romanen Thomas Manns* (Tübingen: Mohr Siebeck, 2008), 211.

29. Michael P. DeJonge, *Bonhoeffer's Reception of Luther* (Oxford: Oxford University Press, 2017); *Bonhoeffer und Luther: Zentrale Themen ihrer Theologie*, ed. Klaus Grünwaldt, Christiane Tietz, and Udo Hahn (Hannover: Amt der VELKD, 2007)

30. Hans Ulrich, "Kapitalismus," *Theologische Realenzyclopädie*, vol 17 (Berlin: Walter de Gruyter, 1988), 604–19.

31. Hans G. Ulrich, "Volk—Nation—Bürger-Sein: Fragestellungen und Perspektiven zur politischen Bildung," in *Arbeitshilfe für den evangelischen Religionsunterricht an Gymnasien*, edited by Gymnasialpädagogische Materialstelle der Ev. Luth. Kirche in Bayern, Folge II, 1993, 3–16.

32. Hans G. Ulrich and Stefan Heuser, "Political Practices and International Order," in *Political Practices and International Order: Proceedings of the Annual Conference of the Societas Ethica, Oxford 2006*, ed. Stefan Heuser and Hans G. Ulrich (Berlin: Lit Verlag, 2007), 8–27.

33. Ernst Wolf, *Sozialethik: Theologische Grundlagen*, ed. Theodor Strohm, 3rd edn. (Göttingen: Vandenhoeck & Ruprecht, 1988); Karl Barth, *Church and State*, trans. G.

The many questions about how to go on swirling in this fractured theological and cultural landscape drove fundamental theological questions to the fore for people in every walk of life. It also hints at why this time was so promising for theology. The theological debates of the 1950s and 1960s continually circled back to the question of the human: What *kind* of humanity ought we aspire to be? Gerhard Sauter's response took the form of a political-hermeneutical theology sharply focused on God and only then on the ways in which humans come to be drawn into God's redemptive story with creation.[34] Theology should never try to hedge itself about with doctrines or concepts that obscure the fundamental fact that the Christian life cannot escape reliance on the ongoing working of a living God. Karl Barth, Sauter suggests, appropriately drew these threads together in the prayer that God may make us capable "to risk the small, yet still so significant, step—away from comfort with which we can comfort ourselves and to hope in you."[35]

Sauter elaborated this starting point as a form of lived expectation. At root Sauter was repristinating a theology of the Word. God's promises are of the type that can be lived into in an active and prayerful awaiting and looking for God's own characteristic works: forgiveness, creation, consolation, merciful salvation, and judgment. The life-giving power that flows from God's Word is not exhausted. Each generation of the faithful can count on it to open up and orient their discerning perception of their own unique context. Paradigmatically, God's Word can be heard and learned ever afresh in the gathered worship of the church. For the individual Christian, what is learned in worship is, at its most basic level, a schooling in how to pray.[36] It is in this way that God's Word has the heuristic power to reveal God's action in our time and place, so facilitating Christian cooperation with a living and active God.[37] This is a methodologically worked out elaboration of how the confession of justification in Jesus Christ, when combined with the individual and ecclesial reliance on the promises of God, can generate a coherent hermeneutics of scripture, doctrine, and historical occurrence.

Ronald Howe (London: Student Christian Movement Press, 1939 [first pub. 1938]); Hans Joachim Iwand, *Kirche und Gesellschaft*, Nachgelassene Werke 1 (Gütersloh: Gütersloher Verlagshaus, 1998 [first pub. 1954]).

34. Sauter's programmatic presentation of his theology can be found in *Das verborgene Leben: Eine theologische Anthropologie* (Munich: Gütersloher Verlagshaus, 2011).

35. Karl Barth, *Gebete* (Munich: Chr. Kaiser, 1963), 40, cited in Sauter, *What Dare We Hope?* 78.

36. Hans G. Ulrich, "Gebet," *Glaube und lernen* (Göttingen: Vanderhoeck & Ruprecht, 1986), 13–21.

37. This set of connections is surveyed in Hans G. Ulrich, "Tradieren von Ethik im Gottesdienst: *Traditio activa—vita passiva*," in *Die Tradierung von Ethik im Gottesdienst: Symposiumsbeiträge zu Ehren von Hans G. Ulrich*, ed. Marco Hofheinz with Kai-Ole Eberhardt (Berlin: Lit Verlag, 2019), 267–300.

Sauter's program appealed deeply to Ulrich, and fundamentally shaped his own theological approach. In a context experienced as an empty wasteland, the theologian inevitably faces a choice deeply intertwined with one's existential relationship to God and the world. In such circumstances some theologians seek a theology that offers stabilizing conceptual structures (ideas like "order," "middle axioms," "teleology," or "foundations") to guide Christians by handing them conceptual tools, theological principles or ontological affirmations by which they can regain their orientation. Sauter's intense focus on the priority of God and God's action drew on the Lutheran-Barthian tradition that was the meeting point of the Confessing Church theologians to chart an alternative route. Theology, he proposed, is the work of discerning what God has for human beings, which particular forms of life and resurrection God is promisingly offering in our own time and place.[38] An eschatological theology of promise that lives from hope in the advent of God's Word being fulfilled in each generation held an obvious appeal in a devastated German postwar context in which all human intellectual, cultural, and moral promises had been shown to be so evidently disappointing.

These were the impulses that led Ulrich to focus on anthropology and eschatology as domains in which the necessity of discovering a new beginning in the created world, led by God's own action, is worked out. In this eschatologically oriented theology themes of promise and hope are not built on any initial critical or negating operation, as most famously pursued in the Frankfurt School of philosophy. God's promise does have critical power, yet its leading edge in human affairs is a fertile novelty. A redeeming God is capable of filling the holes left by the collapse of the plausibility of earlier theologies. In Ulrich's hands, eschatological themes are invoked to display how God's reality and God's story with human beings come to determine human perception, self-narration and so ethical orientation. In this intervention God exposes the covert Gnosticism that animates the modern belief in progress and demands moral assent from all supposedly right-thinking people. In the end, an eschatology that so emphasizes God's action as establishing the story of his people in the world can only be a theology of witness, and witness has become an increasingly prominent *topos* in Ulrich's mature theology.

Publication History

Ulrich has authored three main monographs. His doctoral work was published in 1975 as *Anthropologie und Ethik bei Friedrich Nietzsche: Interpretationen zu Grundproblemen theologischer Ethik*[39] (*The Anthropology and Ethics of Friedrich*

---

38. Wolfgang Raddatz, Gerhard Sauter, and Hans G. Ulrich, "Verstehen," in *Praktisch Theologisches Handbuch*, ed. Gert Otto, 2nd edn. (Hamburg: Furche-Verlag 1975), 602–33.

39. Ulrich, *Anthropologie und Ethik bei Friedrich Nietzsche: Interpretationen zu Grundproblemen theologischer Ethik*, Beiträge zur evangelischen Theologie 68 (München: Kaiser, 1975).

Nietzsche: An Interpretation of Foundational Questions in Theological Ethics). Nietzsche is interesting to the early Ulrich in forcing theological ethics to reflect on its methodological presuppositions. The crucial challenge of Nietzsche to Christian theology and ethics is his demand that Christians recognize their perennial temptation to establish internally coherent theoretical systems that inevitably become self-sustaining and finally atavistic. Theology ossified into system reveals itself in its lifeless anthropology or simplistic moralism. Thus, Nietzsche's work aids theology in warning it of the fatal dangers of self-enclosure, in which no true knowledge of God or the self is achievable. In light of this critique, Ulrich presents the task of a theological ethic as a critical work of freeing human practical reasoning from its sterile entrapment in self-enclosed circularity. Nietzsche and a faithful Christian theological ethics meet in understanding the central problem of Christian ethics as the achievement of a methodologically and theologically coherent approach to self-criticism.

The call in the last pages of the Nietzsche book for a "thoroughly soteriologized" constructive elaboration of Christian ethics was answered in the heavily revised version of Ulrich's Habilitationsschrift published in 1988 as *Eschatologie und Ethik: Die theologische Theorie der Ethik in ihrer Beziehung auf die Rede von Gott seit Friedrich Schleiermacher*[40] (*Eschatology and Ethics: A Theological Account of Ethics of the Word of God since Friedrich Schleiermacher*). Part I of this book asks whether Christians can intelligibly speak of an eschatological divine speaking. Eschatology is positioned as the fundamental context for Christian ethical reflection in being an arena in which Christian moral orientation must be discerned. Part II asks how Christian ethicists today might understand their vocation within the eschatological domain established by God's action through the Holy Spirit. A theological ethics that confesses itself to be grounded in the work of the Holy Spirit must be an ethic of freedom understood in a distinctly hermeneutical key. It is a concrete eschatology in the sense of being a filled out and localized experience of the Holy Spirit's establishment of God's Kingdom. Part III fleshes out how Christian judgment is reshaped by the Christian expectation to be acted upon by the Holy Spirit. Christian discernment, it turns out, is closely related to political ethics, justice being one of the supreme gifts that the Spirit donates into human relations, by calling forth fresh and contextually appropriate judgments by political authority as well as peacebuilding discernments about where social consensus might be found.

Ulrich's third and most widely known work first appeared in 2005, as *Wie Geschöpfe leben: Konturen evangelischer Ethik*[41] (*Living as Creatures: Contours of an Evangelical Ethic*). Here Ulrich's emphases on theological anthropology, eschatology, and pneumatology are drawn together though an elaborated

---

40. Ulrich, *Eschatologie und Ethik*.
41. Hans G. Ulrich, *Wie Geschöpfe leben: Konturen evangelischer Ethik*, 2nd edn., Ethik im theologischen Diskurs 2 (Münster: LIT, 2007); 3rd edn. (2020). *Studies in Christian Ethics* dedicated an issue to the book, vol. 20, no. 2 (2007).

account of the Christian doctrine of creation, or more precisely, the creation of the new creature as redeemed creation. The task of the theological ethicist is now positioned as a critical and explorative work of seeking out the works of God that have been given to particular creatures to witness. Ulrich's previous work on ethical method and an eschatology of revelation are now deployed to offer an account of creation organized around Luther's dynamic notion of the three estates—which Ulrich prefers to call "institutions." Ulrich prefers the language of institutions because the order that concerns him is not creational order as traditionally interpreted in Lutheran order-theology, but the patterns of creaturely activity that God has promised to establish and uphold: the order of churchly worship, human reproduction and feeding, and political peace as discovered in the search for justice around which the institutions of human governance should be organized.[42] This programmatic work displays how much the theologian of revelation can say on material themes in Christian ethics, toward which Ulrich's previous works had been continually pointing but which he had not yet discussed in anywhere near the detail offered in *Wie Geschöpfe leben*.

Ulrich has also edited several volumes of source texts, and arguably the most succinct presentations of his approach can be found in two essays that introduce these collections. His introduction to *Evangelische Ethik*[43] displays the affinity between Ulrich's approach and the postliberal emphasis on story. Because modern Christian ethics has so emphasized progress and optimism, couched in the idiom of universal principles, a faithful Christian ethics today must draw attention to the timeliness of ethical discernment: "now is the time, awake from sleep." The discipline of Christian ethics has its own history, just as the church in various contexts has a story, and God is drawing these stories to Godself in historically particular acts that must be discerned and followed by a worshipping, prayerful ecclesial community. Here the significant impulses drawn from the theological-ecclesiological approach of English-speaking postliberal theologians such as Stanley Hauerwas and Paul Lehmann is also visible. Ulrich's introduction to *Freiheit im Leben mit Gott*[44] offers a particularly clear articulation of the centrality of the theme of "freedom" for an evangelical ethics, succinctly articulating why a genuinely theological account of ethics must resist the dominant universal account of freedom in favor of a materially dense depiction of the freedom that has been, and is being, actualized by God in particular creaturely lives, with all their unique constraints and contextual features.

---

42. Brian Brock, "Why the Estates? Hans Ulrich's Recovery of an Unpopular Notion," *Studies in Christian Ethics* 20, no. 2 (2007), 179–202.

43. *Evangelische Ethik: Diskussionsbeiträge zu ihrer Grundlegung und ihren Aufgaben*, ed. Hans G. Ulrich (Munich: Chr. Kaiser Verlag, 1990), 9–40.

44. *Freiheit im Leben mit Gott: Texte zur Tradition evangelischer Ethik*, ed. Hans G. Ulrich (Gütersloh: Chr. Kaiser Verlag, Gütersloher Verlagshaus, 1993), 9–40.

Outline of This Volume

In the last decade or so, Ulrich has increasingly been invited to address English-speaking audiences. This volume collects various texts originally written in English or translated into English. They therefore represent encapsulations of his mature theological emphases, and have been chosen and arranged to provide English speakers with an overview of his thought as a whole. Almost all of the chapters are composites of essays that were not initially connected, and all have been heavily revised to limit repetition and bring them into line with idiomatic English usage. Many of the chapters amalgamate parts of several essays and talks, and none have appeared in their current form. Ulrich has reviewed and approved the final form of the manuscript.

In the broadest outlines, the chapters gathered in the three sections all tackle a single question from different angles: How does God enter into the fallen human world, transforming or transfiguring empty and destructive patterns of life to make them habitable for living with God? Part one begins with questions about what God's Word suggests about what human beings might hope for, where they might seek renewal, and how they might practically receive God's transforming presence in any domain of life. The second set of chapters focuses this question on the interpersonal aspect of this transforming divine appearance. What should we hope for God's presence to accomplish in reshaping our interpersonal relations and with them the social institutions in which they are embedded? The third trio of chapters engages the question of how God's presence transforms human relations as embodied relations. As the section headings indicate, the grouping of the sections reflects Ulrich's novel interpretation of the Lutheran doctrine of the three estates, with the first section displaying his reading of the *Ecclesia* (the domain of the church), the second of the *Politia* (the domain of interhuman relations and institutions), and the third the *Oeconomia* (the domain of bodily life and its sustenance).

Breaking these sections down into chapters, Part I, "A Christian Ethics of Messianic Presence (*Ecclesia*)," presents a Messianic interpretation of the origin of the Christian ethos. Chapter 1 explains why Ulrich thinks an eschatological orientation is important for Christian ethics, and why a Messianic eschatology best encapsulates the biblical witnesses' understanding of how God's Messianic and eschatological appearance transforms human behavior. Chapter 2 develops these themes by tracing them in the theological ethics of Dietrich Bonhoeffer. This chapter is especially useful in showing how some of the less familiar features of Ulrich's theology (to English-speaking readers at least) are in reality central components of the theological approach of a figure who is relatively well-known in the English-speaking world, Dietrich Bonhoeffer. This chapter also makes especially apparent why the theological path Ulrich has followed is a genuine continuation of the theology of the Confessing Church, and therefore why he has been largely isolated in the German theological scene. Chapter 3 hones in on the question of how God's Messianic drawing near can be perceived and received in the day-to-day life of the Christian. The second part of this chapter may again be especially useful in orienting English-speaking readers in offering a reasoned extension of Oliver O'Donovan's more well-known account of judgment.

Part II, "Christian Witness in the World (*Politia*)," is oriented by questions about how the Christian ethos percolates out to transform the social orders in which Christians live. Chapter 4 engages in a fresh way the old question of how Christians should understand and present their own distinctive views of reality in a secular society that seems to bar them from public discussion. Here Ulrich suggests that a fully theological account of politics not only entails Christian engagement in the political life of the societies in which Christians live, but also reveals the many ways in which secular political thought is dependent on the material insights Christian bring into secular political debates. Chapter 5 extends this discussion into debates about economics and economic policy. Secular economic policymakers need religious voices in order to understand themselves and the operation of the economy. Modern economics, it appears, allows no "outside"—literally everything is part of the economy. The chapter ends with a concrete discussion of how the limitation of the scope of economics held out in the reign of God helps us to see which sorts of approach to business ethics might be most fruitful for Christians to advocate in public today. Chapter 6 focuses on an entity that ought to be outside of the economic domain, the human child. Questions of adoption policy highlight one of the ways in which secular states need religious traditions in order to navigate policy formation. Is it possible for secular states to maintain their neutrality on issues of moral substance and still choose between one adoption policy over another? Ulrich suggests not, showing how a Christian view of children and of family can resource public debates about appropriate adoption policy.

Part III, "Receiving Given Life (*Oeconomia*)," is oriented by three very different engagements in what is today called "bioethics." Chapter 7 engages in some depth with H. Tristram Engelhardt's Christian account of bioethics. Engelhardt criticizes mainstream approaches to bioethics, including those defended by Christians, as having given too much ground to secular liberal political assumptions. Ulrich turns this criticism on Engelhardt himself, though affirming the aims of his project. The issue is how Christians understand history, and here Ulrich's Messianic ethics demands that Christians engaging in bioethical debates think hard about what constitutes medical "progress" in order that their thinking about modern medicine does not lose touch with its origins in Christian worship. Chapter 8 reports on what Ulrich has discovered in the course of a long-running interdisciplinary lecture series on the ethics of genetics and molecular biology. Such public discussions of the minutiae of current genetic science are indispensable for ethical thinking, because this research is raising ethical questions that are relevant to all human beings. Ulrich suggests that a Christian engagement in this discussion will be oriented by an appreciation of the goodness of creation, an orientation that he shows to have surprisingly far reaching practical implications for the practice of genetic research. The final chapter, Chapter 9, explores the implication of the affirmation that human beings are irreducibly embodied. Focusing on the stories told by Christians of being transformed in their relationships with people with intellectual disabilities, Ulrich asks what the reality of these transformations tells us about the embodied nature of all human relationships. Going far beyond the dualistic separation of mind and body so still so widespread today, Ulrich holds bodily presence to be a privileged locus of God's Messianic appearance—even in bodies from whom we are used to expecting almost nothing.

A Reader's Guide

We conclude this introduction with four final comments to orient readers. The first chapter in each section is the most theoretically foundational and also the most conceptually dense. Subsequent chapters tend to elaborate aspects of the fundamental claims introduced in each part's opening chapter.

There are also several terms and turns of phrase that recur throughout the text yet may be unfamiliar to English-speaking readers. The first is Ulrich's regular use of the Latin term *conditio humana*. Ulrich intends the unfamiliarity of the term to hold open an anthropological meta-question: What makes human beings human?[45] Crucially, this intentionally unfamiliar formulation positions scientific descriptions of the human as *contributors* to the discussion without letting them claim the title of *defining* human nature.[46] This linguistic strategy can be understood as an attempt to move beyond the disastrous use of creation order accounts by early twentieth-century Lutheranism as well as the heavy moral freighting of the English term "human nature" by a range of assumptions about the qualities "naturally" possessed by humans. Human beings are part of the material creation, but this does not exhaust what they are called to be. They also are in the unique position of having to investigate their own nature suspended between the finitude of the world and the infinite realms of knowledge and experience.[47] Ulrich

---

45. "Grundbedingung menschlicher Existenz," Ulrich, *Wie Geschöpfe leben*, 311.

46. He assumes, with Gerhard Sauter, that the term *conditio humana* names an investigations of, "the nature of human beings in their life-world, taking into account their basic conditions for living . . . and encompassing studies of human biology, physiology, anthropology (understood as the science of human development), evolutionary psychology, medical anthropology, the science of whole person care, behavioral science, psychology, sociology, education, along with any other science investigating this broad domain. The task is to locate and feel out what is specific and essential to human being, what by and large stays the same, and what we are well advised to preserve." Sauter, *Das verborgene Leben*, 19 (my translation). A similar theological use of the term can be found in Gerald P. McKenny, *To Relieve the Human Condition: Bioethics, Technology, and the Body* (Albany: State University of New York Press, 1997) and in philosophical discourse by Hans-Peter Krüger, "Die condition humaine des Abendlandes," in *Deutsche Zeitschrift für Philosophie* 55, no. 4 (2007), 605–26.

47. The origins of the term in the usage of Pascal is evident in this formulation, *Pensées* 20. See Hendrik Johan Adriaanse, "Conditio humana," in *Religion Past and Present* (Leiden: Brill), http://dx.doi.org/10.1163/1877-5888_rpp_SIM_03187, accessed June 23, 2020. First published online: 2011.

takes all ongoing inquiries into what it means to be human as hermeneutic and reflexive work that should be pursued in public discussion. The purpose of all study and discussion of the *conditio humana* is to better understand, and marvel at, our human condition in its embodied wholeness, which must be continually rediscovered in all its complexity, relations, and coherence. For Ulrich, the human being is not just the human being as material creature, but the redeemed human being, the human being God created us to be.

A second important term in this volume is "transfiguration," which intermingles with the language of "transformation." Both terms gloss Romans 12:2, whose centrality for Ulrich's thinking is signaled by its regular citation throughout this volume. This made the verse a natural choice for this volume's title. In this volume, however, the verse most often appears in the NRSV translation: "Do not be conformed to this world, but be transformed by the renewal of your mind." "Transformation" is a translation of the Greek "*metamorphousthe*." The substitution of the translation "transfiguration" should not be read as aligning Ulrich's work with the Finnish Lutherans, whose architectonic emphasis on deification Ulrich does not share. Though deification sometimes hovers in the background of Ulrich's interest in the human being as an eschatological new creation, the use of the term "transfiguration" as a title is primarily an attempt to highlight the fundamentally theological nature of Ulrich's project in contrast to concepts of change and transformation that dominate German-influenced theology in the wake of Heidegger.[48] The placement of the term "transfiguration" at the head of this volume should therefore be understood both as marking Ulrich's project as an intervention in a post-Heideggerian philosophical context and as an effort to recapture this language for its original sense as a descriptor of the redemptive change wrought in humans by God.[49] The theological issues at stake around the language of metamorphosis and transfiguration are discussed in Chapter 9.

The language of God's word keeping people from "getting lost" in human history that recurs in the chapters of this book point to a third idea that may be unfamiliar to first time readers of Ulrich. Ulrich's various usages of the language of

---

48. As Catherine Malabou has observed of Heidegger's *Nietzsche* lectures, "inversion (*Umdrehung*), reversal (*Umkehrung*), transmutation, transvaluation (*Umwertung*), transfiguration (*Verklärung*), and countermovement (*Gegenbewegung*) are constantly referred to the triad of change—*Wandel, Wandlung,* & *Verwandlung*—which is alone capable of leading back to their foundation," Catherine Malabou, *The Heidegger Change: On the Fantastic in Philosophy*, trans. and ed. Peter Skafish (Albany: State University of New York Press, 2011), 80.

49. Ulrich's use of "transformation" language thus differs both from the Finnish school of theology and from the more widespread Heidegger-inspired anthropocentric formulations that enjoin changing one's life (both individual and political) by altering one's philosophical framework. Adrian Johnston, *Badiou, Žižek, and Political Transformation: The Cadence of Change* (Evanston: Northwestern University Press, 2009); Peter Sloterdijk, *You Must Change Your Life: On Anthropotechnics*. (Oxford, Cambridge: Polity Press: 2013).

"being made real by incorporation into God's story" express a categorical refusal to grant that there is any history or human thought world that people might construct in isolation from the acts of God. Behind this formulation lies a broadly Wittgensteinian view of language and narrative which Ulrich presumes throughout the volume. Language is taken to be constitutive of human sociality. To be part of a family, nation, or culture is to have been born into a form of life held in place by the language and habits constitutive of that community. The stories a community tells itself define its political rationality and ethos by shaping mental habits, conscience, and awareness, through which that life form and political rationale is subsequently handed down to subsequent generations. A "grammar" of intelligible practices is interweaved with linguistic conventions in every community, through which people come to have views about what counts as fitting and unfitting action, as well as what is seen as a positive innovation or a negative deviation. Thus, to acquire a new story or a new grammar of a well-known story is to alter the form of life that it evokes. A different word forms differently acting flesh.

Ulrich harnesses this Wittgensteinian understanding of how human beings acquire an ethos and also how they should expect it to be altered to give flesh to Karl Barth's account of human redemption as an incorporation into God's time. In paragraph 14 of *Church Dogmatics* I.2,[50] Barth explains that Jesus Christ is the full revelation within human history of God's story with the world. God is not *of* our fallen time, but *takes on* our fallen time in a divine act of lordship over it. Beginning with God's incorporation of fallen human beings into God's story yields a sweeping alteration of all familiar conceptions of ethics, which seek to define the good and the true in generic terms. But precisely as accounts of the generic good act, "that which is no problem at all to ethical thought generally, or only a problem which can be lightly pushed aside and left open—the actual situation of human beings . . . their actual commitment to the good, their actual distance from it and the actual overcoming of this distance (not in themselves, but by the actuality of the good itself)—this is the burning problem in Christian ethics, the very aim and content of the whole ethical enquiry and reply."[51] Once it is granted that Christian ethics is oriented by hope for the entry of God's time into ours, why should the ethicist not be instructed by voices and arguments out of the general ethical inquiries ongoing in its vicinity?[52] At this point Ulrich's theological project converges with that of Barth:

"to become obedient," "to act rightly," "to realize the good," never means anything other than to become obedient to the revelation of the grace of God; to live as a human being to whom grace has come in Jesus Christ. But this is the very reason why there can be no change of standpoint or theme when dogmatics becomes ethics, or rather, when it reveals its ethical content.[53]

---

50. Karl Barth, CD I.2, 45–121. The ethical entailments of this account of eschatological time are developed in paragraphs 36 and 37 of CD II.2.
51. Barth, CD II.2, 519.
52. Ibid., 523.
53. Ibid., 539.

In a time of pandemic and increasingly turbulent political and economic crises, Ulrich presents Anglophone readers with a theology forged in a time of cultural devastation and ecclesial struggle over the essence of the Christian gospel. This is theology born from a visceral awareness of the importance, not just of thinking or arguing about, but *living* in eschatological hope. Ours too is a time of dissatisfaction with the limits of the human, in which a deep and widespread desire to be more and better than the human has again become a cultural norm. In such a time Ulrich's emphasis on the ethical importance of wonder and gratitude at the works of God the Creator offers crucial critical insight into a wide range of cultural trends. In being a theology born into a church that had largely lost its way and allied itself with life-destroying ideologies, it is theology acutely aware of the necessity of questioning our theological commonplaces and the ways their meanings are constantly being reshaped and sometimes corrupted by the social context in which we confess them. Ulrich hands on to Christians today a theological approach with the resources needed for harder and more conflictual times, and which has proved itself capable of weathering the temptations and fads that wash over theology in times of easy academic affluence. By inviting us to reconsider the theological legacy of the Confessing Church, Ulrich shows how the historical Christian tradition can still be lived in, can still reveal the world, and is so much more than a moral program or a dogma about the truth. This is theology that cannot rest content until transfigured by a living God.

Part I

A CHRISTIAN ETHICS OF MESSIANIC PRESENCE (*ECCLESIA*)

Chapter 1

THE MESSIANIC CONTOURS OF EVANGELICAL ETHICS

How can Christians today properly articulate what it means to "be in" Jesus Christ? Positioning such a question within the subdiscipline of Christian ethics might at first blush appear to narrow its scope. In fact, it broadens the inquiry far beyond a merely doctrinal investigation in asking what it means to "*live in*" Jesus Christ. This is a question that cannot be investigated without being drawn deep into the whole scope of Christian theology, preeminently, eschatology. This chapter investigates the implications for Christian ethics of different eschatologies, specifically, Messianic and apocalyptic eschatologies. Examining the grammar of two important contemporary accounts of eschatology is another way of asking how best to understand God's creative, reconciling, and redemptive works to be locating the divine condescension to and proximate claiming of the individual believer. In more general terms, we are asking how the immediate encounter with the redeemer situates the believer who receives it within the wider horizon of temporality.

The Barmen Declaration (1934) provides an initial occasion to display the intertwining and importance of Messianic and apocalyptic eschatologies, as well as the political implications of such an approach. The first section unpacks Barmen in order to explain why a theological account of freedom rests in essential ways on an account of divine deliverance. A second section clarifies how human freedom is won in the exercise of the reign of Jesus Christ to liberate human beings from the powers of this world-age. Taken together these first two points suggestively indicate what is at stake for Christian ethics that takes seriously the divine inbreaking as both Messianic and apocalyptic, despite these eschatological positions having been positioned as rival traditions in modern theology.[1] The emphasis in this third section is on describing how each construal of eschatology configures Christian descriptions of the political horizon of human action. A fourth section proposes that the grounding of the Christian ethos in a Messianic-apocalyptic eschatology is centered on the prayer "thy kingdom come." A concluding section briefly clarifies how this approach can generate sharply focused forms of culture-critical theological engagement, effectively reframing human action in a manner that is

---

1. Gerhard Sauter, *What Dare We Hope? Reconsidering Eschatology* (Harrisburg: Trinity Press International, 1999), chaps. 3–4.

highly fruitful for Christian ethics. The elucidation of these connections brings into the foreground what may be called the Protestant character of Christian ethics, the fundamental question of Christian freedom.

Why Freedom? The Protestant Grammar of the Christian Ethos

If there is such a thing as a Protestant tradition of Christian ethics, why should we grant that the question of freedom is central to its definition? The second thesis of the 1934 Barmen Declaration does not introduce the language of freedom. But it does insist on the importance of taking bondage seriously in Christian ethics.

> *"Jesus Christ, whom God made our wisdom, our righteousness and sanctification and redemption"* (1 Cor. 1:30).
>
> As Jesus Christ is God's assurance of the forgiveness of all our sins, so in the same way and with the same seriousness is he also God's mighty claim upon our whole life. Through his grateful service to his creatures a joyful deliverance from the godless fetters of this world freely befalls us [*widerfährt uns*].
>
> We reject the false doctrine, as though there were areas of our life in which we would not belong to Jesus Christ, but to other lords—areas in which we would not need justification and sanctification through him.[2]

The condition of the confession of thanks for "deliverance from the godless fetters of this world" is Jesus Christ having already been made our wisdom, righteousness, and sanctification. At minimum, then, deliverance must concern our "wisdom," our thinking—the renewal of our mind—as we read in Paul's flagship description of the "ethical existence" in Rom. 12:2:

> Do not be conformed to this world [i.e. do not live in accordance with the "patterns" of this world-age], but let your shape of life [your character] become transformed by the renewal [innovation] of your minds, so that you may discern what is the will of God—what is good and acceptable and perfect [or fulfilled].[3]

As we read in the verses that follow in Romans 12, this is a deliverance that is promised to be concretely realized within the Christian community. The third thesis of the Barmen Declaration explicitly emphasizes this entailment of Christ's liberation.

---

2. "The Theological Declaration of Barmen," in *The Constitution of the Presbyterian Church (U.S.A.)* Part I, *Book of Confessions* (Louisville, Ky.: Office of the General Assembly, 1996), 311.

3. My translation.

> "Rather, speaking the truth in love, we are to grow up in every way into him who is the head, into Christ, from whom the whole body [is] joined and knit together." (Eph. 4:15-16)
>
> The Christian church is the congregation of the brethren in which Jesus Christ acts presently as the Lord in word and sacrament through the Holy Spirit. As the church of pardoned sinners, it has to testify in the midst of a sinful world, with its faith as with its obedience, with its message as with its order, that it is solely his property, and that it lives and wants to live solely from his comfort and from his direction in the expectation of his appearance.
>
> We reject the false doctrine, as though the church were permitted to abandon the form of its message and order to its own pleasure or to changes in prevailing ideological and political convictions.[4]

The rediscovery of the theology of "Christ's lordship" we see here in the Barmen Declaration was catalyzed by Ernst Wolf's insistent teaching that "the lordship of Christ which calls us to be His witnesses demands first of all the realization of the deliverance from the bondage of 'Christian ideological and institutional thinking.'"[5] The presumption of any such affirmation must be that the freedom of an ethicist, as a member of the Christian church, will be realized only if God's ongoing deliverance is granted. At root, Christian freedom is an implicate of God's very own freedom as it appears in His story in Jesus Christ and is fulfilled in Christ's actualized lordship. The essence of the lordship of Jesus Christ is to bring deliverance to human beings. Thus, to become part of the story encapsulated in his life and death entails a freeing from all other forms of bondage and all other determinations.

It is important to notice that in the third thesis of the Barmen Declaration the Christian church is addressed as that community in which Jesus Christ is presently acting through the Holy Spirit. To affirm this commits believers to think through how the deliverance that comes through the Holy Spirit accomplishes the "renewal (renovation) of our minds" and "deliverance" from all ideological bondage—every pattern of thinking that conform to this world-age. Wolf's gloss has usefully highlighted that the core logic of the Barmen Declaration rests on Christ's ongoing action to deliver human beings from their bondage to other "sources" or media of living. The liberation promised in the rule of Jesus Christ is to reveal the distortions introduced by everything which we take for granted as an environmental medium

---

4. "Barmen," 311.
5. Ernst Wolf, "Königsherrschaft Christi," *Theologische Existenz Heute* 64 (1958): 60-1. My translation. Wolf had emphasized this point for some decades in his teaching, and this published version of this emphasis appeared a full two years before Ernst Käsemann's groundbreaking essay on the apocalyptic origin of Christian theology, which was influential in establishing this claim more widely in the academy. Ernst Käsemann, "On the Subject of Primitive Christian Apocalyptic," in *New Testament Questions of Today*, trans. W. J. Montague (London: SCM Press, 1969), 108-37.

capable of sustaining us as they diverge from the only true source and mediator of fullness of life.

My central interest is in how the logic or grammar that organizes the Barmen Declaration can be understood as distinctly present within the Christian ethos and so shape contemporary engagement in the discipline of Christian ethics. In what way does God's own living activity remain present within the Christian ethos? In other words, in what sense can it be understood as obvious that the Christian ethos is directly determined by God's living together with us, that is, as God's creatures, partners, and children? This, I would suggest, is the theological feature that may be called the Protestant grammar of the Christian ethos. It is a biblical grammar. When I use the term "ethos" I am indicating that place where human beings experience themselves to be at home, that is, at the right place of living as human beings. I am asking *which* context actually shapes and orients the believer's perception and action. Any further explication of the Christian ethos will demand we examine in more detail the transmission mechanism for human freedom. *Why* must God's deliverance of the human being from bondage be considered the condition of all human freedom?

God's Deliverance as Scriptural Theme

Significantly, in scripture "freedom" does not appear as a noun. There is not even a word for freedom in Old Testament Hebrew. In the New Testament, the language of freedom is strictly linked with the stories of God's deliverance. Gal. 5:1 is typical: "For freedom Christ has set us free." Biblical texts consistently refuse all talk of freedom apart from divine actions of deliverance (*Befreiung*), which are presented as exclusively God's.[6] "Deliverance," insists Ps. 3:8, "belongs to the Lord." Roughly 200 verses in scripture speak of God's deliverance. If we understand the topos of freedom in biblical terms, then, we can take deliverance to be the most characteristic grammar of God's acts. To trace God's works of deliverance is to see the red thread uniting the story taking place between God and Israel, as well as between God and all of those who then participate in this story.

Taking biblical usage of the language of freedom seriously presses the theologian to understand deliverance as deeply integrated with the story of God's characteristic mode of action. In not being entrapped by the dynamics and trajectories of creaturely history, God is free to intervene and free human beings from their bondage to illusory narratives and realties. In other words, if humans are to live in freedom they will only achieve this in living in accordance with God's deliverance and actions as they are revealed to be moments in His story with the creaturely realm—which is not bound to follow the trajectories that secular narratives of historical trajectories may have led us to expect.

---

6. There are only a few exceptions.

In the Lord's Prayer Christians pray, "your will be done."[7] Put more literally, we might say, "your will may, or should, be realized." The question, "Realized by whom?" receives an unequivocal answer in scripture: God's will will be realized by God's own activity, in which he deigns to involve us. The most intensely focused theological description of this connection is found in Karl Barth's account of the "ethos" of Lord's Prayer and its central request, "Your kingdom come."[8] Barth displays how this prayer functions as a permanent reminder that the Christian life finds its orientation in looking for and waiting upon God's very own actions.

Not only is deliverance the core feature of divine action in scripture, but God's acts also differentiate these works of deliverance. God's acts of creation, reconciliation, and redemption are the most obvious acts of divine freeing. Within this set of actions there are also acts of "authoritative speech."[9] Psalm 130 offers a paradigmatic example of a word of forgiveness and judgment that realizes justice and brings renewal (as a renovated mind). All of these divine acts may be called deliverance because they are merciful divine appearances in creaturely reality that make a new beginning. Mercy provides a paradigmatic instance of how God's deliverance renovates the mind. Deliverance is continually thematically described in scripture as an act of God's mercy, with mercy exclusively attributed to God (Jer. 30:18). God's mercies are the acts of faithfulness on which the continuity of God's story rests. The term "mercy" names God's acts of deliverance and rescue by which those held captive are brought back into God's own sphere of action. Only in a derivate sense are human beings asked to be merciful or forgive, and so participate in God's rescuing works. We forgive "in His name" precisely because forgiveness (as mercy) is exclusively God's.[10] We are commanded to be merciful not *like* God, but as *God* is merciful (Lk. 6:36[11]).[12]

Though the grammar of God's characteristic and inalienable actions is present throughout the biblical narrative, it is particularly visible in the prayers of the Psalms. The Psalter honors and praises God because of His manifold and rich activity. Ps. 103:1-6, for example, presents us with a clear list of the actions exclusively attributed to God:

---

7. Matt. 6:10. Compare with the Greek version: "ἐλθέτω ἡ βασιλεία σου, γενηθήτω τὸ θέλημά σου."

8. Karl Barth, *The Christian Life*, trans. Geoffrey W. Bromiley (Grand Rapids: Eerdmans, 1981), 247; *Das christliche Leben* (Zürich: Theologischer Verlag, 1999), 30.

9. As I will note again herein, I take Martin Buber's translation of the biblical language of "Word of God" as "speech of God" to be theologically crucial in keeping constantly in view the theological emphasis that there is no "word" of God which is not addressed to us.

10. This grammar is evident in the story of Joseph and his brothers in Genesis 50.

11. "Γίνεσθε οἰκτίρμονες καθὼς [καὶ] ὁ πατὴρ ὑμῶν οἰκτίρμων ἐστίν."

12. See Hans Ulrich, "Mercy: The Messianic Practice," in *Mercy*, ed. Gerard den Hertog, Stefan Paas, and Hans Schaeffer (Münster: LIT Verlag, 2014), 7–30.

> Bless the Lord, O my soul,
> and all that is within me,
> bless his holy name.
> Bless the Lord, O my soul,
> and do not forget all his benefits—
> who *forgives* all your iniquity,
> who *heals* all your diseases,
> who *redeems* your life from the Pit,
> who *crowns* you with steadfast love and mercy,
> who *satisfies* you with good as long as you live
> so that your youth is renewed like the eagle's.
> The Lord *works vindication*
> *and justice* for all who are oppressed.

Remaining Present with God's Actions

The line of thought just presented clarifies why it makes theological sense to position the heart of the task of Christian witness as keeping God's actions before ourselves and others while emphasizing that they remain *His* free and merciful acts. This can be achieved only by maintaining the connection between God's story with us and His story as a whole, including the whole cosmic array of His actions (see Deut. 6:20-25), as Martin Luther emphasized:

> How can a mere man see, know, judge, condemn, and change hearts? That is reserved for God alone, as Psalm 7 [:9] says, "God tries the hearts and reins;" and [v.8], "The Lord judges the peoples." And Acts 10 says, "God knows the hearts"; and Jeremiah [17:9-10], "Wicked and unsearchable is the human heart; who can understand it? I the Lord, who search the heart and reins." A court should and must be quite certain and clear about everything if it is to render judgment. But the thoughts and inclinations of the soul can be known to no one but God.[13]

Luther wants to focus our attention and analysis on a specific aspect of God, God's "being in action,"[14] that is, on this God who acts continually and who in His freedom shares His story with His people and with us human beings.[15] It is in this way that God becomes present and apparent in human life. The renewal of the mind of the believer depends on the confession that this story of God's active and innovative rescue is everything. The sequence of God's acts of deliverance exhaustively names the reality sustaining the unity of our lives because their

---

13. Martin Luther, "On Temporal Authority" (1523), in LW 45, 107.
14. Or even, following Jean-Luc Marion, a "God without being": *God without Being: Hors-Texte* (Chicago: University of Chicago Press, 1995).
15. DBWE 2, 110–16. The contrast being drawn here is with any "idol" which we identify and address.

very persistence is dependent on the complex nexus of divine acts of rescue and preservation.

God's being in action is therefore a recurrent concern of the biblical writers, and again nowhere more intensively than in the Psalms. The Psalms present God in His authentic appearance.[16] The psalmists focus on what the dogmatic tradition has given the technical description as God's *opera ad extra*, His apparent works or economy (*oikonomia*). In these works we see what I call a "Messianic" (or an "apocalyptic-Messianic") drive in God's will. This drive originates in God's genuine free act of election of human beings as His partners and of Israel as His people. God reaffirms this election by remaining faithful to this calling over time, and also in God's continuous merciful actions of deliverance and renewal (sanctification).

All God's actions depicted in scripture converge and are summarized in the story of Jesus Christ, who is both Messiah and Lord. The designation "Messianic" indicates the aspects of God's mercy as direct, personal, immediate encounter and coexistence. There can be no messianism without a Messiah, nor any true spirituality without God's Spirit. And that this Messiah ruptures the taken-for-grantedness of human lives can be called apocalyptic in being a revelatory inbreaking. Barth continually and rightly stresses the directness and immediacy of the human encounter with this Messiah. The designation "apocalyptic," in contrast, indicates the character of God's story in its totality, encompassing creation, reconciliation, and redemption. Apocalyptic eschatology points to a total or completed narrative breaking open the seemingly iron-clad continuities we observe in our limited world-age.[17] It is important both to distinguish the apocalyptic and Messianic and to emphasize their inseparability in God's action. The apocalyptic and Messianic have too often over the last century been pitted against one another, and too often have been translated into philosophical schema that purports to "find" God beyond, besides, or behind His Messianic-apocalyptic encounter.

The New Testament's language of *en Christo* situates the human "within that apocalyptic-Messianic story and God's actions" (as I propose glossing 2 Cor. 5:17). To be redeemed is to be addressed as people whose true existence is within God's story and who are being made God's witnesses. Conflict with the apparently invulnerable powers and historical realities of this world-age will necessarily follow. It will follow because to have our life-narratives translocated in this way exposes the fact that we do not really exist in the realities that present themselves as rivals to Christ's rule. We no longer believe we are sustained "naturally" or by "progress" or "the human spirit" to name a few of the obvious claimants.

---

16. The Psalms clearly approach the dynamics of the divine appearance from one angle, and the biblical narratives from another. The psalmic authors' emphasis on making God's acts present to moral agents in the present tense converges in illuminating ways with the animating interest driving contemporary debates about the role of narrative in Christian ethics.

17. Barth, *The Christian Life*, 426–7.

Barth's axiomatic claim that the very substance of God's story depends on God's "election" of human beings to be His partners in Christ aims to secure just this point.[18] The New Testament makes two assumptions that are pivotal for Christian ethics:

> The first is that it has a strictly eschatological content and character, that is, that it looks toward an act of God as the goal and end of all human history and of all the history of faith and the church within it. The second is that it has its basis and meaning in the totality of this history, but in a definite event within it, in a specific, once-for-all, and unique history within that history. Coming from this specific history, Christians pray "Thy kingdom come." Hence their prayer is not . . . the expression of a hope manufactured by people and cherished by the human race as such, the hope of a final solution of the complicated problems of world history which takes place in more or less pure transcendence.[19]

Jesus teaches and commands us to pray "Thy kingdom come" in order to bring about the fulfillment of God's own story in its totality. Those who pray this prayer remain active participants in a worshipping community who knows itself englobed by God's reality and story. Barth's recognition that praying is the center of the Christian ethos was an acknowledgment that the Christian ethos is focused on God's honor, and not primarily on the dignity of the human being, yet another popular reification of the human in isolation from God's story.[20]

Thus, the crucial question: How can Christian witness stay within God's story present because it is God's very own action? This is the question of how human beings can continually verify (*bewahrheiten*) or confirm God's faithfulness, as indicated by Hebrew semantics in which the word for "justice" includes "faithfulness" as well as "verification."

Messianic Time

The insights into biblical theology drawn together by Barth in his *Church Dogmatics* are already well-known. What has rarely been asked, however, is what concrete difference it makes to insist on labeling God's presence "apocalyptic-Messianic." The point of this designation is to recognize that when God's story appears at all within this world-age, it appears in its totality. When it appears at all it cannot but apocalyptically confront this world-age, constituted as it is by narratives and self-understandings that people unquestioningly assume to be reality or history.

---

18. ὁ γὰρ νόμος τοῦ πνεύματος τῆς ζωῆς ἐν Χριστῷ Ἰησοῦ ἠλευθέρωσέν σε ἀπὸ τοῦ νόμου τῆς ἁμαρτίας καὶ τοῦ θανάτου (Rom. 8:2).

19. Barth, *The Christian Life*, 247.

20. Ibid., §§ 77–8.

God's real story is always happening amidst the counter-claimants of this world-age, contradicting them and struggling with their processes and conditions. In other words, God's Messianic-apocalyptic story is neither one beyond this world-age nor one that makes no contact with this world-age. It directly confronts every so-called history that claims to be transforming our world-age in the minutiae of daily life. God's faithfulness is to bring His story into this world-age, so provoking what we may call true history.

In his *Ethics*, Dietrich Bonhoeffer also emphasized that this "apocalyptic-Messianic" logic is determinative for the Christian ethos.

> *In Jesus Christ the reality of God has entered into the reality of this world.* The place where the questions about the reality of God and about the reality of the world are answered at the same time is characterized solely by the name: Jesus Christ. God and the world are enclosed in this name. In Christ all things exist (Col. 1:17).[21]

God's own story of the cosmos leaves nothing out, necessarily claiming for his own story the domains claimed by the counter-reality narratives that are constitutive of this world-age.[22] It is the story of Jesus Christ that determines the distinction between the cosmos and this world-age; Christ appears in this world-age as Lord of the cosmos. The evident distinction between the cosmos and this world-age is therefore established by the apocalyptic-Messianic horizon that is itself explicitly treated as a fault line that must be confronted within the biblical story of God's ongoing work of merciful deliverance.

Recognizing the primacy of God's works of deliverance frees Christian theology from several false alternatives: from having to discover or construct the meaning of history, from needing to come to terms with a fate into which we have been thrown, or even from having to flee from the trials of this world-age into a meta-history floating above lived time. In claiming delivery for Godself alone, God delivers theology from its godless bondage to alienated theological methods, and in a way that is of a piece with God's ways of delivering human beings out of the bondage of all rival mediations of God's reality. God's deliverance comes solely by God's personal involvement to draw us directly into God's story by making God's authentic actions present to us.

Even the notion of a secularized world with its search for meaning in history is one of the framing ideas or worldviews from which God liberates humans. Though the modern notion of history does have its roots in the historical Christian tradition (at least in the West) it remains categorically different from the Messianic-apocalyptic grammar of God's story. It was Karl Löwith who presciently

---

21. DBWE 6, 54. See also Larry L. Rasmussen, *Dietrich Bonhoeffer: Reality and Resistance* (Louisville: Westminster John Knox Press, 2005), 16.

22. See Stanley Hauerwas, *With the Grain of the Universe: The Church's Witness and Natural Theology* (Grand Rapids: Baker Academic, 2013).

insisted that God's story can never be "secularized" without losing its essential logic. Precisely because it is an apocalyptic history it can never be translated into a universally accessible secular history.[23]

Reality

The central theological point that has emerged in this discussion is the importance of the claim that God's presence is made apparent exclusively by His actions, which are never alienated from His agency nor handed over to the immanent dynamics of mediating processes or realities. God's actions are exclusively mediated by Jesus Christ, even within and with the Christian community.[24] As Barth observes of baptism in the *Church Dogmatics*, it cannot be the work of humans that is purifying and renewing in this act.

> According to the New Testament, man's cleansing and renewal take place in the history of Jesus Christ which culminates in His death, and they are mediated through the work of the Holy Spirit. The New Testament does not refer to any additional or accompanying history or mediation of salvation. It mentions no duplicate of this one divine act and word.[25]

The ongoing apocalyptic-Messianic drama must not be obscured by any phenomena or reality that we might want to hold to be indispensable for God's self-revelation—including religious phenomena. The Greek word "near" or "close" as we find in the phrase "the kingdom of heaven has come *close*" (Mk. 10:7) draws attention to unmediated directness of God's deliverance.[26] The difference between a philosophy or theology offering descriptions or reflections on these mediating realities and processes must constantly be distinguished from a theology that insists that its task is solely to witness to God's story.

To be made a witness is to have any perceptions of the self or of phenomena that obscure or obliterate God's own actions ripped away. The paradox of deliverance is that in it phenomena that seemed incontrovertibly real are exposed

---

23. Karl Löwith, *Meaning in History* (Chicago: University of Chicago Press, 1957). See also Giorgio Agamben's critique of Löwith's *Meaning in History* in *The Time that Remains: A Commentary on the Letter to the Romans*, trans. Patricia Dailey (Stanford: Stanford University Press, 2005), 63. According to Agamben, Löwith does not admit the distinction between messianic and the apocalyptic time.

24. This is apparent in the third thesis of the Barmen Declaration.

25. CD IV.4, Study Edition, 128. Barth continues: "If, however, baptism is not a sacrament, its meaning, as indicated in the preliminary thesis, is to be sought in its character as a true and genuine human action which responds to the divine act and word."

26. This point is also emphasized in CD, as well as in Giorgio Agamben, *The Time that Remains*, to which I return later.

as fundamentally indeterminate. Seemingly stable and nonnegotiable realities are interrupted and unveiled in their ephemerality. It is astonishing, to take an obvious example, how many theologies of hope and theological eschatologies have been configured by the quest to discover meaning in history, often using Hegel's philosophy as the template. Hegel's approach has continued to attract theologians in spite of the devastating criticisms leveled against it by Nietzsche and Rosenzweig[27] that are not different in kind from those emerging from biblical theology. The way we understand history and its meaning—like any other theory of reality or all-encompassing worldview—offers a telling example of the ways in which the contemporary church never escapes the need of liberation. Christians have been freed from even the most powerful and all-absorbing patterns of thinking that colonize their world-age.

As God's Messianic-apocalyptic deliverance breaks in on us we recognize that our own conceptions of history obliterate God's story, our conceptions of the future obliterate God's coming, our ideas about spirit obliterate God's Holy Spirit, our moralities obliterate God's ethos, our laws obliterate God's commandments, our *ratio* or reason obliterates God's *logos*, and our "relational existence" can obliterate a very specific relation to the one God. In short, our habits of thinking of God by way of mediating ideas in fact obliterate our ability and interest in attending to God's own speech or word.

Put in the simplest possible terms: God's *logos* or Word[28] is a paradigmatically apocalyptic-Messianic reality that breaks in and exposes the indeterminacy, indifference, or "reign of vacillation" that is characteristic of this age.[29] To highlight the apocalyptic-Messianic aspect of God's word is both a call for a paradigm shift within Christian ethics, and also an apocalyptic intervention. It is an act of witness to having made the transition from thinking and reflecting on human agency and its sources[30] and conditions to the recognition of God's own reality and agency, that is, to God's own ethos within which His partners or children participate. It is in this way that we become witnesses to God's story.

---

27. Franz Rosenzweig's 1925 essay "The New Thinking" is an impressive attempt to escape the Hegelian paradigm in which meaning arises through the mediation of historical processes. Franz Rosenzweig, *The New Thinking*, ed. Alan Udoff and Barbara Galli (New York: Syracuse University Press, 1999).

28. Martin Buber is right to translate "God's word" in the Old Testament as "God's speech" to emphasize that God's *speaking* is a living reality.

29. In German, "Regiment der Schwebe." For the background of this pattern, see Vagn Andersen, *Transformationen Gottes: Abwandlungen des Begriffs des Unbedingten in der Moderne* (Aarhus: Aarhus Universitetsforlag, 2008).

30. Including attempts to search for the "sources of the self," as in Taylor's sense. Charles Taylor, *Sources of the Self: The Making of the Modern Identity* (Cambridge: Harvard University Press, 1989).

The Presence of the New Reality and Its Realization

We can now turn to probe more closely how this witness happens. If God's presence is never mediated, how are the acts of God to create God's new reality in this age to remain constantly present to the human agent? In his *Ethics* Bonhoeffer writes

> The subject matter of a Christian ethic is God's reality revealed in Christ becoming real [*Wirklichwerden*] among God's creatures, just as the subject matter of doctrinal theology is the truth of God's reality revealed in Christ. The place that in all other ethics is marked by the antithesis between ought and is, idea and realization, motive and work, is occupied in Christian ethics by the relation between reality and becoming real, between past and present, between history and event (faith) or, to replace the many concepts with the simple name of the thing itself, the relation between Jesus Christ and the Holy Spirit. The question of the good becomes the question of participating in God's reality revealed in Christ.[31]

Bonhoeffer holds the Christian ethics to serve the realization of the reality that is given with the story God shares with us in Jesus Christ. No concept receives more emphasis in Bonhoeffer's *Ethics* than "reality."[32] But why and in what sense is "reality" being emphasized? The short answer is that an emphasis on the realization of God's new reality corresponds to an equally intense emphasis on God's story in its unmediated and determined totality as invading this world-age. The notion of the reality of God invading this world-age requires this stark emphasis on realization if it is to be intelligible. The ongoing drama of the Christian ethos in fact turns on the dynamic reality of this invasion.[33] The drama ultimately concerns the present appearance of God's story with us human beings, in Jesus Christ. This is what constitutes its "Messianic" character, a label that usefully draws together a specific cluster of moments in the biblical narrative and that presupposes a "Messianic" drama or a Messianic time—that is, a Messianic "today" (see Heb. 3:13-15).

---

31. DBWE 6, 49–50.

32. See *Ontology and Ethics: Bonhoeffer and Contemporary Scholarship*, ed. Adam C. Clark and Michael Mawson (Eugene: Wipf & Stock Publishers, 2013). This same emphasis on reality can be found in the ethics of Barth and Hans Joachim Iwand, and throughout Luther's theology.

33. Oliver O'Donovan, "History and Politics in the Book of Revelation," in *Bonds of Imperfection: Christian Politics, Past and Present*, ed. Oliver O'Donovan and Joan Lockwood O'Donovan (Grand Rapids: Eerdmans, 2004), 25–47.

Distinguishing between Apocalyptic Event and Messianic Time

It may still be unclear how, precisely, this emphasis on the apocalyptic-Messianic appearance of God actually contributes to the freedom of the Christian ethicist. The claim that God's story has an apocalyptic logic is itself relatively uncontroversial, given the apocalyptic scenes and resonances clearly present in the biblical texts. What is more interesting are the implications of the positive rediscovery of the apocalyptic grammar of theology that begins with Barmen and is developed by thinkers like Käsemann. My interest is in thinking through this provocation for the practice of theological ethics. The relevance of this exploration comes immediately into view if we note the inherently political character of God's apocalyptic-Messianic as indicated in passages like 1 Cor. 15:25: "For he must reign until he has put all his enemies under his feet." Apocalyptic theology demands that Christian ethics ask how this promise concerns the present time and *our* world.

Recent attention to Paul's letters has renewed awareness of the apocalyptic contours of God's story, sharpening our understanding of the conceptual scope of biblical apocalyptic. As J. Louis Martyn writes in his well-known commentary:

> Paul's apocalyptic is not focused on God's unveiling something that was previously hidden, as though it had been eternally standing behind a curtain (contrast 1 Cor. 2:9-10). The genesis of Paul's apocalyptic—as we see it in Galatians—lies in the apostle's certainty that God has *invaded* the present evil age by sending Christ and his Spirit into it. There was a "before," the time when we were confined, imprisoned; and there is an "after," the time of our deliverance. And the difference between the two is caused not by an unveiling, but rather by the coming of Christ and his Spirit.[34]

Martin is here giving biblical detail to Käsemann's claim that "Christian theology is from its beginning a witness of the 'real' story confronting every 'reality' which we may call world, history, or nature."[35] Martin's account follows the logic of Käsemann's illuminating thesis that "apocalyptic is the mother of theology,"[36] with his own specific accents.

Deliverance occurs as and when God freely invades what is false and obscured with a new reality in its concluded totality. This has always been the grammar of

---

34. J. Louis Martyn, *Galatians*, The Anchor Yale Bible (London: Yale University Press, 1997), 99.

35. Ernst Käsemann: "The Beginnings of Christian Theology," in *New Testament Questions of Today*, trans. W. J. S. L. Montague (London: SCM Press 1969), 82–107.

36. Käsemann's claim is that—since the preaching of Jesus cannot really be described as theology—apocalyptic was the mother of all Christian theology. See Martyn's discussion of this point, "A Personal Word about Ernst Käsemann," in *Apocalyptic and the Future of Theology: With and Beyond J. Louis Martyn*, ed. Joshua B. Davis and Douglas Harink (Eugene, Ore.: Cascade Books, 2012), xiii–xv.

deliverance in its genuine theological logic—the moments in which God shares his story with his people. Precisely in being *God's* reality the apocalyptic narrative encompasses the whole of reality, including the cosmos and we human beings. The apocalyptic narrative must by its very nature be in Messianic confrontation with any so-called reality that opposes it, often denoted by Käsemann and others as the "fallen world." In Jesus Christ fallen reality is determined to disappear as God's works in all things are made luminously present and visible. And this fallen world, what Paul calls the "old reality," has already been overcome, even if this world-age remains having not yet finally disappeared. These are the grounds for the shared insistence of Martyn and Käsemann that apocalyptic entails the affirmation of warfare, an ongoing conflict between God and "the powers"[37] despite the outcome of this clash having already been decided.

That Messianic time is called "today" in the New Testament is a reminder that the divine rescue experienced by human beings is not necessarily the final dramatic end still to come. Messianic time is nevertheless wholly determined by that apocalyptic ending, which has its own passage of time, even though the sequence of events remains hidden to us. To follow Paul's logic as set out in 1 Corinthians 15 is to be made aware of the distinction between the apocalyptic final end and time here and now, that is, a Messianic time generated and determined by the apocalyptic story and thus still characterized by contradiction and struggle. Nevertheless, Messianic time does still have its own genuine Messianic presence. The apocalyptically determined Messianic time is the time of God's ongoing activity and thus the time of the Holy Spirit. It is the Spirit who apocalyptically invades our rational or spiritual worlds, however they may be configured, in order to realize His own work of transformation and creation.

In his commentary on Paul's letter to the Romans, Giorgio Agamben has insisted with special intensity on the distinction between the apocalyptic final end and Messianic time, which he calls "the time that remains."[38] Agamben's point is that Messianic time has its own proper meaning and substance that makes a concrete appearance as a distinct ethos in our present time within the wider apocalyptic story. With this observation Agamben helpfully clarifies how an ethos that is out of step with the present world can appear as Messianic.

Agamben is aware that the apocalyptic story has already begun and concretely determines the present time. His own approach, however, is strongly insistent that the final fulfillment remains deferred or held back.[39] He does so because, unlike

---

37. Or as Bonhoeffer sometimes put it, between God and the devil. See Scott Prather, *Christ, Power and Mammon: Karl Barth and John Howard Yoder in Dialogue* (London: Bloomsbury T&T Clark, 2013).

38. Agamben, *The Time that Remains*.

39. Here Agamben refers to 1 Thessalonians and also to Carl Schmitt's widely influential theory—but one fatally crippled in its refusal of all definite determination within the present time. See Julia Hell, "Katechon: Carl Schmitt's Imperial Theology and the Ruins of the Future," *Germanic Review* 84, no. 4 (2009): 283–326.

Rosenzweig, he does not want to link Messianic time with the community of faith. In biblical terms, Rosenzweig is on much firmer ground in insisting that God's coming into our world-age is inseparably bound to His story with His people. Rosenzweig's emphasis on God's commitment to the people of God is more biblically defensible than Agamben's proposal to locate apocalyptic time on a different level of world history, as a meta-history. Only by following God's story with his people, the story of Jesus Christ with its own Messianic procession, do we remain within the biblical logic.

Like Agamben, Barth too accepted that there is an apocalyptic deferral that needed to be taken seriously in theology. His account of this deferral, however, unfolded a quite different dogmatic logic than the philosophically leveraged deferral proposed by Agamben. As Barth put it in the *Church Dogmatics*:

> The presence of Jesus in His community is full of import for the future. His presence impels and presses to His future, general and definitive revelation, of which there has been a particular and provisional form in the Easter history. Hence even the presence of Jesus in the Spirit, for all its fullness, can only be a pledge or first instalment of what awaits the community as well as the whole universe, His return in glory. But it must never be forgotten that He who comes again in glory, this future Jesus, is identical with the One proclaimed by the history of yesterday and really present to His own to-day. The thorough-going eschatology for which the interim between now and one day necessarily seems to be a time of emptiness, of futility, of lack, of a progressive and barely concealed disillusionment, is not the eschatology of New Testament Christianity. And again, it is only an unspiritual community which can tolerate such a view.[40]

This tying of Jesus' redemptive work cannot be one that provokes enmity. That the goodwill of Jesus Christ is not yet completed

> has its true basis and determination in the fact that it is the good will of Jesus Christ to move from the commencement of His revelation to its completion, not causing the commencement and the completion to coincide, but Himself first to be provisionally who He is and to do provisionally what He does, giving Himself time and place for combat. The world, the community and we ourselves have thus no option but to participate in the fulfilment of this good will of Jesus Christ, to tread with Him the way which He wills to take, to fight with Him the battle which He wills to fight, in short, to follow Him. Since He precedes us, and it is His good will to act as He does, the only possible thing for the world, the community and ourselves, and indeed the only right thing, is to follow Him, to accompany Him on the way to His goal.[41]

---

40. CD III.2, study version, 468.
41. CD IV.3 §69, 329–30.

Barth's deployment of this martial language must not be read as reinscribing the gnostic myth of a dualistic reality constituted by some power capable of holding back God's final fulfillment. Barth's descriptions of the present time as an apocalyptic-Messianic drama in which a fight is ongoing should likewise be read as a refusal of Bultmann-like stances that propose an "apocalyptic disposition" that is essentially a static existential stance. By insisting on the ongoing personal nature of the eschatological conflict Barth frames Christian discipleship within Messianic-apocalyptic contours. Christians are challenged to live within the apocalyptic story in a Messianic way, in a Messianic time—meaning that the apocalypse is not just the judgment of this *aion*, but has its very own positive appearance and determined reality in personal experience. This positivity is the crucial component in our characterization of the apocalyptic-Messianic contours of Christian ethics. Christian ethics is in essence concerned with the Christian ethos as a lived witnessing to God's present working to initiate and realize God's new reality in determinate places, with determinate people.

To this point my description of the basics of Christian ethics in God's Messianic-apocalyptic activity might appear overly abstract. I have been concerned thus far to set out the grammar of God's claiming of human beings. The time has now come to investigate how this grammar concretely appears in our own practices. We have the heuristic key in hand by which these practices may be recognized in their authentically Messianic-apocalyptic contours and substance, which I have already identified as the Protestant character of Christian ethics.

The Ethos of Messianic Time

Barth rejects the idea that the time between the Messianic advent and the final apocalypse can remain an empty, indeterminate *saeculum*. The Christian community that becomes comfortable in the interminable negotiation of the *saeculum*, he has suggested, could only be an unspiritual community. The question is what is entailed in the affirmation that Messianic time is not empty. On the basis of what we have already said, it is clear that Messianic time cannot be empty in the sense of being a continual waiting for an apocalyptic inbreaking, as proposed, for instance, by Martin Heidegger.[42] Determined time is best described as an *enacted* Messianic ethos. Agamben helpfully indicates why this might be so in developing a description of a Messianic ethos out of some central Pauline ideas, such as *klesis* (vocation) and well as the distinctively Pauline idea of the *hos me* ("as if not").[43] This Messianic ethos is even more explicitly described in Barth's ethics, especially

---

42. See Jakob Deibl, *Menschwerdung und Schwächung: Annäherung an ein Gespräch mit Gianni Vattimo* (Vienna: Vienna University Press, 2013), 48–52.

43. See also Gianni Vattimo, "Os mé: Zur Haltung des 'als ob nicht' bei Paulus und Heidegger," *Zwischen Verzückung und Verzweiflung* 2 (2001): 169–82.

1. The Messianic Contours of Evangelical Ethics

his ethics of reconciliation, as well as in the works of Bonhoeffer, Hans Joachim Iwand, and Stanley Hauerwas.

The Messianic Ethos of the Worshipping Community

The question at hand is how this apocalyptic-Messianic reality and ethos remain transparent to God's story in its totality and firmly tethered to God's ongoing actions. The coherence of an apocalyptic-Messianic ethos turns on the integrity with which it can answer this question: How is the freedom of the ongoing Messianic appearance, linked as it is with the freedom of God to act, continue to be driven by the dynamic appearance of God's story among us without losing its (synchronic) wholeness? To answer this question is to find the heuristic key unlocking the genuinely apocalyptic-Messianic contours and substance of theological ethics.

Barth's description of the Messianic ethos focuses on the presence of God in His ongoing actions as His faithfulness to us. The Messianic ethos is the specific ethos generated by God's faithfulness. As already noted, one Hebrew word means both "truth" and "faithfulness" (*emunah*), much as "faithfulness" and "justice" also coincide in one Hebrew word (*tsedakah*). This semantic overlap directly challenges the modern tendency strictly to separate these four concepts.

This semantic overlap points in turn to the Messianic appearance of God's story as an expression of the will of God for coexistence with His partners and children. God and human beings have come together because human truth and justice exist in God's faithful and continuous acting. The Christian ethos is the liturgical existence and worshipping activity of the community as it witnesses to God's ongoing actions—to the actual living God.

It is significant that Barth describes this Messianic ethos as the ethos of the *worshipping* community. As already briefly noted, this is why the defining activity of the Christian ethos is the prayer that asks after the coming of God's kingdom. This prayer is the entry point for God's coming kingdom. Such prayer sustains in a paradigmatic way the awareness that the only reality Christians seek is that which is sustained exclusively by God's actions, and only secondarily by His cooperation with his partners and children. The coming kingdom is God's very own action, and the paradigmatic form of divine action.

Barth calls prayer "the primal and basic form of the whole Christian ethos" given the essentially petitionary character of the prayer, "thy kingdom come." Prayer, simultaneously a genuinely political act of Christians, both in invoking the lordship of Christ and also because it springs from Christ's acts, makes a new beginning of the believer in the Body of Christ (as the first thesis of the Barmen Declaration emphasized). In Barth's language

> Something very special has to have taken place, and to keep on taking place, when certain people may not only be called the children of God but are this, and as such are qualified, entitled, able, and willing to call upon God as their Father, when in this calling, in their thanks and praise and prayer, the Christian ethos

is actualized and maintained and continued and developed. This is not only not self-evident; it is totally inconceivable. We can count on it only as on a fact of unique order that the existence of such people and their action is possible, not once alone, but in the continuity of their lives. . . . What has to take place, and to keep on taking place, if people are to be Christians, is a special movement and act of God in which he gives to the Word of his grace—the Word of the reconciliation of the world to him accomplished in Jesus Christ—the specific power to reach these specific people among the many to whom it goes out and is directed, so that they open themselves up to it in freedom.[44]

Thus is the political actions of Christians, their Messianic-political ethos, birthed in their prayer for God's coming kingdom. It is a prayer concerned with the coming of God's reality in its totality as it has already begun in the unmediated directness of the coexistence of God and His children. The political action that is characteristic of the Christian ethos is embedded in this particular kind of relationship with God. It is the distinctive political action of God's children.

If our praying for the coming of the kingdom keeps us attentive to God's action, so too do the practices of baptism and the Lord's Supper.[45] Here again the worshipping community appears as the community of those living within Christ's acts. In the words of the third thesis of the Barmen Declaration, "The Christian church is the congregation of the brethren in which Jesus Christ acts presently as the Lord in word and sacrament through the Holy Spirit." In word and sacrament, the witness of the Christian church depends upon this paradigmatic worshipping form of the Christian ethos. Christians live within and with Christ's acts. They are under the reign of the Word of God and receive forgiveness and renewal from the Holy Spirit. Christian worship represents the Messianic ethos in its essence. It is in this way that God's reality is realized, to use Bonhoeffer's language.

God's Speech: The Messianic Witness of His Word

Like prayer, preaching too expresses the genuinely Messianic character of the Christian ethos. Luther's description of the focus of the Christian ethos emphasizes the transforming power of by God's word through preaching and being "under the reign" of the Word of God as it mediates God's genuine and constitutive act. We can find expansive descriptions of preaching that emphasize this Messianic character in the ethics of both Luther and Barth. Barth approaches this task in the *Church Dogmatics* by describing the word through which God works on his partners and children.

---

44. Barth, *The Christian Life*, 89.
45. In the unfinished part of his ethics of reconciliation in the *Church Dogmatics*, Barth planned "to describe the divinely willed and commanded Christian life . . . as man's path from the divine foundation to the divine renewal of his required faithfulness, and in this connection as his path from baptism to the Lord's Supper," ibid., 288.

> The Word of God, which the Christian has heard and may, it is to be hoped, hear again, is among all the factors that determine his life the only one that works and speaks unequivocally. In making God known, already in the present it points radically, unbrokenly, and definitively beyond the regime of vacillation and ambivalence that characterizes the present. . . . In the lives of those who recognize it, this gives his Word a distinction, a majesty, a dignity, which marks it off and differentiates it absolutely from all other factors in their lives when it comes among these factors and close to them, no matter how estimable or worthy or significant or positive these factors may be, no matter how seriously they must be taken.[46]

"God speaks his word"—with this act of God's we are in the midst of Messianic worship.

Preaching is a human activity transparent in a paradigmatic way to God's own speech.[47] In its singular focus on God's own speech, the witness of preaching displays the apocalyptic-Messianic character of the Christian ethos as an embodied invasion of God's word in a given time and place. Because hearing the Word of God is the paradigm of that *extra nos*, preaching is revealed as its corresponding form of genuine witness. God's own speaking contradicts every linguistic world that resists, obscures and obliterates God's message.

As a paradigmatic locus of divine speech, the human action of preaching offers the platform from which Christians can consider the transparency of other types of human action to God's acts. The task is to resist confusing God and phenomena, and so misunderstanding God's deliverance. To keep God's action present means to remain continually attentive to God's presence not being muted but *articulate* in human action. Bonhoeffer's description of communal life in *Life Together* is one exploration of the accompanying practices—such as prayer or reading the Bible together—through which God works to cancel out the hermetic tendencies of linguistic worlds that entrap humans in the worshipping community. When the hidden presence of God is not articulated in praying and preaching, we will come to understand what it means to praise God in all things. Conversely, a church whose praying and preaching are not transparent in this way obfuscates God's deliverance in a manner that hinders the congregation's ability to comprehend God's acts.

We may call such a theology Protestant messianism. It is Protestant in that the apocalyptic-Messianic grammar is one that has a protesting or contradicting character. The paradigmatic stance of such Protestantism is articulated by the prayer of Ps. 130:5, with its hopeful yearning for God's speech: "I wait for the Lord, my soul waits, and in his word I hope."

---

46. Ibid., 177; Barth, *Das christliche Leben*, 298.
47. Again, recall Buber's translation of God's word as God's speaking (or even God's preaching) as discussed previously.

The Christian Ethos in Its Determined Reality

The central task of Christian ethics is to attest the priority of God's apocalyptic-Messianic story and its appearance in a form that is determined by God. Christian ethics thus witnesses to the character of the Christian ethos as it becomes real with and within the Christian community. My emphasis has been on the transparency of this witness to God's continuous actions, and in this sense on its Messianic character as part of a worshipping community.

The Christian ethicist must therefore be highly attuned to the ways in which the Messianic-apocalyptic ethos already permeates all aspects of the Christian community through its bodily life, through the habits, character, and the good works of its members. This too is an emphasis that is central in the Barmen Declaration.

> The Christian church is the congregation of the brethren in which Jesus Christ acts presently as the Lord in Word and Sacrament through the Holy Spirit. As the church of pardoned sinners, it has to testify in the midst of a sinful world, with its faith as with its obedience, with its message as with its order, that it is solely his property, and that it lives and wants to live solely from his comfort and from his direction in the expectation of his appearance.[48]

All these features of the church—faith, obedience, message, order—are features of a witness that is transparent to God's activity. Only a transparent church can witness to God's honor, *soli deo Gloria*. A Messianic ethics is irreducibly concerned with God's honor. If there remains a glory that is finally still to come, it is nevertheless one that is beginning to dawn here and now.[49] This is a point emphasized by Jesus himself: "let your light shine before others, so that they may see your good works and give glory to your Father in heaven" (Mt. 5:16). Barth, commenting on this passage, observes that this giving of glory is necessarily before all human beings, and so entails the task of mission and evangelism.

> But Christians cannot be content with this. This call needs a practical commentary in the acts of those who issue it to human beings—just as Jesus Christ himself proclaimed the kingdom of God not only with words but also with significatory acts. People are right in wanting to see the good works of Christians in order to praise their heavenly Father (Mt. 5:16). They also have to be witnesses to him by resolutely being there—and not as the last on the scene—when on this side of the deliverance that God has begun and will complete, in relative antithesis to

---

48. "Barmen," 311.

49. It is thus to be differentiated from Giorgio Agamben's very different distinction between the coming glory and the messianic time. See Agamben, *The Kingdom and the Glory: For a Theological Genealogy of Economy and Government* (Stanford: Stanford University Press, 2011).

human disorder and the lordship of demons, there is wrestling and fighting and suffering for a provisional bit of human right.[50]

The Messianic character of the Christian ethos is concretized in specific acts, in preaching but also in good works, both of which have an apocalyptic invading character. Messianic time gains material substance through no other mediating ideas or practices. The substance of this invasion is nowhere more apparent than in Jesus' works of healing. These works and the habits of Christians in community signify Messianic time—the time of God's coming and presence. In them God's honor reigns.

The Christian tradition has sometimes used the language of "good works" in order to designate the character of a Messianic ethos living in Messianic time. It was that most radical critic of a distorted ethics of good works, Martin Luther, who ultimately offered the most robust defense of an ethos of good works. This ethos is on full display in Luther's exposition of the Ten Commandments:

The Fifth [Commandment]
You are not to kill.
What does this mean? Answer:
We are to fear and love God, so that we neither endanger nor harm the lives of our neighbors, but instead help and support them in all of life's needs.
...
The Seventh [Commandment]
You are not to steal.
What is this? Answer:
We are to fear and love God, so that we neither take our neighbors' money or property nor acquire them by using shoddy merchandise or crooked deals, but instead help them to improve and protect their property and income.[51]

To display these good works in our daily life—this is the Messianic reality that confronts those who are guided by a determined hope. The rediscovery of the apocalyptic logic of God's story thus places renewed emphasis upon the *determinate* character of this reality. As we read in Paul's writings, these are not potential or possible works, but works that confront and claim us in concrete settings:

For by grace you have been saved through faith, and this is not your own doing; it is the gift of God—not the result of works, so that no one may boast. For we

---

50. Barth, *The Christian Life*, 270; Barth, *Das christliche Leben*, 469.
51. Martin Luther, "Small Catechism," in *The Book of Concord: The Confessions of the Evangelical Lutheran Church*, ed. Robert Kolb and Timothy J. Wengert, trans. Charles Arand, Eric Gritsch, Robert Kolb, William Russell, James Schaaf, Jane Strohl, and Timothy J. Wengert (Philadelphia: Fortress Press 2000), 352–3.

are what he has made us, created in Christ Jesus for good works, which God prepared beforehand to be our way of life. (Eph. 2:8-10)

The task of theological ethics is to unfold God's story within concrete and detailed narratives that contradict every indefinite, generalized, independent, and (therefore fatal) process or history. Such processes are present in every supposedly independent phenomenon, including the phenomena of morality or hope, and even in any universalized concept of Messianic ethos that displaces prayerful attention to God's work, as in Agamben's commentary. To keep God's actions present means constantly to recall that God's story has a narrative with a contradicting logic. Christian hope is kept Christian only as it constantly refers to God's story without transforming it into generic utopianism or optimism.

The manner in which the Messianic inbreaking evokes a counter-narrative to the vitalism of a bare-life account exemplifies in a very compressed way the procedure whereby Christian ethics serves God's contradiction and interruption of ideological patterns that demand confrontation through carefully calibrated counter-narratives. As vitalism deprives human beings of the recognition that socially-formed life is part of God's good creation, so too individualism deprives us of the real human person elected into God's story, or futurism and utopianism of our hope for God's own gifted future. Moralism, too, belongs to this brand of ideology in being an attempt to offer recipes to satisfy the insatiable human desire for a justification apart from hope in God's mercy and forgiveness.

The Witness of Broken Indeterminacy

The Christian ethos is best described as a heuristic stance that empowers believers critically to discern the unstable indeterminacy of everything that the world presents as unshakably firm and true.[52]

This brings us one final time to the crucial point of God's invading story in its totality and reality. Christians do not confess themselves believers in some history of ideas with its indefinite contours, but a different story they have been given and that lends determinacy to the phenomenal world. When Christians talk about children, for example, they do not talking about reproduction in the abstract; their talk about dying addresses far more than simply the end of life; taking up the language of identity, they do not collapse into tropes of self-affirmation; so too

---

52. Even philosophers like Axel Honneth have glimpsed the fragility of this ideological indeterminacy. In his reflections on "pathologies of individual freedom," Honneth examines what it means to "suffer from indeterminacy," and seeks strategies for discovering a determined reality that can sustain a concrete ethos. His approach remains, however, within the parameters of the Hegelian search for a meaningful (meaning determined) context for living. Axel Honneth, *The Pathologies of Individual Freedom: Hegel's Social Theory*, trans. Ladislaus Löb (Princeton: Princeton University Press, 2010), 35.

does talk about God's friendship go far beyond formal claims about a relational existence as such.

The indeterminacy of such general narratives and the distortions they introduce into how phenomena appear has been broken apart by the determinacy of God's story. The fulfillment of human life through the apocalyptic-Messianic deliverance achieved by the entry of God's story into human existence operates by shattering the illusion of stability generated by generic descriptions of reality. In the same way the moralism of justification has been broken apart by God's judgment and justice; the processes of obligation by God's merciful forgiving (and our forgiving in God's name); the processes of liberalization by God's own liberating election of His children; and the processes of interpretation by God's own meaningful word.[53]

God's story has captured human action in order to break the bondage of the world of phenomena in indeterminacy. The apocalyptic-Messianic appearance of God's story in its wholeness constitutes the new reality that becomes apparent with it. It is once again apparent why praying is the primary action in the apocalyptic-Messianic ethos. Prayer calls out of a denuding and confusing situation for God to provide a concrete and determinate deliverance. Jesus' prayer at Gethsemane displays how prayer is simultaneously God's act and a call for God's act. Prayer yields an understanding of freedom that does not so much require us to do something (or take responsibility), as to participate in something already being done, to live out God-with-us. Only by recognizing the sequence of action can prayer begin powerfully to impel apocalyptic-Messianic action. Barth's emphasis on prayer as the entry point of the Christian ethos grows from his insistent quest for a description of human action that does not cancel out the inherently dramatic reality of this communicative life with God.

The indeterminate world will disappear. It is the place of an infinite, endless, undetermined waiting for an advent. It fails to recognize—in its blindness—that the advent of God's actions has already been realized in His Messiah. And God's story continues to break the indeterminacies of this world-age. Its witnesses, the church as its witness, expose the ideologies of this world-age *as* indeterminacies. The freedom of an ethics that follows the apocalyptic-Messianic contours of God's story comes from beyond the logic of liberty and limits. An apocalyptic-Messianic ethic itself does not achieve this, but seeks it as a form of transfigured human life initiated and completed with the given determinacy of God's own story.

Biblical language offers a final clue to the centrality of the Messianic-apocalyptic grammar of God's story. The Hebrew concept of "story" overlaps with being born. A story represents, like the birth of child, a beginning, something unique entering

---

53. This description converges with Samuel Wells' description of the manifold transformations that occur with the realization of God's story. Samuel Wells, *Transforming Fate into Destiny: The Theological Ethics of Stanley Hauerwas* (Carlisle: Paternoster Press, 1998).

the world, as Hannah Arendt elaborated in her discussions of "natality."[54] Arendt's account of newness, however, remains bound to the idea of an individual who is still in some sense undetermined. The rabbinic tradition, in contrast, emphasized that newness is only given to a newborn in the stories that the newborn joins. The child receives its own story because it is determined and provoked by the stories into which it is born.[55] Otherwise human beings would be simply another cog in a process of aimless reproduction.

We may go even further, in conclusion, and say that there are stories at all only insofar as there are people who have been determined by God's unique story and initiated into this story by God's mercy. Every narrative in the biblical text is to be seen within the context of all the other narratives the together form the one and only coherent story. It is a story enacted by God, by God's mercy, carried through to completion by His grace and faithfulness. The story begins on the other side of a temporal horizon over which we may be tempted to peek. To indulge this desire would be to embark on a theology of glory. We must remain content with the way of the cross, testifying to the way in which human creatures have been determined to become witnesses to what we have encountered from our own place in God's own story.

---

54. See Hannah Arendt, *The Human Condition*, 2nd edn. (Chicago: Chicago University Press, 1958), 8–9, 11, 246–7.

55. Micha Brumlik, *Messianisches Licht und Menschenwürde: Politische Theorie aus Quellen jüdischer Tradition* (Baden-Baden: Nomos, 2013).

Chapter 2

ETHICAL LIFE

THE FORM AND ITS FORMS ACCORDING TO BONHOEFFER

The Bonhoeffer Phenomenon and the Grammar of His Theology

In this chapter I trace the account of apocalyptic Messianic-ethics in the work and life of Dietrich Bonhoeffer. Today various rival "Bonhoeffers" exist side by side within theological discourse.[1] Being a German theologian of the generation that came of age in the wake of the Confessing Church struggle, reading Bonhoeffer is necessarily more complex than finding in his work one or two useful theological ideas. This is not to suggest that my cultural and biographical proximity to Bonhoeffer provides me with a privileged vantage point on his theology. We are all immersed in theological presumptions that make it impossible to look directly at Bonhoeffer. In reading him the task can only be to discover the contours of the theological universe in which we live and breathe by coming face to face with his uncanny capacity to pry us away from theological presumptions we have unthinkingly absorbed from our contemporary context.

Bonhoeffer's texts have been treated as a sort of scripture by some, who see that his writings are integrally intertwined with his life, especially his letters from prison. Bonhoeffer was a political theologian before he was drawn into resistance to the Nazi regime.[2] This is important because Bonhoeffer had already articulated his views on what the life of a human being looks like when lived in patient and attentive expectation of God's action, ready to surrender to God's will and plan—so becoming a disciple—before he was called to enact his beliefs in a hostile political context. This intertwining of theological writing and lived witness accounts for the richness of Bonhoeffer interpretations, and also raises the question of how to study his life as a source for theological insight—the same question raised as we read the stories and teachings of Jesus recounted in the gospels. Jesus teaches primarily

---

1. Stephen R. Haynes, *The Bonhoeffer Phenomenon: Portraits of a Protestant Saint* (Minneapolis: Fortress Press, 2004).

2. See Stanley Hauerwas, "'The Friend': Reflections on Friendship and Freedom," in *Who Am I? Bonhoeffer's Theology Through His Poetry*, ed. Bernd Wannenwetsch (London: T&T Clark, 2009), 91–114.

through his life—his living with God—as does Bonhoeffer, a parallel on which Bonhoeffer himself suggested later interpreters of his life should reflect.[3]

Unlike Jesus, however, Bonhoeffer's particular life course is not the measure of all subsequent Christian living, but only one instantiation of a life course that displays suggestive points of conformity with Jesus', the measure of faithful Christian living. Approaching Bonhoeffer's life from this angle is suggested by his own account of discipleship. Discipleship, he insists, cannot be taught in a catechetical fashion nor described in a catechetical manner—it is a particular and concrete exercise of living with God, who is present in this life in a way that cannot be foreseen or transformed into a pattern. Each believer can only open themselves in readiness to God's will and plan, giving themselves up in complete submission. Faith is this specific kind of readiness. Catechetical teaching can only highlight the importance of this formed readiness and attentiveness to God's presence; it cannot describe a way of life beforehand that will be given in this submission. The life of faith is an empty space, a stage upon which God can act. This is the life of a saint. Saints can appear anywhere where people pray: "Your kingdom come, your will be done!"[4] Whether a saint exists does not depend on the saint himself, but on whether God's will has been fulfilled and whether God involves the one who prays in His will, as He involved His own Son.[5]

Bonhoeffer's witness would cease to exist if turned into a catechetical text independent of the particular story in which he was involved, shorn from his unconditional dedication to God's will. Put otherwise, Bonhoeffer's witness is different in kind from his "biographical context." Bonhoeffer's witness is not his death but his desire to fulfill the will of God in God's plan for the world. The decisive question is whether any given life is being drawn into God's story or not. The prayer "Thy will be done" is not an interpretation of the gospel stories; it is an act of inviting God to include our own stories into the story of the one who taught this prayer and also lived it in a manner that can be emulated.[6]

"Thy will be done": the realization of this prayer is the subject of all Bonhoeffer's writings. Bonhoeffer is describing a way of life dedicated to God's will, not because he has turned prayer into method[7] but because he sees it as the way God has given

---

3. Cf. Larry Rasmussen and Renate Bethge, *Dietrich Bonhoeffer: His Significance for North Americans* (Minneapolis: Fortress Press, 1990).

4. Mt. 6:10. The Vulgate reads: "veniat regnum tuum fiat voluntas tua sicut in caelo et in terra."

5. This is not to suggest that the Nazis turned Bonhoeffer into a saint, as perceptively observed by Haynes in *The Bonhoeffer Phenomenon*.

6. For a description of the form of biblical narratives, see Franz Rosenzweig, "Das Formgeheimnis der biblischen Erzählung," in *Die Schrift: Aufsätze, Übertragungen und Briefe*, ed. Franz Rosenzweig and Karl Thieme (Königstein: Jüdischer Verlag Athenaeum, 1984).

7. See Ernst Feil, *Die Theologie Dietrich Bonhoeffers: Hermeneutik—Christologie Weltverständnis* (Berlin: LIT, 2006), 302.

as an entryway into life with God. Bonhoeffer wants to lead people not toward a correct description of God, but to the "real thing," an ongoing life in communion with God.

The chapter proceeds in four broad movements. It first outlines what has been called Bonhoeffer's "Christological realism." For Bonhoeffer the central concern of Christian ethics is an encounter with the real. This encounter, second, transforms the lives of those who follow it, who walk along the way it opens. A third section outlines Bonhoeffer's conception of the mandates, and how they organize Christian ethical perception and action. A final section points toward chapter three, discussing the necessary hiddenness of the Christian life and the central role played by discernment within it.

Participation in God's Reality: The Subject Matter of Christian Ethics

"God's reality" as it becomes present in our world is the unique subject matter of theological and ethical inquiry according to Bonhoeffer:

> The subject matter of a Christian ethic is God's reality revealed in Christ becoming real [*Wirklichwerden*] among God's creatures, just as the subject matter of doctrinal theology is the truth of God's reality revealed in Christ. The place that in all other ethics is marked by the antithesis between ought and is, idea and realization, motive and work, is occupied in Christian ethics by the relation between reality and becoming real, . . . or, to replace the many concepts with the simple name of the thing itself, the relation between Jesus Christ and the Holy Spirit. The question of the good becomes the question of participating in God's reality revealed in Christ.[8]

"God's reality" having appeared in Jesus Christ, representing and fulfilling God's story from creation until reconciliation and redemption is the only "reality" for human beings to live in and to find their real existence and determination. "After Christ has appeared," Bonhoeffer concludes, "ethics can have but one purpose, namely, the achievement of participation in the reality of the fulfilled will of God."[9]

The task of any ethics is genuinely a theological one to the extent that it is exploring the "reality" of human life determined as "real" human life according to God's will to establish a communion with human beings. This communion is already fulfilled in Jesus Christ, *the* real human being. "Real" human life, therefore, cannot be an ideal nor a norm, any more than it can be derived from anthropological or humanistic presuppositions. The only norm for Christian ethics is one can only be explored in its real, and formed, appearance and presence in Jesus Christ, the paradigm of a "real" human willed by God. The single question of Christian ethics

---

8. DBWE 6, 49–50.
9. DBWE 6, 212; see also Larry L. Rasmussen, *Dietrich Bonhoeffer: Reality and Resistance* (Nashville: Abingdon Press, 1972), 156.

is therefore how human beings participate in this "reality" and thus become "real" human beings. To deny this fundamental claim is implicitly to grant that human life is "really" determined by one or more of the construed, imagined, demanded or asserted realities that claim to determine or bind human lives.

Christian ethics as a seeking of God's reality is not an extension of a claim to have secured solid ontological foundations for human existence. It can be labeled, at most, a "critical ontology."[10] Christian ethics explores a distinctive reality, the reality of the real human being as given within God's reality as revealed in Jesus Christ.[11] This reality is not immediately available to common sense, being discoverable primarily in the performance of a communal, social, and political living together, in which all human beings are understood as determined to participate.

None of this is meant to suggest that Bonhoeffer's notion of reality has no points of resonance with later philosophies, particularly with that set of philosophical attempts to overcome the dominance of what have been called onto-theologies as most influentially prosecuted by Martin Heidegger.[12] Bonhoeffer's account of the reality appearing in Jesus Christ has been called a "phenomenological Christology,"[13] and it may also be seen as the Christological affirmation of a genuine theological phenomenology of the real presence of divine acts.[14] For Bonhoeffer, Christology explores God's reality as apparent in Jesus Christ, focusing on a distinct appearance that fulfills human life by giving it a new form.

As Larry Rasmussen has observed, "The ontological coherence of God's reality and the world's in Christ leads Bonhoeffer to discuss moral action in two ways that in the end are the same: 'conformation to Christ' (*Gleichgestaltung*) and action 'in accordance with reality' or 'with due regard for reality' (*Wirklichkeitsgemäßheit*)

---

10. Adam C. Clark and Michael G. Mawson, 'Introduction: Ontology and Ethics in Bonhoeffer Scholarship', in *Ontology and Ethics: Bonhoeffer and Contemporary Scholarship*, ed. Adam C. Clark, Michael G. Mawson, and Clifford J. Green (Eugene: Pickwick Publications, 2013), 2.

11. For Bonhoeffer's critique on "ontologies" see Christiane Tietz, 'Bonhoeffer on the Uses and Limits of Philosophy', in *Bonhoeffer and Continental Thought: Cruciform Philosophy*, ed. Brian E. Gregor and Jens Zimmermann (Bloomington: Indiana University Press, 2009), 31–45.

12. Michael P. DeJonge, 'God's Being Is in Time: Bonhoeffer's Theological Appropriation of Heidegger', in *Dietrich Bonhoeffer Jahrbuch 5 / Yearbook 5*, ed. Clifford J. Green, Kirsten Busch Nielsen, and Christiane Tietz (Gütersloher Verlagshaus, 2012), 123–37.

13. Stephen J. Plant, "'In the Sphere of the Familiar': Heidegger and Bonhoeffer," in *Bonhoeffer's Intellectual Formation: Theology and Philosophy in His Thought*, ed. Peter Frick (Tübingen: Mohr Siebeck, 2008), 326.

14. See Brian Gregor, "The Transcendence of the Person: Bonhoeffer as a Resource for Phenomenology of Religion and Ethics," in *Early Phenomenology: Metaphysics, Ethics, and the Philosophy of Religion*, ed. Brian Harding and Michael R. Kelly (London: Bloomsbury Academic, 2016), 181–212.

... The discussion of any and all facets of Christian ethics, then, rests upon the prior assumption of this ontological coherence in Christ."[15]

Despite the widely divergent readings of what Bonhoeffer actually means by the term "reality,"[16] a consensus has emerged among Bonhoeffer scholars that Bonhoeffer sees ethics dedicated to that unique task of exploring God's "reality" as it has been revealed to this "world-age" (Rom. 12:2) in Jesus Christ, the "real" human being in its real "form" or "figure" (*Gestalt*), in its "structure" and given "orders" ("mandates"), its becoming present in the "world" reconciled by God.

Bonhoeffer's conception of ethics is focused on God's real presence "in the midst of history" because only this real presence can rescue human life from all godless entrapments in illusion and unreality. In his own words:

> Only because there is one place where God and the reality of the world are reconciled with each other, at which God and humanity have become one, is it possible there and there alone to fix one's eyes on God and the world together at the same time. This place does not lie somewhere beyond reality in the realm of ideas. It lies in the midst of history as a divine miracle.[17]

The task of Christian ethics is to explore how we human beings participate through Jesus Christ, in God's establishment in love of a real communion with human beings. This is why becoming real must turn on the question of humans finding their place in God's story with creation. Bonhoeffer encapsulates the core of his approach in the words of Pilate:

> Ecce homo—behold God become human, the unfathomable mystery of the love of God for the world. God loves human beings. God loves the world. Not an ideal human, but human beings as they are; not an ideal world, but the real world.[18]

---

15. Rasmussen, *Bonhoeffer*, 22.

16. The centrality of the idea of "reality" for Bonhoeffer has been variously approached. Significantly, André Dumas entitled his depiction of Bonhoeffer's Theology "Dietrich Bonhoeffer. Theologian of Reality," Heinrich Ott his analysis "Reality and Faith," Larry L. Rasmussen "Reality and Resistance," and Friederike Barth her extensive interpretation of Bonhoeffer's ethics Die Wirklichkeit des Guten ("The Reality of the Good"). André Dumas, *Dietrich Bonhoeffer: Theologian of Reality*, trans. Robert McAfee Brown (London: SCM, 1971). Heinrich Ott, *Reality and Faith: The Theological Legacy of Dietrich Bonhoeffer* (Philadelphia: Fortress Press, 1972). See especially DBWE 6, 179, 270–75. Rasmussen, *Bonhoeffer*. Friederike Barth, *Die Wirklichkeit des Guten: Dietrich Bonhoeffers 'Ethik' und ihr philosophischer Hintergrund* (Tübingen: Mohr Siebeck, 2012). Clifford Green, 'Book Review: Interpreting Bonhoeffer: Reality or Phraseology?' *Journal of Religion* 55, no. 2 (1975): 270–5.

17. DBWE 6, 82.

18. Ibid., 84.

The Resistance of Thought to Reality

Bonhoeffer sometimes criticized "thinking" as one of the chief barriers to human beings inhabiting the reality of Christ.[19] The critique is not built on a distinction between "theory" and "praxis," but between a reality encompassing our entirely lived existence and those "realities" we have constructed and manipulated. He is restating the famous claim of Luther in his Heidelberg disputation: *theologia crucis dicit quod res est* ("a theology of the cross names/points out what is real").[20] A theological understanding of "reality" (*Wirklichkeit*) must not be reduced to *ideas about* reality.[21] *Das Wirkliche ergreifen* ("grasping what is the real") is thereby distinguished from positivistic accounts focusing narrowly on defensible ideas *about* God in favor of a form of thought that is attentive to a reality that is not graspable in thought but is recognizable—the reality that is given for us within God's will. In *Ethics*, Bonhoeffer emphasizes that God's plan and story have, before our arrival, been embedded in reality; otherwise we would be able to make the creaturely cosmos what we, whoever we pretend to be, intend or think it should be.

Bonhoeffer's premise is therefore, at base, very simple. Understood cosmologically, reality is God's reality, and we are involved in that reality already, whether we know and admit it nor not. All thought that is not aiming to apprehend this reality will miss it and be led into sterile considerations of the possible or of fantasy, as the promise of Gen. 8:21 presumes: "I will never again curse the ground because of humankind, for the imagination of the human heart is evil from youth."

Bonhoeffer's insistence on the real presence of Jesus Christ to the believer presumes a critique of religion. No one and no thing can represent God or divine things. The logic of religion is to offer representatives, a logic that also generates political theologies and ecclesiologies, on the assumption that there is something on earth representing God's action or gifts.[22] But a representation of God must be distinguished from God's presence. The idea that God is present includes the idea, for Bonhoeffer, that God also represents us to God by standing in our place. This is something that humans must suffer, because in being represented by Christ we are carried along, can no longer determined our actions. We can only stop acting,

---

19. Bonhoeffer was not unique in raising this sort of criticism. See Martin Heidegger's 1951/1952 lectures *What is Called Thinking?* (New York: Perennial Library, 1968) and Hannah Arendt's *Thinking: Life of the Mind*, vol. 1 (London: Seeker & Warburg, 1978).

20. Heidelberg Disputation, Thesis 21, in LW 31, 40, 53.

21. See DBWE 6, 47–75; DBW 6, 31–61.

22. The only representation in our Christian worship is found in the bread and the wine, which is why Luther insisted on the real presence of Christ in bread and wine, rejecting a religious representation. For Bonhoeffer's critique of religion, see Wüstenberg, Ralf K. *A Theology of Life: Dietrich Bonhoeffer's Religionless Christianity*. Grand Rapids: Eerdmans, 1998; and Bernd Wannenwetsch, "A Love Formed by Faith: Relating Theological Virtues in Augustine and Luther," in *The Authority of the Gospel: Explorations in Moral Theology in Honor of Oliver O'Donovan*, ed. Robert Song and Brent Waters (Grand Rapids: Eerdmans, 2015).

stop fighting, and hand ourselves over to God. Freedom, Bonhoeffer is suggesting, is not throwing ourselves open to a plurality of options; freedom is something experienced at those places (stations) where we can expect God's guidance and action. It is the freedom of disciples who expect God. Our aimless thinking and endless reflecting that lead nowhere are thereby confronted and reclaimed. That is our freedom.

Christians today (academic theologians especially) often couch questions of ethical orientation in terms like "having a vision" rather than as a seeking after God's will. But for Bonhoeffer Christian freedom is found only in involvement in the reality in which God is actively at work. "Staying involved," in this sense, means discovering what specific acts are required to remain part of God's working in the world.[23] This focusing on the necessity of human action does not imply activism because for deeds to be good they must be rooted in our dedication to God's will, to His beginning and to His reality. The deeds given for Christians to do can never be deduced from antecedent conditions, nor justified as having been necessary in a given context nor for having produced good outcomes. They are defined by a unique logic of responsibility. Being responsible for Bonhoeffer is not, as in the ethics of Max Weber, defined in terms of how one has responded to other people, and how well what we have done can be justified rationally. For Bonhoeffer the most politically responsible deeds are ones which are freed from the burden of responsibilities as Weber defines them. Jesus's example and teaching proclaim:

> "You stand before the face of God, God's grace rules over you; you are at the disposal of someone else in the world and you must act and work for God. So be mindful in your actions that you are acting under God's eyes, and that God's will needs be done." The nature of this will of God . . . can only be clear in the moment of action, and to that will realized in surrender to God's will.[24] Good works manifest a disciple's worldly vocation "supported only by God's commandments and your faith."

Conformation to Jesus Christ in His Communion with God

As is now clear, Bonhoeffer's basic account of Christian ethic foregrounds the question how human beings become "formed," "figured" or "conformed" to Jesus

---

23. Luther's ethics of good works is presumed here. See *Treatise on Good Works*, LW 44, 15–114.

24. Dietrich Bonhoeffer, "What is a Christian Ethic?" in *A Testament to Freedom: The Essential Writings of Dietrich Bonhoeffer*, rev. edn., ed. Geffrey B. Kelly and F. Burton Nelson (San Francisco: HarperCollins, 1995), 348. Insofar as the Christian's ethical action is God's will, it can be described as love. But this is not a new principle; it derives from our place before God. For Christians, there are no ethical principles by means of which they could perhaps civilize themselves. For more on the meaning of "responsibility," see also "After Ten Years," in DBWE 8, 37–52.

Christ, the "real" "figure" (*Gestalt*) of human existence. His emphasis on this term is polemical. He is highly resistant to any idea of humans being responsible for "self-formation," or as responsible for making meaning by giving history or nature a fitting form. The German phrases *Weltgestaltung* (world shaping) and *Lebensgestaltung* (life shaping) both emphasize the habit of thinking that assumes responsibility for giving form to reality this common idea or even ideological habit. Bonhoeffer insists that it cannot be up to human beings to "form" substantially the "real" world.

> The word "formation" [*Gestaltung*] arouses our suspicion. We are tired of Christian agendas. . . . We have seen that the forces which form the world come from entirely other sources than Christianity, and that so-called practical Christianity has failed in the world just as much as so-called dogmatic Christianity. Hence, we must understand by "formation" something quite different from what we are accustomed to mean, and in fact the Holy Scripture speaks of formation in a sense that at first sounds quite strange. It is not primarily concerned with formation of the world by planning and programs, but in all formation it is concerned only with the one form that has overcome the world, the form of Jesus Christ. Formation proceeds only from here.[25]

Bonhoeffer's suspicion amounts to a pointed criticism of Nazi jargon which prominently emphasized the importance of *Gestaltung* ("formation").[26] The Nazi ideology intended to impose "form" (*Gestalt*) on human lives and institutions. Bonhoeffer grasped that this Nazi ideology of formation pointed forward to the world that has in fact emerged in which governments assume that the whole of existence, not least bodily existence, must become subject to absolute limitless technical and governmental formation policies.[27]

"Conformation" to God's "reality" as it becomes present in the only "real" figure of the human being, Jesus Christ, is the focus of the inner logic of theological ethics. Bonhoeffer articulates pointedly in his *Ethics*:

> Formation occurs only by being drawn into the form of Jesus Christ, by being conformed to the unique form of the one who became human, was crucified, and is risen. This does not happen as we strive "to become like Jesus," as we customarily say, but as the form of Jesus Christ himself so works on us that it molds us, conforming our form to Christ's own (Gal. 4:19). Christ remains the only one who forms. . . . Christ is the one who has become human, who was

---

25. DBWE 6, 92.

26. Dolf Sternberger, Gerhard Storz, and Wilhelm E Süskind, *Aus dem Wörterbuch des Unmenschen* (Hamburg: Claassen, 1957).

27. See for that context Brian Brock, *Christian Ethics in a Technological Age* (Grand Rapids: Eerdmans, 2010).

crucified, and who is risen, as confessed by the Christian faith. To be transformed into his form is the meaning of the formation that the Bible speaks about.[28]

It is in faith that this conformation becomes actualized, as Bonhoeffer presents it in his *Ethics*.[29] Faith names the substrate of obedience to Christ which orients the believer in their encounter in other human beings of the "real" Other whom they are called to follow. Only the call of the paradigmatic "person" heard as an encounter with Jesus Christ, can be adequately followed by faith and obedience. This encounter and call are the condition for human living that is no longer captive to its own devices but is ready to become transformed into a new life and communion with God.

To make sense of the "conformation" to Jesus Christ in His *Gestalt* as Bonhoeffer understands it entails some understanding of the complexity of the semantic field assumed in his language of "form" and "formation"; "the richness of the German *Gestalt* and *Gestaltung* or *Gleichgestaltung* is not immediately obvious from the English 'form' and 'formation' or 'conformation.' The connotations in German are those of dynamism and alteration in the process of an organism's growth, while yet remaining the same organism."[30] If, then ethics is centrally understood as the dynamic exploration of God's reality, "formation" (*Gestaltung*[31]) must be understood as for Bonhoeffer a verb, not a noun. "Ethical life" is a *becoming* "formed" or "figured." Ethics as a discipline is positioned as a practice of ethical reflection, thinking, judging, discerning, and communicating determined by the contours entailed in living in conformity with God's reality. Such an ethics must unfold according to its own theological meta-ethics in distinction from all meta-ethics or moral theologies that ground themselves outside of God's constitutive story.[32] Human ethical life is being formed by God in its entirety, including the

---

28. DBWE 6, 93. To prefigure what will be developed later in this chapter, Bonhoeffer denies that formation is properly conceived in individualistic terms, which always collapse into questions about how placeless isolated "moral subjects" beyond the real human being can constitute themselves. For Bonhoeffer, humans become real only in the exploration of given structures of living together.

29. See especially Christiane Tietz, *Bonhoeffers Kritik der verkrümmten Vernunft: eine erkenntnistheoretische Untersuchung* (Tübingen: Mohr Siebeck, 1999), 129–31.

30. For an acute study of that linguistic problem see Vivienne Blackburn, *Dietrich Bonhoeffer and Simone Weil: A Study in Christian Responsiveness* (Oxford; New York: Peter Lang, 2004), 93–104.

31. See for key aspects Nadine Hamilton, *Dietrich Bonhoeffers Hermeneutik der Responsivität: ein Kapitel Schriftlehre im Anschluss an Schöpfung und Fall* (Göttingen: Vandenhoeck & Ruprecht, 2016), 312–16.

32. See for this central implication Philip G. Ziegler, "'Completely within God's Doing': Soteriology as Meta-Ethics in the Theology of Dietrich Bonhoeffer," in *Christ, Church, and World: New Studies in Bonhoeffer's Theology and Ethics*, ed. Michael G. Mawson and Philip G. Ziegler (London: Bloomsbury T&T Clark, 2016), 101–17.

person's habits, mental and psychic conditions, as well as in the forms of communal life that are constitutive of "real" human cooperation. Put in these terms, it is clear that Christian ethics will have to speak in terms of "the" form of ethical life which entails wider circles of determinatively configured forms and institutionalized structures.

The most fundamental "structure" that is promisingly prefigured in the life of Jesus Christ's life is the "structure of responsible life." Bonhoeffer's *Ethics* is concerned both with how human beings become "real" human beings as well as how they do so by exploring structures given within God's work that give determinate form to the ethical lives of human beings.

The term "ethos" helpfully signifies human life in its ethical form,[33] recalling that the Greek roots of the term indicate that environment in which human beings experience themselves of being "at home." Human life is not at home in rules about proper action or any other abstract set of concepts. Humans are only at home in the restored form of sociality promised in Jesus Christ. God's will is fulfilled in God's inalienable work of forgiving, reconciliation, and sanctification to create a holy and sanctified world. In the time between the times, ethical life is life discovering itself enclosed in that salutary divine work. To become conformed to Jesus Christ, therefore, flows from participation on God's salvation in Jesus Christ.[34] We may call the reformed and lively human community prefigured in Jesus Christ in accordance to God's will the *conditio humana* in order to distinguish it from "human nature" as understood today in secular thought as primarily a biologically determined species. (I will retain this terminological distinction throughout this volume.)

The crucial ethical question, then, is how the "form" and its entailed "forms" of human being can be discovered by beings estranged by forms of life that seek to proceed without reference to God's reality. Bonhoeffer presupposes that this figure or form cannot be grasped by norms, ideals, or models generated by human beings. The "real" figure is by definition resistant to all activity of forming, transforming (*Gestaltung*), or even manipulating human life organized by any human other than submitting to God's "reality." This is not a constricting limitation, because in focusing formation language exclusively on conformation to Jesus Christ, the "real" human being, it is experienced as liberation. In Jesus Christ human beings are revealed as God's creatures. Creatures have been determined to participate in God's "reality" as it becomes present in this world, that is, within the whole story of God's creation, judgment after the fall, reconciliation, and redemption. This whole story has been definitely realized in Jesus Christ the real "figure" (*Gestalt*) of human beings. "The unity and differentiation of incarnation, cross, and resurrection should be clear. . . . Christian life means being human [*Menschsein*] in

---

33. Rasmussen states: "In my judgment Bonhoeffer is speaking about Christian ethos, not ethics." Rasmussen, *Bonhoeffer*, 157.

34. For this fundamental implication in Bonhoeffer's *Ethics*, see Ziegler, "Completely within God's Doing".

the power of Christ's becoming human, being judged and pardoned in the power of the cross, living a new life in the power of the resurrection. No one of these is without the others."[35]

The explicitly theological contours of this approach to ethics is by definition differentiated from all worldviews built on alternative metanarratives. For Bonhoeffer, looking for human life outside God's reality inevitably means the disappearance of real humanity.[36] Even humanity's fall is only intelligible as an episode within God's reality.[37] The relentlessness with which Bonhoeffer insists on Christian ethics as the exploration of that "real" life of human beings within God's "reality" complicates attempts to read his *Ethics* as a version of Christian humanism.[38]

The discipline of Christian ethics, in its way of witnessing, presenting, and communicating the Christian ethical life in its unique form, itself follows this ethos of becoming conformed to God's reality and becoming resistant to any other conditions or forces affecting the forms of human creaturely life. This is the genuine disposition of theological ethics as Paul has defined it in Rom. 12:1-2 (NRSV):

> I appeal to you therefore, brothers and sisters, by the mercies of God, to present your bodies as a living sacrifice, holy and acceptable to God, which is your spiritual worship. Do not be conformed to this world, but be transformed by the renewing of your minds, so that you may discern what is the will of God—what is good and acceptable and perfect.

"Be not conformed to this world"; that is, "be not conformed to the patterns, the formations of this world age," a world-age, which doesn't follow its determination by God's "reality" and embeddedness into God's story with the world reconciled by God: this is the critical focus of theological ethics as it is promisingly grounded in the "transformation by the renewing of one's mind." The hopeful perspective behind Paul's *paraclesis* is eschatological and apocalyptic: "The present form of this world is passing away" (1 Cor. 7:31). God's reconciliation of his "world" bursts into this passing world-age.[39]

---

35. DBWE 6, 158–59.

36. "The message of God's becoming human attacks the heart of an era when contempt for humanity or idolization of humanity is the height of all wisdom, among bad people as well as good." DBWE 6, 85.

37. DBWE 3, 115–20, 146.

38. See for the discussion of that question Tietz, *Bonhoeffers Kritik der verkrümmten Vernunft*. See also Jens Zimmermann, *Dietrich Bonhoeffer's Christian Humanism* (Oxford: Oxford University Press, 2019).

39. The apocalyptic substrate of Bonhoeffer's ethics is ably defended in Philip G. Ziegler, "Dietrich Bonhoeffer—an Ethics of God's Apocalypse?" *Modern Theology* 23, no. 4 (2007): 579–4.

The eschatological "renewing of one's mind" is the context of practicing "ethics" which has the demanding work of exploring God's will in its fulfillment within the rival stories and habits of the patterns of a fallen world. The success of this exploration can never be achieved shorn of its contact with the world of divine reconciling action. The renewal of the mind can only take place within the "worldliness" of ethical life.

> The figure [*Gestalt*] of the reconciler, of the God-man Jesus Christ, steps into the middle between God and the world, into the center of all that happens. In this figure is disclosed the mystery of the world, just as the mystery of God is revealed in it. No abyss of evil can remain hidden from him through whom the world is reconciled to God.[40]

As there can be no separation nor dualism between "world" and God's "reality" nor can the "secular" subsist outside God's "reality." Though this "world-age" (Rom. 12:2) is passing away, the premise of the whole biblical story is that God's reconciled world will be preserved eternally within God's own story. Even as it is passing away, this world is simultaneously being taken up, reconciled, and preserved as part of God's own story. Insofar as it is something penultimate, it is being ultimately determined by God's will and work, being made part of God's reality in its full eschatological extension.

God's Presence Is Freedom

Bonhoeffer designates the essential character of human life lived in communion with God as "freedom." Freedom will only be fulfilled by God.[41] God himself acts with us, instead of us, in our place.

In his poem "Stations on the Way to Freedom,"[42] Bonhoeffer succinctly outlined the components of the formed freedom he was imagining. Living with God means submission, dedicating oneself to God's will and action in any walk of life, and thus does not rise above everyday life. Nor is this submission a form of fatalistic submission to whatever happens, a position closely allied to the deist submission to a God who has set in motion all natural occurrences. Yet again, it is also not submission to a God who is the author of a history that we can fully understand and map out. Bonhoeffer, like Job, refuses to submit to God collapsed into any of these abstract patterns, instead insisting on gaining knowledge of God's judgment

---

40. DBWE 6, 83.

41. "In view of what is coming, I'm almost inclined to quote the biblical dei, and I feel that I 'long to look' like the angels in 1 Pet. 1:12, to see how God will go about solving what seems beyond any solution. I think it has now come to the point where God will arise and accomplish something that we, despite our inner and outer involvement, can only take in with the greatest astonishment and awe" (DBWE 8, April 30, 1944, 361).

42. DBWE 8, 512–14.

and will directly, face to face. In this sense, Bonhoeffer's account of ethics presumes a life *coram Deo*, a life "before the face of God," a life within the drama, in which God is involved with us.[43]

Bonhoeffer suggests that there are specific places for submission: discipline, action, and suffering. But in considering these places, we must consider carefully the word "stations" that Bonhoeffer chose for his title. The German word "Stationen" has many meanings, not all of which are captured by the English words "stage"[44] or "stations." For Bonhoeffer "stations" are places of submission to God's will, where God's presence can be expected and experienced. Because these "stations" are places where discipleship happens, Bonhoeffer's account draws close to the traditional concept of "orders," "estates," or "institutions," which Bonhoeffer often referred to with the language of "mandates."[45] This understanding of discipleship is what makes Bonhoeffer a Lutheran theologian.

Discipleship within the Community of Saints

The worldliness that proceeds from God's reconciliation of our world gives the Christian ethos its political character. For Bonhoeffer *Nachfolge* ("discipleship") is the ethical form within which the conformation to Jesus Christ is actualized.[46] This ethos takes shape as human beings faithfully welcome God's salutary and sanctifying work, which forms the community of saints, visible in the church-community. This community is given with Christ's communion with God, because Jesus Christ himself is not an isolated "subject." Jesus Christ surrendered to God's will and love in order to establish communion with human beings. Jesus Christ's established communion with God thus entails the community of saints, the community of all human beings surrendered—realized in faith—into God's work of love.

On these grounds Bonhoeffer considers the form of Christian ethical life to be intrinsically communal, social, and political both inside the community of faith, and in that community's relations with all human beings. The individual is, nevertheless, addressed by God's judgment, only together with that community of those whom God has chosen to be God's beloved human beings.

---

43. Bonhoeffer, "What Is Christian Ethics," 345–51.

44. As it appears in some translations. It was translated as "stations" in other editions: Dietrich Bonhoeffer, *Letters and Papers from Prison*, ed. Eberhard Bethge, Enlarged edition (London: SCM Press, 1953), 370–1.

45. See for that topic: Brian Brock, "Why the Estates? Hans Ulrich's Recovery of an Unpopular Notion," in *SCE* 20 (2007): 179–202; and Bernd Wannenwetsch, "Luther's Moral Theology," in *The Cambridge Companion to Martin Luther*, ed. Donald K. McKim (Cambridge: Cambridge University Press, 2002), 120–35.

46. See Florian Schmitz, *"Nachfolge": zur Theologie Dietrich Bonhoeffers* (Göttingen: Vandenhoeck & Ruprecht, 2013).

> Thus we find that the Christian community of love has a unique sociological structure: the mutual love of the saints does indeed constitute "community" as an end in itself, that is, community in the strict sense of the word. But this brings us again to the problem derived from the thought that the community is, after all, not an end in itself insofar as it seeks only to realize God's will. However, since God wills precisely this community of saints, the problem is solved; it is therefore not the case that community in the strict sense would still have an end outside itself—a case that would be sociologically possible—but community (in the broader sense) is actually organized for a single purpose, namely to accomplish God's will. But since this realization of God's will consists in the community itself, it is an end in itself.[47]

Because theological ethics is tasked with describing the ethical life of human beings in its becoming conformed to Jesus Christ, the church-community in its visible form is "real"—meaning reconciled—not separated from, but within the "world-age" that is passing away. The "worldliness" of Christian life is given only within this "real" eschatological-apocalyptic determination of the world of this world-age as in truth encircled by God's own reconciled reality.[48]

The "worldliness" that corresponds to the irruption of the reconciled world highlights the intrinsically political character of the Christian ethos with its distinctive forms of living together, freedom, and responsibility. No categorical difference can be established between the disciple and the political human being: "The disciple helps to define the citizen, and vice versa."[49] In Bonhoeffer's words,

> Since the church-community is the city on the hill, the "polis" (Matt. 5:14), established on this earth by God and marked with a seal as God's own, its "political" character is an inseparable aspect of its sanctification. The "political ethics" of the church-community is grounded solely in its sanctification, the goal of which is that world be world and community be community, and that, nevertheless, God's word goes out from the church-community to all the world, as the proclamation that the earth and all it contains is the Lord's. That is the 'political' character of the church-community.[50]

This is not an ideal or utopian community striving to always incompletely conform to a general ideal but that "real" community where God's unique work is present even if under eschatological strain: his judgment, his forgiveness, and his command addressed to all human beings. In this it is being transformed into the image that is held out to all humanity, because "What takes place in the church

---

47. DBWE 1, 176.
48. DBWE 4, 249–51.
49. Stefan Heuser, "The Cost of Citizenship: Disciple and Citizen in Bonhoeffer's Political Ethics", *Studies in Christian Ethics* 18, no. 3 (2005): 65.
50. DBWE 4, 261–2.

happens vicariously and representatively as a model for all human beings."[51] It is in this manner that the political aspect of the church is revealed to be an entailment of Bonhoeffer's initial affirmation that the ethical life is prefigured in Jesus Christ. In Him every human being is determined as God's saint.

The Forms of Ethical Life

Conforming to Jesus Christ, human life finds its definitive, distinct, and concrete form as "ethical life." Conformation, consequently, will reveal itself in the character that people develop.[52] There have been several attempts to apply this character ethics approach to Bonhoeffer's *Ethics*,[53] though Bonhoeffer did not himself conceive the form of ethical life explicitly in terms of "virtue ethics" in its typically Aristotelian or Thomistic formulations. To do would have involved unacceptable concession to the definition of the political community of virtue formation in these accounts, which is the context of Bonhoeffer's occasional positioning of himself as an opponent of virtue. In the letter "After Ten Years," for example, he outlines a number of ethical forms that have proven to be of limited value during the ten years under National Socialism: the reasonable ones, the fanatics, the dutiful, those who act on their own freedom, and finally those who "attain the sanctuary of private virtuousness." Bonhoeffer, instead, holds that the only ones who stood firm during this time were those people:

> whose ultimate standard is not his reason, his principles, conscience, freedom, or virtue; only the one who is prepared to sacrifice all of these when, in faith and in relationship to God alone, he is called to obedient and responsible action. Such a person is the responsible one, whose life is to be nothing but a response to God's question and call. Where are these responsible ones?[54]

Given the unique focusing of Bonhoeffer's notion of "form" and "conformation" of the ethical life on the fulfillment of God's will to establish a communion with His human beings, it is best understood not by looking at the character acquired by the Christian. We understand his point better, by asking about the "simplicity" and "prudence" or "wisdom" with which the believer attends to God's will. For Bonhoeffer it is clear that such qualities are not good in themselves; rather, they assist reflection and deliberation that accords with reality (*Wirklichkeitsgemäßheit*). To act and reflect in accordance with reality, for Bonhoeffer, means to participate

---

51. DBWE 6, 97.
52. Stanley Hauerwas, *A Community of Character: Toward a Constructive Christian Social Ethic* (Notre Dame: University of Notre Dame Press, 1981).
53. Jennifer Moberly, *The Virtue of Bonhoeffer's Ethics: A Study of Dietrich Bonhoeffer's Ethics in Relation to Virtue Ethics* (Eugene: Pickwick Publications, 2013).
54. DBWE 8, 40.

in God's own reality that is drawing human beings into their genuine ethical form. The Christian yearns not to develop an individual profile, but simplicity and wisdom.

> But what is simplicity? What is wisdom? How do the two become one? A person is simple who in the confusion, the distortion, and the inversion of all concepts keeps in sight only the single truth of God. This person has an undivided heart, and is not a double-psyche, a person of two souls (James 1[:8]). Because of knowing and having God, this person clings to the commandments, the judgment, and the mercy of God that proceed anew each day from the mouth of God. . . . The person is wise who sees reality as it is, who sees into the depth of things. Only that person is wise who sees reality in God. Knowledge of reality is not just knowing external events, but seeing into the essence of things.[55]

The divinely granted qualities of simplicity and wisdom assist those "who take their stand in the world in their very own freedom, who value the necessary action more highly than their own untarnished conscience and reputation."[56] "Freedom" appears within this demand to act in simple obedience according to God's will and to God's reality even in the face of opposition. It is in this sense that one's conscience is considered binding only to the extent that it reveals the "unity" of that person bound equally to her conscience and to the obedience to God's will and reality. Similarly, "conscience" is also for Bonhoeffer no inviolable authority justifying extraordinary decisions for the isolated individual but a locus of attunement to God's will. It is truly operative when revealing an inner unity of the person in their faithful and humble waiting for God's will.

Conformation to Jesus Christ also includes the more disciplinary specific practices associated with ethics, its forms of reflection, judgment, discernment, and attempts to verify God's promises. These practices may even be called methods or an ethical methodology so long as they are understood not as constructed by given with the form of ethical life. Some might consider Bonhoeffer's emphasis on simplicity and wisdom, combined with his decentering of conscience, to produce a fatal methodological uncertainty. This would be to miss the fact that Bonhoeffer is looking for a categorically different mode of certainty, not rooted in any kind of supposedly fundamental convictions but in simplicity and wisdom. Simplicity and wisdom situate the certainty of ethical judgment not in the personal assurance of the individual but in conformity to the structure of responsible life embedded in the given structures of human life revealed by the mandates and natural contours of a real human being established and preserved by God. Participating in God's reality is a "suffering divine things" with Jesus Christ who also suffered God's will. The Christian form of ethical life is entirely encapsulated in that "passivity."

---

55. DBWE 6, 81.
56. Ibid., 79.

The Suffering of Faith

For Bonhoeffer, history is the revealed story of God's secret. The cross is the emblem of this divine secret in its resistance to reduction by theological interpretation. God can never be exhaustively decoded by reason, which always stands at one remove from the acts of Christian living. Bonhoeffer does not espouse a negative or apophatic theology of God or history. The methodological coherence of his theology grows from an unbroken faith in the promise the real, positive, contradiction, and resistance of God to human bondage. Bonhoeffer's is a theology of a positive breaking of historical continuity by a God whose presence is redeeming, not a God whose hiddenness is threateningly present in the dark side of history, and leads into the abyss.[57]

Faith is trust in God's plan. Its opposite is *Anfechtung*, a Janus-faced temptation to, on one hand, stabilize one's moral universe by embracing a false certainty about right and wrong, and on the other hand, to become entrapped in doubts whether or not an act is God's will. The simplicity of faith grows from the refusal to surrender to any of the permutations of temptation that make their appearance in *Anfechtung*.[58]

Nowhere more than here are we at the core of Bonhoeffer's ethics. When torn between *Anfechtung* and the desire for simple obedience, the faithful believer can identify with Jesus' prayer in Gethsemane: "He went away for the second time and prayed, 'My Father, if this cannot pass unless I drink it, your will be done'" (Mt. 26:42). The Greek rings more literally, "let *your* will be realized." In this prayer the one who prays is implicitly asking: By whose power? There is an act which must be undertaken by a human agent who knows they do not have the will to do it. At the same time, there is a promise of fulfillment attached to the act.[59] In such—perhaps brief—moments, freedom, Bonhoeffer suggests, will "embrace your spirit with rejoicing." Such rejoicing freedom is the opposite of all forms of "spiritual freedom" that aim to lift the human spirit above the limitations of earthly existence. In such moments our spirit is embraced by God's freedom to do God's will. In fulfilling God's will, guided by his commandments and by all we are invited to believe, we participate in God's own freedom. We are incorporated into God's freedom not in a way that warrants the boast that "God is with us," but in the prayer that we will let, "Thy will be done"—God's will as it is articulated in His commandments.

---

57. "The courtier in Acts 8, Cornelius (Acts 10) are anything but persons in desperate straits. Nathanael is 'an Israelite in whom there is no deceit' (Jn 1:47), and finally there are Joseph of Arimathea and the women at the tomb. The one thing they all have in common is their sharing in the suffering of God in Christ. That is their 'faith.' There is nothing about a religious method; the 'religious act' is always something partial, whereas 'faith' is something whole and involves one's whole life. Jesus calls not to a new religion but to life" (DBWE 8, July 18, 1944, 482). Cf. "After Ten Years," DBWE 8, 37–52.

58. Cf. The Lord's Prayer as presented in the Book of Common Prayer: "And lead us not into temptation."

59. See DBWE 5, 166; DBW 5, 125, where Bonhoeffer refers to Psalm 22.

To be incorporated into God's will can by definition only be a suffering of God's action. The inability to master and change events causes suffering, raising the further question of whether or not to allow one's self be transformed (*Verwandlung*) by voluntarily embracing such a loss of the power to act. In Bonhoeffer's view this constriction of our sense of power to act is a crucial station of transformation in that only here can we discover the freedom that comes in handing over our "right doing" to God. Such a handing over of our deeds and ends to God will become for us a new place for the presence of God's freedom. Wherever we do the right, involving ourselves in reality by such suffering action, the comfort we experience is especially obviously the fruit of God's own power of fulfillment. This is what Reinhard Hütter has called the "suffering divine things," that necessarily attends our earthly lives in that God's reality is not beyond or above the conflicts and contradictions of this world-age.[60] God has involved Godself in that reality.

This account of simple faith as an active suffering of God's allows Bonhoeffer to speak of human beings as instruments in God's guiding of history. In Bonhoeffer's hands, however, the language of "directing history" follows an entirely different logic than progressivist theologies of history that understand it as a theater for the ongoing revelation of God's triumph.

What comforts the Christian with simple faith comes through that faith, not through "knowledge." This is the secret of Christian freedom.[61] Here again we find the Lutheran grammar of Bonhoeffer's theology.[62] Christians are justified only by faith, by active trust in God's justice, that is, his trustworthiness to his people. This faith includes comfort for our human life. The German term for "comfort" Bonhoeffer uses is *Trost*, cognate to the English word "trust," and which Luther constantly deployed in his translations of the Bible. In doing what is right, Christians hand themselves over to God's righteousness, to God's promise to bring forth political justice. "Isn't God's righteousness and kingdom on earth the center of everything," Bonhoeffer wrote on May 5, 1944, "and isn't Rom. 3:24ff. the culmination of the view that God alone is righteous, rather than an individualistic doctrine of salvation?"[63]

---

60. Reinhard Hütter, *Suffering Divine Things: Theology as Church Practice*, trans. Douglas Stott (Grand Rapids: Eerdmans, 2000).

61. Bonhoeffer writes, "If only during this time . . . we learn, indeed, that personal suffering is a more useful key, a more fruitful principle than personal happiness for exploring the meaning of the world in contemplation and action. But this perspective from below must not lead us to become advocates for those who are perpetually dissatisfied. Rather, out of a higher satisfaction, which in its essence is grounded beyond what is below and above, we do justice to life in all its dimensions and in this way affirm it," DBWE 8, "After Ten Years," 52.

62. Bonhoeffer refers to the "this-worldliness" of Luther's theology, cf. DBWE 8, 486.

63. DBWE 8, 373. In his final letters from prison, Bonhoeffer argues that the "religious interpretation" is "metaphysical" and "individualistic" but not, in a biblical sense, political, cf. DBWE 8, 372–3.

The Structure of Ethical Life: Responsibility

In distinction to all conceptualizations of a self-constituting moral subject, Bonhoeffer points to the "real" human being in its always provoked conformation to Jesus Christ, the "real" human being and the paradigmatic "responsible" human being. In Christian theology, the definition of responsibility emerges out of the way of living taught and realized in Jesus Christ. In Jesus' "real vicarious representative action," Bonhoeffer suggests, "he is the responsible human being par excellence. Since he is life, all of life through him is destined to be vicarious representative action."[64] Jesus Christ is "the responsible human being par excellence" because of Jesus Christ's real vicarious representative action.

> "Come, you that are blessed by my Father, inherit the kingdom!" This the Lord will say to no other than the one to whom he says: "I was hungry and you gave me food, I was thirsty and you gave me drink. . . . Just as you did to one of the least of these who are members of my family, you did it to me."[65]

Jesus displays the form of flourishing human life for all human beings, setting them free of the task of self-construction. "Responsibility" appears to be the core of human beings' conformation to Jesus Christ. It is the very form of "ethical" life. Responsibility includes one's living, acting, and suffering vicariously for others. In responding to the demanding "other" human being, the believer in faith fulfills "real" humanity within God's reality.

Human life conformed to Jesus Christ in His way of being surrendered God's will and work is absolutely non-violent in being bound to faith in God's very own unique power to act, to judge and to speak, and relinquishing all other forms of power to effect events. Nonviolence may be seen as the fundamental grammar of ethical life, the signature ethical characterization of the political form taken by human life made real in God's action.[66]

Bonhoeffer's account of the "structure of responsibility" does have some points of convergence with the ethics of Emmanuel Lévinas.[67] Lévinas insists on an absolute asymmetry between a person and the encountering "other."[68] Lévinas

---

64. DBWE 6, 258–9.

65. Dietrich Bonhoeffer, "Thy Kingdom Come: The Prayer of the Church for the Kingdom of God on Earth," *A Testament to Freedom*, 92.

66. Stanley Hauerwas, *Performing the Faith: Bonhoeffer and the Practice of Nonviolence* (Grand Rapids: Brazos Press, 2004).

67. See also Brian E. Gregor, "Shame and the Other: Bonhoeffer and Lévinas on Human Dignity and Ethical Responsibility", in *Ontology and Ethics: Bonhoeffer and Contemporary Scholarship*, ed. Adam C. Clark, Michael G. Mawson, and Clifford J. Green (Eugene, OR: Pickwick Publications, 2013), 72–85.

68. For a most intensive and convincing synopsis, see Clark J. Elliston, *Dietrich Bonhoeffer and the Ethical Self: Christology, Ethics, and Formation* (Minneapolis: Fortress Press, 2016).

gives priority to the other in order to overcome ontological accounts with their intrinsic tendency to reduce different to sameness. Bonhoeffer's treatment of responsibility overlaps with the account of Lévinas in avoiding beginning from a "self" understood a subject able to establish or justify one's existence.[69] Both thinkers insist that human beings receive what moral continuity they might have by way of external forces that constitute them and grant them form, and external formation Bonhoeffer insists is given in Jesus Christ. All encounters and demands arising from an "other" are invitations for the individual (as well as the church-community) to participate in Jesus Christ's responsible action for all human beings. Participating in Christ's responsible action frees the individual "self" from enclosing the "other" within his or her own identity. The externally grounded "self" has to become the "other's" as Christ becomes his/her deputy and even taking over guilt by acting as the deputy, should acting unavoidably include taking on guilt. The focus of the person who has been brought into a relationship of responsibility by Jesus Christ to an encountering "other" is one that is embraced in faith without reservations, whether about the justifiability of one's act nor taking into account the demands made by the innate desire to live (*conatus essendi*).

Bonhoeffer's account of the structure of responsible life includes reciprocity within a fundamental asymmetry between the responsible person and the "other." In this he differs from Lévinas, who holds that to affirm reciprocity is to abolish the absolute asymmetry of the ethical relation to the other. In Bonhoeffer's ethics, however, the topic of reciprocity embedded in the theological concept of "orders" or "mandates" is conceived as the divinely given matrix for ethical life and living together. Bonhoeffer conceives the asymmetries of the encounter with the "other" to preserve within the framing of specific aspects of life provided by the different mandates.

The structure of responsible life is one in which responsible life can be understood as genuine and good in its proper limited domain within God's reality in contrast to the dominant forms of ethics and their abstract formulas for justifying moral claims. The most basic form of the ethical life, is thus, for Bonhoeffer, twofold:

> by life's bond to human beings and to God, and by the freedom of one's own life. It is this bond of life to human beings and to God that constitutes the freedom of our own life. Without this bond and without this freedom there can be no responsibility. Only the life that, within this bond, has become selfless has the freedom of my very own life and action. The bond has the form of vicarious representative action and accordance with reality [*Wirklichkeitsgemäßheit*]. Freedom exhibits itself in my accountability [*Selbstzurechnung*] for my living

---

69. For that distinction, see Bernd Wannenwetsch, "'Responsible Living' or 'Responsible Self'? Bonhoefferian Reflections on a Vexed Moral Notion", *Studies in Christian Ethics* 18, no. 3 (2005): 125–40, https://doi.org/10.1177/0953946805058804.

and acting, and in the venture [*Wagnis*] of concrete decision. This, then, is the framework [*Disposition*] within which we have to consider the structure of responsible life.[70]

Bonhoeffer has intentionally located "freedom" within the structure of responsible life. There can be no freedom that is not bound to human beings and to God. It is this twofold bond that exhaustively determines ethical human action, according to Bonhoeffer. All other types of responsibility nest within this twofold bond.

> There is also a responsibility for things, conditions, and values, but only by strictly keeping in mind that the origin, essence, and goal of all things, conditions, and values is determined by Christ (John 1:4), the God who became human. It is through Christ that the world of things and values is given back its orientation toward human beings, as was originally intended in their creation. The frequent talk about responsibility toward a cause is legitimate only within these limits. Outside these limits it serves in a dangerous fashion the inversion of all life through the dominance of things over people.[71]

Concrete Ethics

Responsible life can only be realized through engagements with specific neighbors within their concrete reality.[72] God's reality is actualized within ongoing human actions that are concretely performed in the face of permanent contestation.[73] There is a critical realism that attends ethical life, Bonhoeffer insists, a realism that springs from the irreducibility for Christian ethics of attending to the ongoing drama of God's "reality" as it is present in concrete human lives. The eschatological-apocalyptic drama of God's "ultimate" reality plays out in the concrete determination of the "penultimate" by the ultimate. Thus,

> For those who act responsibly, the given situation is not merely treated as the raw material on which they want to impose and imprint their idea or program, but instead it is included in their action as the formation of the act itself. . . . the self - denial of those who act responsibly includes choosing something relatively better over something relatively worse, and recognizing that the "absolute good" may be exactly the worst. Responsible people are not called to impose a foreign

---

70. DBWE 6, 257.
71. Ibid., 259.
72. Ibid., 261.
73. Peter Dabrock, "Responding to 'Wirklichkeit': Reclaiming Bonhoeffer's Approach to Theological Ethics between Mystery and Formation of the World," in *Mysteries in the Theology of Dietrich Bonhoeffer: A Copenhagen Bonhoeffer Symposium*, ed. Kirsten Busch Nielsen, Ulrik Nissen, and Christiane Tietz (Göttingen: Vandenhoeck & Ruprecht, 2007), 49–80.

law on reality. On the contrary, their action is in the true sense *in accord with reality*.[74]

Because Bonhoeffer's account of reality is strictly that reality that appears in Jesus Christ, it invites concrete performances according to God's will for the sake of His human beings. Responding to reality is therefore to be responsible, with responsibility being, "always a mutual relation between persons, derived from the responsibility of Jesus Christ for human beings, so that the origin, essence, and goal of all reality is the Real One, who is God in Jesus Christ. Based on this foundation, . . . we call *appropriate to the subject matter* [*Sachgemäßheit*]."[75]

For Bonhoeffer responsibility is thus a hermeneutic activity, in that dedication to responding to God's reality is a form of responding to a "reality" that may very well be hidden to the eyes of the "others" to whom one is responding. Reality has to be discovered and attended to and then acted into in the context of the messiness characteristic of the fallen, penultimate world. To act in accord with Christ is to act responsibly toward reality in that God's reality, "allows the world to be world and reckons with the world as world, while at the same time never forgetting that the world is loved, judged, and reconciled in Jesus Christ by God."[76] This is not the working out of a clash between two principles, or two contrasting societies, but between a world entrapped in its own unfreedom and the God who delivers human beings by granting them fullness of life.

The Mandates: Prefigured Forms of Human Life

In Bonhoeffer's writings he sometimes parallels the traditional ethical concept of "orders" or "institutions"—"mandates," as Bonhoeffer came to refer to them— with the language of "stations." Bonhoeffer's "stations" are public places, places of public existence, visible to the world, where the secret of God's guidance and action are explicitly stated. These places of meeting God's action are located in the midst of the world that God has not given up. That these "stations" are public places—the fora—of God's presence, highlights the thoroughly political nature of Bonhoeffer's theology, which is impelled by the promise of Jesus Christ to bring concrete freedom and life to the whole world. "The mandates are historical forms of the *Gestalt Christi* which embody and direct the normal processes of life. The ethical as a theme arises when "who Christ is for us today" becomes questionable at the point of our behavioral response to his changing forms among men."[77] God's command is addressed to human beings by way of specific "forms" of living and living together. Ethics, then, has to explore how to live within that institutionalized

---

74. DBWE 6, 172. Emphasis original.
75. Ibid., 269–70.
76. Ibid., 264.
77. Ibid., 30–1.

and formed "reality" which does have the promise of God's protection of a transformed new life according to God's will.

The central concern of Christian ethics is with the form the kingdom of God assumes within the *oeconomia*, the *politia*, and the *ecclesia* in discipline, action, and suffering. Bonhoeffer's understanding of the Church cannot be separated from his appropriation of the Lutheran scheme of the three stations. As the *oeconomia* is the place where we are involved in God's all-embracing work, and as the *politia* is the place of action in its fragmented freedom and involvement in God's will, so the *ecclesia* is the place where human beings hear of their transformation by God's action and involvement in His story. Bonhoeffer is talking about a visible Church, which is at the same time political in praying and enacting justice.[78] The Church is present where God's people stand in for others in the experience of freedom in discipline, action, suffering, and death for God's world, which he has not given up. This happens in any sphere of our human life where God's presence is expected: in the *oeconomia* of life, in the *politia* of action, and in the *ecclesia* of being transformed. The Church does not replace the *politia* as would be the case in "religious" political theology, because God's kingdom is present in different ways, including those deeds that belong to the *politia*. God's kingdom belongs to the secret of freedom.[79] The Church suffers in place of the world, stepping in for the world, which God has not given up. The witness of the Church is not "beyond" the world, but actively reveals the immediate presence of God.

Understanding Nature (Oeconomia)

Loss of touch with God's reality brings in its train the loss of nature. Bonhoeffer was highly critical of the loss of a theological notion of "nature" within the main stream of Protestant theology in his day. Bonhoeffer fundamentally rejected the dualism between "nature" and "human spirit" common in his time (promulgated by Dilthey), which he held to wrongly treat "nature" as the resistant substrate of human spirit in need of being given rationalized form. The concept of the natural was in dire need of a theological recovery.

---

78. See Stanley Hauerwas, "Dietrich Bonhoeffer—Ekklesiologie als Politik," in *Kirche, Ethik—Öffentlichkeit: Christliche Ethik in der Herausforderung*, Ethik im Theologischen Diskurs—Ethics in Theological Discourse, vol. 5 (Münster: LIT-Verlag, 2002), 99–130.

79. "How do we go about being 'religionless-worldly' Christians, how can we be ek-klēsia, those who are called out, without understanding ourselves religiously as privileged, but instead seeing ourselves as belonging wholly to the world? Christ would then no longer be the object of religion, but something else entirely, truly lord of the world. But what does that mean? In a religionless situation, what do ritual [Kultus] and prayer mean? Is this where the 'arcane discipline' [Arkandisziplin], or the difference . . . between the penultimate and the ultimate, have new significance?" DBWE 8, April 30, 1944, 364–5.

More recently, Agamben's account of "bare life" has drawn critical attention to those forms of politics that have been called biopolitics, in which the citizens of a political community are treated as a resource, as "nature" in need of formation for productivity.[80] Bonhoeffer and Agamben are both concerned with a set of perspectives that inflate life into a universal reality descriptor in a manner that leads directly to the loss of awareness of that reality that we have seen as essentially determinative. Because the resurrection of Christ is part of God's apocalyptic story, its invading appearance breaks up all forms of vitalism that suppose the indeterminacy of life in order to overrule and to dominate it. In his *Ethics*, Bonhoeffer explicitly criticized such vitalism as an obvious example of the ways that generalized worldviews and ideas destroy human life and freedom:

> Natural life is formed life. The natural is the form that inheres in and serves life. If life severs itself from this form, if it tries to assert itself in freedom from this form, if it will not allow itself to be served by the form of the natural, then it destroys itself down to its roots. Life that makes itself absolute, that makes itself its own goal, destroys itself. Vitalism ends inevitably in nihilism, in the destruction of all that is natural. . . . It is movement without end, without goal, movement into nothingness. It does not rest until it has drawn everything into this annihilating movement.[81]

The description of "movement without end" is also applicable to God's story, as long as we understand this to be the movement of the resurrected Christ becoming present and sanctifying the worshipping community. This counter "movement without end" is liberative in contradicting every rival description of movement that presents itself as ruling and determining human life.

Bonhoeffer is suggesting a radically Christological criterion for recovery of a theologically defensible account of the natural. "The natural is that which, after the fall, is directed toward the coming of Jesus Christ. The unnatural is that which, after the fall, closes itself off from the coming of Jesus Christ."[82] "Nature" has to be seen in its explicitly promising givenness, which is not separable from its own given form (*Gestalt*). Bonhoeffer's understanding of the givenness of the material world is not a covert version of naturalism or vitalism nostalgically evading the work of alteration that humans have already visited upon the natural world. In Bonhoeffer's theological account, "nature" is neither raw material needing to be given meaningful form nor is it pristine wilderness. The laws of responsibility to it are not displayed on its surface, which is why one of the tasks of Christian ethics is to discern the natural as it has been given and preserved by God.

---

80. Giorgio Agamben, *Homo Sacer: Sovereign Power and Bare Life* (Stanford: Stanford University Press, 1998).
81. DBWE 6, 178.
82. Ibid., 173.

Life's form is tied up with the activity of God's preservation, which resists all kinds of human formation destroying life. To follow nature in its preserved form is the task of reason (*ratio*, *Vernunft*[83]) and wisdom.[84]

> The reason for this is that the natural is also the true protection of preserved life. Thus, the recognition of the natural by "reason" corresponds to the affirmation of the natural through the "basic will" of preserved life. Furthermore, it is not as if this "basic will" were a divine remnant in human beings, uninjured by the fall into sin, and thus able to affirm the divine order. Instead, this basic will is just as embedded within and immersed in the fall and the preserved world as is reason. Therefore. it concerns itself exclusively with the content of the natural and affirms it because there it seeks and finds the protection of life. The natural guards life against the unnatural. In the end, it is life itself that tends toward the natural and ever again turns against the unnatural and breaks it down.[85]

Bonhoeffer regains an ethics of the natural as that part of God's reality which is—under fallen conditions—"directed toward the coming of Christ." With this move he recovers a crucial ethical distinction between the natural and the unnatural by naming as unnatural that which "closes itself off from the coming of Jesus Christ."

Ethical life in the natural realm is a hermeneutical one, demanding ongoing human work of judgment and discernment. Forms of ethical life frame Christian ethics in its exploration of the concrete ways in which God's reality has become present in Jesus Christ within God's whole story from creation to reconciliation and redemption. Bonhoeffer's claim appears to be in some accordance to those discourses in biosciences which follow a hermeneutical approach to "nature" as it became acute especially within the context of genome analysis and all the issues and problems of its "reading," "understanding," and, then, also its "correcting" by human intervention.

The Kingdom and the Kingdoms (Politia)

Bonhoeffer always stressed that God—because of Jesus Christ—has not given up this world but in Christ has been reconciling the world to Himself (2 Corinthians 5). The Church steps in for the world, living the redemption in Christ and participating in his sufferings. In the Church's suffering, God's will for his world appears, and in the powerlessness of the Church God's power becomes visible. The Church steps in for the world by being involved in its affairs, which are transformed into God's affairs through the Church's involvement. This standing up as the place holder for God's acting in the world by the Church does not establish it as the new

---

83. See ibid., 174.
84. See ibid., 81–2.
85. Ibid., 176.

polis.[86] The Church is the place of transformation, the place of change, the place of giving oneself over to God: a station on the way to freedom, on the way to God's heavenly kingdom.

The "stations on the way to freedom" are not the biographical stations of an individual, but rather places where God's presence is to be expected, where God's people meet and come together in order to meet God. The church, as Stanley Hauerwas has often emphasized, is always the "visible Church."[87] It is the visible Church of people who hand themselves over to God and who are therefore free from any other occupation or condition. The Church is not a religious space where God is represented but the people who live this freedom and witness to it—through discipline, action, and suffering—within and to the worlds. This Church therefore is visible, and this visible Church is the obvious presence of God's hidden kingdom. But the Church only exists where and when we find people on the way to freedom in discipline, action, and suffering. It is an actual, particular Church, a Church of today and tomorrow, a Church of this actual worship. It does not represent something universal, something beyond these stations.[88]

This "living in transformation" has to be witnessed to the world as it in this age by a church displaying a renewed mind, and so proving what is the will of God in action (Rom. 12:2). Proving what is the will of God is not an intellectual task. It is our experience of God's will taking the place of our own will. The Church is the place of that reversal. With the fragmentary presence of God's freedom within the stations God's kingdom is also present. God himself will remain within the secret and be visible in discipline, action, and suffering.

> The kingdom of God is not to be found in some other world beyond, but in the midst of this world. Our obedience is demanded in terms of its contradictory appearance, and, then, through our obedience, the miracle, like lightning, is allowed to flash up again and again from the perfect, blessed new world of the final promise.[89]

Though the kingdom of God assumes form in the Church, it does not do so in a manner that is abstracted from the state.

---

86. It can possibly be understood in the logic of a "negative" political theology, as Bernd Wannenwetsch has suggested: "Representing the Absent in the City," in *God, Truth, and Witness: Engaging Stanley Hauerwas*, ed. L. Gregory Jones et al. (Grand Rapids: Brazos Press, 2005), 167–92. Yet, the problem with a "negative" political theology might be that while it remains in a dialectical way within the logic of a political theology by refusing any "representation," it may still not fully overcome this "religious" logic.

87. Stanley Hauerwas, *Performing the Faith: Bonhoeffer and the Practice of Nonviolence* (Grand Rapids: Brazos Press, 2004).

88. This account is close to Luther's description of the *notae ecclesiae*, the defining marks of the Church: *Authority of Councils and Churches*, LW 42, 3–178.

89. Bonhoeffer, "Thy Kingdom Come," 92.

The kingdom of God exists in our world exclusively in the duality of church and state. Each is necessarily related to the other; neither exists for itself. Every attempt of one to take control of the other disregards this relationship of the kingdom of God on earth. Every prayer for the coming of the kingdom to us that does not have in mind both church and state is either otherworldliness or secularism. It is, in any case, disbelief in the kingdom of God. . . .

The kingdom of Christ is God's kingdom, but God's kingdom in the form appointed for us. It does not appear as one, visible, powerful empire, nor yet as the "new" kingdom of the word; on the contrary, it manifests itself as the kingdom of the other world that has entered completely into the discord and contradiction to this world. It appears as the powerless, defenseless gospel of the resurrection, of the miracle; and, at the very same time, as the state that possesses authority and power and maintains order. The kingdom of Christ becomes a reality only when these two are genuinely related to each other and yet mutually limit one another.[90]

The Church and the Logic of Responsibility (Ecclesia)

The God of Israel and the Church is not a God who avoids reality. Just as God fulfilled His will with Jesus, He does it continually with His disciples who follow him. He is still the God who let His Son suffer. He stands in our place in His Son—and enlists His disciples to stand in the place of others. Being responsible means standing in for somebody in order that God's will might be fulfilled.[91]

Such a position cannot fit within any political theology interested in representing God's achievement—including "religious" triumph, whether on earth or beyond time. Religion is always about triumphant representation.[92] And any such political theology is religious because it sets up a positive representative, so causing rivalries about what or who can provide proper representation. Does peaceful behavior of the Church represent God's peace? Does doing right represent God's righteousness? In contradiction to this logic of representation, God himself overcomes our ways with his own. Bonhoeffer understands Jesus not as the last triumphant representative of God but the one in whom God himself suffers, stepping into our human powerlessness and loneliness.[93]

---

90. Ibid., 91–2.
91. For the theological logic of responsibility, see Wannenwetsch, "'Responsible Living' or 'Responsible Self'?"
92. Cf. Niklas Luhmann's definition of religion as *Kontingenzbewältigung* ("coping with contingence") in *Funktion der Religion* (Frankfurt: Suhrkamp 1977).
93. "Whatever human weaknesses, miscalculations, and guilt there are in what precedes the facts, God is in the facts themselves. If we get through these next weeks or months alive, we shall see very clearly afterward that it was good for all of us that things turned out just the way they did. The idea that many hard things in life could have been avoided if we

This was the logic behind Bonhoeffer's involvement in the plot against Hitler. In his eyes, this involvement was a stepping in for the other. It was neither an act of last resort nor even a defensible act of revolution. It was a situation in which it was no longer possible for "right" to be done. Someone had to kill the tyrant. This was "the end of human action" a handing of everything over to God, remaining powerless, casting aside the "powerful deed," and, in this case, embracing the ethically "wrong." Bonhoeffer had no intention of justifying in principle the use of violence in order to achieve power. In his view the plot was an admission of powerlessness, submission to God, and suffering whatever the consequences might be. Bonhoeffer could accept himself becoming a victim, but he could not accept that the other should have to become a victim. This is a thoroughly Lutheran logic: one may give up one's own rights, but cannot expect the same abstinence from the other, even to the point of being willing to incur guilt by acting one's self.

To resist the evil means to do good works (Romans 12), to do what is right. However, this can also mean "the end of your action" and hence suffering. To suffer means to give oneself over to God and his story, which through Jesus has already been revealed to be precisely that suffering. One's suffering must be part of that story if it is not to be an act of inventing our own story. This stands in opposition to a political theology which points to a politically significant representation of God, which is beyond His presence in bearing us on the way to freedom. It stands, of course, also against any church that pretends to be beyond suffering in following God's presence. Such a church would not be an invisible church, but one that was visible in all the wrong ways.

The uniqueness of Bonhoeffer's political theology as well as his approach to political ethics springs from its fundamental grounding not in ontological claims or structures but in God's economy and rule. He never loses sight of the claim that God's ruling in freedom must be experienced as challenging the representations of God offered in all political theologies. What is essential is that God's political presence enters into and takes over our fallen reality, transforming it thereby. God's ruling is actualized in this giving over of all that we do to God.

The Secret and the Understanding

Freedom has to be experienced. But it can be experienced only at the stations of God's presence and guidance. Consequently, freedom remains secret, a secret of God. Freedom is not the result of processes of liberation. It lies beyond our human condition, beyond the chains and walls of our body and mind, beyond the blindness of our soul, and beyond the (religious) practices that attempt to overcome such boundaries. Freedom is the secret of a new life with God, face to

---

had not kept going forward courageously is really too craven to take seriously even for a moment," DBWE 8, January 23, 1944, 265.

face with Him. This is the goal of God's will and not the fulfillment of our own. Freedom is alien to us, *libertas aliena*. Where God is present, there is freedom. Consequently, freedom is found at these stations, where God is present in various ways. Bonhoeffer's whole theology is permeated by a quest for God's presence in our world. God has not—as Bonhoeffer constantly stresses—given up the world, which is still his very own, in which he wants to reign through Jesus Christ in all times and places. This is the secret of freedom, which is promised to us found in the stations on the way to the eternal freedom.

Yet the freedom of God remains enclosed in a secret. We cannot have a firm "knowledge" of it, but must simply have faith in both its existence and creation through the stations. The secret of freedom cannot be disclosed by any kind of liberating reflection, pronouncement of conscience, or enlightenment. Freedom is a possession given to God's chosen children (Rom. 8:21) who have become acquainted with God's presence: because freedom belongs to God. That freedom is "secret" does not mean that it is beyond our horizon or that it is a closed reality we cannot reach. Rather, it is the present secret of a kingdom to which we are called, along whose way we journey.

Bonhoeffer sometimes maintained that the whole of human life is a yearning to gain cognition of all that God has prepared for us. As long as we—like Job or Jesus—do not fully see God's plan and will, we are experiencing the secret of freedom. Bonhoeffer's few hints about a "discipline of the arcane" concern this problem, which inevitably attends a theology that explores God's secret will and plans rather than the human religious conscience, language, and thoughts. It is the discipline of living in God's revealed secret—whose reality we have experienced with certainty. It is revealed to us as a secret; the secret of freedom that we know already through discipline, action, and suffering.

We can have insight into God's secret only when we are face to face with God, as the apostle Paul emphasized in 1 Cor. 2:7-10:

> But we impart a secret and hidden wisdom of God, which God decreed before the ages for our glorification. None of the rulers of this age understood this; . . . as it is written, "What no eye has seen, nor ear heard, nor the heart of man conceived, what God has prepared for those who love him," God has revealed to us through the Spirit.

Knowledge, face to face with God, is the final goal on the way to freedom, because this is the only way to gain knowledge of what happens to us, of what reality is about. Such understanding is not generated by interpreting history—as theologians often have done, pretending to know God's will, or pretending not to be able to know and looking for some supra-temporal knowledge.[94] We can find understanding

---

94. "God's beyond is not the beyond of our cognitive faculties. The transcendence of epistemological theory has nothing to do with the transcendence of God. God is beyond in the midst of our life" (LPP, 282).

only through our submission to God's own reality, which is not separated from our human reality—a submission, finally, to our own death. Bonhoeffer is critical of all theologies that seek God at the borders or limits of our human horizon. The only "beyond" is the Other who has entered our history, and involved us in God's story. "God is the beyond in the midst of our lives."[95]

Theology, on the one hand, has to preserve the secret instead of transforming it into the religious, and on the other, it must learn to follow God's reality instead of transforming it into piety or theological descriptions. "An 'arcane discipline' must be reestablished, through which the mysteries of the Christian faith are sheltered against profanation. The positivism of revelation is too easygoing."[96] At the very least, the Church must learn not to replace God's reality with religion, seeking instead to be involved with God's presence wherever and whenever it appears in our reality. Such formed attention to God's presence will lead, in the end, to understanding.

In Jesus Christ, God stands in our place in our deeds, sufferings, and guilt. We do not stand in for Him or even serve as representatives for Him. We are not Christ—however much we share God's sufferings.

> Christ, so the Scripture tells us, experienced in his own body the whole suffering of all humanity as his own—an incomprehensibly lofty thought!—taking it upon himself in freedom. . . . We are not lords but instruments in the hands of the Lord of history. . . . If we want to be Christians it means that we are to take part in Christ's greatness of heart, in the responsible action that in freedom lays hold of the hour and faces the danger, and in the true sympathy that springs forth not from fear but from Christ's freeing and redeeming love for all who suffer.[97]

Christian faith is faith in God's presence, as it was the faith of those who stood under the cross at Jesus' death. We are disciples in no other way.

The dynamics of the secret, freedom, and the vicarious suffering of Christian discipleship are highlighted by a literally fatal mistake of one of the conspirators of the July 20 plot against Hitler. General Oster refused to destroy the files outlining the conspiracy because he wanted to have material after the war to justify the plotters against the possible accusation of having acted too late. Oster's desire

---

95. Ibid.
96. DBWE 8, May 5, 1944, 373.
97. DBWE 8, "After Ten Years," 49. Almost two years later he applied this analysis to his own participation in the plot against Hitler. "The human being is called upon to share in God's suffering at the hands of a godless world. Thus we must really live in that godless world and not try to cover up or transfigure its godlessness somehow with religion. Our lives must be 'worldly,' so that we can share precisely so in God's suffering. . . . It is not a religious act that makes someone a Christian, but rather sharing in God's suffering in the worldly life. . . . But what is this life like? this life of participating in God's powerlessness in the world?" (DBWE 8, July 18, 1944, 480, 482).

for justification meant that the files were hidden carelessly in a garden and later discovered by the authorities. This, of course, can only be said as an aside, and not as a judgment on Oster. The fact is, however, that this is how things happened, in direct contrast to Bonhoeffer's understanding of the proper form of Christian responsibility. There was also a Judas working in the context of God's plan— who was paralleled from the other side by the courageous soldier who delivered Bonhoeffer's letters, including his prison poems, at the risk of his life. Because of the acts of this one soldier, Knobloch, we are able to hear the messages Bonhoeffer penned for others while in prison. These messages would have been lost without a human being unconstrained by human law who was free enough to deliver them. In the freedom of Knobloch, and the comfort he undoubtedly afforded the imprisoned Bonhoeffer, we see in microcosm both the counterintuitive suffering of faith and the this-worldly concreteness of God's faithfulness.

Chapter 3

EXPLORATIVE THEOLOGY

DISCOVERY AND DISCERNMENT

What Is Theological Research? Questions New and Old

In the hurly-burly of discussions about research in the university, as research emphases are established and research plans formulated, the question of what is to be considered research often arises. It is a question that is rarely pursued with any seriousness, however, and almost never out into the terrain of questions about whether the practices of research in different disciplines are describable within any single logic.

In the scientific disciplines a trickle of public discussion has emerged about how such a question might even be formulated and tested according correspondence or coherence criterion. The description of this understanding of science has been offered by Paul Feyerabend, who held up for inspection the science of pluralism as his method.[1] But above all, it is Jean-François Lyotard who has successfully indicated that the prioritization of knowledge inquired after, and the way this knowledge is legitimated, is based on the criterion of what is marketable.[2] After Lyotard, the dominant master narrative shaping modern scientific research, in which science is narrated as a series of steps on the way to the emancipation of humanity, has lost its power to legitimate scientific projects. Furthermore, narratives or metanarratives of scientific advance, like the one Thomas Kuhn developed in *The Structure of Scientific Revolutions*,[3] do not comprehend many fields and dynamic processes of scientific activity, even though people continue to use the language of paradigms and paradigm shifts as marking the progress of scientific research. Lyotard's analysis may well overreach itself, however, in that the framing story of technological progress itself, which produces knowledge,

---

1. Paul K. Feyerabend, *Wider den Methodenzwang: Skizze einer anarchistischen Erkenntnistheorie* (Frankfurt am Main: Suhrkamp, 1976).

2. Jean-François Lyotard, *The Postmodern Condition. A Report on Knowledge*, trans. Geoff Bennington and Brian Massumi (Manchester: Manchester University Press, 1984).

3. Thomas S. Kuhn, *The Structure of Scientific Revolutions*, 3rd edn. (Chicago: University of Chicago Press, 1996).

continues to a great extent to morally and socially legitimate the scientific search for knowledge.

I will not engage these debates about how best to describe current legitimating narratives and their relationship to scientific method (which include debates about how such narratives might be constructed[4]). Nor will I delve into historical reconstructions of the ways in which the theoretical discourses of science have penetrated theology in the last twenty years. I will, however, draw one line of theological interpretation of such narratives, in particular that of Joachim Track. Using language theory, he has shown the sense in which theology should be considered a science within the terms of contemporary discussions. Though there are theologians who have attempted to conform their theological approach according to current accounts of scientific investigation, Track defines theology as a science by taking its own scientific and linguistic theoretical reflections seriously.[5] This weighty contribution to the understanding of theological language and religious speech helpfully highlights the possibility of a genuinely *theological* investigation of the generation of knowledge in the medium of language.

These debates show how the history of research can be analyzed in order to locate ourselves and our methodological proposals today. In this chapter, however, I do not take a route that builds from a genealogical starting point. Instead I directly pursue the question of how and in what way we—in theology—should consider formulating anew the question of what theological science and theological research is, can be, or should be. The demand that all university faculties formulate research aims or knowledge production makes this an urgent task for academic theologians negotiating a highly fluid university context with its attendant changes in the context of university research, and above all a radically changing redefinition of what is counted as "scientific community."[6]

The language of research and knowledge production is ubiquitous not only in universities but also in public discourse in general, a fact that is rarely interrogated by theologians. Yet across the various subdisciplines represented in departments of theology or religious studies, we continue to describe our work as exegetical research, of Pentateuch research or Pauline research, or in even more narrowly defined research areas. Much of this research self-evidently coincides with and overlaps with research in other departments in multifaceted ways. This raises the question of this chapter: is there within all these areas something that might be called a special *theological research*? Restated: is there any form of research that demands theological reflection if it is to be aptly characterized? We will lose the force of this formulation of the question if we translate it into the more familiar

---

4. Aspects of this are found in Jürgen Mittelstraß, *Die Häuser des Wissens. Wissenschaftstheoretische Studien* (Frankfurt/M.: Suhrkamp, 1998).

5. Joachim Track, *Sprachkritische Untersuchungen zum christlichen Reden von Gott* (Göttingen: Vandenhoeck & Ruprecht, 1976).

6. Compare with the most recent discussion of *Unterwegs zur Wissensgesellschaft: Grundlagen-Trends-Probleme*, ed. Christoph Hubig (Berlin: Sigma, 2000).

question of whether there can be a specifically theological method. We lose it in a different way if we position it as repeating the old question of the relation between theology and the sciences. Our guiding question of what is to be called theological research in exegesis, church history, or systematic and practical theology directs attention to a more fundamental conceptual question of whether the word "research" used in all these self-descriptions by theologians shares any single logic of investigation, and whether this logic bears any relation to theological claims and categories.

That scientific theory, like language theory, has enclosed theological reflection in the modern period is largely beyond dispute.[7] Given this widely shared reading of the state of theology today, there is therefore every reason to ask about a theological understanding of research, and especially to ask about a *theological* understanding of theological research.

The task of this chapter is to show how contemporary academic descriptions of research open up into the question of what genuinely theological research might look like. Jumping off from the premise that academic research is an inquiry aiming to discover new knowledge, I suggest that Christian faith too can be understood as a process of discovery of the reality exposed when human beings are claimed by the name of the God of Israel and Jesus. In Jesus Christ God's reason has entered the rationalities of this world, exposing the reality of creaturely occurrence anew. In the entry of God's reason into the world, reality is exposed in a manner that can be discovered (and so sought, researched), and inhabited. The second half of the chapter further elaborates the semantic fields of "research" and "discovery" by way of an engagement with Oliver O'Donovan's account of Christian "ways of judgment." O'Donovan's account of judgment is presented as grounded in biblical ideas of "discernment" and the act of "rendering judgment" that are constitutive of the scriptural wisdom traditions. Taken together, these themes and keywords clarify and concretize the anchoring of Christian ethics in discerning activity in which the mind of the believer is transformed by the drawing near of Immanuel, "God with us"—that reveals the world and generates new knowledge.

Research: ars inveniendi

The extensive discourse within scientific theory about research has spawned distinctions for parsing what counts as science that are even at a first glance not

---

7. This is articulated in very informative ways in the treatise from Track, *Sprachkritische Untersuchungen*. His language theory is a case of a language critique approach called "modified nominalism," which implies a theological reflection: "God and experience are heard together. We are discovering who God is in immediate experiences, which will be enabled and created through God's history of disclosure. Here our language-critical proposition is affirmed once again by theological reflection; that in immediate experience the understanding and reality of God is at risk" (312f.).

without theological explosiveness. One is between *searching* and *demonstration*, as Kuno Lorenz has indicated in his article "Research."⁸ The initial step of research is to *investigate* reality so that we *"become aware."* What follows is a descriptive activity that safeguards the validity of what has been observed in order that what has been ascertained becomes comprehensible (learning in order to teach).⁹ One can relate this difference to the traditional differentiation between the *ars inveniendi* (the art of invention of new theories) and the *ars iudicandi* (the practice of justifying theories): research is in the first instance about locating or discovery, and not a single activity of proving, justifying and presenting.¹⁰ Scientific activity can be legitimately called research when it is locating of and getting to know objects—discovering reality— and also when it is representing and converting the novelty that has been glimpsed into terms comprehensible within the framework of previous knowledge. Research is thus two sided: it aims at discovery, at perceiving what is not yet perceived, but also in naming and giving description of that which is not yet known.

These observations describe research in terms that should raise the interest of theologians. They do so because they highlight the necessity of asking directly what research itself might be, a question that will not be answered by procedures that assume that there is one universal "logic of research."¹¹ To understand what research means in any given field will entail describing a wide range of research tasks, which will generate an understanding of research that is differentiated in character. Close attention must be paid to the question of how formerly unknown and even unimagined objects "come into existence," appear for the first time as objects at all. It is at this point that the function of language becomes critical, since it is in language to some extent that objects "come into existence" in linguistic accounts or linguistic conventions prior to their being observed in the material world.¹²

---

8. Kuno Lorenz, "Forschung," in *Enzyklopädie Philosophie und Wissenschaftstheorie*, vol. I (Mannheim: Metzler, 1980), 663–4. Compare also Jürgen Mittelstraß, *Die Häuser des Wissens*.

9. "This will not be identified in the mode of demonstration according to the logic of coherence (in which what is systematic is defined as rational, thus understanding knowledge as produced by human reason), or the mode of research that substantiates by identifying and recovering coherence (here equating historical with empirical, and defining knowledge as related to understanding causes), because demonstration as meta-competence depends on object competence [conformity of knowledge to the entity being described]." Lorenz, "Forschung," 664.

10. Compare also as *ars inveniendi* the aspect of nature, which we search but do not find: *quaerit se naturam sed non invenit*; Wolfram Hogrebe, *Sehnsucht und Erkenntnis* (Erlangen/ Jena: Zweigniederlassung der Unibuch Erlangen-Jena OHG, 1994), 17.

11. Compare this with Rüdiger Bubner, Dialektik als Topik. Bausteine zu einer lebensweltlichen Theorie der Rationalität (Frankfurt/M.: Suhrkamp, 1990).

12. See here Track, *Sprachkritische Untersuchungen*, especially the themes Metaphern und Metapherbildung. Also see Hans G. Ulrich, "Metapher und Widerspruch," in *Metapher*

Fundamental research is not directed at things as they already are, but searches for that which is not yet an "object," what has not yet "appeared" or been identified. More usually research unearths only what presents itself according to the measure of that which is already understood to be present, or the measure of immediate apprehension. This regular research only augments what is already understood; it will not locate the unknown or discover the unexpected. Properly speaking, therefore, the concern of pure or fundamental research is with the question of how the unknown and unrecognized comes into our world, how the new appears *as* unknown and unrecognized.[13] When, to take one example, black holes were first discovered in physics, it was by no means clear *what* it was that had been discovered. It was not yet clear whether the novelty of such an entity was an artifact of our never having come across one before, or because of the challenge it levied on our theories of the sort of thing that might possibly exist in the physical realm. In such cases it is not immediately apparent how the new and the unknown come into visibility. These questions are also appropriate in reference to the "discovery" of the gene. *What* exactly was discovered? When scientists (such as James Watson[14]) call it an "information carrier" that will allow us to decode the mystery of life, such descriptions highlight the reality that the designation of the object is not yet settled. It is this unsettledness that demands metaphors be harnessed in order to depict the novel.

The science that inquires after the novel is not necessarily successful as a philosophy that takes wing at twilight with the owl of Minerva. Rather, it is science that is no longer searching to display and stabilize the coherence of current concepts of what there is but investigates instead what might not yet be comprehended by these concepts. Such science is also not reflexive in the sense of emphasizing the self-awareness of the observer or the trajectory of the history of science; it is not concerned with the safeguarding and securing of what is already known, or compiling records on the basis of what is otherwise given (coherence justification). Its sole concern is to find the place of the genesis or the appearance of the given—in order to position itself to study the novel.[15]

---

und Wirklichkeit: Die Logik der Bildhaftigkeit im Reden von Gott, Mensch and Natur; Dietrich Ritschl zum 70 Geburtstag, ed. Reinhold Bernhardt (Göttingen: Vandenhoeck & Ruprecht, 1999).

13. Compare Joachim Track's positioning of the task between the "retreat" of assertive speech and the logic of hypothesis formation and verification. In itself the latter form of speech is deficient. "Assertive" speech is *itself* identified by Track as the discovery. Such speech contradicts perception which means that the speaking of God is—in a formal, functional sense—hypothetical speech. It is exactly this positioning which we are once more following out, as we search here to clarify the understanding of "*fides quaerens intellectum*." *Sprachkritische Untersuchungen*, 275f.

14. James Watson, *The Double Helix. A Personal Account of the Discovery of the Structure of DNA* (New York: Scribner and Sons, 1998).

15. See Track, *Sprachkritische Untersuchungen*, 256f.

Science so described regularly finds itself on adventurous paths in its search for virginal soil where there appears to be none. It is explorative. The means or "method" needed in this pursuit are categorically other than those which are utilized to safeguard and to communicate current frameworks of knowledge. Thus, fundamental research as the search for the novel is at the same time a seeking after a way.

Method as an approved scientific procedure for perception and knowledge exploration will always emerge when the main aim of research is to render validation. Such validating work foregrounds the repeatable conditions for others, so that they too can approach the location of the novel. On this view scientific methods function as guideposts remembering routes by which one recovers what has been found. To speak of a "heuristic" method as a method of investigation is a contradiction in terms to the extent that we are talking about investigating entities that are as yet unknown by deploying familiar methods. How can familiar methods help us to discover the unknown?

Theology as ars inveniendi

Is theology an *ars inveniendi*, an art of discovering novelty? Could we even say that theology is the art *par excellence* of the discovery and investigation of the novel? Or is it rather more like the philosophy whose owl flies in the twilight—having something to say only when other theories are losing plausibility? The connection with science lies in the object of theology being something which already exists. God has already established His reality, theology only searches to understand it. Is this not especially the case if we are allowed to say that God is also treading this path in making appearances?[16]

The history of theology is replete with assertions that God in His abundance precedes everything we can investigate. On these grounds it is often then suggested that the whole comprehensible object of theology is the faith (or the religious consciousness) that God has given out of his abundance. The only question then is how and to what extent this object, which is given in faith, can be represented, how it becomes present and understandable in more distinctly and in increasingly differentiated and comprehensible ways, and also how it comes into language. Theology understood as research into faith cannot be considered the work of investigating a novelty. It is more like regular scientific research in explicating and presenting the faith that is well-known and is granted to humans. Schleiermacher explicitly presents this as the task of a "positive science," a science of the given, of the *positum*, in this case of the *positum* of living faith and its forms of devotion.

---

16. For an eagle-like view of the differences in the sciences, the owl and science, see Jürgen Mittelstraß, *Natur und Geist*. On dualistic, cultural, and transdisciplinary forms of science, in *Die Häuser des Wissens*, 91–158, especially 13f. Mittelstraß, oddly enough, does *not* make reference to Nietzsche's eagle.

Karl Barth's interpretation of Anselm of Canterbury's identification of theology as *"fides quaerens intellectum"* works with a very different account of research. Barth asks how the *ratio* of God which precedes human understanding and knowing becomes an object in faith and understanding. For him research turns on the success of this transfer, the successful entrance of God's *ratio* into our reality. Barth has a place for investigations seeking the novel that is distinguishable from other tasks such as the providing of justification.[17] The question is how Barth understands this to work.

Fides quaerens intellectum

Is theological research an analysis appended to, or is it the explication of what is given in faith—so becoming "doctrine"? It is in the latter terms that Anselm of Canterbury is often understood to have brought "fides *quaerens intellectum*" as a theological task back into view. Theology explicates—*per rationem, per intellectum*—a *positum*. This is the (rational and intelligible) reality of God given to faith and contained in faith.[18] Theology thinks about what is already given in faith (but not yet contained in the intellect). It does not search behind that which is given in faith as reality.[19]

On this interpretation it is possible to hold that theology acts on the assumption of an *unchallengeable faith* (although this is to be distinguished from a deposit of faith). One can then underscore, as did Karl Barth in his exegesis of Anselm's "*Fides quaerens intellectum*," that in this respect the believer and the unbeliever are in the same situation: neither want to nor are able to bring about their own faith. The seeking of greater understanding by the nonbeliever aims to gain greater insight into Christian faith without coming to have that faith. Believers, on the other hand, seek deeper intellectual insight into what they believe, knowing that this insight does not add anything to faith.

Thus, along with *sola fide* is an inescapable *sola ratione*—or *solo intellectu*. Nothing else can sustain insight, because insight itself cannot be based upon anything given. When one speaks of experience, then only the insight itself or the faith itself can be considered the experience (not being an experience which is added to faith). This being the case, we will speak of an *experience of faith* or an *experience of insight*. The theology which seeks to articulate *this* insight does

---

17. Karl Barth, *Anselm: Fides quaerens intellectum: Anselm's Proof of the Existence of God in the Context of His Theological Scheme*, trans. Ian W. Robertson (London: SCM Press, 1960). Compare also the distinction between discovery- and justification-rationales in the theology of Gerhard Sauter, "Die Begründung theologischer Aussagen—wissenshaftstheoretisch gesehen," in *Erwartung und Erfahrung* (München: Gütersloh, 1972).

18. This is also suitably understood as the speech of God as the "object" of theology.

19. For a sophisticated discussion of these problems see Dietrich Ritschl's posing of questions about "implicit axioms." See also *Implizite Axiome. Tiefenstrukturen des Denkens und Handelns*, ed. Wolfgang Huber, Ernst Petzold, and Theo Sundermeier (München: Gütersloh, 1990).

not think "after" what is already given in faith: faith itself consists in the seeking and encounter with the novel—and so faith makes its appearance as insight. Understood in these terms, faith "originates" in and with the discovery of the not-yet-appearing. It is in faith that the object to which faith holds is "given." Through faith a reality appears that will need to be understood (*intelligere*).

Such an account of the discovery of faith is not that of an individual alone because the *object* that is discovered is available to everyone who is situated on the path leading to this discovery.

The crucial difference between the understanding of research presented by Schleiermacher and Barth is Barth's emphasis on an understanding of faith *itself* as a work of seeking those places where the object will be attained, where the new *will* be present—in that place where, as Kuno Lorenz has put it, *object competence* (becoming aware of the object) counts. Faith places itself where the object will be discovered, not at the place where the given is already held to, arranged, vindicated, or arranged for presentation. The place of faith is the place where it is necessary to be in order to be aware of God in His partially encountered fulfillment. The place of faith is these *learning situations*.[20] Incidentally, we may call the traditional theological use of the "*assertiones*,"[21] as analogous to the statements of certainty that scientists use to guide other people back to the novel that they have observed. Theological assertions are thus not statements of unassailable proof or indisputable givens but are reports of discoveries that have also been in some respect understood. These reports are true assertions, despite being in need of further substantiation.

Faith and ars inveniendi

What might the process of such discovery look like? Faith follows the Word, which allows the object belonging to the reality of God to become present. This is the basic procedure of discovery. Various biblical texts discuss this process of discovery. Psalm 82 provides an initial example of the processes by which the specific contours of justice come into language. Israel discovers the reality of justice by being told to discern the neighbor in his distress. God Himself is understood to appear in this distress in order to call for justice. The origin of this learning situation of faith is God's entrance onto the scene. God's address is the means of locating such learning situations—because God's address enables perception of

---

20. See for instance the meaning of the teaching and learning situation in the acquisition of language, Track, *Sprachkritische Untersuchungen,* 281. Track speaks here on the meaning sense of the "teaching and learning situation of faith."

21. See this topic as discussed by Martin Luther in "On the Freedom of the Will (De servo arbitrio) 1525," in *Martin Luther, Ausgewählte Werke,* ed. H. H. Borcherdt and Georg Merz (München: Kaiser, 1962), 11–14. See also Günter Bader, *Assertio: Drei fortlaufende Lektüren zu Skepsis, Narrheit und Sünde bei Erasmus und Luther* (Tübingen: Mohr Siebeck, 1985).

a particular form of justice that could not be perceived without this clue. Justice itself consists precisely in this changing of view: discerning *means* to do justice to the reality of the other.[22]

The Word generates discoveries, through the primal naming of the "*vox significans rem.*" God's voice speaks what justice is. This is not a *predicament* in the sense of Wittgenstein's "this is (also) a tree." It is much more a creative word, a speaking forth of things: this word, and nothing else, articulates "justice." The justice so articulated is to be distinguished from the exercise of law and force in all its forms, though these different exercises of justice name and discover their own forms of novelty because it is in the process of dispensing justice that the novel is revealed. In such activity the way in which the *ratio Dei* enters into human reality becomes explicit. In all strands of the biblical tradition this activity is presented as a dramatic discovery—culminating in the epiphany of Christ in the stories of the Gospels. Stories such as that of Jesus' baptism allow the listener directly to hear, "This is my beloved Son" (Mt. 3:13-17). In this statement Jesus appears as something new to the people in the textual narrative and to the reader; God's Son is discovered through this divine word. We have here an example of an "object competence" that can be followed by listeners in faith. It is a word that makes explicit that the object of faith is in no way brought into appearance by the faithful but emerges into view only by the creative word. With the revealing of the object of faith, faith itself is brought forth as a specific realization, a heard realization of what has in this way become present as reality to the one who has faith. This particular object now stands as a faith-object. The origin of this faith is coeval with the appearance of the object. Thus, the discovery is of faith itself. Faith is the place and mode of the discovery.

Hence the crucial point: faith stands against the confusion of the object with any other memory, experience, or motivation that might have been present and so could be used to explain the appearance of the faith-object. This faith has its "telos" (its essence) in *sola fide*. A faith which supports itself in some other way is no faith. Only this faith—*sola fides*—has "object competence" of this type.[23] "Faith" is a conceptually precise name for this object competence: provided an object is genuine in faith, it is being included in its own logic and is not derived from another object. In this way the object unmistakably proves itself *not* to be revealed by any genealogical account or unmasking. Justification—as Nietzsche describes

---

22. On this exegesis of the Psalms see Martin Buber, *Right and Wrong*, trans. Ronald Smith (London: SCM Press, 1952).

23. This is pivotal for a perception theory of faith as it becomes clear through the miracle accounts in the New Testament, such as walking on the water. The miracle is not the overcoming of physical laws (das Bodenlose), nor is it the irrational for which we can give no reasons (das nicht Begründbare), but centers on the disciples' radical exposure in the context of the new appearing. Miracle is the giving of space to the novel. Yet a miracle is no guarantee that the new will appear.

it[24]—is a projection of ressentiment. The attraction of ressentiment is it justifies by reference to what it understands as incontestably justified reasons, with the final aim of putting one's self in the moral right instead of receiving what one is actually due. But self-justification of this sort hides its own arbitrariness by constructing a rival account of power and authority. This example displays, like innumerable others, what it is necessary to "investigate" here!

The discovery of a new reality in faith is consummated at the same time in the intellect. The "*intelligere*" is not necessarily a "given," but is itself a discovery. This means that *understanding* is not necessarily directed toward a *given* "object" but is a perception of an object in the mode of discovery. The *intelligere* of the subject comprehends the discovery: the *intelligere* follows anew the dramatic of this discovery—in no other way than as faith.

The *intelligere* is itself the consummation of the discovery in its own way: it is a matter of the fulfillment of the object acquisition in the intellect. It is in this sense that *vox significans rem in intellectu*. The "*res*" originates here, the new "*res*." The word establishes a new context out of the same objects by transforming them into faith-objects. Here deeper insight is fulfilled as faith, and faith as deeper insight. Faith is thereby that point in the process of perceiving whereby what is acquired anew by the *intellectus* is anticipated and carefully preserved. This understanding in faith, the *ratio fidei* or *intellectus fidei*, is the exercise of this (specific) object competence. This exercise allows the meaning to become present of *what* is necessary to be understood. But this becoming-present is also necessarily a discovery.

The immense richness of such discoveries in the biblical and Christian traditions is available for us to explore. These records of discovery, these signposts to the object of faith, can be investigated. They invite us to ask anew: On which path is "justice" to be discovered? How will "freedom" be uncovered in our time? How will we discover "humanity"? How will we glimpse real "creaturely-being"? The question is no less complex which asks how a Christian "ethic" might be discovered. The gospel story of the rich man displays the essential process of all such discoveries. A new way is opened for him into what it means to be perfect and good. This discovery is then integrated into a dramatic story. Stories like that of Job, of Psalm 82, or of the rich man show us a human being entering into virginal territory, through the hearing of the voice, the word, which "says what is" (*dicit, quod res est*). To hear this word is to have uncovered something new.

Discovery in the Name of God

Karl Barth drew his interpretation of theological research from the program of Anselm of Canterbury. Anselm's procedure was to

---

24. Friedrich Nietzsche, *On the Genealogy of Morals*, trans. Douglas Smith (Oxford: Oxford University Press, 1996).

meditate upon a particular article of the Christian *Credo* by itself, that is, to investigate the meaning of what it contains that he may place it in its relation to all the other articles or to the one next to it, comparing and connecting it with them and allowing them to illumine it. All this he does with the intention of himself conceiving by reflection the hidden law of the object of faith about which this article speaks, that thereby he may show it forth and so be able to know the thing believed: the noetic *ratio* becomes the discovery of the ontic *ratio* in so far as it follows after it; in which case the remaining articles of the *Credo* point the way along which the ontic precedes the noetic *ratio*, along which the noetic *ratio* has to follow to discover it.[25]

Thus, Barth clearly articulates the intertwining of reflection and discovery in theological research: the *intelligere* (the noetic ratio) attains the object as it already exists in *ratio dei* (already present in reality). Discovery names the moment of insight as simultaneously thought about what has been revealed through the appearance of God's rationality. Theological discovery is not the subsequent work of portrayal or confirmation, clarification nor the displaying of newly discerned distinctions.[26] Given this intertwining of noetic and rational discovery, the insight that comes with faith is necessarily dramatic. The dramatic of discovery is rooted in faith being beholden to what God has said and what can be discovered. God is not the object of theological discovery, but God does become "objective" in this event. Theological research need not to withdraw itself from either faith or perception. Neither does it proceed by consciously bracketing the insights that are incipiently glimpsed in the very first words grasped by faith.

At any given moment the first word grasped by faith opens a *new way* for perception because this first word is an as-yet not entirely heard word that brims with creativity. God's reality-revealing word is not illustrative, verificatory, or mediatory—since it relies on no more basic legitimating narratives, such as progress or liberation. This is why research understood in this way must be considered as fundamentally discovery of the new, since it is not the application of an old word or method that can reveal nothing novel, or only corroborate what is already known. These path-finding words are creative in the sense of generating perception in those who hear them of the relevant "*significatio rei*" ("signifying properties") in their context or situation. As indicated in the words of the baptism of Jesus "This is my Son," the first of these path-crating words is naming, or name-affixing. This applies also for God's name, which Anselm of Canterbury designates the object of theological science.[27] Discovery of the name

---

25. Karl Barth, *Anselm*, 53. Translation slightly modified.

26. Compare Oswald Bayer's account of the proximity of Barth to Hegel in *Theologie* (München: Gütersloh, 1994), 330f. Hegel understood dogmatics as the thoughtful *displaying* of faith.

27. See Barth, *Fides quaerens intellectum*, 77. The transaction depicted here lies very near the interconnection sought by correspondence language theories and linguistic

of God precedes all other theological discoveries. Because God is the source of the world's novelty, the annunciation of his name is creative both for faith and *in intellectu*.[28] This name giving opens the way for the one who hears it to become a creature.

Anselm presents this creative naming as paradigmatic in that it allows the affixing of a designator to God as "something greater than which cannot be conceived."[29] The name of God is thus not a proposition, hypothesis, or explanation of who God is, but purely a designation. As such, this name cannot be independently conceived or deduced. The name says this itself. Because it is God's name, revealed by God, it has a precise purpose:

> All that can possibly be expected from this Name is that, in conformity with the program of Anselm's theology, it should demonstrate that between the Name of God and the revelation of his Existence and Nature from the other source there exists a strong and discernable connection. Only in that way and to that extent will statements about the Existence and Nature of God inevitably follow from an understanding of this Name.[30]

Because the name of God is a designator and not an explanation, to receive it in faith continually opens up discoveries and allows them to be immediately distinguishable *as discoveries*. Anyone who follows in the dramatic opened up by the name of this "something greater than which cannot be conceived" *will* discover the novel. Those who follow other names than God's will make different discoveries: some of these will be of false names of God, golden calf-like substitutions of explanations and hypotheses for God's own given name, perhaps calling God the "Author of all things" or "the Ground of Being" to name two contemporary appellations.

Quaerens intellectum

The decisive point to grasp is that the insight gained in following God's name is not of the type that protects the one who receives it, nor does it validate them against attack, nor is it a mediation of God in things, nor is it a portrayal of reality. This insight into the form of theological insight is itself a discovery—provided

---

critiques. See Track, *Sprachkritische Untersuchungen*.

28. This is to say, "When he (Anselm) gives God a name, it is not like one person forming a concept of another person; rather it is as a creature standing before his Creator." Barth, *Fides quaerens intellectum*, 77.

29. "Aliquid quo nihil maius cogitari possit." See Barth, *Fides quaerens intellectum*, p. 77. In addition, see Eberhard Jüngel, *God as Mystery of the World. On the Foundation of the Theology of the Crucified One in the Dispute Between Theism and Atheism*, trans. Darrell L. Gruder (Edinburgh: T&T Clark, 1983), section IV, "On the Speakability of God."

30. Barth, *Fides quaerens intellectum*, 75–6.

that the name, no matter what it brings into view, has actually generated hitherto undiscovered perceptions of the novel.

It is at this most sensitive point that misunderstandings arise ever anew. Unless "understanding" is conceived as reflective in the sense that the name has itself appeared as a reality, then the work of understanding will inevitably be devoted to validating one's own knowledge, to proving one's possession of that knowledge, and to pursuing other lines of investigation that verify that already known (but false) name of God. Insofar as *"intelligere"* ("understanding") is a *"probare"* ("testing") it should be considered a theological demonstration, as Barth reads Anselm.[31] Whatever happens, and for the reasons discussed earlier, insight is both *sola ratione* and *sola intellectu* which has taken place. The implication is that this *intelligere* and *probare* are the execution of discovery, not of instrumentality and illustration. Discovery and giving reasons are crucially different activities.

Understanding defined in this way is an inquiry after the discoveries that appear in the ways that are opened up by the name of God. This name allows a whole new reality to be discovered, which awaits discovery as long as the one who seeks does not shift their focus to the activity of trying to secure or give reasons for what is found. Discovery will continue as long as discovery is not displaced by the activity of justifying and displaying what is discovered—precisely as in scientific exploration.

Anselm of Canterbury aims to win non-Christians by taking them along the route to discovery, not by offering them justifications or legitimations by way of translations of Christian faith-claims into the terms of their own names for reality. Anselm's program thus resists all apologetic strategies as invitations not to discovery but to self-assurance. What is necessary is to call people to explore the way opened up by faith in God's name. The entrance onto the way of discovery is thus identical for Christians and non-Christians to hearken to the name of God.

Theological Research—Explorative Theology

What follows as a consequence of this fundamental heuristic? How does it configure the task of searching after and discovering in theology, and what sort of theological research results? We can now say more precisely that theological research is essentially devotion to exploring the reality that exists in the presence of God's name. It follows in the way, seeking the traces, of the reality this name draws into itself.[32] In so doing it takes up the traces and follows the signposts left by those who are also following this way.

---

31. See ibid., 61f.

32. See especially Christian Link, *Die Spur des Namens: Wege zur Erkenntnis Gottes and zur Erfahrung der Schöpfung* (Neukirchen: Neukirchener, 1997).

It is constitutive for any discoveries of what this name draws together that what is considered "real" is understood as all that is drawn together with this name, that set of realities the name has permitted to be associated with itself, everything that the name makes available and accessible.[33] To affirm this is not an act of self-reassurance about the capability of this name to generate expert knowledge through which we can connect ourselves with God. It is rather a mode of testing and exploration of the novel that has come into the world. It is a seeing what happens and what has happened where people are seized by this name, by the God of this name.

The paradigm of this process is the story of Jesus, who was rendered available to faith as the Messiah according to this dramatic of discovery. It is paradigmatic novelty for God's Son to come into the social and imaginative world of human beings who, when they grasp what has happened, make a discovery that no prior skill or knowledge could have led them to expect. This coming generated a new experience,[34] and theological research follows the dramatic of this genesis. Theological research is only competent to explore those things of which it has been made aware: with the arrival of this Jesus a new form of life comes into the world, a new love, a new justice, a new hope, a new story. This is the life form of the one who is able to say the Lord's Prayer, and in doing so says, "Thy will be done."

The discovery of the life form that is drawn together by the name of Jesus grasped as the Messiah is dramatic, and only intelligible because its novelty is fleshed out in the story of Jesus. Jesus listened to the voice of the One who sent him on this way of discovery. When we in faith retrace this way, when we catch hold of the name spoken by this voice, hear the call, then *"in intellectu,"* we can in our understanding and testing discover this new life form in a way that coheres with Christ. An *explorative theology* springs exclusively and perennially from this point of transfiguration into the novel. Were the new form of life in Christ no more than a moral or ascetic ideal (as Friedrich Nietzsche suggested[35]), then nothing could be discovered by following Christ except a moral system. But for those who expect that this name will yield this new form of life, "something greater than which cannot be conceived," they understand that it will be discovered by following what happens after the prayer, "Thy will be done." Whoever articulates these words has discovered the new life form. They expect not an ideal, but to experience particular disclosures in their own places of the entailments of the name of God that Jesus embodied in the world. To trace the testing of this life form in all areas of human reality, a testing which plumbs every region of that reality, is the task of an

---

33. For an understanding of the opening up function of the speech of God see Track, *Sprachkritische Untersuchungen*, 83f.

34. This is identified as "experiencing as experience." This is meant here in the sense that there arises a new explorative experiencing of experience.

35. Nietzsche, *On the Genealogy of Morals*, Third Essay.

explorative theology.³⁶ The work of understanding faith, bypassing the attempt to reassure one's self of being in the right or having knowledge, directs itself to testing and probing the veracity of human reality in and under God's name.

In Rom. 12:1-2 Paul presents the topic of theological research that I have so rudimentarily and sketchily laid out here:

> I appeal to you therefore, brethren, by the mercies of God, to present your bodies as a living sacrifice, holy and acceptable to God, which is your spiritual worship which follows the *Logos* and the *ratio Dei*. And let your life-forms be changed by the renewing of your mind, in order to find out what is the will of God, the good and acceptable and perfect.

To follow the discoveries of faith is to probe and investigate human living in a manner that will always and again be experienced as novel. Such an exploration will gravitate to those areas, for instance, where various people are testing the statement (*assertio*), "I believe that God has created me, together with all creatures." Theological research seeks to test this confession amidst the many domains in which people currently are radically changing the conditions of their existence, even though they are not able to state what the foundation of their existence is. We live in a world where many aspects of human lives are being radically changed under many names, such as "financial efficiency" or "the alleviation of suffering." But at a more fundamental level speechlessness, if anything, is ascendant. Theological research enters this fray to locate and make accessible to language what it means to be God's creature. An example for this possible theological research aim is all those projects which investigate anew the phenomenon of human existence—from within the perspective of the certainty that we humans are allowed to be God's creation.³⁷

The Ways of Discernment

Christians also confess that human beings are allowed to live at peace with one another. Oliver O'Donovan's book *The Ways of Judgment*³⁸ develops an analysis of human political judgment that allows us to flesh out this account of theological

---

36. This alternative conception of ethics understands ethics as instruction in the probing of the Christian life form by those who themselves exist in the testing of God's will.

37. See as an example of an explorative theology of the activity of blessing and the blessing Dorothea Greiner, *Segen und Segnen: Eine systematisch-theologische Grundlegung* (Stuttgart: Kohlhammer, 1998); and on the phenomenon of being born, Karin Ulrich-Eschemann, *Vom Geborenwerden des Menschen: Philosophische und theologische Erkundungen* (Münster: Lit, 2000).

38. Oliver O'Donovan, *The Ways of Judgment* (Grand Rapids: Eerdmans, 2005).

discovery in a more obviously horizontal and interpersonal direction, and in more concrete terms.

O'Donovan's basic proposal is that there is an act of judgment that theology must describe if, in a kind of reverse apologetic, it is to speak to the world about what "the ways of judgment" are and should be. If he is correct in this, as I think he is, may it not also be the case that there are further basic "acts" which should be described and which would also serve, paralleling the ways of judgment, as a reminder in an apologetic reinterpretation of other phenomena or institutions which are also fundamental for our human life? Would it not also be appropriate to reflect through a similar method "the ways of understanding" and "the ways of discernment" that would serve as a reminder of what "science" or "knowledge" is really about?

O'Donovan notes at the beginning of *The Ways of Judgment* that there is

> a crisis that is more pressing on unbelievers than on believers ... In our days it is not religious believers that suffer a crisis of confidence. Believers *did* suffer a serious one two or three generations ago, and the results of that crisis in small church attendance and the de-Christianizing of institutions are still working themselves out around us. But that crisis was precipitated by the presence of a rival confidence, a massive cultural certainty that united natural science, democratic politics, technology, and colonialism. Today this civilizational ice-shelf has broken up, and though some of the icebergs floating around are huge—natural science and technology, especially, drift on as though nothing has happened—they are not joined together anymore, nor joined to the land.[39]

Here a new apologetic task opens up, that of recalling to their proper orientation the fundamental acts that constitute human existence, in order to ensure that they preserve the fabric of human life. Might this apologetic approach even do substantial work in the case of the icebergs of "science" and "technology"? In my work I have continually found this to be of particular interest, as my own collaborative work over many years with people from the fields of technology and the natural sciences has repeatedly raised the question whether theology might have the resources to remind them of their "orientating" task.

The Ways of Judgment

It is significant that O'Donovan's book is not merely about "ways" of judgment but about "*the* ways" of judgment. Human judgments proceed down certain discernible "ways," as long as we do not deviate from these "ways" they have the power to direct us in our judgment and open up the landscape of particular orderings of justice for particular contexts. "Ways," in my reading, does not mean "manners"

---

39. Ibid., xii.

(even if this meaning is not totally excluded), but ways for walking along within specific social domains. I am now concerned with the domain of justice, the sphere or the "context" in which we human beings live according to our human condition as social and politically at peace.

O'Donovan's usage of the language of "way" and "the ways" of judgment can be even further elaborated by going further into the highly differentiated semantic field offered in biblical language. There are "the ways of God (YHWH)" which we, human beings, cannot understand even though they are the very ways in which God is leading us. There are also the ways of the just which God alone knows (cf. Psalm 1). Furthermore, there are "the ways" down which God led Israel from Egypt, and in doing so challenged Israel to follow these ways and not deviate from them. The ways by which God leads his people are at the same time the ways of the Torah. It would be inappropriate to assume that the way of living as presented in the Torah is no more than a metaphorical transposition of Israel's one supposedly original way through the desert. Rather, the decrees of the Torah offer a way of living that is at the same time the way of life and the way we are to live, as recent exegetical work on the semantics of "way" in the biblical traditions has highlighted.[40] The Hebrew phrase *derech chaiim* or *orech chaiim* has at least a threefold meaning, all running together in the Torah, which teaches the way of life, the way of living, and the way we are to live.

Israel has learned the Torah by following God's leading out of Egypt and by learning the Torah anew in other situations. In a further step of reflecting the reality of living, the Torah appears as the second creation, as we read in Ps. 19:7: "The law [*Torah*] of the Lord is perfect, reviving the soul; the decrees [*edut*] of the Lord are sure, making wise the simple."

To follow the Torah implies the growth of wise understanding. There is no Hebrew word for obedience other than the word "listen" (and then "preserving"—not "observing"). The way of life held out in the Torah has to be taught, and this teaching must be understood, it must generate discovery and insight. In Ps. 119:34 we read, "Give me understanding, that I may keep your law and observe it with my whole heart." Those who follow the Torah become wise. To be wise means to be experienced in the Torah. Martin Buber translates what the English version calls "decrees" (*edut*) as *Vergegenwärtigungen* ("re-presentations") (Ps. 19:8; Deut. 6:17; Jer. 44:23).[41] The Torah provides the context of living as it is constituted by God's

---

40. For overviews, see Kathrin Liess, *Der Weg des Lebens: Psalm 16 und das Lebens- und Todesverständnis der Individualpsalmen*, Forschungen zum Alten Testament, Reihe 2, 5 (Tübingen: Mohr Siebeck, 2004); and Markus Philipp Zehnder, *Wegmetaphorik im Alten Testament: Eine semantische Untersuchung der alttestamentlichen und altorientalischen Weg-Lexeme mit besonderer Berücksichtigung ihrer metaphorischen Verwendung*, Beihefte zur Zeitschrift für die alttestamentliche Wissenschaft, vol. 268 (Berlin: de Gruyter, 1999).

41. Martin Buber and Franz Rosenzweig, *Die Schrift und ihre Verdeutschung* (Heidelberg: Schneider, 1954).

presence. This context has to be understood if the people of God are not to lose their way.

The Act of Discernment (Understanding)

As the first part of the chapter outlined, the key biblical term "understanding" points to an act, and this act is one with multiple connections to the language of "judging."[42] Psalm 82, for instance, defines unjust rulers as ones do not "understand." The NRSV translation has it that they "have neither knowledge nor understanding" (v. 5). The Hebrew text, however, uses the language of acts: the act of getting knowledge and the act of understanding. The unjust do not understand, meaning that they do not act in a way that displays understanding. Thus, by connecting "understanding" with O'Donovan's description of the act of judgment, it becomes clear that there must be further basic acts in which human beings follow the name of God.

"Understanding," however, is a rather vague translation of the Hebrew word we encounter here, which is very often translated in English Bible versions as "discern." This translation is quite close to the Hebrew word can also be translated as "distinguish" or "differentiate." The act of "discernment" is about distinguishing with clarity issues, phenomena, and things with its antonyms being indifference and confusion. Within the biblical grammar, the act of discernment is positioned as the basic act of the wise person as they gain insight into reality in its given differentiation. The Hebrew word finds its Greek equivalent in *krinein*. Significantly, this Greek word covers both the act of judgment and the act of discernment. It would be a story of its own to describe the semantic field of *krinein*,[43] and for now I will focus on the implications of the Hebrew language, in which the New Testament usage in the Greek is rooted.

Because the act of discernment is tightly connected with the act of judgment Solomon asks God for a "heart" able to "listen" (1 Kgs 3:9). God adjudges this a pleasing request and grants to Solomon the heart that is discerning and wise and enables him to judge rightly (1 Kgs 3:12). This is an example displaying how an act of discernment is the central act of wisdom. Wisdom is a practice of discernment.

As far as the various Hebrew words in this semantic field are concerned, Gerhard von Rad has shown the importance of bearing in mind that there are no sharp

---

42. The Hebrew Bible shows around 170 references.

43. Cf. Ingeborg Bertau, *Unterscheidung der Geister: Studien zur theologischen Semantik der gotischen Paulusbriefe* (Erlangen: Palm & Enke, 1987). See for its meaning especially in O'Donovan's work: Gerard C. den Hertog, "Urteilen als Kernaufgabe des bürgerlichen Regiments: Ein Vergleich von Johannes Calvin und Oliver O'Donovan," in *Kirche, Theologie und Politik im reformierten Protestantismus: Vorträge der 8. Emder Tagung zur Geschichte des reformierten Protestantismus*, ed. Matthias Freudenberg and Georg Plasger (Neukirchen: Neukirchener Theologie, 2011), 37–50.

distinctions between some of the Hebrew words used here.[44] The manifold richness of this semantic field reflects the complexity and importance of the phenomenon of wisdom in Israel. One of the words for wisdom pointedly denotes the act of "discernment." This act characterizes or should characterize those responsible for making judgments. It is not enough to know the rules of law; judgment is only just that understands these laws via an appropriate hermeneutics of the lived context. Discernment is the core act anchoring an appropriate hermeneutics of the lived context: it is "understanding" growing from being observant about the ways in which underlying distinctions are determining a given context of living.

In *The Ways of Judgment*, O'Donovan highlights this connection between judging and understanding. His chapter on imperfectability, for instance, describes the role of "contextual truth," that is, the understanding of circumstances and situations. This understanding is, he notes, "in principle unlimited."[45] In practice, however, there are limits, for otherwise there would be no effective judgment possible. He gives as an example how some aspects of a case under discussion might well call for more extensive discussion and consideration of their human effects, not to mention what a theological consideration might reveal, but neither the court nor the legislative chamber is the place to undertake that discussion and exploration. Judges and legislators have to cut things short and act.[46] Along with this practical limitation is the transcendental priority of "divine insight": all human acts of judgment are, one might say, positively and beneficially limited by God's insight and God's final judgment, that can only be made present to us in God's own time.[47]

The "context of living" in which discernment, understanding, and judgment take place thus includes both the beneficially limited context of human understanding and judgment as well as the overarching context that encompasses it of God's own "understanding" and His characteristic acts of judgment. Only because human and divine judgments are thus distinguished are human discernment and judgment possible in a clearly determined form. (We return later to the theological implications of judgments having these limits.)

Discernment and Judgment—Related to God's Acts

The act of discernment as linked with judging does not focus on the clarification of general distinctions but solely those distinctions exposed by God in His active presence. The act of discernment seeks the way of life that corresponds to the reality in which human beings find themselves. The act of discernment turns on

---

44. Gerhard von Rad, *Wisdom in Israel*, trans. James D. Martin (London: SCM Press, 1972).
45. O'Donovan, *Ways of Judgment*, 22.
46. Ibid.
47. See the story of Cain and Abel discussed in ibid., 28.

grasping the distinctions necessary for our remaining within God's presence and guidance. As we read in Ps. 16:11:

> You show me the path of life.
> In your presence there is fullness of joy;
> in your right hand are pleasures forevermore.

In the biblical traditions "discernment" is this particular discernment of this particular "path" (*orech*). This is true for the individual and for God's people. Both find themselves wandering through the desert. Every place is a desert that contains no divinely given way. This is why the coherence and continuity of the path has to be marked in order to be followed by an ongoing discernment, as taught through God's guidance and judgment. This interpretation is a rejection of another reading of the language of the way in contemporary biblical studies, in which it is taken as a call to prolong sacred rites and customs into the rest of life.[48] The continuity of tradition is ensured only in explicit acts of handing over, of teaching the word along with the context-sensitive discernment through explicit acts of handing over—as the Greek word for "tradition" denotes in being a cognate of *paradidonai*, the ongoing practice of handing over.

In seeking the point of meeting for discernment and judgment we meet in significant respects with Hannah Arendt's posthumously edited work on judging, *Das Urteilen*.[49] As with thinking and willing, judging, according to Arendt, is one of the three basic acts of the human mind. In partial agreement with Immanuel Kant, she locates the act of judging in the context of a common world that is the context of all political action and interaction.[50] The human practice of reaching shared understanding is constitutive of any common world. The question that follows from this observation is: Where—within what practice—will we find a common world if we bypass reflection on the geography of the limits beneficially granted by God's acts. This question crops up again when we ask about the ways of teaching and learning. Those who have heard God's name perceive that the

---

48. Contra Zehnder, *Wegmetaphorik im Alten Testament*.

49. Hannah Arendt, *Das Urteilen: Texte zu Kants Politischer Philosophie* (Munich: Piper, 1985). Translated as *Lectures on Kant's Political Philosophy*, ed. Ronald Beiner (Chicago: University of Chicago Press, 1982). An important discussion of this text can be found in *Judgment, Imagination, and Politics: Themes from Kant and Arendt*, ed. Jennifer Nedelsky and Ronald Beiner (Lanham: Rowan & Littlefield, 2001).

50. See further her essay "Verstehen und Politik," in *Zwischen Vergangenheit und Zukunft*, ed. Ursula Ludz (München: Piper, 1994), 110–27; translated as "Understanding and Politics (The Difficulties of Understanding)," in *Essays in Understanding, 1930–1954: Formation, Exile, and Totalitarianism*, ed. Jerome Kohn (New York: Schocken Books, 1994), 307–27. Arendt is also very instructive on the relation between judgment and opinion, the role of opinion (as opposed to scientific knowledge) in politics, and the relation of judgment and the *vita contemplativa*.

common world is only understood within the context of creation, renewal, and redemption. They are learning to distinguish a common world and the context of living which are grounded in God's acts. Arendt's account of understanding is without these limits. She understands the work of judgment as an unlimited activity in which we seek to find a common world so that we can "reconcile" ourselves with that world, coming to terms together, for instance, with the terrible events that have occurred in recent memory, such as the Holocaust and Nazi totalitarianism. Here again Arendt's account of the work of "understanding" again converges with a theological account in seeking reconciliation—itself, it should be noted, is one of the animating ideas of a traditional concept of hermeneutics.[51]

The Biblical Tradition of Discernment

Reflecting on Arendt's account of judgment brings to attention the importance of distinguishing between the common world of public discourse and the common reality determined by God's acts. In particular, as Bonhoeffer emphatically reminded us, it is determined by the fact that God has reconciled "the world": our world is constituted by an act of God, thought this can only be understood by the renewal of our minds that gives rise to a new awareness of the reality granted by God.

No reality exists in which God's people can live separated from God and His acts—at least as it is presented in biblical traditions and theological reflections on these traditions. To be outside this reality is to be separated from the acts of God alone that constitute our human world. These acts are addressed to His people. Cut off from these acts we His creatures can neither live nor live together. "If you, O Lord, should mark iniquities, Lord, who could stand?" reads Ps. 130:3-4, continuing, "But there is forgiveness with you, so that you may be revered." Who could stand without receiving forgiveness from God? It is a wise act to raise this question. To subject of wisdom is the relation and distinction between God's acts and human affairs, and—crucially—the distinctions that arise at this boundary and so mark out the contours of the way of living God has for us.

It takes wisdom to discern what needs forgiveness, to take one example, forgiveness that Psalm 130 says God alone is able to grant. God's forgiveness alone enables and authorizes human beings to forgive, in the way Jesus hands on in the Lord's Prayer. Forgiveness is one of the acts whereby God constitutes a common human world by beneficially marking the limits of all human action.

Coming from a very different (secular) vantage point, Jürgen Habermas has recently shown the practical importance of this limitation of human acts when

---

51. Arendt, "Verstehen und Politik." Arendt, Hannah: "Understanding and Politics," *Partisan Review* 20, no. 4 (1953), 377–92

encompassed by God's acts. The loss of the horizon of God as the only truly just one has left contemporary language of justice mired in irritating confusions.

> When sin was converted to culpability, and the breaking of divine commands to an offense against human laws, something was lost. The wish for forgiveness is still bound up with the unsentimental wish to undo the harm inflicted on others. What is even more disconcerting is the irreversibility of past sufferings—the injustice inflicted on innocent people who were abused, debased, and murdered, and which reaches far beyond any reparations available to human power. The lost hope for resurrection is keenly felt as a void. . . . The unbelieving sons and daughters of modernity seem to believe that they owe more to one another, and need more for themselves, than what is accessible to them, in translation, of religious tradition—as if the semantic potential of the latter was still not exhausted.[52]

Habermas's view is based on a taken-for-granted distinction between religious and nonreligious traditions. Believers and nonbelievers are distinguishable by observing the terms of the "more" that they seek. The biblical traditions mark this distinction in contrasting the wise person and the fool. The one who may be called a fool might feel no void, but has lost the way of wisdom, because there can be no wise discernment outside God's acts, that is, outside an active confidence in God's acts, God's forgiveness, God's judgment, God's *edut*, God's reconciliation. In particular, reality is disclosed exclusively by those acts of God which are focused on the sacrifice of His Son. As Paul says, wisdom appears as the wisdom of the cross. It is the wisdom of a *theologia crucis*, as Martin Luther puts it, which alone "declares what reality is" (*dicit quod res est*). The distinction between wisdom and foolishness indexes to that confidence and trust in God's present acts.

Von Rad's description of the biblical reflection on the "limits of wisdom" shares much with O'Donovan's description of the limits of judgment.[53] Referring to Prov. 19:21 ("Many plans are in a man's mind, but Yahweh's decree [*azat*] endures"), von Rad observes:

> Here, too, it is a question of limits of which a man must remain aware in his attempt to master life. There is no thought, however, of the well-known and much-lamented limitation of man's range of vision. That would be something still comparatively harmless. It is a question not of something which a man does not know, but ought to know and perhaps even could know, but of something which he can never know. Once again this simply establishes the fact as such. What it means for a man is left open. One can almost suppose that in the case of

---

52. Habermas, "Faith and Knowledge," in *The Future of Human Nature*, trans. William Rehg, Max Pensky, and Hella Beister (Cambridge: Polity Press, 2003), 110–11.

53. See Gerhard von Rad, *Wisdom in Israel*, trans. James D. Martin (London: SCM Press, 1972), esp. his chapter on imperfectability, 97–110.

this limitation, where it becomes clear that even in every human plan God still has the last word, the wise men saw, rather, something beneficial. God could protect man even from his own plans. . . . The ancients became aware of this limitation in that utterly incalculable and therefore mysterious factor which seemed to intrude between the preparation of a project and its realization. Here, so the teachers thought, one can experience the hand of God. Of course, such sentences do not purport to be sound doctrines about the theological distinction between human and divine activity (man in planning, God in action). They are simply examples from life by means of which one can demonstrate clearly the intervention of the divine mystery.[54]

Wisdom emerges out of openness to that always present mystery, von Rad continues. Biblical wisdom has its own distinctive contours and limits, tied to the bounded capacities of creatures to discern their own way in the absence of divine guidance. The limit of human discernment is thus not a complaint about creaturely limitation, but an awareness of rudderlessness of all human capacities outside of ongoing dependence on God's acts.

When did Israel ever complain of this mysterious presence of God in every human activity? This divine presence, on the one hand limiting human planning, on the other carrying men beyond the goal which they had envisaged—to experience human limitations in this way was, in the last resort, a comforting doctrine. By this dialectic of the two points of view the wise men have influenced the religious thinking of the entire Western world.[55]

The signposts of scripture generate an expectation that the way of wise discernment will be marked by conflicting or even contradictory experiences. The wise person will be aware of and even expect these conflicts and will resist in such moments giving way to forms of certainty that dispense with the need for trust in God's acts. That kind of certainty is foolish. Put in other terms, foolishness is the rejection of the dialectical tensions of waiting to discern God, a failure to be open to different experiences and to the renewal of one's mind (Rom. 12:2). Wisdom, in contrast, is constituted by an openness much richer than a humane open-mindedness in being is rooted in the expectation of encountering the novel. Wisdom is sustained in the recognition of God's acts, in particular His acts of teaching and transforming our minds.

As the ways of judgment (with their constitutive sightings of the novel) have to be realized in ways of representation, so too do the ways of wise discernment have to be realized in ways of teaching and learning. Wisdom must be taught and made explicit. It becomes real in its articulation.

---

54. Ibid., 100.
55. Ibid., 105–06.

Learning the Practice of Wisdom

The wisdom of discernment is one that must be learned. This wisdom as presented in the scriptural traditions is not conceived as a detached knowledge about the differences between God and humankind nor some gnosis about a mystery. Wisdom is a practice, a discerning practice that is able to remain in the tracks opened by God's ways. One of the distinctive characteristics of this wisdom is its capacity to integrate different and even contradictory experiences. In this it differs starkly from the "purifying" processes of gaining knowledge through increasingly abstract generalizations typical of the modernist scientific mentality.[56] Von Rad marks the difference. Wise men in scripture could not provide

> practicable directions for the road. They were aiming at something much more important: by means of their teachings, derived from experience, they set the pupil in the midst of the constant oscillation between grasp of meaning and loss of meaning, and in this way they induced him to make his own contribution in this exciting arena of knowledge of life. In this way they probably achieved more than if they had trained their pupils to find a better solution for theological problems. Reduced to its bare essentials, these regulations of theirs for a fruitful life seem determined by a remarkable dialectic. . . . [On the one hand] do not hesitate to summon up all your powers in order to familiarize yourself with all the rules which might somehow be effective in life. Ignorance in any form will be detrimental to you; only the "fool" thinks he can shut his eyes to this.[57]

On the other hand, if you give yourself to learning all the rules of life you encounter around you, experience will teach you that the acts of living can never be certain. To be wise is to remain eternally open for a completely new experience. Without learning this one will never become really wise, for, in the last resort, this life of yours is determined not by rules but by God.

God's Acts and the Wisdom to Discern God's Acts

The only "reality"[58] in which human beings can live as God's creatures is constituted by those acts of God which we not only presuppose (or have to presuppose) in our living but in which we are all along engaged. To believe otherwise would mean following very different rules of living. The biblical traditions articulate manifold acts of God. Theological traditions have cataloged these many acts as acts of creation, of government and preservation, of salvation and reconciliation, and

---

56. Bruno Latour, *We Have Never Been Modern* (Cambridge, MA: Harvard University Press, 1993).
57. Von Rad, *Wisdom in Israel*, 106.
58. See Gerhard von Rad's critical reflection on "order" in ibid., 106–7.

of redemption. All are acts that are exclusively God's. We become aware of this universe of divine action in the first instance through God's act of forgiveness and judgment. All God's acts are not a presumptive fundamental condition for human living, but an actual reality that we can engage and experience because we have immersed in and surrounded by these acts our whole lives.

We must affirm this, at least, if we take seriously what the biblical traditions of wisdom teach us, as reiterating in Jesus' teaching as recounted in Mt. 6:25-30.

> Therefore, I tell you, do not worry about your life, what you will eat or what you will drink, or about your body, what you will wear. Is not life more than food, and the body more than clothing? Look at the birds of the air; they neither sow nor reap nor gather into barns, and yet your heavenly Father feeds them. Are you not of more value than they? And can any of you by worrying add a single hour to your span of life? And why do you worry about clothing? Consider the lilies of the field, how they grow; they neither toil nor spin, yet I tell you, even Solomon in all his glory was not clothed like one of these. But if God so clothes the grass of the field, which is alive today and tomorrow is thrown into the oven, will he not much more clothe you—you of little faith?

It is unwise to imagine the human condition in terms that screen out all the things we human beings receive from God. Any of God's many acts can open our eyes to this actual context of human living.

Take the topic of health as an illustrative example. Mt. 9:2-8 teaches that health is inseparable from the need for forgiveness from God, which only Jesus has authority to grant. The assumption here is that the health of God's creatures is badly understood when perceived as merely physical strength. As Jn 9:3 teaches, even blindness is not understood if it is reduced to physical blindness: the blind man belongs to God's story with His people as blind. Despite the suggestion of some exegetes, biblical wisdom does not distinguish between a physical, material sphere and a spiritual sphere. The distinction is rather between God's acts as they define our human condition and much more restricted perceptions of reality that lose their orientation and understanding in being focused by false questions such as the question about the relation between guilt and illness. The central question remains how forgiveness—or the renewal of our minds (Rom. 12:2)—constitutes a new way of life.

This is one of many examples of the manner in which awareness of living within the context of God's acts enables people to discern the differences that mark out a truly human way of life. "Is not life more than food?" Jesus teaches. Only within the context of God's reality does Jesus's teaching foster wise discernment; outside of such a context the command not to worry about one's life would be arbitrary and apparently self-destructive.

Further discernments emerge for those who keep in sight the reality that God's acts are raising up a coming kingdom, as we hear in Mt. 6:31-33:

> Therefore, do not worry, saying, "What will we eat?" or "What will we drink?" or "What will we wear?" For it is the Gentiles who strive for all these things; and

indeed, your heavenly Father knows that you need all these things. But strive first for the kingdom of God and his righteousness, and all these things will be given to you as well.

This consoling admonition calls on us to discern between bodily needs that are unquestionably basic on the one hand and the righteousness of the Kingdom of God on the other. But only because this pronouncement is declared against the background of God's trustworthiness to act does it avoid being an arbitrary or even cynical teaching. Only within this context is it possible to discern between fundamental worries (as the Greek word indicates) and daily tasks of care and providence.

Notice that Jesus is teaching a fundamental distinction organizing concrete human acts of discernment. The distinction is not between what can and cannot be perceived given the limits of our human capacities, but between what can and cannot be perceived if we are not aware of the acts of God that positively limit our duties and requirements and so transform them.

In the same way that we can find such significant distinctions in Jesus's teaching, so too do we find many further distinctions throughout the New Testament, not least in Paul's letters. Take the distinction between *soma* and *sarx*, or between freedom and liberty. Consider too the different meanings of justification, between different meanings of conscience, and all the other distinctions Paul makes in his various letters. All of these distinctions take their point of orientation from the acts of God: His act of justification, His act of liberation, His act of vocation, His act of judging, His act of reconciliation, His act of forgiveness, His act of communication, and so on. Together these distinctions offer to those who follow them the way of life. Moral theology has to represent these distinctions: this is the task of its acts of discernment. The ethics of Dietrich Bonhoeffer provide some especially fine examples: consider, for example, his distinction between the natural and unnatural on the one hand and the "contra natural" on the other.[59] The logic of this discernment—as of other discernments in his ethics—is rooted in the awareness of God's acts as they are focused in the story of Jesus Christ as constitutive for our real context of living.

The Question of Wisdom Also Concerns the Ways of Discernment Themselves

Have we yet understood the proper object of understanding and discernment? Are we clear about "the ways of discernment"? This question implies that understanding and discernment can coalesce—but can only do so in the concrete realization that we are on "the ways" that have been predetermined for us.

For those granted this understanding, the next step is to describe for others the ways of discernment as O'Donovan has explicated the possibility to hand on traditions that shape people for ways of judgment. As there are appropriate

---

59. The implications of this distinction are developed in detail in Chapter 8.

institutions to support just judgment so too must discernment be "realized" by practices (and institutions) of teaching and learning. Discernment must be taught, or rather what has to be taught is the concrete meaning of the claim that God himself is the one who teaches us His ways of discernment. Following the same logic that demands we describe legislative and judicial institutions of "judgment" Christians must also concern themselves with the "institutional" forms of teaching and learning wisdom. And as Gerhard von Rad has observed, this Israel did not neglect to do. Institutional forms are intrinsic to the character of wisdom insofar as wisdom is constituted by God. The prayer for God's teaching that we read in Psalm 16 or 25 are recognitions of this relation between individual wisdom and the institutions that hand it on. We have here the clue we need to understand the sense in which all teaching has its paradigmatic location within the church. The ways of discernment pass through this teaching if the church, the people of God, His still wandering people.

The institutional form of handing on the practice of discernment parallels the institutions that teach judgment in one final and all-important respect. Wisdom comes only through the gift of "new hearts of wisdom." This is the eschatological fulfillment already present in God's acts, the divine renewal of understanding that Jer. 31:31-33 describes as already standing before us:

> But this is the covenant that I will make with the house of Israel after those days, says the Lord: I will put my law within them, and I will write it on their hearts; and I will be their God, and they shall be my people. No longer shall they teach one another, or say to each other, "Know the Lord," for they shall all know me, from the least of them to the greatest, says the Lord; for I will forgive their iniquity, and remember their sin no more.

Part II

CHRISTIAN WITNESS IN THE WORLD (*POLITIA*)

Chapter 4

THE PUBLIC APPEARANCE OF RELIGION
GOD'S COMMANDMENTS AND THEIR POLITICAL PRESENCE

Ethics in Traditions: In Lutheran Perspective

Political ethics always inhabits a traditioned domain, as Oliver O'Donovan has insightfully observed:

> Communications are sustained by tradition, and tradition is a continuity of practices, learned, repeated, and developed. In specialist communities these practices revolve around skills and around the knowledge that supports skills. But what kind of practice forms the tradition of a whole society, the matrix within which many specialist communities cohere within a given place? Supremely, the practice of recounting. History sustains the identity of societies, not only the history of the distant past, but that of the immediate past, too.[1]

Are the practices and habits that form traditions capable of shouldering the burden of being "the tradition of a whole society"? For some this remains an open question while others seek to discover, or recover, a tradition they understand as *the* Christian political tradition. Approaches of this latter type have the advantage of squarely facing what Hannah Arendt called the problem of a lost tradition, namely, the grand Western tradition of political thinking which has been the only one so far to succeed (for a time) in sustaining the political forms of a whole transnational society.[2] At the same time, the tenability of this reconstructive project has been rendered decidedly more precarious by the terrible passages of modern Western history. Arendt met these challenges by proposing that "human dignity needs a new guarantee which can be found only in a new political principle, in a new law."[3] This is a reminder we are well served to heed, and one that I will be directly engaging in the main body of this chapter. Before pursuing a traditioned

---

1. Oliver O'Donovan, *The Ways of Judgment* (Grand Rapids: Eerdmans, 2005), 69–70.
2. Hannah Arendt, "Tradition and the Modern Age," in *Between Past and Future: Eight Exercises in Political Thought* (New York: Penguin Books, 1977), 17–40.
3. Hannah Arendt, *The Origins of Totalitarianism* (Orlando: Harcourt, 1968), ix.

account of law, however, I will first address the pre-political work of defining tradition in the first place, and in a way that includes an indication of which practices are necessary to maintain them.

My own orientation in this terrain derives from the Lutheran-Reformed tradition, which I understand to itself be a manifold dialogue with multiple elaborations.[4] It is represented by a range of thinkers from whom the practice of critical understanding is centrally important to their procedure, such as Karl Barth, Ernst Wolf, Joachim Iwand, Dietrich Bonhoeffer, or George Lindbeck, along with many others within the English-speaking world, who have helped to mark out the path of that tradition.

For our purposes here, what is most important about the Lutheran-Reformed tradition as I understand it is the richness of ethical thinking it has developed around the *topoi* of law and justice. These pivotal themes for political ethics are also ones in which the most fundamental theological issues converge. When asking about Western political traditions it makes logical sense to do so by first admitting that one's own formulations of ideas and starting points have been nurtured by one of the specific traditions populating that clearing, each of which has its own particular logic. Taking such a tradition-focused approach offers an opening for dialogue to develop between different traditions in which members of each tradition can consider how they might meet one another or how their traditions may converge and therefore serve, at least in some elements, to constitute or maintain a common tradition for a whole society.

Every tradition, more or less explicitly, transmits presumptions about the "ground" of ethics, understood as a pre-existing social reality that frames the individual's experience of the fullness of life, its meaning and telos. I assume that ethics is a work of understanding and exploring this existing reality as it is communicated and determined by a tradition. When we say that we "understand"[5] we make a linguistic gesture indicating that we are able to follow the rationale of a tradition. In such cases, what we are following can also be called the grammar of a tradition, since traditions are carried on through language and can be inhabited like a language.[6] This is true in even more obvious ways for a theological tradition in which reading the Word of God, living with it and in it, is explicitly understood to be a constitutive practice. Understanding, furthermore, occurs within concretely articulated practices, and tradition may be best understood as the crystallized and intelligibly linguistically articulated

---

4. Wolfgang Lienemann, *Gerechtigkeit* (Göttingen: Vandenhoeck & Ruprecht, 1995), presents a decidedly ecumenical consideration of current developments.

5. Hannah Arendt, "Understanding and Politics," in *Essays in Understanding 1930–1954*, ed. Jerome Kohn (New York: Harcourt, Brace & Co., 1994), 307–27.

6. See Hans G. Ulrich, "On the Grammar of Lutheran Ethics," in *Lutheran Ethics at the Intersections of God's One World*, Karen L. Blomquist (Geneva: Lutheran World Federation, 2005), 27–48. See also George A. Lindbeck, *The Nature of Doctrine: Religion and Theology in a Postliberal Age* (Philadelphia: Westminster Press, 1984).

forms of those practices. To follow the articulations in a tradition is to follow its grammar, which is equivalent to its rationale, its logos. This is the logos within the word, the logos within the logos.

To understand demands making judgments, and judgments are acts that can be shaped to become describable practices. When rendered in Greek, judgment, *krinein*, means to distinguish, to discover distinctions and criteria, as well as to follow them out, that is, enact to critical understanding in deployment. As we will see, this emphasis has direct implications for assessing political structures, in highlighting the irreducibility of the forms of judgment that theological ethics must disclose.[7] This is, in summary, the intellectual practice I have presupposed as basic in political ethics. Political ethics is a practice of critical understanding. It takes concrete form in the practice of making judgments according to the distinctions that must be discovered within that Word of God, distinctions that will at points necessarily cut across and judge other distinctions that we may once have held.

A critical hermeneutic of this type is constitutive of those theological traditions that maintain that the paradigmatic practice of theology is to understand and explore the Word of God as it becomes present to His people in their worship— and through the testimony of the congregation to all human beings. Theology is the study of the grammar of that word. To follow the grammar of that word also entails being prepared to give reasons for it, communicating it to those outside the tradition, as 1 Pet. 3:15 makes clear: "But sanctify the Lord God in your hearts, and always be ready to give a defense (ἀπολογίαν, *apologian*) to everyone who asks you for a reason (λόγον, *logon*) for the hope that is in you, with meekness and fear."[8] A complex ethical task understood in this way will contain a range of elements within it. Apologetic explanation aims to display the context of living as it is given with the Word of God in its biblical tradition, and in so doing to become clearer about which distinctions best foster the believer's critical understanding.

These preliminary considerations converge to yield this chapter's central constructive question: What intellectual practice is appropriate when we investigate a subject like divine law or divine command or inquire into the ground of ethics? What could be the appropriate vantage point from which to fruitfully engage questions about the ground of ethics? With what, precisely, is such inquiry concerned?

When such fundamental questions arise at those points where the context and nurturing ground of our human living are at stake, the task of ethics has been to bring into view the essential environment within which—as apprehended by critical understanding—human beings may come to terms with the grammar of their living. To talk about the "ground" in this way, and with it corresponding practices, namely that of critical understanding, differs, of course, from other

---

7. O'Donovan, *The Ways of Judgment*, xiii.
8. See O'Donovan, *The Ways of Judgment*, for the apologetic task.

practices and approaches that might be possible, with the different opening questions they yield; for example, the question of searching for a "foundation" for ethics put perhaps in terms of a quest for some "external," given ground, beyond the context that may have crystallized in a living tradition.

The Need for the Public Appearance of Religion

What does it mean for "religion" to appear in "public"? Both terms are understood in highly divergent ways in contemporary discussions taking place around the globe. This question is therefore one that cannot be answered without asking about the context in which it is asked, what are the conditions under which it is asked, and from what perspective it is being asked. Some of these factors converge in some discourses in Western Europe and the English-speaking countries of the Atlantic.[9] In this discursive space some agreement can typically be achieved among the different discussants about the features that would qualify a set of practices as a "public religion."[10] Any theological engagement with this question is forced to decide which are the various political, social, and cultural reasons that might be adduced in calling something a "religion in public," and must do so by seeking a definition that can be squared with its own particular (for instance, Christian) religion, its traditions, languages, and practices. Such a procedure is necessary in order to avoid letting the discussion drift into vague generalizations about "religion." A theological approach to this question must therefore inquire after the specific sense in which "religion" becomes intelligible as understood in a specific way within a tradition that has a distinctive "public" appearance. Put differently; What will the term "public" mean within the grammar of a determinate and living "religious" language? To put the question in this way is to raise the further question of what the referent might actually be of "religion" as a general category, given that any general concept is already bound to quite specific constellations of "religious phenomena" already in the public sphere that are already in specifically configured confrontations between the articulate presence of the particular religions and their traditions.[11]

This then is our revised question: In what sense is a particular "religion" like the Christian religion to be understood as having a "public" appearance, and how does that tradition's own account of the public figure in the definition of both terms? The Lutheran tradition provides an especially good forum to answer this

---

9. William H. Swatos and James K. Wellman, eds., *The Power of Religious Publics: Staking Claims in American Society*, Religion in the Age of Transformation (Westport: Praeger, 1999).]

10. James E. Wood Jr., "Public Religion Vis-a-Vis the Prophetic Role of Religion," in *The Power of Religious Publics*, 33-51.

11. Charles Taylor, *Sources of the Self: The Making of the Modern Identity* (Cambridge: Harvard University Press, 1989).

question, not only because the tradition has a highly elaborate political ethics but also because this tradition itself includes an ongoing internal debate of the terms "religion" and "public."[12]

The Public Presence of Religion in Society

The way I have proposed to engage the question of the public appearance of Christian religion relates to, but must be sharply distinguished from, the well-known location of religion as private or individual practice and belief in liberal political theory. It is an opposition that has its own problematic historical origins.[13] The Reformation movements were especially resistant to the privatization of religion, in the sense of relegating it to a partitioned domain distinct from the public and political sphere, and insisted that Christian worship is definitely not private. All Christian religious practices or habits are, in principle, related to the church's worship, which is not private but public. In the modern Lutheran tradition the public nature of Christian worship has been an important and productive element of political theology on the understanding that in it a congregation gathers to listen to Word from the One who is the ruler of their hearts—and their political lives.[14] This use of the language of the heart is not meant to suggest that the congregation is just a gathering formed of individuals who have elected to gather. The gathering itself is understood as political, a public assembly that occupies social space.

I am suggesting that the Lutheran tradition so described should be understood as a genuine representative of the Christian religion in general and highlights some of its constitutive components, such as its characteristic understanding of itself as being present in public and the grounding of this self-understanding in concrete practices such as preaching. We cannot grasp the coherence of any religion by screening out the practices by which it instills in its members a sense of the coherence of their tradition through institutionalized practices such as prayer, preaching, baptism, and the Eucharist. Even the concept of "institution" has a theological grounding in the Christian tradition, developed out of the various hints in the biblical sources that God has provided places which carry in a special way the promise of God's presence. Thus, the public nature of these places

---

12. For a significant recent contribution to that discourse that surveys the internal discussion as well as what I have called the "Reformed-Lutheran" tradition of political ethics, see Bernd Wannenwetsch, *Political Worship: Ethics for Christian Citizens*, Oxford Studies in Theological Ethics (Oxford: Oxford University Press, 2004).

13. Jürgen Habermas, *The Structural Transformation of the Public Sphere: An Inquiry into a Category of Bourgeois Society* (Cambridge: Polity Press, 2002).

14. *Worship and Ethics: Lutherans and Anglicans in Dialogue*, ed. Oswald Bayer, Theologische Bibliothek Töpelmann (Berlin, New York: Walter de Gruyter, 1996); *Lutheran Ethics at the Intersections of God's One World*, ed. Karen L. Bloomquist (The Lutheran World Federation, Department for Theology and Studies (LWF-Studies) Geneva, 2005).

in which God promises to meet his people are highly formative for Christians' understanding of political ethics, in forming the lived basis of their particular experience of political realism.[15]

It is in this way that what is typically called "religion" within political theory (as described from a viewpoint outside any religious tradition and its language) screens out the specifically public definition of religion characteristic of particular traditions, in this case the Christian "religion." What is screened out in the discourse of political philosophy is, specifically, the institutionalized practices that belong genuinely to Christian faith. These are practices whose specific contours, even historically understood, have in fact been essential contributors to the constitution and development of the "public sphere" (*Öffentlichkeit*) as we know it in liberal societies today.[16] Christian practices of worship were not incidental to but essential components of the creation of the modern understanding of citizenship and in which Christians had their own particular understanding of their place within the public sphere of citizenship.[17]

From the perspective of the Christian faith, any practice, including prayer and meditation, must be understood as a public practice in precisely configured senses. Any prayer addressed to Jesus Christ, the "Lord," or to God, the Creator, entails a public and political dimension. Reading the Word of God, like other elements of worship, constitutes a public reality by holding open a social space that can be entered and inhabited by anyone who engages in those particular practices. Meditation, too—as in the meditation on God's word—must be understood as a form of participation in God's creation and governance of the world and therefore emphatically not a private matter. In a Lutheran political theology, different practices can be distinguished as having primary reference to either the spiritual or worldly side of reality and does not admit that there is any private sphere than can be detached from the public sphere of human relations.

Attempts to detach the characteristic practices of Christian worship from the sphere of public relationships typically rest on abstract concepts of the public sphere. These abstract definitions of the public often presuppose that the public is that space of indeterminate human interactions that lie beyond the social and political realities determined by economic and governmental oversight. Here the public sphere is assumed to be de facto created and constituted by multiple "civil" and "civic" activities and institutions, such as the "family" (whatever the term "family" might be assumed to mean in different contexts), public schools, health care activities, art, and so on. From the perspective of this abstract account of the public, religious practices, like any other civil/civic activity, ought not to be treated as different in kind from the formative practices that make up the traditions that

---

15. Hans G. Ulrich, *Wie Geschöpfe leben: Konturen evangelischer Ethik*, 2nd edn. (Münster: LIT-Verlag, 2007).

16. Ted A. Smith, *The New Measures: A Theological History of Democratic Practice* (Cambridge: Cambridge University Press, 2007).

17. Wannenwetsch, *Political Worship*, 235–75.

constitute these other civic institutions—even though such views almost always assume that religious practices, strictly defined, are actually the voluntary acts of specific individuals. As we have seen, however, this definition of religion does not fit Christian practice as Christians would understand it.

In short: debates about the supposed privatization of religion, its withdrawal from public engagement, have tended to overlook the formation of the very concept of secularity itself as an institutionally separated (and therefore supposedly also "secular") state or government on one side, and its opposite, the Christian public worship and a "church," rooted in this worship, on the other. The secular state as we know it today presupposes this opposite as its "positive" limitation. In this account the church as an institution embodies a politics organized around shared, substantive ontological and moral commitments in contrast to the liberal state whose political institutions are grounded specifically in the exclusion of any agreement about ontological and moral commitments. Far from being opposites, they are symbiotically related conceptions and social domains.[18]

The Utility of Public Religion for the State

It should by now be clear that it is a mistake to confine the concept of the "public" nature of religion to officially established state churches we find in various European countries like Denmark and Sweden, where the church as an institution is written into the constitution in a way that no other religions—or religion in general—are. It is not difficult to find phenomena that fit the description of public religion in many places and practices, and in ways that can be distinguished from well-established religious groups. Some candidates for the label of public religion are commonly held and enacted values, such as "solidarity," "nation," "liberty," "welfare," and "happiness," which are perceived as values not least because of their religious implications.

Likewise, there are various public rituals that take on a religious air, such as confessions of collective guilt, the celebration of shared memories, and ritualized enactments of reconciliation. Secular rituals that modify describable religious ritual patterns also often accrete around pivotal moments in human life like birth, marriage, death, and burial. The label "religious" can also be meaningfully applied to the more or less numinous aspects of the state's own founding documents, such as the concept of "sovereignty" that have historical roots in the Christian tradition. It would be possible to cast the net even more widely by looking at the ways in which some human phenomena accrue a religious valence in being media of important modes of human relations, in the way we can observe in the economic sphere in general, the market. At this level, the "religious" aura of a medium of human interconnection emerges from its capacity to connect people at

---

18. Brian Brock, "Government, University and the Category of Religion," in *Religion as a Category of Governance, and Sovereignty*, ed. Trevor Stack, Naomi R. Goldberg and Timothy Fitzgerald (Leiden: Brill, 2015), 228–47.

a deeper level than explicitly political institutions. The phenomenon of patriotism is another example of this deeper form of human connection even though it is dependent upon constitutionally guaranteed conditions of living. In this (perhaps hidden) sense, secular public religion is constantly doing material political work.

For our purposes it is sufficient to define "public religion" as the set of phenomena that arise from the aim to integrate all people into a specific political community. This unifying power of religious phenomena is well recognized and is often drawn upon as a political modality by modern secular states in the belief that public religion not only offers unique tools for integrating citizens or enjoining obligations on them but does so in a manner that offers common ground on which all citizens can meet since it embodies its own independent authority. When defined in this way, public religion must be understood as a rival to the Christian religion in being a community formed by already committed members embedded in institutionalized practices. Such a definition of public religion also generates conflicts with religious traditions (such as the Roman Catholic tradition) that understand themselves as similarly constituting a general or even universal public sphere rather than defining themselves as a community of committed members. And it is also a view with significant internal tensions. The most obvious inner tension is between the commitment to a religiously neutral state allowing a plurality of religious practices and ways of life and the task of governing that state. Governing necessarily requires acts of judgment about allowable and prohibited expressions of those religious comments, judgments that flow from prioritizations about what sorts of activity are seen to move the community forward and which impede it.[19] At the level of political governance it is clear that strict neutrality is not possible, even about religious (theological) insights and interpretations of human life, which are necessarily implicated in such judgments.

Religious Traditions, Civil Society, and the Necessity of Forming Citizens

Further areas of tension emerge when we look more closely at the impact religion has on the habits of the heart, daily life, and institution formation—what is often called "civil" society. Civil society can be seen as a grouping formed by people who commit themselves to any task that is of interest to other people. Such civil societies are also fundamentally important in a political sense to the extent that the political community is rooted in a civil society. Given that it is people's concrete daily ways of life that constitute a civil society, the question will inevitably arise for government whether some practices are matters of private and/or personal, or even individual, decision and therefore not a matter of political public interest and so also not a matter of the ethics that emerge from public religion that is oriented around such public interest.

This question, however, brings us back to the initial discussion of this chapter of how to conceive the relationship between specific religious traditions, with

---

19. O'Donovan, *The Ways of Judgment*.

their own "thick" accounts of reality, and the ways of life that they call forth. Here we are brought back to many basic questions of how to evaluate and live out the practices of human life. The contemporary debates about the legal order of marriage highlight the relevance of such questions. People regularly present their decision to marry exclusively in terms of individual (private) considerations. There nevertheless remain significant public (political and governmental) responsibilities for overseeing and maintaining the institution of marriage, through, for instance, granting tax breaks to married couples. The felt responsibility to tend the legal structures of marriage is sometimes seen as grounded in the expectation that children, the coming generation of citizens, should grow up in a family, and that marriage law stabilizes the institution of the family. There are even more fundamental reasons for such interventions in maintaining the institutions of marriage than such pragmatic ones, reasons that may even be relevant for people who insist they are exercising their individual options in entering the state of marriage. One aspect of the ethical meaning of marriage, according to the Christian (and also to the Lutheran) tradition, is its paradigmatic status as an analog to God's covenant with human beings. It makes good sense even for secular thinkers to ask what it means for a society to have people in it who live in lifelong commitment, and what this means for the way their political lives are shaped and take longstanding, stable forms. Similar considerations would apply to other areas of burning public interest, such as healthcare and education, domains in which this deeper ethical sense of institutionalized forms of life can be seen to be essential for a well-functioning public realm in defending interests beyond, for instance, purely economic rationales.

In some religious traditions, for instance, the education of children is essentially connected with religious education, illustrating yet another facet of the public importance of religion. It is becoming widely accepted that public education systems cannot replace the learning emerging in everyday life—and which necessarily includes our religious life. This insight repositions what is meant by "education." In a broader sense, education is concerned with how youth acquire "character," which in fact boils down to becoming a human political character. We need to think about character formation and the educational institutions which best serve it because nations are not (best) served by citizens who have been formed according to cultural need or predetermined social interest, despite the fact that there will always be an explicit public interest in educational processes. Within the Christian tradition, education is connected with the renewing of human minds (Rom. 12:1-2) through critical interaction with all merely imposed and human patternings of human life. Because the Christian tradition includes the fundamental concept of human beings as "created" and "shaped" in the image of Christ—in opposition to imposed patterns of life—it is resistant to all programmatic concepts of "public" education. One of the paradigmatic roles of education in the Christian view lies in its promise to generate citizens with the capacity for contradicting the political and public status quo in a manner that serves their renewal. The public importance of the Christian religion is thus most obvious at the point where it resists the self-understanding of law or social patterns as they currently exist.

This line of analysis reveals that many fundamental characteristics of our human life may be important for a civil society, and may also be religiously determined by religious practices or religiously conditioned "habits of the heart."[20] These religious sensibilities and practices often create fine-grained tensions with, and sometimes even oppositions to the societies within which they exist. When we call society "civil" we point to the manifold and often intangible tasks and habits that must be carried out in a society in which each citizen feels cared for and has their needs supplied. The question is the extent to which the practices that sustain this total environment of a good political society need rooting in a particular religious context that can hand on such a "civil" interest in the needs of others. The concept of an "ethics of profession" is another one of the places where answers to this question have been practically worked out. The significance and presence of the habits of "profession" in the various civil tasks is almost immeasurable. This has again and again been exemplified in the profession of doctors, politicians, teachers, and other sorts of workers who have felt the need to constitute themselves as a guild of "professionals," despite the reality that today the idea of a professional guild comes into increasing conflict with modern managerialist accounts of their role in serving the good of the political community.[21] The issues at stake are sufficiently compelling to have recently sparked a lively discussion of the need for modern bureaucratically managed states to programmatically promote a "civil" society as an alternative to intensifying all-embracing governance by means of governmental or organizational processes and structures, homogenizing the professions in the process. To be concerned with such questions as a Christian today can be understood as the late flowering of the Reformation emphasis on the hallowing of daily life.

Politics Proper: What Goes on the Agenda?

In contradistinction to the more diffuse and granular characteristics of a "civil" society there is also a more precisely defined "public sphere" in which people explicitly communicate and cooperate and negotiate the *res publica*, "those things that are affairs of the public." The *res publica* should not be reduced to any specific public phenomena. Rather, correctly understood, the *res publica* is that which belongs on the agenda of explicit public discourse. Explicit public discourse is not reducible to, but does depend on institutional forms, such as the press. This basic idea of a public discourse is inflected in different ways by different institutionalizations. The institutional forms for public discourse in political liberalism, for instance, differ from the Agora and Forum that institutionalized

---

20. Robert N. Bellah, *Habits of the Heart: Individualism and Commitment in American Life* (Berkley: University of California press, 1985).

21. David Martin, *On Secularization: Towards a Revised General Theory* (Aldershot: Ashgate, 2005).

public discourse in ancient Greece.[22] The public agenda does not encompass every possible question in the public sphere but is confined to the essential political questions of justice and equal opportunity required to sustain life together.

Here again in this more precisely delimited domain of public discourse we are invited, or provoked, to ask what is contributed by "religion," churches, religious groups, and religious people. What are the issues of the contribution religious people and religious institutions must discern? And how is this contribution understood from the viewpoint of modern political liberalism?

In the European context it is easy to find many significant examples where the *res publica* is at stake beyond the moral questions that arise around family ethics, bioethics, medical ethics, and ethics of social justice. In all these domains the debates that arise are not about "public religion," but arise because people with religious convictions are active in the specific sense of making a contribution to public discussion by defending an account of what constitutes the good of the *res publica*. We come at this point to a crucial and philosophically irreducible question: to what extent can, or should, certain kinds of issues be on the public agenda at all? Which issues do we think legitimately relate to the public concern?

If we answer that the public agenda in any given social domain should be set by the goal of achieving justice in it, we run immediately into the dynamics that emerge from the fact that achieving justice requires putting in place some content-rich view of what is good for human beings. When we designate achieving justice as the criterion for letting subjects onto the public agenda, in practice this almost leads to a tendency to circumscribe practices of letting everyone contribute to setting that agenda. A particular view of justice comes to dominate in a society, and even if it is misshapen, it will often coalesce into a political consensus that will not openly listen to all contributing voices, especially those that lie outside the consensus or contradict that consensus. Indeed, one of the problems of achieving actual (rather than just procedural) justice, even in liberal societies, is this tendency that even bedevils democracies to systematically silence the voices of the marginalized. The practice of (in-)justice that is characteristic of such societies is in dire need of another voice that comes to them from outside their dominant views. This, at least, is what the Lutheran distinction between the public and the church would lead us to expect—as long as by this we mean a church which can speak up on the issue of justice denied because it is itself listening to the "other" word, the Word of God, which is constitutive of its political character.

Profiles of a Public and Political Commitment: Religiously Rooted Citizenship

The fundamental role given to listening to the "other" word, the Word of God, has led Lutherans to develop the ethical concept of a civic Christian. The citizen who finds him or herself appointed to a task in the political community is understood

---

22. John Rawls, *Political Liberalism*, Columbia Classics in Philosophy (New York: Columbia University Press, 2005).

as having shouldered a vocation in a religious sense. This does not mean that the Christian with a political vocation understands their work as fulfilling an explicitly "religious" task, but that their work is rooted in their own religiously grounded freedom. For Christians, freedom of religion is not reducible to a spiritualized liberty standing apart from its political appearance, but becomes manifest in a genuine freedom for other people, in a political vocation, to serve the task of discovering what makes in a given society for political freedom. The Christian in a political role is thus not pursuing a religious agenda, but living out the freedom of a citizen to seek justice for his or her neighbor, the *iustitia civilis*, by doing those works that support other citizens and fulfill the law. What is crucial, however, is that the Christian does so not according to the letter but the material purpose of human law to uphold human life, because they have been freed from the bondage to denuding and reality-obscuring ideologies. This Christian freedom is discharged solely for existing citizens, with the implication that it forgoes any appeal to the "common good" or to the "greatest good," or to the "meaning of life" as the goal of political action, since each of these goals runs the risk of losing this focus on concrete justice for the other, which cannot be postponed or suspended in favor of a greater good.

We are left with the question of whether or not our social groupings and political communities fundamentally depend on servant-citizens of this kind, or whether they finally put their trust in laws or protocols to ensure that they are protected from the malfeasance of their political officeholders. These questions are becoming acute in Western European cultures, in which formerly self-evident religiously shaped patterns of life will only be maintained as Christians develop an explicit and politically engaged witness to their vision of the *conditio humana*. The burning questions of today, the ones that may or may not make it onto the public political agenda, have to do with how human life is understood and treated, rather than the tired debate about the public function of "religion" in general. According to the Christian paradigm I have just set out, drawing on the Lutheran tradition, religion does not have to constitute a church as a *polis*[23] that is intentionally contrastive with the "secular" *polis*, but must coexist with and provide a creative tension with the *polis* that needs, safeguards, and appreciates people who are experienced citizens.

Law for the People: Understanding the Conditio Humana *in Its Political Form*

These, then, are the foundations of Christian political engagement. My opening emphasis on the importance of forming citizens is not to be understood as a

---

23. Arne Rasmusson, *The Church as Polis: From Political Theology to Theological Politics as Exemplified by Jürgen Moltmann and Stanley Hauerwas* (Notre Dame: University of Notre Dame Press, 1995).

disparagement of politics as a governed and law-regulated human activity along libertarian lines. The remainder of this chapter outlines how the focus of the first half of the chapter on the political vocation of the Christian calls forth an account of law that supports and extends it. The starting point of such an account emerges from the centrality within the biblical traditions of the relation of God's law to His people. "Law," as articulated in the commandments, was first for God's people, the commandments being addressed to them particularly, as exegetical work in the Lutheran-Reformed tradition has understood it.[24]

Grounding a Christian account of law in biblical usage presupposes a particular relation of "law" (*Gesetz*) and "commandment" (*Gebot*): God's "law" is understood as becoming present to his people as commandment.[25] When heard as commandments, the law is perceptible as God's self-articulation of God's desires for the life of the people. The law is a gift in providing a location for the emergence of the command. As a document it provides the context of the unity of the people in God and demarcates the "sphere of living"[26] for God's people. The commandments are the medium of God's covenant[27] that have emerged in the course of God's story with his people, and which points forward to his will for their lives in all its dimensions. Thus, the testimony of this people is that they have discovered the covenant as offering a context in which all human life can flourish. If understood in these very specific terms, we may therefore legitimately say that the covenant carries forward God's understanding of the *conditio humana* sufficient for each generation and for all human beings. The covenant conveys God's outline of the conditions necessary for human beings to remain human in the fullest and most politically elaborated sense. In sum, theologically understood, it is legitimate to say that the universal *conditio humana* is embodied in a particular story; this story is entrusted to humans and institutionalized for humanity in the commandments.

We use the term "institution" here framed by the theological tradition I have already indicated. To establish and maintain an institution is to set up a contoured sphere of interaction between humans that sustains them. There has been some discussion of whether a distinction should be drawn between the terms "order," "mandate" (Bonhoeffer), and "institution" (Wolf), each of which are attempts to draw attention to the commandments as the divinely given ground of political life. I use the term "institution," to designate the space opened up by God's governance, and which expresses God's promise to rule His people. The promise of the law, however, is only intelligible when embedded within the story of God's interaction

---

24. See especially Gerhard von Rad, *Old Testament Theology* (New York: Harper, 1962–65). Von Rad's exegesis has to be seen throughout as a commentary to the Lutheran-Barthian tradition.

25. I am drawing on Karl Barth's elaboration of this distinction as presented in his *Ethics* (New York: Seabury Press, 1981).

26. Von Rad, *Old Testament Theology*, 194–5.

27. See David Novak, *Covenantal Rights: A Study in Jewish Political Theory* (Princeton: Princeton University Press, 2000).

with His people. To establish a context of living by giving a particular commanded and taught "law," is what is meant by the Hebrew language of "Torah" (Ps. 19:8). The complex story of linguistic interplay between the Greek "law" and Hebrew "Torah"[28] may be read as itself a confirmation that the biblical law has served as a reliable context of living, and of living together, because in it God's commandments become articulated.

As Luther observes in his Genesis lectures, this context of living was established in the Garden of Eden, immediately after the creation of the first humans. Law as graciously given command is not a response to the fall. Yet the fall does bring about a change in the law, which now becomes two-sided as a response to the newly problematized social horizon of human life. The fall brings about a need for an explicitly institutionalized political status to be instituted within the law's description of the contours of living with God. This is the origin of the *"politia."* Against this protological background, any given state must be understood as nothing more than one quite specific enactment of the political status ascribed to human beings. That humans have been created political means that they can never escape the need for the actual forms that their political existence has taken to be critically assayed against the grammar of the *politia* called forth in God's law.

Along with the calling forth by the divine law of a political institution comes another explicit institutionalized political existence of the people of God in a worshipping community, the *"ecclesia."* This too was already established in the Garden of Eden. Founded for the first humans in the state of innocence, on a theological reading, the *ecclesia* must also be understood as an indicator of the true *politia* as it is hoped for, as it is yet to come.[29]

It would be legitimate to approach these frame-setting questions by elaborating other theological approaches to the disposition of the given "law" as, for example, in Karl Barth's attempt to unpack the Trinitarian dimensions of ethics by means of descriptions of three spheres or phases of God's story with creatures: the commanded law to God's creatures, to His people within His covenant, and to His children.[30] In each of the three phases the commanded law is understood as the specifically tailored medium for political togetherness configured so as to take into account the particular dynamics of different phases and aspects of God's story with humanity. In other words, in a theological view there is no reason to define the Law of the Old Testament in atemporal or transcendental terms, as beyond or outside the political context in which human life is lived, as a "moral" law or "morally" grounded law—as most influentially defined by Kant. The commanded

---

28. Frank Austermann, *Von der Tora zum Nomos: Untersuchungen zur Übersetzungsweise und Interpretation im Septuaginta-Psalter* (Göttingen: Vandenhoeck & Ruprecht, 2003).

29. On this aspect of Luther's theology, see Bernd Wannenwetsch, "Luther's Moral Theology," in *The Cambridge Companion to Martin Luther*, ed. Donald K. McKim (Cambridge: Cambridge University Press, 2003), 120-35.

30. See Nigel Biggar, *The Hastening that Waits: Karl Barth's Ethics* (Oxford: Clarendon Press, 1995).

law is given within and with specific political realities, mediated by their practices, procedures, relations, and institutions.[31] By definition, law is something that must be articulated and pronounced, an explicit communication. The public legibility of law is the condition of its being interpreted, of being used to motivate people by appealing to them. Only an explicitly stated law can be explored, learned, taught, or guide acts of judgment.[32] In sustaining all these practices (and more) human relationships are shaped into a form that can be relied on to support life-sustaining patterns for people who live together. We can even go so far as to say that all human practices are grounded in and related to some given law. Legislators have no place to stand except the institution that is built in the articulation of a law.

Such an account of the public appearance of the commanded law stands in some tension with a range of other groundings of ethics, not least, to take one prominent example, the idea of a "moral man" who has been rendered reliable and calculable in having internalized moral rules given by someone else. Such realist accounts tend to embrace precisely the function of law in Christian morality attached by Nietzsche. The aim of God's commanded law is not to produce reliable human beings in general but is an expression, most fundamentally, of *God*'s loyalty, reliability, and commitment to his people. In giving the commanded law God both displays a concrete act of loyalty and confirms it through subsequent acts of guidance that facilitate God's people remaining loyal in return, keeping their focus of attention on their only reason for existence, namely, *God*'s loyalty. The law is thus a divine response to desire of God's people to remain together, and one which graciously shapes the *way* in which they remain together. The law configures their lives together as a way of life rather than death, not only in the face of the many threats and uncertainties that face God's people but also in explicitly delimiting the boundaries of the sphere granted by God's good governance and government. These emphases are all implicated in their most condensed form in the first commandment, which our tradition has recognized as the key to that understanding of the ground theological ethics has to unfold into the many spaces of human activity: "You shall have no other gods before me" (Exod. 20:3).[33]

The Lutheran tradition's reading of the biblical traditions understands human law first in its relationship to God. God is not seen primarily as the authority legitimizing human laws by matching them to a "divine law" from which good human laws might be deduced. In this Lutheran tradition human laws are seen as particular articulations of God's reliable government for a particular grouping of people, and so as a genuine medium and of God's governance and salvation for all human beings. In this approach, human lawmaking is understood as always beholden to the conditions of living experienced by specific groupings of human

---

31. In modern political theory, this distinction is typically marked by the distinction between "law" and "morality."
32. See Patrick D. Miller, "Divine Command/Divine Law: A Biblical Perspective," *Studies in Christian Ethics* 23, no. 1 (February 1, 2010): 21–34.
33. See Martin Luther, *Treatise on Good Works* (1520), LW 44, 15–114.

beings; the laws that articulate the contours of their political life never transcend constant critical assessment as to their suitability in service to that community. Not every law that obliges and presents itself as a social medium binding people is granted authority as an aspect of God's government, governance, and salvation. God's will is not arbitrary; it has been publicly articulated in the commandments. In them people encounter God's will in the way God has already determined it to be.

One of the key insights of Luther's treatise *On the Bondage of the Will* is that, despite appearances, human beings are shown in Christ that they are not bound by any law or obligation that is not from God. God's people are embedded in God's will; they have to probe it and to follow it according to the given commandments; they will not encounter God's will outside of the space opened up by God's governance and they are not in a position to make a decision for or against it as a whole. They already exist within a political worship and service, a realm that exists because God's active guiding and ruling has already preceded them. In this understanding "political worship"[34] is not understood as one aspect that arises when human beings drawn together by the things that they love (to cite one popular formulation). Here political worship is defined as the active human recognition and discovery of God's ruling activity through experience and practice when people gather to listen to God's word. In such worship the people of God give themselves over to God's rule, as paradigmatically presented by Paul in Rom. 12:1-2:

> I appeal to you therefore, brethren, by the mercies of God, to present your bodies as a living sacrifice, holy and acceptable to God, which is your Spiritual worship. Do not be conformed to this world but be transformed by the renewal of your mind (*nous*), that you may prove (*dokimazein*) what is the will of God, what is good and acceptable and perfect.

Paul's formulation highlights why the main theological concern of political theology must arise from Christians' experience of God's mercies. To experience this mercy and liberation is the only possible beginning for the Christian, and the only possible way forward from them must be oriented by the question of how God's people are to *remain* in God's "mercies," that is, in His good government, governance and salvation. Only by remain within the domain of God's ongoing merciful works do they remain God's people. No church, as a political entity, can ensure this remaining with God: it must be continuously practiced in the congregation of those who participate in that "political worship" which is listening to God's word and gathering in the community of their present Lord.

Learning in the ecclesial setting is thus affective and praxeological, it is something emotively engaged and physically enacted. In political worship Christians are learning how it feels and what practices are called forth from human beings as they stand under God's governance, government, and salvation. It is also intellectual,

---

34. See for this topic: Bernd Wannenwetsch, *Political Worship: Ethics for Christian Citizens* (Oxford: Oxford University Press, 2004).

as the experience the "transformation" of their life-form (metamorphosis) brings with it the renewal of their minds. The *ecclesia* in its political worship is ordered toward this transformation, paralleling the practices of the *politia* that aim to provide what is needed for the human condition in its political form.

If we follow the lineaments of Paul's theological account of transformation as parsed in Reformation theology, what emerges is that the ground of togetherness with God in worship is centered on God's "justice." In scripture God's justice was seen as attested through God's loyalty and commitment to his people.[35] Human beings participate in that justice by being justified, that is, brought back into God's justice, brought back into the sphere of God's commitment to them. In principle then, to be justified entails the "transformation" of people's "life-form" on the basis of or within the "renewal" of the minds, that is, the *intellectus*, the way of understanding. Experience within this political worship is the *new* "ground" from which the believer can "prove (*dokimazein*) what is the will of God."

To have one's form of life transformed in being justified entails being freed from the selfishness that makes fallen human beings so terrible at human relationships. The political power of justification in the Lutheran tradition is its breaking of the authority of sin to free the human being for a genuinely political existence, free to be a *citizen*. This work of being re-formed in freedom comes by way of the specific renewal of the mind that allows the selfish and incurved human being to become genuinely aware of the needs of the other—as Luther highlighted in his "Freedom of a Christian."[36] To become transformed by justification makes its public appearance in this form of trust and faith in God's work, which is the genuine political form of the people of God. It is in this sharply defined sense that faith can be said to focus this ethical-political tradition.

In his Large Catechism, Luther sees the first commandment of the Decalogue to insist that God's people trust God's governance and government and no other. The first commandment demarcates the sole sphere of living upheld by the government of the God who has called his people to live with him. This is the promise of God's law.[37] As he puts this point in his Large Catechism: the first commandment requires

> that one's whole heart and confidence be placed in God alone, and in no one else. To have a God, as you can well imagine, does not mean to grasp him with your fingers, or to put him into a purse, or to shut him up in a box. Rather, you lay hold of God when your heart grasps him and clings to him. To cling to him with your heart is nothing else than to entrust yourself to him completely.[38]

---

35. See von Rad, *Old Testament Theology*, 370–2.
36. See Martin Luther, "The Freedom of a Christian" (1520), LW 31.
37. See Martin Luther, *Treatise on Good Works* (1520).
38. Martin Luther, "The Large Catechism" (1529), in *The Book of Concord: The Confessions of the Evangelical Lutheran Church*, ed. Robert Kolb and Timothy J. Wengert (Minneapolis: Fortress Press, 2000), 13–14.

Although much that is good comes to us from human beings, nevertheless, anything received according to his command and ordinance in fact comes from God.[39]

To trust in God's governance and government is not only right worship, it is genuinely political worship. Luther explicitly understands trust in God's governance to oppose every human attempt to hold the "world" together by one's own power, which inevitably becomes imperialistic. The first commandment (which comprehends all the rest of God's commandments) thus positions as false worship all other attempts to govern human living together by promulgating obligations based on other grounds. In this analysis when Luther says "heart" he does not mean subjective inner feelings. For Luther the "heart" signifies the "inner man," human existence insofar as it is completely entrusted to God.

It is in political worship that human beings are drawn into political practices that engender the trust in God that exposes the anti-political forces at work in trusting all other false laws and duties as Paul describes the practice of salvific transformation in Romans 12:1. The *paracletic* sermon that instructs or counsels (*paraenesis*) is paradigmatic of all ecclesial practices of trust-formation in that its central aim is to publicly recall God's mighty acts as they call forth congruent human action. This is why Christian political freedom is rooted and situated in worship. From the vantage point of Christian worship, human beings come to understand themselves as outside or distanced from all the laws and cultural norms that arise independent of that worship and which in worship become visible in their negation and contradiction of the grammar of God's word.

The universal claim of the first commandment is that God's governance and government offer the only sphere of living suited to human beings. This implication applies both inside and outside the community of the church. Thus, the commanded law has to be seen in its relation to general habits, rules, and customs of living—the "ethos" (*aethos*)—articulated in the human laws of a political community. None of what I have said is intended to suggest that the laws of the political community are "founded" on some additional foundation, perhaps on a *conditio humana moralis*, or on democratic consensus. Rather, each community must seek the political form that is appropriate to it, deploying a critical hermeneutic that aims to discover the *conditio humana* in its genuine political form as preserved in the commanded law attested by God's people.

Political ἔθος (ethos)–Political ἦθος (aethos)

One way to precisely locate the context of human living is with the Greek notion of "ethos," which our analysis suggests could even be an illuminating translation of the Hebrew "Torah." Terminologically speaking, there is a significant, if fine, distinction between the two meanings of the Greek "ethos," and both could be

---

39. Martin Luther, "The Large Catechism," 26.

said to be equivalents to the idea of Torah as I have presented it. On the one side is the sort of political ἔθος (*ethos*) that unifies a political community. We can say that this form of ἔθος (*ethos*) has directly to do with the political form of the *conditio humana*. In distinction to this ἔθος (*ethos*), we have on the other side the worship of God's people, which is the form and context of Christian living: we may conceive this ecclesial form of political life with the Greek concept ἦθος (*aethos*). ἦθος (*aethos*) signifies the context to which people belong, in which they are at home. It designates the unfolded life-form as it is granted and continually reshaped in the sphere of living whose contours are determined by the commandments. Christians who are at home in the *ecclesia*, therefore, are freed as critical citizens in not needing (existentially) to be "at home" within the political communities to which they also belong.

The responsibility of Christian ethics entails displaying the importance, and appropriate grammar of *both*, the ἔθος (*ethos*) and the ἦθος (*aethos*).[40] To some extent the distinction I am emphasizing parallels the distinction between *moralisch* and *ethisch* in German. Likewise, the distinction between ἔθος (*ethos*) and ἦθος (*aethos*) to some extent also parallels the distinction between "law" (Gesetz) and "commandment" (*Gebot*). In sum: law can be said to articulate what binds a specific group of people together and generates institutional practices like government offices and procedures of legislation, with all the richly detailed practices of understanding that attend them. Commandment binds in the first instance the people who participate in political worship as their life-form, a life-form that also entails a political contour governed by God in convergence and divergence with the given laws made by humans in a given community.

God's Twofold Kingdom

It will come as no surprise that this distinction between ecclesial and political domains of human association is described in the Lutheran tradition with the language of God's "two kingdoms"[41] and of the "estates"[42] as Luther described them. The two kingdoms (and the estates) signify God's one government, governance, and salvation in its differentiated coherence and emphasize that God's justice does become present in the word for all human beings. It is in the story of Jesus Christ that the addressing of God's rule as His government to all human beings becomes most transparent. The story of Jesus Christ announces God's will to bring all human beings back into God's justice. God rules by bringing to life, in Christ, the "inner man" (as Luther has called this side of the *conditio humana*). The "inner man"

---

40. See Brian Brock, *Singing the Ethos of God: On the Place of Scripture in Christian Ethics* (Grand Rapids: Eerdmans, 2007).
41. For an explanation, see Wannenwetsch, "Luther's Moral Theology."
42. For that element, see Brian Brock, "Why the Estates?" *Studies in Christian Ethics* 20, no. 1 (2007): 179–202.

signifies the *conditio humana* as it is embedded in God's justice in its realization through God's people who participate in God's justifying work.

God's will for justice for all human beings as announced in Christ leads Christians to resist the entrapment of the "world" in the clutches of those powers that are other than God and so obscure his rule. It is important to clarify what is meant when we speak of the "world." In the Lutheran grammar, the world is not a designation of secularized social domains in distinction from religiously dominated institutional, moral, and social domains. In a Lutheran grammar there is no secularized world which God has left on its own; rather, what we today call secular social spaces and orders are domains in which God has preserved human life despite its orientation to immanent rather than transcendent reality ("worldliness"),[43] yet without acceding that it be surrendered to any other agencies offering to save human life. This God-related worldliness requires an appropriate institutional form, and it is in this respect it parallels, but is not an analog of, the political worship appropriate to God's people, since it does not receive the witness of the people of God and is not prepared to remain within God's kingdom.

The central concern of this theological tradition is to confront the loss of ability of those in the world to generate a context of living that is hospitable for extant human beings. A world without God must cast about for *political* configurations that flow from their current imagination of the *conditio humana*. The orienting concern of the theological response to this condition is focused on ensuring that human beings are not forced into forms of life that demand more than they can bear. Which kinds of worldly institutional forms and patterns are capable of genuinely hosting and providing for human lives? Who can establish the space of this interpersonal agreement and secure that provision? What or who can preserve the *conditio humana* according to God's will by winningly engaging and reshaping the *res publica*? These are questions that, from a theological perspective, will not be answered by extrapolations from concepts like "human nature," definitions of the "political animal," or any other asserted "reality." When questions about the *res publica* are submitted to "reality," however conceived, they flee from the essentially interpersonal task of political action, from the constitutive "ground" of political cohabitation. This "ground" is explicitly established ever anew in political worship and—in accordance with its political nature—the "institution" of the *politia* is established at the same time, since it is included in what Christians confess the *ecclesia* to be. God's law is not above but is *embodied in* these institutions and articulated in the commanded law for his people. They attest God's rule to the world, which is prepared to receive this witness because of these institutions. What is communicated in God's commanding activity reveals the *conditio humana* in its political form, which, in essence, is life lived in trust in God's good governance and government.

At the heart of this political ethics lies a singular focus on the question of how, practically, specific human beings will *remain* within the given "ground"

---

43. For this concept, see Dietrich Bonhoeffer, DBWE 8, 364, 480.

of their living. God's people both preach to recall God's acts before the church and world, calling people onto this ground of flourishing human life, and also continue to listen to God's word that they may continually follow and not drift away from it. Both movements happen as it is declared and pronounced to God's people in worship. Such an ecclesial pronouncement is more than an offering of some trustworthy good beside God. When in the church we hear what God has pronounced good, what we hear only becomes visible to the world as in fact good because of the institutional form it takes in the church, as it lives out in practice the rationale of what it preaches. The institutional and praxeological form taken by the Christian community must be publicly recognizable if the witness of God's people, via its critical engagement with society, is to be seen as an offer of a life-giving political practice for the political community.

Human Law

It is here where human law comes into play (according to our tradition). Human law is one of the main directions in which human beings have elaborated the ethical task. Christian ethics is the work required in this domain as the work of probing God's judgment and government as it is institutionally present in the *politia*. Put otherwise, for Christian ethics, the task is to query specific laws and institutional forms to discover if they are believable representations of the grammar of God's government for political communities.

Again, political worship offers Christians the crucial insight into the essence of all human laws. Christian worship preserves and draws attention to the *telos* of human political life by keeping it explicitly present to those engaged in judgment and legislation. In this work its interest is in keeping human beings within God's good governance, government, and salvation. It is concerned to draw given political realities, as represented by institutions onto the ground of God's government. It is therefore concerned with the political setting of all human life (its ἔθος, *ethos*). Human law crystallizes in specific *content*, which becomes apparent as particular distinctions are deployed to circumscribe the contours that given actors perceive of the *conditio humana politica*.

Human Law: Bodily Life and the Common Good

The decisive critical question in relation to human lawmaking, then, is whether specific laws provide and protect this *conditio humana politica*, that is, forms of living that accord with the first commandment. In a political realm, however, human law can only be concerned to shape the political life of the "outer man," that is, human beings in their *bodily* constitution, which must be provided with goods which only God can grant—as the first commandment affirms. No one should be prevented from receiving the necessities granted by God, nor should anyone prevent his neighbor from receiving them. Bodily life, the "outer man," is the status that fallen and worldly human beings present to one another in their social and political interactions.[44] The distinction derives from Luther.

> A man is abundantly and sufficiently justified by faith inwardly, in his spirit, and so has all that he needs, except insofar as this faith and these riches must grow from day to day even to the future life [*ecclesia*]; yet he remains in this mortal life on earth. In this life he must control his own body and have dealings with men [*politia*]. Here the works begin.[45]

Here is how Luther then goes on to describe Christian good works in the context of the *politia*: "A man does not live for himself alone in his mortal body to work for it alone, but he lives also for all men on earth; rather, he lives only for others and not for himself. To this end he brings his body into subjection that he may the more sincerely and freely serve others."[46]

The good works of the Christian are oriented by the needs of my neighbor in his bodily life. The condition of these good works is trust in God's governance and government, so fulfilling the first commandment. In other words, good works in political community flow from the Christian's awareness of God's abundance granted to all human beings. Such good works shape human laws, and as Romans 13 indicates, they also are responsive to the human laws that exist. This dual focus grows from the Christian affirmation that human law is designated by God to provide for human life, and so is good, but also fails according to this standard, and must be contradicted by Christian citizens. This duality is again an expression of the theological claim that God's justifying work runs in tandem with God's governing of all human societies, which can be summarized with the formula, "the *politia* coexists with the *ecclesia* in its political worship."

In this scheme it is impossible for any of our neighbors to lose their political status, because that status is not dependent on me, on my willingness or moral attentiveness, but on my neighbor's claim as a rightful recipient of my good works according to the needs of her bodily life, for which God has promised to care. Good works recognize "the right of the neighbor" that rests on God's active promise to care for this neighbor. The bodily life of any citizen must not be deprived of this context of rights as these come to be articulated in human laws. Thus, to appeal to any human law entails standing up for all the rights of the neighbor in his or her status as a citizen.[47] This is the goal of legislative activity, theologically conceived, as well as providing a critical hermeneutic for judging the justice of any given law.

---

44. See Luther, "The Freedom of a Christian," LW 31. See also Dietrich Bonhoeffer, DBWE 3, 79.

45. Luther, "The Freedom of a Christian," LW 31, 358.

46. Ibid., 364.

47. Hannah Arendt, "The Perplexities of the Rights of Man," in *The Origins of Totalitarianism (1951)* (New York: Harcourt, 1968), 290–302.

Thus, as developed in the Lutheran tradition, "the right of the neighbor,"[48] oriented both the critical and constructive impulses of a political-social ethics devoted to exposing this political reality.

Natural Law

Our tradition has had its own way of negotiating the quest for a universal meaning or rationale of the commandments which has traditionally been carried out under the heading of "natural law."[49] Put more pointedly, our tradition substitutes this account of political performance for the sake of the other within the "institutions" (or "estates") for the quest for universality that is the central aim of natural law accounts. The account of the institution I have offered differs in an analogous way with the concept of "orders of creation" found at this point in other Lutheran ethics. As I understand it, the language of "institutions" is a circumlocution for the commandments. Natural law understood in these terms is taken to be universally applicable but without undermining or presenting an alternative to a theology of the Word of God. When so understood it connects organically with the lineaments of the Lutheran tradition.[50] Within this account, the "state" is characterized (by Karl Barth) as "the order, sanctified by the actual presence of the Word and Spirit of God, in which, by the grace of God, the rules are set up and upheld for common life."[51]

The binding content of the natural law—essentially concerned with bodily life—takes form in practices that follow the rationale of the estates. The estates are a divinely given means of continually awaking human beings to the "right of the neighbor" commanded in God's law and witnessed to by explicit works. This is the sense of the politics assumed in passages like Eph. 2:10, which speaks matter of factly about the "good works, which God prepared beforehand that we should walk in them." Within these good works the Christian citizen cooperates with God through the Christian's (new) heart becomes governed by God ("created in Christ Jesus for good works," Eph. 2:10).

---

48. Erik Wolf, *Recht des Nächsten, ein rechtstheologischer Entwurf*, 2 vols (Frankfurt am Main: Klostermann, 1958).

49. Markus N. A. Bockmuehl describes the history of this development, *Jewish Law in Gentile Churches: Halakhah and the Beginning of Christian Public Ethics* (Grand Rapids: Baker Academic, 2003), see the conclusion, 173. For an enlightening discussion with respect to Karl Barth's *Ethics*, see Nigel Biggar, "Karl Barth and Germain Grisez on the Human Good: An Ecumenical Rapprochement," in *The Revival of Natural Law*, ed. Nigel Biggar and Rufus Black (Aldershot: Ashgate, 2001), 164–83.

50. See, for further discussions, David Novak, "Karl Barth on Divine Command: A Jewish Response," in *Talking with Christians: Musings of a Jewish Theologian* (Grand Rapids: Eerdmans, 2005), 127–45.

51. Barth, *Ethics*, 518–19. For further discussion, see also Stanley Hauerwas, *With the Grain of the Universe: The Church's Witness and Natural Theology* (Grand Rapids: Baker, 2001), 141–7.

So positioned as a set of political performances mediated by good works, it is possible to speak theologically of something like the "common good"[52] as hinted at in Romans 13. In this construal the common good is another name for the *conditio humana* as it is present in that bodily life in its political shape. The concern for the common good finds its corresponding practice in a critical hermeneutic of laws, following distinctions which belong to the grammar of God's commanded law and signify the *conditio humana*. This grammar remains present in the world through the witness of God's people.

Critical Hermeneutics: Related to the Conditio Humana

To call for such a theological practice of critical hermeneutic engagement meets constant challenges in many areas of legislation and judgment. Hence it is crucial that the orienting question for this practice of critical engagement remain crystal clear: How do human beings remain God's people within the techniques of medical care, how do they remain God's people within their own techniques of life-management, and so on. Put succinctly, how do they remain the people for whom God has promised all the goods they need, according to His will (Rom. 12:2)? The material questions exposed by such a critical question are treated in other familiar veins of ethical discussion: issues of social justice and welfare, and not least the area of labor legislation. Here again the question for Christian ethics is both clear, and has its own distinctive contour: how do people remain safe from exploitation, how do people come into possession of what their work yields because God has cooperated with it to make it fruitful (Psalm 127)?

These points of theological orientation provide a fresh entry point into familiar questions about what "justice" means within the field of juridical judgment and legislation, and also how this human justice is grounded in the officeholder's appointment to be responsible to the right of the neighbor. In order not to lose all that we have gained as we turn to practical questions it is crucial that we not forget that this appointment to the right of my neighbor is not located or rooted in some conceptual schema or theoretical affirmation, but in the practices of political worship that allow people to gain a feel for justice through the practices engendered by the work of divine justification that has freed them from slavery to their own desires and interests. They have experience of that divine justice and the practices that accord with it.

This is the living "ground" of human laws and justice. From this ground there are practical reasons to work, for instance, for the development of a welfare state concerned to establish social justice.[53] Should such a state in fact be established, this does not absolve the Christian from the responsibility to explicitly attest

---

52. See, for that issue, O'Donovan, *The Ways of Judgment*.

53. Philip Manow, *Religion und Sozialstaat: Die konfessionellen Grundlagen europäischer Wohlfahrtsstaatsregime* (Frankfurt am Main: Campus-Verlag, 2008), describes the development in Europe.

and speak up for the right of the neighbor. On the contrary, any existing welfare state will only serve the right of the neighbor to the extent that it is continuously regenerating and correcting its grammar in relation to the welfare of its existing citizens. What is decisive is that laws preventing social injustice correspond to good works and coexist necessarily with good works, not only compensating for injustices suffered but also keeping the grammar of the right of the neighbor, that is, the ethical meaning of the welfare state, alive.⁵⁴ It is this necessity for the institutions that serve justice to be "living" that displays how important it is for the ἔθος (*ethos*) of social justice to be continually resourced by the ἦθος (*aethos*) of political worship.

Acute Conflicts Expose Existing Political Rationalities

We can expect conflicts to arise at those places where legislation or governmental activity impinges on what are called "forms of life" (*Lebensformen*). Forms of life are not conceptual descriptions (whether philosophical or theological), but currently existing patterns of living, whether in family life, "reproduction" (as it is called), education, health care, relations of generations, or expression of religious belief. In contemporary public discourse, all these domains are assumed to be ones that may be shaped or even robustly governed by governmental activities and legislation.

In all these domains of contemporary human practice it is worth attending to the fact that none of these domains is ever discussed as a domain in which we are concerned with anything so grand as "the human condition." This is crucial to note because what I have been calling the *conditio humana* will never appear on the agenda for discussing how these forms of life should be governed by human law, unless wrapped in other languages, such as that of "values." So even if there is political controversy over how to handle an issue in one of these domains, and even if the substance of these debates touches directly on the *conditio humana* as I have defined it, it will receive no critical attention in our public discussions. The liberal democratic ideology of the moral neutrality of legislation renders speaking about "life-forms" out of bounds. The rules of discourse have been configured in such a way that these life-forms and their elements as they appear in our political institutions and practices—family life, health practices, "reproduction"—cannot be discussed in substantive terms, even when they clearly have implications for our "human condition" and common good.

In his lecture *The Future of Human Nature*, Jürgen Habermas has illustrated what may be at stake in cases like this, and how different kinds of intellectual practices emerge from different accounts of the ground of political reasoning.⁵⁵ Habermas is concerned with the loss of a common sense of the *conditio humana* as mediated by rational reflection, which he also understands as taking the

---

54. For this topic, see Stefan Heuser, *Instrumente des Guten* (Erlangen: Habilitationsschrift, 2009).
55. Jürgen Habermas, *The Future of Human Nature* (Cambridge: Polity, 2003).

political contours of the *conditio humana* into account. In his view appropriately rational reflection on political questions must be open for political insights from all traditions, not least to "religious" insights that may, in fact, offer considerations that are essential for understanding the political *conditio humana*. Habermas's general admonition is:

> Only if the secular side, too, remains sensitive to the force of articulation inherent in religious languages will the search for reasons that aim at universal acceptability not lead to an unfair exclusion of religions from the public sphere, nor sever secular society from important resources of meaning. In any event, the boundaries between secular and religious reasons are fluid.[56]

Habermas resists human cloning on the grounds that, as a reproductive technique, it would destroy the apparent fact of an equal origin of human beings. Habermas takes this equality of origin as the indispensable—transcendental—presupposition for the equal political status of all human beings, since introducing multiple origins of human beings would entail generating different categorizations of human beings. Some people would have come into the world by apparently random genetic combination, the other dependent on some human beings' decision about what is valuable in human genetic inheritance. The rational God-human distinction, for Habermas, warrants rational conceptions of duty to maintain human beings as of only one kind. On the basis of a rational insight into a given distinction, an insight into the grammar of a "religious" distinction (between a God and a human) Habermas has defined a common good in terms of the *conditio humana politica*, which, he argues, can only be intelligibly understood when related to its "ground."

Habermas's insight is that the ground for ethical understanding is given with a language. Languages preserve insights into what is essential for the *conditio humana*. Habermas extracts from a basic theological distinction a transcendental presupposition that human beings are equal. In so doing he does not solve questions like whether this transcendental grounding of human equality can be falsified by the empirical fact of human beings arising who have been cloned or created in other ways. The point is that Habermas grasps that the practices we take up or resist toward our human bodily life in its determined contours will always have a bearing on the *conditio humana*.

This example, one of many, suggests that the reason for listening to articulated religious traditions is that they preserve grammars that are fundamental for the political and the maintenance of its rationale. It behooves us to assume that every articulated tradition has an intelligible rationale that can be understood by patient attention even if the inner coherence does not originate in an *a priori* rational construction. Human communities carry and hand on the rationale of their life-forms in their practices. The rationale carried in traditions arises from

---

56. Habermas, *The Future of Human Nature*, 109.

what is given and entrusted to people who live the creaturely life of people that has been appointed to all by God. It is futile—as comparative religionists are wont to do—to try to extract valuable insights, languages, and so forth, by appeal to mental habits or naturally given sensitiveness (perhaps of those with a supposedly "sensitive conscience"), because the content and rationales of living people are inextricably tied to the life-form that they inhabit. This is not a theological defense of "human nature" simply in terms of its givenness by God. It emerges, rather, as a discovery and attestation of the political existence that first became tangible in the specifically configured worship of a linguistically and conceptually elaborated practice of worship. It is an attestation spoken out of the sphere of living avowedly circumscribed by God's commanded law. This praxis and its ἦθος (*aethos*) preserve the ἔθος (*ethos*), the needed morality and its rationale for the political sphere.

On the "Ground" of Ethics: Ruled by the Spirit

The context for living that Christian ethics is called to display is articulated in God's commandments. They are not a higher context of legitimization but a context of discovery of human life that differs from other political conceptions and experiences. We can even go as far as the Lutheran tradition understands it—political worship is, in fact, the only context in which that which determines and defines our human existence and that God's people are called to attest, to explore in their living, and to communicate by their critical understanding can be discovered. The motor of this account is the claim that "justification" happens when people find themselves transformed within God's justice, that is, by God's practice of justice and judgment. This experience bequeaths the germinal insight into all human political existence—that it is not, in reality, ruled or governed by any other "power." There is no "divine law" suspended in the transcendental heavens, nor a "natural law" encoded in the natural world: there is only the law given by God in his active works of governing human societies, bringing justice, and rendering judgment.[57]

By traveling with the Lutheran tradition of political ethics we are led, finally, to Paul's reflections on law, specifically his exhortation: "But if you are led by the Spirit, you are not under the law" (Gal. 5:18). Luther's translation draws out the political horizon of this verse, which he translates: "If you are *ruled*, governed by the Spirit." Bernd Wannenwetsch has insightfully observed that this is in no sense a spiritualization of political existence, because Paul's invocation of the

---

57. The elaboration of the topic of "justification" within Luther's work and within the mainline Reformation and its further tradition orbits around this political existence. This was also the focus of the rediscovery of the Reformation in the twentieth century. Karl Barth has articulated it in his essay on *Church and State*. German: *Rechtfertigung und Recht*. Karl Barth, *Church and State* (London: Student Christian Movement Press, 1939).

Spirit includes God's whole political activity and work as addressed and concretely communicated to his people.[58] Nor is there any opposition between "law" and "spirit" here, only an explication of the "law of the Spirit" (Rom. 8:2).

The "fruit" of "being ruled by the spirit" consists in those habits or virtues which characterize human existence in its political form: "But the fruit of the Spirit is love, joy, peace, patience, kindness, generosity, faithfulness, gentleness, and self-control" (Gal. 5:22–3). These "virtues," as they have been called, are the form within which the people of God live together, are set into already-configured relationships with each other. Love, joy, peace, and so on are not about a moral status distinct or separated from the political status. It is significant that this status receives its contour, its shape, through a "law." The "law of the Spirit" is no antinomian attitude; it is, quite the contrary, the ground for a political existence determined to live within the rights of the neighbor. Every "spiritualizing" interpretation will find itself generating new demands for norms and laws that aim to control that "Spirit." Luther was acutely aware of the dangers on both sides, from both legalism and antinomianism.

This perspective gives us fresh ears to hear Jesus in the Sermon on the Mount:

> You have heard that it was said to the men of old, "You shall not kill; and whoever kills shall be liable to judgment." But I say to you that everyone who is angry with his brother shall be liable to judgment; whoever insults his brother shall be liable to the council, and whoever says, "You fool!" shall be liable to the hell of fire. So if you are offering your gift at the altar, and there remember that your brother has something against you, leave your gift there before the altar and go; first be reconciled to your brother, and then come and offer your gift. (Mt. 5:21-24)

The grammar of the commandment "You shall not kill" reaches deeply into political existence, which is threatened by any practice or attitude that is unaware of the status afforded the neighbor within God's governance and government. To call the neighbor a "fool" is to deprive him of his *conditio humana*, not because he has been disrespected, but because these actions threaten the political form of neighborly togetherness, for these practices both share in coexisting within God's justice and judgment. This coexistence has not only to be accepted (as something imposed externally by law), but actively received and flowing out into good works that serve and protect the neighbor in his *conditio humana*. This is ultimately the theological trajectory Luther was following in his Small Catechism as he sought the implied positive claim in the negative prohibitions of the Decalogue.

---

58. Bernd Wannenwetsch, "'Ruled by the Spirit': Hans Ulrich's Understanding of Political Existence," *Studies in Christian Ethics* 20, no. 2 (2007): 257–72.

"You shall not kill." What is this? Answer: We are to fear and love God, so that we neither endanger nor harm the lives of our neighbors, but instead help and support them in all of life's needs.[59]

"We are to fear and love God." In this way the first commandment reveals the grammar of the rest. This implication is only visible when this fear and love understands itself as resting on trust that all human actions are embedded in God's governance and government. God's commandments make explicit all the ways in which human beings should guard against losing interest in God's granted context of living.

The commandments do negate, but through Christ, Luther saw in these negations a yes, a life-giving gospel—impelling the believer into active works of serving the neighbor's experiencing fullness of life. The context of living described in and granted by the Torah emphasizes the abundance of God's governance and government for all human beings. This abundant divine governance as encapsulated in the Torah is confirmed in its enacted work of justification through Jesus Christ. Jesus himself encapsulates this grammar: "Do not think that I have come to abolish the law and the prophets, I have not come to abolish but to fulfill." "Fulfill" is a translation of the Greek πληρῶσαι (*plerosai*), which this points to the abundance (πλήρωμα, *pleroma*) of God's granted law. The law as the primary institution of human political life contains the resources needed for the government and legislation of every human community. It thus offers a starting point for a political ethics that proceeds by way of the critical hermeneutic practice which ferrets out substantial insights into the *conditio humana* that are continually granted and realized in God's justifying work.

---

59. Luther, "The Small Catechism" (1529), in *The Book of Concord: The Confessions of the Evangelical Lutheran Church*, ed. Robert Kolb and Timothy J. Wengert (Minneapolis: Fortress Press, 2000), nn. 9–10.

Chapter 5

HUMAN ECONOMIES AT THEIR LIMITS, BUT GOVERNED WITHIN THEIR LIMITS

To speak about economics is immediately to encounter a thicket of urgent problems related to both contemporary practice and theoretical description. On almost a daily basis our political discourses engage questions of how, or whether, economic growth needs to be balanced against accumulating national debt (today a burning question in the Eurozone), and even the question of whether the infinite growth of economies is a good idea can arise in these discussions. Questions of economic growth quickly slide into debates about how economic growth is already or might possibly be steered toward more equitable distribution of economic gains, and how the problem of equitable distribution links with ever-shifting problems of unemployment and income development. Behind all these practical and theoretical questions looms the even more perplexing question of whether our modern global system of finance is even governable at all.

Many of these problems are inherent in the concept of economy as it is understood in modern economic theory, and recognizing this, we may even go so far as to view our conception of economics as in a state of disarray, or even in a permanent crisis, since there seems no realistic way to satisfactorily address many of these problems. When we try to grasp the concept of economy theoretically (as various theories of capitalism do), the theories that emerge today are not ones susceptible to straightforward intellectual critique, hampering our best intentions to fine-tune or seriously consider alternatives to our present capitalist systems. When, as an ethicist, I have found myself in discussions with economists or people from the finance sector, I have frequently been confronted with serious suggestions that our current economy is not even governable, neither at the micro-level of business ethics nor at the macro-level of the ethics of economics systems. Thus, underneath all our debates today about practical economic decisions there are clearly bubbling serious questions about whether the structural characteristics of the market we have built are resistant to our best efforts to change it. If we cannot, my conversation partners sometimes conclude, then our only option is to learn to live within the specific limits our concept of economy places on what we can do and how we can live.

Such pessimistic conclusions are not accepted by everyone in this field, and other thinkers in the field of ethics are doubling down on their efforts to find ways effectively to govern economic processes by improving political levers, clarifying conceptual frameworks, and better understanding the role played in economies by civil institutions and practices.[1] "Governance" is a key term in all such efforts, a recognition that when it comes to the economy, political power and governance are severely limited in a wide range of ways. There are limits of the kind of political power that can be applied to economic behavior, there are limits to what legislation and the courts can do to shape economic patterns, there are limits to the legitimacy governments can establish regarding their right to intervene in economics, along with ideological, moral, and systematic limits. Theorists discussing economics have invariably discussed these limits, given their direct connections with the question of the way in which economy is governable or even capable of being significantly changed. It is beginning to many to look like the *only* limits that can be imagined to the economy are the limits imposed by the environmental conditions of human life. Even this limit—which allows discussions of sustainable economics to get off the ground, for instance—presuppose notions about human life, its characteristics, its quality, and its determination, as well as raising questions about the extent to which environmental conditions themselves can be controlled or governed.[2]

Such discussions reveal how the quest to understand economy brings us inevitably before the fundamental phenomenon of human life on the one hand embedded in practical ethical questions about how to handle it on the other. Though it is logically possible to make this distinction between fundamental reflections about the phenomenon of human life and the ethical question of how to handle it, in the end, these two levels or dimensions cannot be sharply separated. Insisting on this inseparability, as I will do in this chapter, is one way to keep constantly in view the reality that economy is not value-free, but is always organized by human ethical impulses even if the terms we use to describe these impulses systematically diminish the role played by them (as when we speak of "processes of economic development," to take one example). Such an integrated approach may appear, at the outset, to rule out ethically guided governance, but as we will see, if we follow this approach, we discover fresh and important points of view from which more ethically reflective notions of governance and change appear.[3]

As the role of the economy has come to increasingly determine the courses taken by Western developed societies, the reality that economic questions in fact

---

1. See especially Luigino Bruni and Stefano Zamagni, *Civil Economy: Efficiency, Equity, Public Happiness* (Bern: Peter Lang, 2007).

2. See Donella H. Meadows et al., *The Limits to Growth: A Report for the Club of Rome's Project on the Predicament of Mankind* (New York: Universe Books, 1972); and updates: Donella H. Meadows, Dennis L. Meadows, and Jørgen Randers, *Beyond the Limits* (White River Junction, VT: Chelsea Green Publishing, 1992); Donella H. Meadows, Dennis L. Meadows, and Jørgen Randers, *Limits to Growth: The 30-Year Update* (White River Junction, VT: Chelsea Green Publishers, 2004).

3. Niklas Luhmann, *Paradigm Lost: Über die ethische Reflexion der Moral* (Frankfurt am Main: Suhrkamp, 1990).

have to do with the basic shape of human life has become much more obvious, pronouncedly so within current philosophical and theological discourses on "business ethics." It is no longer surprising to find oneself on explicitly theological ground in discussions of economics, given that there are so many points at which our economic lives are grounded in faith rather than knowledge. It is in this way that we find economy being rediscovered as a fundamentally theological concept by those in the academic field interested in the ethical issues it raises—and in a different mode by people engaged with in its public contexts, entrepreneurs, corporations, and civic institutions.

Economy and Theology: Three Approaches

There are several theological accounts that remind us that there are conceptions of economy in the Christian tradition that have been worked out in an explicitly theological and biblical context. In the body of this paper I will set out three ways in which the relationship of theology and economics has been articulated: first by way of a genealogical account of the origin of economic concepts in theological concepts, and then by way of a theology of economy. Finally, I suggest that the most important insights of both approaches can be drawn together in what I am calling a "Messianic ethics of economy" that approaches the economy as a domain in which human work strives to discern and embrace God's provision for human life.

In line with the theological approach set out in earlier chapters, this Messianic ethics of the economy is, at root, an attempt to develop strands of the biblical witness to which the Lutheran theological tradition draws our attention. The case is complicated when approaching the topic of economy because it is not a term that appears in the Old Testament—though the idea as presented in the New Testament is certainly present in the Old. There is no direct equivalent in the Hebrew of the Old Testament for the Greek *oikonomia* of the New, despite the fact that it is considerations rooted in the Old Testament that provide the context for specific approaches to a theologically reflective account of economics.[4] We may say that there is a genuinely biblical tradition of economic thinking only in the sense that there is a theologically and philosophically elaborated Christian tradition of engaging this theme by drawing on a range of biblical citations. I have already set out (in Part I) the reasons why I will be reading the biblical texts as centrally presenting God's work and story with his people with the aim of demonstrating that God is understood by believers as a God committed to becoming present in the world of humans from the very origins of God's being as Trinity.

---

4. See especially Franz Segbers, *Die Hausordnung der Tora: Biblische Impulse für eine theologische Wirtschaftsethik*, 3rd edn. (Darmstadt: Wissenschaftliche Buchgesellschaft, 2002).

My premise, then, is that human talk about economy should be oriented toward the activity of God toward the world, traditionally called his economic activity. God's acts toward the creation are independent, of course, of all human theological descriptions while being intrinsically connected with God's being and inner life (the so-called imminent relations of the Trinity). Theological thinking that endeavors to root itself in God's working, is liberated from the outset from deterministic views of economics, even if widely held views of economics are experience as a burdensome heritage that has determined our human history so far. In distinction to the "iron cage" in which many economic theories seem to place human beings, according to the Christian tradition, *oikonomia* names a reality that flows from God into the world. Because God's economy is distinct from human economic theories and practices, it can and does contradict the various configurations of economic phenomena that confront us today. The continuity of God's care for human life is more trustworthy than the iron cage of economic theory and practice—a claim that has important implications for how we understand economic ethics today.

God's Oikonomia *and Economy: The Genealogical Approach*

My approach to the topic of theology and economy takes as its starting point the specific usage of *oikonomia* in Eph. 1:9-11.

> He has made known to us the mystery of his will, according to his good pleasure that he set forth in Christ, as a plan [*oikonomia*] for the fullness of time, to gather up all things in him, things in heaven and things on earth. In Christ we have also obtained an inheritance, having been destined according to the purpose of him who accomplishes all things according to his counsel and will, so that we, who were the first to set our hope on Christ, might live for the praise of his glory.

When the NRSV translates *oikonomia* as "plan," they get to the heart of the concept as it has been elaborated within the Christian tradition. The *oikonomia tou theou* is God's well-planned action for our salvation, in which God enacts and continues God's story with His people. *Oikonomia* names God's plan of salvation as progressively revealed to his people through the ages and definitively realized in the story of Jesus Christ.

Christian theological traditions of thinking about *oikonomia* incorporated aspects of the Greek usage of the word which also allow us to translate it as "the governance of the household [*oikos*]," in which we human beings live, along with all other creatures.[5] The linkage of God's plan with the Greek notion of household governance might at first blush look rather dubious, there being no obvious link between the divine *oikonomia*, with its supposedly theological meaning, and our human economy, particularly given its complex saturation by the urgent problems

---

5. The Old Testament understanding of this notion is described in, Segbers: *Die Hausordnung der Tora*.

of theory and ethical practice already noted. Nevertheless, several substantial figures have discovered precisely this linkage as they excavated the "hidden genealogy" linking the Christian tradition of *oikonomia* to our human economy, and then going on to identify how its characteristics might have developed into the modern context. The genealogical approach to the background of modern economic language first developed by Nietzsche and elaborated by Foucault has been meticulously followed by Giorgio Agamben in his book *The Kingdom and the Glory*.[6] Agamben's core argument is that, if we look closely at Western uses of the language of *oikonomia* we are led back to the realization that the basic logic of theology as a description of God is in fact about economy because it is about God's *life*. According to Agamben, because Christian theology is concerned with eternal life, it is continually interested in the question of how life is fulfilled. Thus,

> From the beginning theology conceives divine life and the history of humanity as an *oikonomia*, that is, that theology is itself "economic" and did not simply become so at a later time through secularization. From this perspective, the fact that the living being who was created in the image of God in the end reveals himself to be capable only of economy, not politics, or, in other words, that history is ultimately not a political but an "administrative" and "governmental" problem, is nothing but a logical consequence of economic theology. Similarly, it is certainly more than a simple lexical fact that, with a peculiar reversal of the classical hierarchy, a *zoe aionios* and not a *bios* lies at the center of the evangelical message. The eternal life to which Christians lay claim ultimately lies in the paradigm of the *oikos*, not in that of the polis.[7]

This observation clarifies why Agamben's genealogical work centers on how the message of eternal life as the fulfillment of life has come de facto to be the impelling driver of modern views of the necessity for development of our human economy, and thus how this notion remains a part of our present political and economic reality.[8]

Theology of Economy: God's Economy as a Paradigm for Human Economy

In distinction from genealogical approaches to the question of the link between theology and economics, a second approach might be labeled a *theology of economy* approach, which I will refer to as the "ethical approach." It is much closer to what I called political theology in Chapter 4. This second approach draws on

---

6. Giorgio Agamben, *The Kingdom and the Glory: For a Theological Genealogy of Economy and Government*, Homo Sacer II, 2, trans. Lorenzo Chiesa and Matteo Mandarini (Stanford: Stanford University Press, 2011).
7. Agamben, *Kingdom and the Glory*, 16.
8. For a different interpretation of Agamben's work, see Thanos Zartaloudis, *Giorgio Agamben: Power, Law and the Uses of Criticism* (New York: Routledge, 2010).

biblical strands to conceive economy as a reality determined by God that precedes human action and provides a context for human action. The economy of God's interactions with creatures is perceived in this theological-ethical perspective as a model or paradigm for understanding human economy. More precisely human economies *ought to* accommodate the divine economy.[9] In this approach the moral claims ordering human economic activity arise from the agent's location within the context of "God's household." Martin Luther saw Psalm 127 as clear evidence for this understanding.

This approach takes both sides of the equation to be dynamic, requiring constant discerning attention by human beings to God's activity as well as to developments in human economic behavior. Thinkers like Rowan Williams and Larry Elliott in their *Crisis and Recovery*, as well as Douglas Meeks's *God the Economist* and Franz Segbers's *Die Hausordnung der Tora* are examples of this theology of economics approach.[10] Each of these—in some ways quite different—theologies of economics take two questions to be key. First, what is the aim of the *oikonomia tou theou*—in what sense does it focus on the fulfillment of human life? The second is: How might we grasp the continuity of God's *oikonomia* with our human economy in its current form?

Since these questions are ones that inquire into the content (or *telos*) of God's *oikonomia* they converge with the genealogical approach of Agamben, whose research uncovered a direct connection in the Christian tradition between the *oikonomia tou theou*, and human economy. What is distinctive about this second approach, is its presumption that a theologically reflective *aethos* (as defined in Chapter 4) is necessary if the real connections between, not the ideas of divine and human economy but the real points of God's *oikonomia* and human economic activity are to be grasped. A theology of economics approach thus brings a number of subsidiary economic topoi into view, types of human activity that are seen as receiving special concern in God's economy, and therefore ought to be part of human concern with economics as well. These include human work with its means of production and institutional arrangement, human needs in their relation to property,[11] and, more fundamentally, articulating the central characteristics of a genuine economic praxis. Each of these approaches assumes that a critical account of economy, or a specific economic *ethos*, must address configurations of human work, human needs, and property—such as practices of charging interest—and, in particular, the specific contours of our economic praxis, analyzing, for instance, the implications of current economic models and assumptions.

---

9. See also Tomas Sedlacek, *Economics of Good and Evil: The Quest for Economic Meaning from Gilgamesh to Wall Street* (Oxford: Oxford University Press, 2011).

10. *Crisis and Recovery: Ethics, Economics and Global Justice*, ed. Rowan Williams and Larry Elliott (London: Palgrave Macmillan, 2010); Douglas Meeks, *God the Economist: The Doctrine of God in Political Economy* (Minneapolis: Fortress Press, 1990).

11. These themes are especially prominent in Meeks's *God the Economist* and Segbers's *Hausordnung*.

What unites this second set of ethical approaches is their insistence on taking as their point of reference a *reality* that is determined, or should be determined, by God's actions and God's will as articulated in scripture and as it is paradigmatically present, or should be present, within the Christian community and its worship. Rowan Williams, for instance, explicitly presents Christian worship as a paradigmatic exemplification of an economy displaying an alternative to existing economies. Williams's account suggests that, as in the last chapter we spoke of a "political worship," it makes good sense to speak in terms of an "economic worship"—which is of course not different from, but another aspect of, political worship.[12] To speak in this way raises the question of whether the experiences Christians have in economic worship can meaningfully be said to offer paths forward for economic practices in other arenas of human life. If this were not the case, then Agamben's genealogical research must be wrong—theological practice cannot have shaped "real" economic behavior.

This last observation highlights the fundamental difference between the genealogical and the ethical approaches, rooted in their different definitions of life. Agamben's reconstruction of a (hidden) genealogy between the *oikonomia tou theou* and our present economy is led by the fundamental idea that economics concerns the fulfillment of life. As is well known, Agamben resists all talk of "life" as bare, physical life (*zōē* in Greek), separated from fulfilled life in which physical life is understood as praxeologically formed and having a constitutive biographical narrative (signified by the Greek word *bios*). As Agamben puts it, the Greeks, "used two terms that, although traceable to a common etymological root, are semantically and morphologically distinct: *zōē*, which expressed the simple fact of living common to all living beings (animals, men, or gods), and *bios*, which indicated the form or way of living proper to an individual or a group."[13] Fulfilled life—the unity of *bios* and *zōē*—is, according to Agamben, the very *telos* of God's *oikonomia*, articulated in the promise of "eternal life." Human life can be said to be fulfilled when God's *oikonomia* and political reign are no longer separated but are eschatologically realized. The world we live in today is organized by the very different presupposition that political sovereignty, especially that of a state, does not have the power or remit to rule over human life in this more encompassing sense of unifying *bios* and *zōē*. Contemporary governments therefore take themselves to be governing human life as bare life (*zōē*) without any thought of the destiny of human life to glorify God to be life for the glory of God that was a staple of Western political thought in the centuries of Christendom.

This intentional negation at the heart of modern political theory is starkly opposed to the vision of human fulfillment presented in passages like Eph. 1:5-6: "He destined us for adoption as his children through Jesus Christ, according to the

---

12. Bernd Wannenwetsch, *Political Worship: Ethics for Christian Citizens* (Oxford: Oxford University Press, 2004).

13. Giorgio Agamben, *Homo Sacer: Sovereign Power and Bare Life* (Stanford: Stanford University Press, 1998.

good pleasure of his will, to the praise of his glorious grace that he freely bestowed on us in the Beloved." One commentator on Agamben's work, Thanos Zartaloudis, goes directly to what is at stake in this disjunction between the biblical view and modern views of governance:

> Contrary to the long held Western assumption that the world is governable, what is shown, instead, in the current phase of the global political spectacle, is that the world's government or even self-government (through, for example, the apparatus of the free market) has always been founded through what can be described philosophically as a *negative metaphysics of a ground that prescribes or commands nothing* (nothing other than the mere presupposition of governability).[14]

That is, the fulfilled human life has been conceived as a ground or foundation in modern political theory only as *an absence*, while its messengers and administrators (the benefactors of humankind) act or govern as if it was always present, or at least available. The result is a pseudo-paradoxical state of affairs in which the self-governing of the world is predicated on the premise that mere governability is sufficient for reaching the goal that is not avowed. That is, fulfilled life is believed to be reachable by standing on *no other foundation than the absence of a foundation*, a bare—absolute—ground without content.[15]

Agamben's reconstruction focused on a specific fundamental concern with our human economy, that it, with its complicated intertwining with our politics, has lost its very meaning, that they have has lost their *telos* or—to put it another way—that they have given up the very idea of a telos by which any contours or genuine limits of economic activity could be discerned. In this he offers Christians a salutary reminder that their own tradition has read the biblical traditions as assuming that a fulfilled human life, in which *zōē* and *bios* are unified, is intended to glorify God—and that glorification is a political activity. In the end, everything is about the glory of God, at least according to the New Testament, Agamben argues.[16] Human life is destined to be fulfilled by finding its form as eternal life to the glory of God. This is the transformation that de facto drives the transformation of human economies.

The function of genealogical reconstructions is to open the reader's eyes to hidden paradigms that inescapably determine the patterns of our relationships, in this case, our economic relationships. Agamben's deployment of this method is an attempt to demonstrate how the attempt to bring the fulfillment of life through human economy is an aspiration formed out of a substitution of the telos to glorify God and His economy for a glorification of other actors and processes. This substitution leads to a forgetfulness—or occlusion—of reality the attempt

---

14. Zartaloudis, *Giorgio Agamben*, 155.
15. Ibid.
16. See Agamben, *The Kingdom and the Glory*, 77.

being made to fill up the empty space created by the rejection of the human work of conforming to God's *oikonomia* is so concerted. This is how human economic activity comes to offer the unfulfillable promise to offer fulfillment of human life in all its dimensions. The economy of God has been co-opted by the generation of every kind of "value" that can be thrown up by human desire.

To this analysis Agamben adds that the mass media have honed substitute practices of acclamation for political authorities that pick up leftover aspects of the political "glory" and "glorification" that humans were once understood to owe to God. In this way conceptions of "reign" and "government" are united to form a modern substitute that only resembles the eschatological fulfillment assumed in scripture.

> In opposition to the ingenuous emphasis on productivity and labor that has long prevented modernity from accessing politics as man's most proper dimension, politics is here returned to its central inoperativity, that is, to that operation that amounts to rendering inoperative all human and divine works. The empty throne, the symbol of Glory, is what we need to profane in order to make room, beyond it, for something that, for now, we can only evoke with the name *zoe aionios*, eternal life. It is only when the fourth part of the investigation, dedicated to the form-of-life and use, is completed, that the decisive meaning of inoperativity as a properly human and political praxis will be able to appear in its own light.[17]

If we accept Agamben's theologically attuned genealogy of economy—in order to hear this prophetically articulated voice—we are bound to take a more critical stance toward the biopolitical assumptions (*zoe*politics) that have become the driving force in the development of our human economy. We should affirm instead that economy is and should be the precise place where we hope to experience the fulfillment of life.[18] But what follows from that?

What follows at minimum from this philosophical suggestion is that a fundamental and radical conversion is needed—here Agamben is following in the footsteps of Nietzsche, Heidegger, and others. All these thinkers prophetically announce an alternative world that cannot be brought about by human effort. What is crucial to note about these philosophical prophecies is that even though they do have a decidedly eschatological outlook as they point beyond the reality we know, they lack a positive perspective or point of reference and so what we would call an "ethical perspective" on what is to come.

Philosophers such as Oliver Marchart have criticized this kind of doom prophecy for expelling even the repose that is part of all Messianic hope (paradigmatically in

---

17. Ibid., xiii.

18. It is here that a theological analysis of the methods by which marketers calibrate what they promise consumers is highly illuminating. See Emily Beth Hill, *Marketing and Christian Proclamation in Theological Perspective* (Lanham, MD: Lexington/Fortress Academic, 2021).

ideas like Adorno's negative dialectics).[19] Such empty eschatologies announce only the perversion of politics and economic life as we know it.

In his commentary on Paul's letter to the Romans, Agamben reflects on Paul's notion of a "fulfilled" time as the very beginning of a new world. As he does so he discovers in it the distinction that I have suggested is crucial between "eschatological time" and "Messianic time," the time of the final end and the time of ending (*Endzeit*).[20] He finds this distinction put sharply in Gal. 6:10: "So then, whenever we have an opportunity [*kairos*], let us work for the good of all, (and especially for those of the family of faith)." Galatians 6 speaks quite literally of an "opportunity" or *kairos* that has to be understood and lived into as fulfilled Messianic time. Significantly, Paul speaks here of our "work for the good of all"—the real task for human action lived within this *kairos*. Hence Agamben too stumbles on the crucial question about the content of the Messianic time, bringing us round yet again to the question of the essence of God's *oikonomia*—and finally how coming to terms with this reality leads to an ethical perspective.

God's Present Reign

It is genuinely remarkable that theological discussions of economics so rarely engage the question of what God's *oikonomia* for this world is all about. Nor do we often hear of investigations of what the Christian tradition, developing the biblical traditions, might have to say regarding God's present reign and economy within the Messianic time—let alone how this reign shapes our human economic practices.

Agamben himself draws attention to the Trinitarian logic of the theology-economy link in the *logos* of God in his being (*theologia*) and in his presence (*oikonomia*). These are distinct but inseparable dimensions of God's being. Agamben is critical of current theology for abandoning this Trinitarian logic and, as a consequence, finding God's *oikonomia* unintelligible. Though this criticism is overstated, the question is a good one: How is *oikonomia* part of Christian affirmations of the Trinity, particularly as it is related to the Messianic time? I suggested at the outset that *oikonomia* may be understood as God's plan to save the world, to reconcile the world with Himself, as foregrounded, for instance, in 2 Cor. 5:17–19:

> So, if anyone is in Christ, there is a new creation: everything old has passed away; see, everything has become new! All this is from God, who reconciled us to himself through Christ, and has given us the ministry [*diakonian*] of

---

19. Oliver Marchart, *Die politische Differenz: Zum Denken des Politischen bei Nancy, Lefort, Badiou, Laclau und Agamben* (Berlin: Suhrkamp, 2010), 224–5.

20. Giorgio Agamben, *The Time That Remains: A Commentary on the Letter to the Romans* (Stanford: Stanford University Press, 2005). For my own reasons for thinking this distinction important, see Chapter 1.

reconciliation; that is, in Christ God was reconciling the world to himself, not counting their trespasses against them, and entrusting the message of reconciliation to us.

According to this biblical reference, God's *oikonomia* is directed to God becoming present in Jesus Christ. The concern of God's *oikonomia* is the real arrival of God's "new creation" or "new life." Its telos is nothing other than this *adventus* of Messianic time, with all the implications of a new reality determining our present time that come with it. On this matter, Agamben notes:

> Paul speaks of a Plan of God that has not been spoken of for eons but that has now become manifest in Christ: the mystery of God and Christ that has become manifest to the world through Christ's appearance. It is at this point that the ways of a philosophy of revelation become possible. It must not be understood, like mythology, as a necessary process, but in a way that is fully free, as the decision and action of a will that is most free.[21]

While Agamben freely admits that in the New Testament the arrival of Messianic time is a revelation of God's mystery in Jesus Christ this admission does not substantially determine how he then goes on to reconstruct *oikonomia*. His philosophical vantage point does not allow him to see the *oikonomia* as fully determined by a Trinitarian logic and provoking an *ethos* that accords with it. In Agamben's view God's *oikonomia* concerns the ultimate, eschatological fulfillment of human life, the gift of eternal life, and this is a view which continues to be the hidden motor of our thinking about human economies today—ignoring the biblical claim that the Messianic *kairos* is explicitly presented as an already given fulfillment.

Another Eschatological Paradigm: Toward a Messianic Ethics of Economy

What if we begin with what Agamben overlooks? His account usefully highlights the real-world implications of an eschatology of post-temporal fulfilled life within God's *oikonomia* as well the perversions that arise when this Christian understanding of eschatological fulfillment is turned into a rhetorical cipher for all the things that human economic activity can offer. Agamben gives us a clear sense of how the transmutation of an eschatological into a materialist account of fulfillment is the root of the puzzling contemporary presumption that economics pervades every dimension of human life. Agamben himself sees this de facto "concrete eschatology" as an alternative to the theological accounts of political life of Erich Peterson and Carl Schmitt. Their failure, in his view, springs from their insistence on an "eschatology of the *katechon*," an eschatology of suspension, the

---

21. Agamben, *The Kingdom and the Glory*, 6.

"retainer" holding back the universal flood of salvation and eternal life which is the decisive promise of God's *oikonomia*.[22]

Agamben understands Schmitt and Peterson to be intentionally repressing the account of concrete eschatology he favors in order to strengthen the legitimacy of the political sovereign to govern human life in Schmitt's case, and the legitimacy of the church's government in Peterson's work. Their respective arguments for a suspended eschatology function conceptually by creating an empty space between God's *oikonomia* (as it is fulfilled in Jesus Christ) and its final consummation. For them, in the time between the times, political theology must grant either that the sovereign de facto governs human life (Schmitt), or that over the state stands the church, whose pastoral or moral insight is the guarantor that human life is well governed in light of what the church knows about the fulfillment promised by God (Peterson). This rivalry, it is worth noting, seems to set up a competition between the state and church about who holds the reins of political governance— understood as biopolitical management. The central move of Agamben's counter-proposal is his claim that God's eschatological work is not in abeyance, but is very much at work in a substitute form, a concrete eschatology that—by substitution— is taken to be giving all the good things to humans that were once understood to flow from God's plan. Thus, for Agamben, Schmitt and Peterson lose any purchase on the characteristic theological valences of contemporary political and economic life.

So, while Schmitt and Peterson claim that eschatology is inoperative, and Agamben that it is operative as a secular materialistic horizon of hope and aspiration, Agamben still operates with a restricted view of the *concreteness* of eschatology. Agamben is aware—as highlighted in his commentary on Paul's letter to the Romans—that Messianic time is important, but he has no grasp of the appearance of this time as a contentful *adventus* concretely opposing the ways of living and thinking that assume that human economic activity is bringing about a universal (eschatological) transformation of the world. What Agamben is missing is the concreteness that is assumed in the New Testament notion of Messianic time as *kairos*. This concrete Messianic time is clearly not a suspension (*katechon*), but the particular consummation of God's *adventus oikonomia*. The New Testament's language of *kairos* ensures that eschatology is not a distant or conceptual reality, but a worldly "Messianic phenomenon" of God's fulfilled *oikonomia*. God's *adventus* in Jesus Christ is the guarantee that there is no such thing as a merely formal or materially empty *kairos*.[23]

Agamben is highly sensitive to the historical efficacy assumed in different eschatological accounts. He nevertheless is not himself able to transcend the alternatives that dominate contemporary academic discourse between utopian and *katechontic* (or *saeculum* accounts) accounts of eschatology. I want now to turn in more detail to the suggestion that it is Messianic time itself that opposes

---

22. See ibid., 6–11.
23. See Agamben, *The Time That Remains*, 41.

an eschatology of a universal economic fulfillment of life on the one hand as well as a katechontic eschatology of a real—but formally empty—fulfillment on the other. It is precisely here that we should begin to look for answers to the question of what we are doing when we seek a faithful *ethos* for our present time, our human economy and politics—that reckons with its own, historically and geographically given contours.

In contrast to this theory of an empty Messianic time (with its corresponding empty throne), the biblical Christian traditions offer a picture of an already-realized *adventus* of God's *oikonomia*, which clearly has political entailments—as well as a corresponding and necessarily implicated *ethos*. Scripture warrants us placing *oikonomia* as the opposite of all concepts of *katechon*, which the advent of God's presence reveals to be an illusion.[24] To take this assertion seriously will mean banning all talk about a God "behind" human powers or authorities (as an invisible hand or a vague "Providence") in favor of looking for a God who is visibly reigning and governing the world through his people insofar as they remain attentive to his direction in his Word. The Christian ethos is the place we must look to understand the concreteness of God's reign.[25]

The Ethos in Messianic Time

In opposition to Agamben's notion of eschatology, the New Testament holds that God's *oikonomia* has been fulfilled in Jesus Christ. Eph. 1:11–12 addresses the question that immediately follows about how we are to live in correspondence to that fulfillment: "In Christ we have also obtained an inheritance having been destined according to the purpose of him who accomplishes all things according to his counsel and will, so that we, who were the first to set our hope on Christ, might live for the praise of his glory." The fulfillment of human life already given in Jesus Christ is not "empty," but politically content-rich, since the *adventus* of his Kingdom is by definition the operation of God's *oikonomia*. Jesus Christ is Lord— or, put slightly differently, God reigns over the world with Jesus Christ—through His people.

The advent of Messianic time sets God's people in concrete opposition to the powers of the *katechon*. The truth of the language of *katechon* is its highlighting that the way rule is carried out today often looks very like a "state of exception" in which everyone assumes that nobody reigns over the world and, within this empty space, power, construed primarily as that of "the" economy, establishes its law (or *nomos*) for human life. The insight into the *katechon*, the suspension of eschatology, allows us to see how the economy as we experience it today is a law (*nomos*) unto itself, ruling over, but not ruled by human agents. There has in fact

---

24. For a dogmatic elaboration of this notion, see Friedrich Mildenberger, *Biblische Dogmatik. Eine biblische Theologie in dogmatischer Perspektive*, 3 vols (Stuttgart: Kohlhammer, 1991–1993).

25. See Zartaloudis, *Giorgio Agamben*, 39–40.

been significant critical discussion of whether, in moments of economic crisis, the law of economics in fact has the power to claim a *political state of exception*, presenting itself as having the legitimate right to govern or even take over the government.[26] In such moments of economic crisis, we are absolutely warranted in asking what the crisis actually is. It is a question that cannot be answered without recourse to the theological meaning of "crisis," as any "crisis" inhabits an undetermined state that may in time be revealed as a moment decay—or of rescue.

When we reflect on the message the Christian tradition might have for the politics and economics of our world, we ought to recall the uniquely critical relation of the Christian *ethos* to our political and economic reality, with its hidden and problematic genealogy. What is clear is that the biblical traditions emphatically contradict the idea of a state of exception in which any government or power claims to have the right to step outside of the responsibility to uphold justice and righteousness. It is the articulateness of this refusal in passages like Psalm 82 that led Martin Buber to describe this Psalm in particular as the psalm for the twentieth century.[27] The ethos called forth in the biblical traditions, in short, positions the ethical question as one of how we live in response to and in accordance with the advent (or *kairos*) of God's *oikonomia* with its telos in bringing human life to fulfillment. This formulation of the ethical question presents us with a reformulated, and highly productive, relation of eschatology and ethics relevant for political as well as economic ethics.

In his *Ethics*, Bonhoeffer articulated in a paradigmatic way how we might approach material questions when starting in this way. Human labor, he suggests, is one of the crucial places to examine to understand the convergence or divergence of human economy in its coexistence with God's *oikonomia*. In his own words,

> The work founded in paradise calls for co-creative human deeds. Through them a world of things and values is created that is destined for the glory and service of Jesus Christ.... Through the divine mandate of work, a world should emerge that – knowingly or unknowingly—expects Christ, is directed toward Christ, is open for Christ, and serves and glorifies Christ. That the descendants of Cain should fulfill this mandate casts a deep shadow over all human work.[28]

For Bonhoeffer, human labor is destined (dedicated) to "glorify" Christ—that is, to enact an *eschatological* task in present Messianic time. This task is not oriented solely to the fulfillment of life as a material entity with material needs. The *telos* of labor is the praxis of coexistence with Christ in a reconciled world. Labor, for Bonhoeffer,

---

26. Ulrich Bröckling, "Human Economy, Human Capital: A Critique of Biopolitical Economy," in *Governmentality: Current Issues and Future Challenges*, ed. Ulrich Bröckling, Susanne Krasmann, and Thomas Lemke (New York: Routledge, 2012), 247–68.

27. Martin Buber, *Right and Wrong: An Interpretation of Some Psalms* (London: SCM Press, 1952), 23–33.

28. DBWE 6, 70, 71. "Instituted": *begründet*.

aims to bring about a different material *and* social world. Labor is a "mandate" because it is an arena in which human beings actively wait for Christ's arrival. This waiting is not empty, nor is it handed over to humans to configure according to reason in the era of the *saeculum*, the time of the suspension of God's fulfillment, Instead, labor is a theological mandate because labor, theologically understood, strives to embrace God's will to reveal in the most concrete terms that it is our world—and no other—that has been reconciled. *This* world has been reconciled, and so a site wherein we may glorify Christ. In labor too human beings can receive the word of the Sermon on the Mount, "Let your light shine before others, so that they may see your good works and give glory to your Father in heaven" (Mt. 5:16).

A vista opens up here into an alternative ethics of labor and economy as a whole. In the time of waiting for the consummation all things, humans have been endowed with "mandates." In distinctions from all anonymous law (*nomos*), the mandates, or commands, are productive *institutions* established by God as context for flourishing human living. They thus suggest fruitful ways forward for the institutional character of economy as a whole.[29] Economic activity is determined by the task of preserving the world in its waiting for Christ. It does not serve a never-ending fulfillment of physical need. The eternal life promised to human beings within God's economy does not culminate in merely endless biological existence but in a definitive coexistence with God—which is already present. This is so, as Jesus teaches in Mt. 6:25–26 because,

> I tell you, do not worry [remain not in fundamental sorrow] about your life, what you will eat or what you will drink, or about your body, what you will wear. Is not life more than food, and the body more than clothing? Look at the birds of the air; they neither sow nor reap nor gather into barns, and yet your heavenly Father feeds them. Are you not of more value than they?

This is the *telos* of economic justice, which is why it is a message that can be proclaimed to the poor without implying any justification of their disenfranchisement from the economic orders that currently exist.

I have suggested that the economic orders in which we live are driven by a basic desire for an endless and in a sense limitless life and its final fulfillment. Agamben's genealogical reconstruction has provided one plausible account of how we have arrived at this understanding of our economic lives. But this status quo, whatever its historical origins, fundamentally contradicts the eschatological and Messianic logic of God's *oikonomia*—and vice versa. God's *oikonomia* flatly contradicts every idea—and practice—of a limitless human economy. It does so because God's *oikonomia* is organized by its telos in living with God. Because it is focused on this coexistence with God, it is indestructibly and without any moments of exception concerned with righteousness—and the political and economic justice that it entails. As we read in the Sermon on the Mount: "Strive first for the kingdom of

---

29. See Chapter 2.

God and his righteousness" (Mt. 6:33). The prophetic insight of the community practicing economic worship is that economics can never be just if it is organized around any hidden force, including desire. Economic activity is only just when pointing to coexistence with God. This is the insight unfolded in the theological tradition of God's twofold governance. God's people are led and "governed" by God through his word. This is not a legitimation of human power, but a mandate for human government and governance, which is constantly actualized and supported by God's word.

This theological positioning of economy follows from an understanding of God's *oikonomia* as it is articulated in the message of Jesus Christ. It will only be sustainable as Christians continually turn to the Word of God, with the practices of conversion and repentance that it entails, in which we are constantly shown—and turned away from—our trusts and reliance on other convictions and desires, especially from the "desire of desire."[30]

Institutional Configurations: Limits of Economy, Limits for Economy

Having laid out the necessary background distinctions, we are more prepared to revisit the question of the limits of economy. The determination of economy as a site where a reconciled world and coexistence with God is *instituted* allows us a new purchase on how to conceive of the limits of economy in a specific sense. Limits are now to be understood as the contours offered in the divine mandate with its own ordering and determination by its *telos*.

There is no shortage of expert discussion today about the limits of economy, its systemic, ecological, and moral limits. These discussions have typically been focused by the problem of gaining a theoretical vantage point on the economy as a whole in order then to propose how the economy so understood might be governed or even fundamentally altered. In these discussions the economy is almost always conceived of as a "system" having a range of describable parameters and yet is not susceptible to truly effective or comprehensive governance. What is probably more important to note, however, is the dependence of all these discussions on the idea that there is some parameter or index that, if it is modified, will affect the whole system in a meaningful way. If, however, we look at the institutional forms that economic processes and practices have taken in the last century we will soon grasp the limits of thinking of economics as a system that can be moved by finding the single right parameter (perhaps interest rate manipulation, for example).[31]

---

30. Bernd Wannenwetsch, "The Desire of Desire: Idolatry in Late Capitalism," in *Idolatry: False Worship in the Bible, Early Judaism and Christianity*, ed. Stephen Barton (London: T&T Clark, 2007), 315–30.

31. See, for example, Elinor Ostrom, *Understanding Institutional Diversity* (Princeton: Princeton University Press, 2009); Francesco Duina, *Institutions and the Economy* (Cambridge: Polity Press, 2011).

The institutional forms taken in modern economies are limited by definition in that they are committed to incommensurable particular tasks, for instance, to provide the opportunity for everybody to earn one's living and at the same time to intensify growth and wealth for investors and also contribute to the appropriate distribution of profits. These incommensurable inner tensions are one of the reasons that ensuring corporate "compliance" is a growth industry, whose increase seems more and more necessary. This growth is significant in revealing that law and moral limits are not really the natural outflowing of economic activity as we have institutionalized it but are imposed on it as external restrictions. What we need to be looking for are institutions that are just and distribute wealth equitably without such constant correction by external regulations.

Following an exhaustive analysis of global businesses, Daron Acemoglu and James A. Robinson have suggested that, historically speaking, the most important factor in whether nations become rich or poor is the extent to which their economic institutions are "extractive" or "inclusive."[32] Inclusive institutional forms even appear to have greater impact on economic development than available resources or environmental conditions. Both authors hesitate to describe the optimal institution outright, preferring instead to suggest incremental improvements. They confidently agree, however, that attention to institutions is decisive for any fundamental and sustained positive economic change.[33] Their way of thinking is very close to what we have been calling an ethics of traditions, which draws attention to the reality that sustainable and just practices are dependent on continuous attention to, and discerning alteration of, ongoing institutionalized practices.

Such thinking about the institutional constitution of economic practice is closely related to the question of how economies might be "governed" at all.[34] As the language of "inclusive institutions" suggests, the institutional character of economic activity hones in on describable "interactive activities" and the rules that shape it between visible and accountable actors on all the different level of economic practice, from the individual entrepreneur to the corporation to the national as a whole. Such investigation is especially invested in fostering transparency in all these institutionally configured economic interactions.

These considerations merge with familiar but typically vague ethical pleas for economic systems to be made more mutual and/or reciprocal—and therefore more likely to flourish in localized economies. Far from being unrealistic, this ambition to give greater economic prominence to local economies has deep roots in institutional arrangements of economic activity that have dominated

---

32. Daron Acemoglu and James A. Robinson, *Why Nations Fail: The Origins of Power, Prosperity and Poverty* (New York: Crown Publishers, 2012).

33. Their procedure is most clearly laid out in their critique of China's developmental model.

34. See, for example, Duina, *Institutions and the Economy*.

the Christian theological tradition of thinking on economic questions.[35] Biblical sentiments like that expressed in Psalm 82—which criticizes unjust rulers who do not recognize the other and are not aware of their needs—have contributed to this theological background and the corresponding notion of justice behind the calls for a more localized institutionalization of economic activity. To be just means to be tangibly aware of the other and to meet his *particular* needs, a need which by definition is not grasped by any universal or general norm. Seen in this way, such a theological constitution may be deployed through reflection on the theological tradition of *oikonomia* in which *oikos* refers to "institution" and by extension to a reliable coexistence of people. The analysis of Acemoglu and Robinson shows that where there is an identifiable parameter that can serve as the focal point for change, there is a reasonable hope for a positive wider effect on economy. From a theological perspective, we might say that an *established* hope is what counts—an established hope that is concrete and practical enough to mount an explicit resistance to whatever forces are currently driving the inevitable, and inevitably constant, interventions in the institutional configurations of economic practice.

Civil Economy and the Relative Merits of Business Ethics Approaches

Philip Blond has observed that economy in this limited sense appears for the first time as one limited field of activity among others rather than an all determining reality. This more modest account of economic practice is one that is determined by specific tasks focused on tangible parameters, such as "institutions" or "contracts," Blond adds. This more limited definition of economics, as a theory, has been called "civil economy."[36]

From such an economic viewpoint, Blond argues, "it appears more realistic to try and achieve a moral market than to limit an amoral market by a more bureaucratic and interventionist state. It is also a far higher ethical aspiration."[37] He goes on to ask:

> Can we not ensure a basic, just distribution at the level of the economy, thereby minimizing the need for political redistribution in order to correct economic injustices? This is all the more desirable because redistribution is necessarily always limited and unstable and involves the additional coercion of the state. Besides, because the market logic seeks always to expand its scope, redistribution is a bit like trying to push back the tide with a broom.[38]

---

35. Philip Blond, "There Is No Wealth but Life," in *Crisis and Recovery: Ethics, Economics and Justice*, ed. Rowan Williams and Larry Elliott (London: Palgrave Macmillan, 2010), 77–99.
36. For an elaboration of this concept, see Bruni and Zamagni, *Civil Economy*.
37. Blond, "There Is No Wealth but Life," 88.
38. Blond, "There Is No Wealth but Life," 88.

Later he adds,

> Through civil enterprises, a new type of market regulation becomes possible via shared ethos rather than state imposition. This can come into effect by example and influence—when the ethical firms turn out to be more economically successful than nonethical firms. We need to stop seeing all contracts as amoral and grounded in mutual egoism; once this notion is overthrown, there will be less inclination to form monopolies. This is already true at a local level in many parts of Europe, because small and medium sized local firms are often content with sufficient profits and a relationship of reciprocity with their suppliers and consumers.[39]

This general perspective on a civil society and the moral parameters it espouses (like the local dimension of mutuality and reciprocity) is in fact being elaborated in innumerable discourses and concepts that can be understood as not only in accordance with a theological understanding of economy but one of the most suggestive avenues that might be implemented on the basis of a theological view of God's *oikonomia*.

Having reached this point, it is relatively straightforward to elaborate and more fully unfold the implications of the lines of approach already developed by showing how various concepts of economic ethics and business ethics do very much fit into an analysis focused on institutions, if only minimally modified. The concept of "governance ethics"[40] for business is one such promising literature amenable to a theological reading, given that in it businesses are taken to be institutional forms in which dimensions of cooperation, communication, and mutuality are all important. Other similarly promising ways of talking about economic ethics can be found in literatures around topics like "corporate citizenship" and "corporate social responsibility."

In all these conceptions of ethics we find the notion of an *ethos* that insists on *visibility*, performance, and accountability as a prominent emphasis.[41] It is an *ethos* in marked contrast with approaches that emphasize governance by anonymous laws and is different again from those which seek more effective regimes of external regulation. Conceptions of business ethics that are focused on virtue ethics also lead in similar directions as long as the account of virtue offered is compatible with the theological localization of economy within its limits.

All these different approaches to business ethics share an interest in the integration of the human *ethos* and economic activity. Such integration is one that

---

39. Ibid., 90.

40. See, for example, *Behavioral Business Ethics: Psychologie, Neuroökonomik und Governanceethik*, ed. Josef Wieland (Marburg: Metropolis-Verlag, 2010).

41. Richard Higginson presents an equivalent and promising theological conception, *Faith, Hope and the Global Economy: A Power for Good* (Nottingham: Inter-Varsity Press, 2012).

should not be assumed to be present *a priori*, but I have tried to indicate why it may be discerned in these different literatures with some critical reflection—and illuminated by the theological background I have described earlier with its critical realism based on a grounded hope. The existence of any *ethos* presupposes its realization in the patterns taken by the lives of living people. This is why it will always remain decisive how people are guided and governed, and how they behave, given the institutionally shaped contours and conditions provided to them by the economic institutions in which they must live.

Chapter 6

ADOPTION

A Theological Account of Political Responsibility to Entrusted Lives

Contemporary political culture has a decided tendency to understand children primarily as "our future." It is a view that permeates the way the state understands the importance of governing the oversight of families, of reproductive policies, and also of fostering and adoption policy. Individuals also often understand the importance of children in a not dissimilar way, as necessary to continue one's family name or line. These views are also ones that are taken up by Christians and church governing bodies, as I discovered while on a committee tasked with preparing a church statement on the importance of children for the German Lutheran Church some years ago. Even though many in our church felt the need to speak into the public debates on declining German birthrates in order to encourage people to consider having children, we discovered it was extremely difficult for this working group to become clear about what the church's message was supposed to be.

Even a cursory knowledge of the biblical and Christian traditions, however, immediately reveals that thinking of children as "our future" fails to articulate essential aspects of those traditions' assumptions about the role and vocation of children within the people of God. Delving into these traditions highlights the ways in which asking about children theologically leads quickly from legal and moral questions into the whole of the biblical message about God's story with his human beings, as we may find summarized in Ps. 78:5-8 (KJV):

> For he established a testimony in Jacob,
>   and appointed a law in Israel,
> which he commanded our fathers,
>   that they should make them known to their children:
> That the generation to come might know them,
>   even the children which should be born;

who should arise and declare them to their children:
> That they might set their hope in God,
and not forget the works of God,
> but keep his commandments:
And might not be as their fathers,
> a stubborn and rebellious generation;
a generation that set not their heart aright,
> and whose spirit was not steadfast with God.

Children are depicted here not as "our future," but as participants in God's story to which others must witness in order to encourage them "to set their hope in God, and not forget the works of God." The premise of the Psalm's approach to children is that they are part of the people tasked with carrying on God's story with the world, which should be remembered and continued by all children to come. All questions about the vocation of children orbits around the responsibility to uphold the continuous praxis of "testimony" from generation to generation. The testimony established by God is the basic ground on which all human welcoming of children must rest according to scripture—there is no other purpose or telos. This biblical insight offers a significant place to begin to think theologically about what the church might have to say to a world struggling to find good reasons to have children, and so about how the church might think about the practice and legal regulation of adoption today. The biblical traditions reveal children as a divine announcement of promise, and this chapter, after tracing this biblical thread, then moves to indicate how this biblical promise can orient political activity and policymaking in contemporary political communities.

Toward a Positive Ethos of Adoption

One approach to the practices and institutions of adoption frames it as a matter of Christian "morality."[1] In this literature adoption is clearly related to the needs, interests and rights of children and is not subordinated to other purposes, interests, and demands, not even parental hopes and wishes surrounding procreation. Instead, as Brent Waters puts it, the intent is

> to illustrate the need for religious, moral, and legal forms of discourse that portray adoption as an act grounded primarily, though certainly not exclusively, in charity rather than reproduction. The fact that adoption is driven by a complex set of motives is readily granted; I am not arguing that only saints should be eligible to adopt. But there should be a public perception that the

---

1. See *The Morality of Adoption: Social-Psychological, Theological, and Legal Perspectives*, ed. Timothy P. Jackson (Grand Rapids: Eerdmans, 2005).

actual performance of adoption is a uniquely moral act that is sanctioned by both religious conviction and legal approbation.[2]

Waters's account highlights the importance of discussions about the morality and legal institutions surrounding adoption attending closely to questions like: Who should be considered suitable to adopt, and on what conditions? What is the role of government in legitimating practices of adoption? How should the prospective adoptive parent's perspectives, gifts, duties, abilities, sources, and resources to adopt be weighted in relation to the needs and rights of children to be adopted by approved parents? Many theologically significant insights and distinctions emerge from the Christians ethics discourse that seriously engages such questions,[3] which is immensely helpful in critically sifting the wide range of positions and interests with which the marketplace of adoption is awash. This Christian ethics discourse might fruitfully be considered an expression of public conscientiousness about children taking linguistic form.

This literature often approaches the morality of adoption by way of the Kantian categorical imperative that every human being deserves to be treated as an end in themselves, and whose interests must not be subordinated to the aims or interests of others.[4] The most familiar move here is to translate Kant's negative moral injunction into a positive ethos in which children's differentiated spectrum of needs, interests and (human) rights can be elaborated that correspond to responsibilities of parents and so provide an agenda by which to formulate institutional procedures for adoption. In many cases this Kantian-based formulation will make allowances for "religiously" grounded considerations and motives. Many of the authors contributing to discussions about adoption from within Christian ethics discourse assume that their basic orientation is derived from Christian traditions, even if their grounding Christian ideas or sensibilities are supplemented by drawing on various philosophical and sociological insights into parenthood, childhood, education, and identity. Many aspects within this still developing framework of an "ethics of adoption" or an "ethos of adoption" remain still to be developed, given the many aspects of the discussion which remain controversial. More importantly, the discussion of adoption is one that goes much deeper than the mere regulation of adoption practices in society: it is yet another domain in which these pragmatic and moral questions are only the surface appearance of the more fundamental task that I have highlighted in this volume, to understand and deal discerningly with the *conditio humana*. We touch on these deeper theological issues when we ask, for instance, whether or not it should matter for human existence to have some

---

2. Brent Waters, *The Family in Christian Social and Political Thought* (Oxford: Oxford University Press 2007), 50.

3. See especially, Amy Laura Hall, *Conceiving Parenthood: American Protestantism and the Spirit of Reproduction* (Grand Rapids: Eerdmans, 2008).

4. Immanuel Kant, *Grounding for the Metaphysics of Morals*, translated by James W. Ellington, 3rd edn. (Indianapolis: Hackett, 1993 [1785]), 30.

contact with or knowledge of "birth parents." To ask this question is another way to probe in a concrete form the question of whether human "identity" should be seen as related in any way to someone's "natural" origin.[5]

An Evangelical Message?

Within this differentiated and still developing discourse my own interest is in the *message* of adoption, that is, in the "evangelical" message, the good news that is announced in the practice. Such an interest aims neither to meet the familiar problem that contemporary society seems to lack motivating reasons to seek adoption nor to offer more stable conceptual foundations for ethical deliberation about adoption. I also do not aim to develop a more effective way of morally legitimating current adoption practice. Instead, I want to ask which aspects of, and perspectives on, our human existence and condition are disclosed in the practice of adoption. I am asking about the sense in which adoption can be considered a gift to human beings in offering particular moments in which our human condition is exposed to view and confirmed so that we understand better who we are and what belongs to us. To ask after the gift in adoption practice is by no means a suppression of the manifold experiences of suffering that attend it. On the contrary, asking about the gift-nature of adoption may particularly open our eyes to the genuine suffering that might attend the loss of "natural parents," or the sorrows and responsibilities that arise in practices of foster parenting. Yet it is not always clear what this suffering is actually about, leaving us unclear what a consoling message to those who suffer in such contexts could be. I am not, of course, presenting "consolation" and "comfort" as alternatives to real help and care. Rather, consolation and comfort are the fundament of care in a theological account of adoption, the medium in which care finds its orientation. In such an insight we can already hear a promising hint that understanding God's care and consolation in the domain of adoption may even reveal in an especially potent way the core meaning of all parenthood and childhood as a divinely gifted relation.

Hence the question: What is the divine message that not only provokes human practices of adoption but can bear them through trials? What "promise" impels human adoptive activity? Such questions immediately imply another: What is the promise given to parents and children, for suffering children and for suffering parents—and who is authorized, destined or asked to convey that promise to children, to witness to it and to stand up for it?[6]

---

5. See also Karin Ulrich-Eschmann, "The Importance of Knowing Where You Come From," in *A Graceful Embrace: Theological Reflections on Adopting Children*, ed. John Swinton and Brian Brock (Leiden: Brill, 2018), 107–18. For the discussion in Germany, see *Adoptierte suchen ihre Herkunft*, ed. Regula Schmidt-Bott, Transparent 16 (Göttingen: Vandenhoeck & Ruprecht, 1995).

6. This formulation is indebted to the treatment of Karl Barth in CD III.4, §54, 277f.

Children and Human Rights

Recent treatments of "the child in the Bible"[7] and "the vocation of the child"[8] have offered important insights into the preeminent position children have in the biblical and (to a certain extent) in theological traditions. What the biblical and theological traditions do not include is the claim that children are someone's "future," nor do they present children as the guarantee that a family will have a future. These treatments also suggest that the language of human rights and dignity cannot encompass all the morally relevant aspects of the position occupied by a child within the human family.

What this literature does highlight is the focusing of the biblical narratives on the needs of "orphans" to receive justice and "just judgment" (*mishpat*). Thus, in Psalm 82, we read about God's judgment on unjust "powers" who draw God's ire for their manifest injustice toward orphans and widows. Justice for orphans and toward widows emerges as a fundamental ethical demand throughout the biblical texts. We can even say that this form of justice is the paradigmatic case by which the justice or injustice of human judgment is revealed. Justice for orphans and widows plays this central role as a heuristic for judging all authorities and acts of judgment because of its focus on human beings who are totally dependent. Orphans and widows need to be able to rely on something more than the private virtues of other individuals and so their sheer existence exposes the necessity of a society to foster just conditions and to build institutions that can support justice. Here too we meet the question of what the promise might be that can bear this much needed justice for orphans. Is there a promise that can be detected within the command to do justice to orphans (Isa. 1:17)?

In the biblical context, to "give justice"[9] (*mishpat*) means to be faithful and loyal to a relevant relation and community.[10] Orphans are unquestionably members of the community. There is no question of their needing to become a member or to need acknowledgment as an equal member. Orphans, like widows, belong self-evidently to the political community, the community of God's people. "To give justice" means to respond to this reality. The biblical traditions therefore suggest that the most threatening danger to widows and orphans is that they will be neglected, oppressed, and treated unjustly, so—pivotally—be deprived of their entitled inheritance. Though this emphasis on inheritance may strike us today as counterintuitive, biblical scholars such as Walter Brueggemann have confirmed

---

7. *The Child in Christian Thought*, ed. Marcia J. Bunge (Grand Rapids: Eerdmans, 2001).
8. *The Vocation of the Child*, ed. Patrick McKinley Brennan (Grand Rapids: Eerdmans, 2008).
9. The NRSV translates: "Give justice."
10. Gerhard von Rad, *Old Testament Theology*, vol. 1, *The Theology of Israel's Historical Traditions* (London: SCM Press, 1975), 371-5.

that the adoption of orphans was primarily understood in the biblical traditions as a recognition of their inheritance and in this way protecting their security.[11]

What all these traditions assume is that it is fatal to justice when doubts are allowed to emerge about whether or not an individual belongs to the community of rights. This ineradicable belonging is the fundamental moral substrate of life for everyone living with Israel, including the stranger (Deut. 24:21; 26:12). It is this given form of political coexistence that is mediated and realized in the act of specific Israelites "giving justice" (*mishpat*). It is important to notice that this activity of serving justice is not construed as flowing from the agent's personal virtues. Nor is this active doing of justice toward orphans considered an act of hospitality since it is not defined by the virtues of the one doing the act, but as a human response to a self-evident state of affairs, namely, the need of the orphan as a member of the community.[12] These considerations suggest that in this biblical emphasis on "doing justice" we meet a fundamental message of the whole biblical tradition. It is a message that concerns the indispensable institutional medium of a community which sustains and shapes a community's ongoing practices of doing justice.[13] If this medium is destroyed (Ps. 82) God pledges God's own honor on reestablishing it. "Father of orphans and protector of widows is God in his holy habitation" (Ps. 68:6, NRSV).

There are many ways of recognizing this divine reality by creating and supporting institutional forms in given communities, which includes particular adoptive practices. What this approach absolutely rejects is any talk of "displaced persons." Theologically understood, the doing of justice is never positioned by the grammar of inclusion and exclusion. It is exclusively linked with the grammar of acceptance and rejection. In the biblical tradition orphans are understood as a reminder that every human being belongs *a priori* to a community constituted by rights and maintained by justice that protect it from being thrown back onto mere "natural" or "biotic" status (the status of a *homo sacer*). Theologically speaking "community" is not a "natural" given reality (in the sense of a "nation") but a bequeathed and discovered common ground of coexistence that has been recognized in the formation of institutions.

It was Hannah Arendt who developed this logic into a rights formulation by asserting that there is only one single indispensable human right: the right to have rights, to be part of a constitutional community, and not to be reduced to a bare human being.[14] On her view—derived from the biblical logic—to be an orphan by definition includes having a legally defined position within the community, to

---

11. See Walter Brueggemann, "Vulnerable Children, Divine Passion, and Human Obligation," in *The Child in Christian Thought*, ed. Bunge, 399–422.

12. See for the meaning of "hospitality" in the Jewish tradition: Jacques Derrida, *Adieu to Emmanuel Lévinas* (Stanford: Stanford University Press, 1999).

13. See Chapter 3.

14. Hannah Arendt, "The Perplexities of the Rights of Man," in *The Origins of Totalitarianism* (London: Allen & Unwin, 1958/1961), 290–302.

already have a relation to others mediated by rights. Arendt is picking up on the axiomatic status of the biblical traditions' rejection of all formulas that justify there being people without any legal status in any community. It is this logic that makes the rights and practices of offering asylum in the biblical traditions intelligible.[15]

It is in bringing the reality of inalienable political belonging to the surface that orphans remind us of a fundamental presupposition of human existence.[16] This makes it significant that "adoption" (or, as we will soon discuss, its equivalents in the biblical tradition) serves the end of preserving the inheritance (and so security) of those children who have lost their parents. This Old Testament background sheds light on the reasons why God is spoken of in the New Testament as one who understands all human beings as His children (Greek: "*huiothesia*"). God is one who is intensely concerned with preserving the believer's inheritance in relation to the community of God's people: "The Spirit Himself bears witness with our spirit that we are children of God, and if children, then heirs - heirs of God and joint *heirs* with Christ, if indeed we suffer with Him, that we may also be glorified together" (Rom. 8:17, NKJV; see also: Eph. 1:11-14; Gal. 3:15-18; 4:4-6). It is because human beings participate in God's *huiothesia*—because they are heirs—that the continuation of God's ongoing story is ensured. The concern of *huiothesia* is thus in the first and most basic instance the participation of the believer in the heritage to which God has given testimony.

In other words, the heritage that is the promise of human life is grounded in the common story that all human beings share with Israel. The main theological task is to understand how this heritage is mediated by the Torah, which is given in the first place to Israel to organize this particular relation between God and His elected people Israel. This is to understand the Torah not as "Law" (*Nomos*), but as the divinely given context in which the coexistence of God and Israel takes place.[17] *Huiothesia*, then, indicates how this wonderful relation is inherited, according to God's will.

The story of God's mission in Jesus Christ is the dramatic story of the extension of God's inheritance to all the nations, and the notion of *huiothesia* encapsulates the dramatic nature of this extension. *Huiothesia* indicates that the inheritance of a privileged status is mediated by God's first-born child, Jesus Christ. In him there is established a way of *huiothesia* for all human beings by adoption (Eph. 1:5): "He destined us for adoption as his children through Jesus Christ, according to the good pleasure of his will." If Jesus Christ is the name of the dramatic inclusion of gentiles in Israel's inheritance, we cannot immediately translate the Greek *huiothesia* (υἱοθεσία) as "adoption." Because the referent of this term is ultimately

---

15. For the Jewish tradition on these themes as represented by Emmanuel Lévinas, see Derrida, *Adieu to Emmanuel Lévinas*.

16. This presupposition is related theologically to a modern theology of rights in texts like Karl Barth, "Church and State," in Karl Barth, *Community, State, and Church*, ed. Will Herberg (Gloucester: Peter Smith, 1968).

17. My understanding of law is presented in Chapter 4.

the heritage that is the continuation of the children of Israel, it cannot be severed from the question of how God's story will be continued with them. Christian uses of the language of adoption cannot, and must not, be abstracted from the semantic entanglement of this New Testament usage with the whole biblical witness to God's relation to his people as a "family" and a "household."[18]

Children: God's Heritage

I understand this divinely established status for all human beings within God's story with His people to encapsulate what I have called the *conditio humana*—the basic reality of the human. The biblical story of God's relation to a community, and to practices of justice, suggests a logic that must not be subverted by the introduction of a logic of inclusion or exclusion. Taking this seriously is to render the question of how to understand children and the practices of adoption thus: In what sense do children encounter their "parents" within a specific promise? In putting the question this way, we see that it is a formulation that can be considered paradigmatic for every human being. The promise that undergirds the parent-child encounter is one uttered by God, and which confirms and fulfills the *conditio humana* within God's real, explicit story with His people and all human beings.

To affirm that it is in the quotidian encounter of a child with a parent that the redeemed shape of human life can be discovered within God's promises generates a new set of questions. These heuristic questions differ in significant ways from the questions about responsible oversight of contemporary adoptive practice that we have seen to be characteristic of mainstream approaches in Christian ethics. I have suggested that we ask: What is the promise given to children—and given together with children? What is their vocation or dedication, and how may parents correspond or respond to that promise? In what way does their response establish them as parents? To put the question this way is not to introduce by the back door the much more common question of what parents may be capable of confidently or faithfully pledging to a child. Every adoptive act must be understood as a promise to the child within the logic of God's promise to the child as a procreative act (if we do not reduce procreation to mere reproduction).[19] Who, and in what respect is someone entitled, authorized, or blessed to follow that promise? If an adult's pledge to faithfully embrace a child were grounded in the parent's own confidence, it would only be as secure as their own steadfastness. Children would be hostage to the insecure vagaries of their parent's continued willing. Far more promising is the biblical suggestion that the parent's promise to a child can only be meaningfully

---

18. For a broader exploration, see Trevor J. Burke, *Adopted into God's Family: Exploring a Pauline Metaphor*, New Studies in Biblical Theology 22 (Downers Grove: InterVarsity Press, 2006).

19. Jana Bennett, *Water Is Thicker than Blood: An Augustinian Theology of Marriage and Singleness* (Oxford: Oxford University Press, 2008), chs. 5–6.

rooted and grounded in a promise given to them. Both children and parents can then understood the promise of parents to be faithful to children as a response to what has been divinely given—or entrusted—to parents.

To formulate the parent-child relationship in these terms touches on the question of the sense in which children are in the first instance *God's* "heritage," as they are presented, for instance, in Ps. 127:3 ("Sons are indeed a heritage from the Lord").[20] It also raises further questions about how to read the command of Gen. 1:28, to "be fruitful and multiply." What is the promise here? It is clearly no guarantee of the "future" of mankind, nor is it a (new) categorical imperative as thinkers like Hans Jonas have proposed, "there shall be a mankind."[21] What we have already established is that this command too must be part of human life as a context of communal living, within which children play a specific and indispensable role.

Post Christum: The Continuing Story and the New Beginning

Because God's story has been fulfilled, children are destined both to participate in as well as give testimony to the truth of this story. In the volume on ethics in *Church Dogmatics* vol. III, Karl Barth elaborated an account of the parent-child relation rooted in God's story with His people and all creatures as fulfilled in Jesus Christ. The fulfillment of God's story with the created world in Christ means that the basic requirement of human life has been fulfilled: human beings will no longer be forced to live in separation from God's faithfulness, so losing the freedom of God's creatures and children to experience God's gracious gifts.

In starting from God's fulfillment rather than a view that springs from fear about the future of humanity Barth nevertheless meets the question raised thinkers who focus on fear for humanity like Hans Jonas: "Why children?" Before Christ this was a question that could not be meaningfully raised, and after Christ, to ask it is to point to an answer already given. After Christ children remain most welcome gracious gifts of God. There is, notes Barth, one more important implication of this fulfillment.

> In the sphere of the New Testament message there is no necessity, no general command, to continue the human race as such and therefore to procreate children. . . . Post Christum natum there can be no question of a divine law in virtue of which all these things must necessarily take place. On the contrary, it is one of the consolations of the coming kingdom and expiring time that this

---

20. In the Hebrew text we find "Sons." Luther translates "children," and so does the King James Version. For Calvin's understanding, see Barbara Pitkin, "The Heritage of the Lord: Children in the Theology of John Calvin," in *The Child in Christian Thought*, ed. Bunge, 160-93.

21. Hans Jonas, *The Imperative of Responsibility: In Search of an Ethics for the Technological Age* (Chicago: University of Chicago Press, 1984).

anxiety about posterity, that the burden of the postulate that we should and must bear children . . . is removed from us all by the fact that the Son on whose birth alone everything seriously and ultimately depended has now been born and has now become our Brother. . . . Parenthood is now only to be understood as a free and in some sense optional gift of the goodness of God. It certainly cannot be a fault to be without children.[22]

Martin Buber raises a similar point when discussing education, and in a way that exposes an important tension with Barth's presentation. Buber insists that there is divine grace in the reality that the human race is beginning every hour in the birth of each child.

> In every hour the human race begins. We forget this too easily in face of the massive fact of past life, of so-called world-history, of the fact that each child is born with a given disposition of "world-historical" origin, that is, inherited from the riches of the whole human race, and that he is born into a given situation of "world-historical" origin, that is, produced from the riches of the world's events. . . . in spite of everything, in this as in every hour, what has not been invades the structure of what is . . . —a creative event if ever there was one, newness rising up, primal potential might. This potentiality, streaming unconquered, however, much of it is squandered, is the reality *child*: this phenomenon of uniqueness, is more than just begetting and birth, this grace of beginning again and ever again.

> What greater care could we cherish or discuss than that this grace may not henceforth be squandered as before, that the might of newness may be preserved for renewal? Future history is not inscribed already by the pen of a causal law on a roll which merely awaits unrolling; its characters are stamped by the unforeseeable decisions of future generations. The part to be played in this by everyone alive to-day, by every adolescent and child, is immeasurable, and immeasurable is our part if we are educators. The deeds of the generations now approaching can illumine the grey face of the human world or plunge it in darkness . . . —how much it can do this cannot be guessed, but only learned in action.[23]

Barth insists that God's story is fulfilled, that beyond Christ's coming there is no need to hope any longer for new conditions for human life. Yet Christians nevertheless must also affirm with Buber that every child nevertheless brings a new beginning within that new story. The telos of that story has been fulfilled, but every child must be given the opportunity to experience this story for themselves, to be recipients of faithful people's witness to it, so that she or he might discover

---

22. Barth, *CD* III/4, 266.
23. Martin Buber, *Between Man and Man*, trans. Ronald Gregor-Smith (New York: Routledge, 2002), 98-9, emphasis in the original.

their own specific role in this story and to become, in turn, witnesses to the generations to come.

Bringing Barth and Buber together thus reveals the "mandate" of teaching and education. Education cannot be a process of entrapping the new human being in the status quo, quashing their newness by forcing them to support and shore up the forms of living that precede them and into which they are born. Instead, after Christ, every child is offered the opportunity to be part of the "new creation," presented with the opportunity to experience the new creation in Christ for themselves. In Christ—and therefore in our educational efforts—they are not doomed to confirm the old reality with all its ways of proceeding and modes of progress. Children's position in the world of adults is thus that of a carrier of the freedom of a new beginning. For an adult to receive a child cannot, therefore, be a matter of extending one's own story. Properly understood, it is an active affirmation of God's new beginning within the continuity of His story with us human beings. These considerations helpfully clarify what Jesus means when he promises, "Let the little children come to Me, and do not forbid them; for of such is the kingdom of God. Assuredly, I say to you, whoever does not receive the kingdom of God as a little child will by no means enter it" (Mk. 10:14-15, NKJV).

To witness to the new creation thus entails embracing as a work of God the new beginning that is intrinsic to every birth when understood according to God's story and His coming kingdom. Because children are destined to be heirs and witnesses of God's work (Psalm 8), they present us with paradigmatic exemplifications of creaturely existence. Their existence is an anticipation of the encounter that is promised to them through God's work and story with them. It is this promised fulfillment in Jesus Christ that demands the question "Why children?" not be answered by appealing to our own desire for offspring. The promise of the new creation intrinsic to God's story with human beings includes an answer to the "why" at the root of the continuing existence of children. On what other basis could we explain to our children why they are born? They are God's heritage. The wider story of this heritage concerns God and His honor, which is secured in the course of God's multigenerational continuation of God's story with God's people. It was out of commitment to continuing this story that God sent His Son, who was both Jewish-born and at once bound to all human beings. In Jesus Christ, God makes all human beings heirs of God's story with His people.

When we approach the phenomenon of the child from the priority of the divine adoption, we are enlightened about what it means to call someone a parent in its true theological meaning, in the same way that we might call some people prophets, apostles, and witnesses. Speaking about "parents" is in reality to point to two entities who are together embracing a new beginning—on one side a community with an institutionally elaborated common life, and an "individual," the singular human existence. Enclosed within this theological grounding we discover the fundamental meaning of parenthood. Parenthood is a vocation, which falls to birth parents as well as other configurations of parenting.

Every child comes into existence as and with a new beginning. Along with this new beginning they also are born into a context, with a body. In this sense birthparents are a part of every human life. Precisely because each child begins a new story, however, a child's story with their birth parents may not be the only one that will determine their story. To be true to the vocational reality of parenthood—whether we are speaking about parents by birth or adoption—we must allow space for God's very own story with the child. From a theological perspective, then, the basic question underlying all practical questions about adoption is who will take up, or who will be called to take up, the divine heritage that appears in every human child. A theological perspective is opening up here that includes the contributions and contribution between birthparents and other parents. Such forms of cooperation in parenting may be realized in some forms of adoption, perhaps in the practices of hospitals who facilitate adoptions in order to avoid abortions. Within a theological perspective such cooperation, in which birth parents give up a child, may be rightly understood as an enacted recognition that God has his very own story with every child given by Him.

God's Heritage: An Eschatological Reality and Our Response

The human longing for children is rooted in a range of dispositions, each of which throws up its own answers to the question "Why children?" The rich and contradictory diversity of these several answers indicates why no abstract realm of philosophical or theological speculation can ever answer this question uninterested in the human desires, hopes, and self-understandings that permeate discussions of childbearing and adoption. Which of these desires is to be embraced and which should be resisted will need a word from outside them, such as the promising testimony of Psalm 78 with which this chapter opened. The core of this biblical promise is that children are *God's* heritage, as Psalm 127 stresses and as we have seen Barth explicate. God molds each child in the womb (Psalm 139) and God promises children, the biblical narratives tell us, for the sake of His ongoing story with His people—paradigmatically in God's committing His son to Mary. This is a paradigmatic handing over of a child if we read Ps. 127:3 ("Sons are indeed a heritage from the Lord") as a proto-evangelion—a proclamation of "Jesus" as "the child" entrusted to Mary, as the composer Claudio Monteverdi suggested in weaving these two passages together in his "Vespers for the Blessed Virgin" of 1610.

When we come face to face with the child as such an "encountering reality" (as Buber called it) and are asked how we will respond to it or understand it—only then and in this sense are we prepared to ask: "Why these children?" and "For what purpose is this wonderful heritage entrusted to us?" What then is our mandate as we respond to this reality? Because God's story is already fulfilled in Jesus Christ, the appearance of children does not present an imperative for some adult to fill up an empty "not yet." At the same time there remains a "not yet" presented in the encountering reality that is the child, and this "not yet" is a positive one. In Chapter 1 I suggested that Christian eschatology does not teach Christians to persevere while awaiting Christ's (delayed) second coming. A Messianic eschatology allows us to perceive the new beginning that comes with a child as a marvelous site of living anticipation of concrete continuation of God's story of reconciliation.

God's reconciliation with human beings within their earthly and worldly life will appear for every human being and become abundantly real in every human life. It becomes real for the sake of God's glory on earth, confirming His story with his people as His very own story. Every child is a standing invitation and enacted confirmation of this story. This claim is not presented as an inevitability, but as an expression of faith in the inexhaustibility of the concrete content God has in store for all human beings called to be His people, as we read in Romans 12—the good, the pleasant, and the fulfilled are prepared for everyone. God's will is that we human beings should be given time to hear this promise, to try it out—and so to encounter God's fulfilled Messianic time. This also implies the necessity of witness; where people are not in the place to look for this Messianic appearance, they should be helped and supported by others. The need for witnesses is an expression of the tension between the time of God's fulfilled story and the necessity that God must testify to, and so reveal, that story to those who do not hear or receive it. That we too are those who do not yet hear it is also attested by the need for our repentant engagement in the open-ended progress of that story as it unfolds in our own places and times.[24]

God gives us the space and time to respond to that promising heritage: the present time of waiting for the coming Christ. We can therefore say that children are an eschatological reality. With them comes a task, a mandate, to respond faithfully. This is the paradigmatic task in which we can see what it means, practically, to receive God's heritage. This need to receive the heritage presented to us is constitutive of our "human condition." In abstraction from this divine offer, we would be forced to affirm that there is no "human condition" because there are no indisputable grounds on which to establish who the "human" might be who could be addressed as such. The promise of children *as a divine heritage* is in this way to be understood as establishing the conditions by which humanity might be affirmed: "humanity" is what we can call those creatures whom God has drawn into his explicit story. These creatures remain in God's story not because they preserve some heritage of norms or ideals that they must fulfill if they are not to slip back into being sub- or in-human. The objective reality of their remaining human is that they are in fact given children in whom this divine-human story will be continued. The only appropriate response to that given reality is to recognize it as a mandate laid on us all. It is a mandate grounded not in a moral code, but which presents itself with the arrival of concrete children, understood as representatives of God's heritage. With what, then, is this mandate concerned, specifically?

---

24. See especially Hall, *Conceiving Parenthood*, 398–400.

6. Adoption

The Promising Task of Raising Children

Despite my earlier discussion, Barth's discussion of parents and children does not neglect the topic of raising and educating children. His treatment of this topic parallels my own in emphasizing that the parent's responsibility is to work toward each child having the opportunity to encounter the gracious God. Parents' mandate is to facilitate this encounter.[25] They do so by acting in a way that lets God's work in their children's lives become apparent to them. The aim of parental responsibility, Barth writes, is to

> give their children the opportunity to encounter the God who is present, operative and revealed in Jesus Christ, to know Him and to learn to love and fear Him. The greatest and smallest things, the most serious and the most trivial, which can happen between parents and children, can become for parents an occasion to present to their children this opportunity. No one else has so many manifold and intimate occasions over what is normally so long and continuous a stretch of time to put this opportunity before another human being as do parents in relation to their children. And no one again has these occasions at a period which is so formative and usually so decisive and fundamental. This time and its opportunities must not be missed.[26]

Barth's insight is that children present in a special way a form of life ready to experience and encounter God's work. In this sense all human beings are destined to be "children of God," not per se, but through God's calling each into His story and His further life with Him. God's children are called to "have a part in the history in which God is their partner und they are his partners."[27]

The mandate of parents finds its focus as it responds to the essential contours of this form of life. Parents will never be able to produce the divine encounter for a child. On the contrary, their task is to get out of the way, to act in a way that God's calling, his very own creativity and cooperation, can be experienced by children and entrusted to them so that they may be claimed by that divine determination. All their actions enact the commitment of the child "to the hand of the God from whom they have received him, to the Holy Spirit of God who alone is able to make their weak testimony efficacious to him and to ward off the influence of evil spirits, some of which may well be parental in origin." In the last resort, Barth concludes, the best a parent can do for a child is to "direct their conduct in harmony with the fact, that the Holy Spirit is the true Author of the good to which they as men can only direct their children."[28]

---

25. On this point, see also Pitkin, "The Heritage of the Lord," esp. 193.
26. Barth, *CD* III.4, 283.
27. Barth, *The Christian Life*, 104. See John Webster, *Barth's Ethics of Reconciliation* (Cambridge: Cambridge University Press, 1995), 116–73.
28. Barth, *CD* III/4, 284–5.

Unfolding Creaturely Life as Encountering God's Work within His Story

Creaturely life within God's story must always be approached and understood according to the positive "not yet" that is bestowed in God's presence. There is no objective standpoint from which human beings' response to this presence can be explained. It is something which must be experienced from within, and to which those who have become involved in life with God witness. The biblical texts are organized by the stories told by the canonical witness to such a life which echo through the stories believers tell today. All these stories orbit around the trust in God that Jesus succinctly encapsulates in the Sermon on the Mount.

> Therefore, I tell you, do not worry about your life, what you will eat or what you will drink, or about your body, what you will wear. Is not life more than food, and the body more than clothing? . . . But strive first for the kingdom of God and his righteousness, and all these things will be given to you as well. (Mt. 6:25, 33)

This is how creaturely life looks when understood within God's story as it appears in the light thrown on it by the coming kingdom. This is the way of life that is appropriate for God's people, and which should therefore be paradigmatic for their children. Within the promising mandate of raising children, and within the eschatological reality that children are, every parent is called to become childlike, allowing a new beginning for witness to be born in them; a new story to be lived out by concretely probing, and verifying, the veracity of God's promise.

The act of adopting a child is an act of sharing the mundane activities of creaturely life as activities within God's story. Thus life together becomes a joint participation in that eschatological reality. In the practice of adoption one of the deep continuities of God's story with creatures rises to the surface: the continuity constituted by God's graceful commitment to redemptive new beginnings. One of many biblical examples of a redemptive new beginning is the adoption of Moses by the daughter of Pharaoh. In the birth of this child is a new beginning for Israel, a breaking of the historical patterns expected by Pharaoh, and so the emergence of a Messianic redemption of the people of God. In the adoption—as well as the birth—of Moses, God persists in God's commitment to continue the story of God with us.

Despite the fact that English Bibles use the term "adoption" for a variety of Hebrew words, within the biblical grammar "adoption" does not refer to an institutionalized practice with a specific aim as ensconced in modern family law and practiced by adoption agencies. In the biblical witness there are a range of adoption-like ways of taking responsibility for children that are understood as activities of "doing justice" to orphans and widows whether or not they are legally recognized as such. Precisely as works of doing justice they are understood as responses to the divine promise to console and provide for all human beings. It is God's stated will that no human being be lost—each being a sheep in God's flock. The whole soteriological drive of the story of salvation history speaks of God's determination to draw humans back into God's story with His people as it is fulfilled in Jesus Christ. This name is also God's call to remain with God as God's grateful creatures. This is the consolation that God is to enact in the unfolding stories of every child on this earth.

Discerning How to Receive Children in Context

I have developed my considerations in this chapter by focusing sharply on the perspective of children and their position within God's will and plan as it is related to His people. The perspective I have explored does, however, raise crucial questions about whether concrete practices of adoption in any given society are adequate as responses to God's heritage and mandate. It would be almost inevitable that a theological investigation of this evaluative question engages many of the other discourses that cross the territory of adoption, discussions about the ethics of adoptive practices, their justifications, and strategies for taking people's biographical particularities seriously. In this all parents—whatever their motives and desires may be—are challenged to consider whether they are living up to their mandate and authority in relation to a child. Adoptive parents, like birthparents, are challenged by the promise embodied in the birth of Jesus Christ to realize the good works that are given to them to do toward a child. Thus all parents must constantly ask how best to respond, how best to correspond to the heritage and mandate that has been entrusted to them? They must continually be attentive to the critical force of the question of what they have to "offer" to the child other than their grounded confidence that God has acted graciously toward them. Thus to respond to the promise of a child can never escape daily questioning as to whether one is truly ready to receive God's promising heritage and to follow His mandate?

Such a question ought not be morally paralyzing, and indeed, relieves potential parents of embarking on the project of moral self-justification by which they believe that they will be made fit to parent if they take on the burden of living up to whatever moral norms currently define "responsible parents." What is more important is the way this account focuses the attention of prospective parents on the telos of adoption, to allow children to experience the life within God's story that is promised to them. When this telos is recognized, all sorts of cooperation between parents according to their different mandates for the child may come to be recognized as work that is pursued among several people and groups as part of the "good work" of cherishing God's heritage. Cooperation between adoptive parents and birthparents, for instance, can emerge in this perspective as equivalent to the cooperation between God and every parent in being united by a concern to provide a secure place for children to experience their life within God's story with His people.

In sum, the urge to consider adoption drives us toward the "good work" prepared for each believer by God (Eph. 2:10). Adoptive practices reach out toward the promise of the mandate that attends the birth of every child. This mandate is not an expression of a morally grounded way of life which must be shouldered by an act of will. It is instead a paradigmatic enacted acknowledgment of the human condition as defined by its context in God's story. The adoption of a child is thus understood in its truth: as an act of joyful acknowledgment of this particular child as God's heritage—and so God's own eschatological presence.

Part III

RECEIVING GIVEN LIFE (*OECONOMIA*)

Chapter 7

GOD'S STORY AND ENGELHARDT'S BIOETHICS

CHRISTIAN WITNESS IN MODERN MEDICINE

It is hard to imagine a more profound challenge to bioethics as it is conventionally understood today than the work of H. Tristram Engelhardt, Jr. Engelhardt not only offers a range of acute criticisms of this status quo but also presents a genealogical description of the field of academic bioethics that lays bare its contradictions of the Christian tradition and its distinctive understanding of human nature, the *conditio humana*. Engelhardt's work cannot be neglected if ethics, and therefore also bioethics, aims to present itself as part of the Christian tradition and the message to the world that it bears.

Engelhardt identifies the heart of the Christian message as a call to conversion to the original Christian faith and its morally thick account of reality.[1] Engelhardt's presentation of that message is embedded in a reconstructed genealogy of Christianity from the perspective of true Christian worship. The celebrants of Christian worship are, through this activity, grounded in God's story and given orientation to remain within that story. This chapter digs deeper into the implications of Christian worship for bioethics, drawing out and highlighting the critical and epistemic resources of that Christian tradition. For the reasons I discussed in detail in Chapter 4, the public and secular discourse of bioethics cannot afford to neglect the insights of religious traditions if it is interested in understanding the *conditio humana* rather than simply resting content to define humans according to the functional data–driven picture of the human assumed by the apparatus of bureaucratic management of medical institutions.[2] There remain

---

1. Gerald McKenny has highlighted this as the core theme of Engelhardt's work in "Desire for the Transcendent: Engelhardt and Christian Ethics," in *At the Roots of Christian Bioethics: Critical Essays on the Thought of H. Tristram Engelhardt, Jr.*, ed. Ana Smith Iltis and Mark J. Cherry (Salem: M&M Scrivener Press, 2010), 110. This chapter has many points of agreement with the analysis of the field of bioethics McKenny develops in *To Relieve the Human Condition: Bioethics, Technology, and the Body* (Albany: State University of New York Press, 1997).

2. See Jürgen Habermas, *The Future of Human Nature* (Oxford: Blackwell, 2003); Habermas, *Between Naturalism and Religion: Philosophical Essays* (Cambridge: Polity Press,

fundamental insights into what it means to be human that are inextricably and exclusively linked with the Christian tradition, to which Christians bear witness within the universal community of discourse, Christian or not.[3]

A critical engagement with the more problematic implications of Engelhardt's genealogy of bioethics requires revisiting some of the characteristic terms that are under dispute in his debate with the status quo in bioethical discourse, fundamental ideas like "secularity" and "modernity." Hans S. Reinders has convincingly shown that Engelhardt's rendition of philosophical bioethics too quickly dismisses secular morality, which is "much richer than liberal morality allows us to acknowledge."[4] Reinders's strategy of using Engelhardt's philosophical bioethics to draw out the moral content of liberal thought parallels the work I will undertake in this chapter. I will go further than Reinders, however, in suggesting that, regardless of whether the practices characteristic of secular morality practice morally richer than it can admit in theory, nevertheless, citizens in the secular domain still need the witness of Christian bioethics and its corresponding ethos.[5] My interest in this chapter is in showing why the question that is left on the table in the dispute between Engelhardt and Reinders is the crucial one. To what extent can modern secular citizens experience their own moral beliefs as more content-rich than their political theory as Reinders describes it (including the experience of the transformation of understanding) without an explicit encounter of conversion as understood in Christian bioethics and the distinctive epistemology that attends it?

My interest is in showing how Christian engagements in all these discussions are shaped by the context in which they take place, and how Christians might go about seeking to point them in more promising directions, as viewed from the Christian tradition. The work of this chapter should therefore be understood as prolegomena for bioethical discourse initiated by, and exemplified in, Engelhardt's work. It is, at the same time, also a critical engagement with Engelhardt's enterprise, indicating some of its questionable moves within the overarching goal of sharpening and augmenting the main thrust of his work.

This critical engagement will also raise questions about the extent to which Engelhardt's deployment of genealogical method overdetermines his message. I will suggest that this question arises out of my concern with how Christian

---

2008); and Brian Brock, "Seeing through the Data Shadow: Communing with the Saints in a Surveillance Society" *Surveillance and Religion* 16, no. 4 (2018): 533-45.

3. In this chapter I use the term "Christian" with more ecumenical breadth than other chapters in this volume, to include all other Christian traditions (i.e., the Roman Catholic or Orthodox traditions) insofar as there can be a consensus presupposed among them. I do so, of course, as one primarily traditioned by the Reformation Christian traditions.

4. Hans S. Reinders, *The Future of the Disabled in Liberal Society: An Ethical Analysis* (Notre Dame: University of Notre Dame Press, 2000), 55

5. Engelhardt has at times also pointed in this direction. See *Foundations of Christian Bioethics*, which appeared in the same year as Hans Reinders' critique (Lisse, Netherlands: Swets & Zeitlinger, 2000).

worship functions as a witness to the world: in what respect does the work of ethics, as expressed in the discourse of bioethics, belong to this good work of witnessing to the world? What is implicated in this sort of work as a practice that prominently includes what is sometimes called practical reason? How does the activity of Christian witness lift the burden imposed by secular thinking to make practical reason into a general theory, and so a replacement for, or equivalent to, the story of God and its unique grammar?[6]

In so formulating the question of how to understand bioethics today this chapter is another attempt to follow the path opened by Paul's hopeful *paraenesis* in Rom. 12:2: "Do not be conformed to this world-age (*aion*), but be transformed by the renewing of your mind, so that you may discern what is the will of God— what is good and acceptable and perfect."[7] The Christian exploration of God's will seeks renewed understanding (*nous*) which it witnesses to the world, in turn, in this case in the biomedical domain.

The pivotal question to be addressed in this chapter is how this Pauline disposition relates to Engelhardt's Christian epistemology and genealogical diagnosis of Western Christianity. I will propose that Engelhardt's suggestion that the problem with bioethics is primarily epistemological underplays the noetic work that accompanies the Christian work of ethics as seeking good works grounded in God's story. The underrepresentation of this positive witness raises, in turn, questions about the prominence Engelhardt gives his genealogical history of Western Christianity and its ethics. Where, we must ask Engelhardt, is the genealogical account itself located? How does the Christian witness to God's story, with the reconciliation of the world (cosmos) that lies at its heart, relate to his genealogically reconstructed history of medicine and the West? The question, at base, is whether we will understand the Christian witness in the domain of medicine to be fundamentally a matter of the real presence of good works addressed to the world (including the good work of "ethics" and "bioethics" and its noetic task), and whether those works depend on or are justified by a genealogically reconstructed history. I will suggest that the witness of good works cannot rest on any theoretical construct but only on the liberating and transformative inbreaking of God's own

---

6. The most developed contribution to the story concept as I am use it here can be found in Dietrich Ritschl's work. For a summary, see Ritschl, "Nachgedanken zum 'Story'-Konzept: Die Koagulation Wiedererzählter 'Stories' auf dem Weg zu differierenden theologischen Lehren," *Theologische Zeitschrift* 61 (2005): 78–91.

7. Engelhardt underestimates the importance of reading *nous* as an equivalent to the Hebrew word for "understanding," as it is used, for instance in Psalm 82, which is not a human rational faculty in a modern sense. "The traditional Christian account of knowledge is that the *nous* is the perceptive ability of which the Gospel proclaims, "Blessed are the pure in heart [*kardia*], for they shall see God" (Mt. 5:8). This invocation of heart identifies the central faculty of understanding, which when opened and oriented to God transforms us so that we are restored by grace," Engelhardt, *The Foundations of Christian Bioethics*, 168.

story, with its distinctive grammar, by which God continues God's story with His people and with us human beings.

Thus, despite my general agreement with Engelhardt and my aim to both endorse and place his work in its overarching theological context, my central theses in this chapter will be that his criticisms of modern liberal politics do not go far enough, since he embraces an empty procedural account of the justice that can be achieved by the state. Cannot insights and practical trajectories growing from the ethos of the witnessing community lend some ethical *content* to modern governance? I propose that this is precisely what happens in the good work of the Christian, including in the domain of biomedical ethics.

The Inability of Reason to Engineer the Human

We begin with the question of how to understand the relationship between faith and reason in the biomedical domain. How can reason grasp and understand nature—especially given that we are part of whatever we say that nature is? These are questions that are brought into sharp focus by recent debates about radical genetic engineering, in which acute questions are raised about the capacity of reason to properly articulate the *conditio humana*.

In these debates about how "human nature" is affected by techniques of reproduction and reconstruction, the problem arises, once again, of how to distinguish between "history" and "nature." Can we, as human beings, actually understand ourselves within a history fundamentally constituted by human achievements, especially if that history is seen as bearing no relation to "nature" as an orienting normative point of reference? These are the questions about the "future of human nature"[8] raised by developments in the biosciences that press for a more substantive understanding of the operation of what is often called practical reason.[9] Does it even make sense to talk about the moral dimensions of "human nature" and its "future" or about the *conditio humana* within a

---

8. Habermas, *The Future of Human Nature*. For a theological account of this problem see especially Gerald P. McKenny, *Biotechnology, Human Nature, and Christian Ethics* (New York: Cambridge University Press, 2018). McKenny's approach is at several points quite close to mine. The crucial question, however, is the extent to which he understands "human nature" within God's story. McKenny does speak about the "eschatological fulfillment" of human nature (4–5), and holds, "I will argue, humans image God, and they have been given their particular biological characteristics by God because these are precisely the characteristics that suit them for the form of life with God and with other humans for which God has created them. Normative status thus attaches to human nature as a condition for this form of life with God and with other humans" (10).

9. Stephan Kampowski evokes some profound observations from Habermas on this topic in *A Greater Freedom: Biotechnology, Love, and Human Destiny: In Dialogue with Hans Jonas and Jürgen Habermas* (Eugene: Pickwick, 2013), 156–7.

historical frame? This question vastly complicates what we are asking about when we try to understand the historical embeddedness of human practical reasoning.

To ask about the "future of human nature" thus provokes a range of questions about human morality and its rational grounding by challenging practical reason to become more aware of which elements of the *conditio humana* are (contingently) given, and which are available for modification. When and where ought we to consider the historical circumstances to definitively provide the frame for the new technologies and their applications? We come here before fundamental questions about the limits of morally licit interventions into human nature, and even more fundamental questions about how any limits at all could be established purely on the basis of an ethics of practical reason. As Jürgen Habermas has observed, "The decoding of the human genome opens up the prospect of interventions that cast a peculiar light on a condition of our normative self-understanding, a condition that, although natural and thus far unthematized, now turns out nonetheless to be essential."[10] Biomedical innovations force us to revisit the very foundations of our ethical thinking.

Thus, questions about whether or how to alter the human genome demand that bioethics revisit its assumptions about the meaning of terms like "history," "nature," and "practical reason." It is an open question whether the discourse of bioethics can confine itself to practical reason, perhaps understood as a "renewed" practical (moral) reason that integrates the wider horizon of a new genetically modified human nature. What is crucial, I will suggest, is that the practice we call "bioethics" remain embedded within an ethos—a transcendent Christian ethos—that offers guidance about both the right and the good, while also preserving or even rescuing the human condition in the fullest sense, including dimensions, limits, and determinations of its given state which otherwise would be lost. Here Engelhardt is prescient.

> With the secularization of morality, a new gulf emerges between the ideals of moral action and the broken character of the world. The physical world is deaf to human suffering, and tragedy is unredeemed.... Worse yet, the struggle for survival, out of which all life is seen to have evolved, is characterized by suffering, death, and the frustration of the deepest yearnings of both humans and animals. Without the metaphysical force of Christian redemption, the world apart from God is unredeemed from non-moral as well as moral evil. After all, in the long run, without God all is obliterated.... Without God and immortality, why should one sacrifice those whom one loves on behalf of abstract commitments to the right and the good? Kant recognizes this difficulty. However, Kant only in part acknowledges the depth of the tension between morality and reality.... Moral ideals that had been nurtured in the expectation of eternity are now placed in an indifferent if not hostile cosmos.

---

10. Habermas, *The Future of Human Nature*, 12–13.

Thus runs the genealogical history. Engelhardt continues to the Christian alternative:

> In profound contrast, traditional Christianity recognizes that the broken character of the universe, rooted in the free choice of Adam and Eve, finds its restoration through the free choice of a second Eve and a second Adam. The second Eve submits and gives birth to the second Adam, Christ, who as God and man reconciles the cosmos with God, guaranteeing full reward for human moral striving. All of morality and human history are embedded in a narrative defined both by human freedom and God's infinite power. Human choice and its consequences are real, including the free choices of the God-man Christ in conformity with the will of the Father and in the Holy Spirit. In this cosmic narrative in which God plays the cardinal role, the right and the good are in the end fully integrated, the various goods placed in concert, and the motivation for justified moral action secured (e.g., through eternal punishments and rewards). Tragedy is real, though redeemed. Against such expectations, secular morality is at best broken and incomplete.[11]

This is how Engelhardt interweaves "history" and God's story as presented in the Christian witness, the "cosmic" story that encompasses both the *conditio humana* and also the task and horizon of practical reason (reflecting the right and the good in its unity). If we are to gain an adequate vantage point to discuss the relationship of faith and reason, it will only be at the complex intersection of these two types of narrative and their rationalities. We will have to examine the premises of the historical notion and genealogy of Western Christianity as it converges and conflicts with a Christian understanding of the *conditio humana* understood within the Christian narrative of God with the world. Christians are bound to follow God's story and witness to it in their ethos and worship. As they do so it is inevitable that they will perceive the *conditio humana* to be "hidden," or as Engelhardt puts it, "embedded" in that story,[12] rather than delivered by way of a history of the rise or fall of secularization processes.[13] The question is how these two stories are integrated, and Engelhardt's account appears to "embed" the secular in the eternal in a rather disjunctive manner. For Engelhardt, in effect, the entry of God's "integrated" story appears to be an (unnecessarily) all or nothing affair.

---

11. Engelhardt, *The Foundations of Christian Bioethics*, 79–80.
12. The procedure I am suggesting for a theological exploration of the *conditio humana* parallels that of Gerhard Sauter, *Das verborgene Leben: eine theologische Anthropologie* (München: Gütersloher Verlagshaus, 2011).
13. Jürgen Habermas and Benedict XVI, *Dialectics of Secularization: On Reason and Religion* (San Francisco: Ignatius Press, 2007).

History versus God's Story

Engelhardt has presented us with a multifold interweaving of issues and approaches that are nevertheless admirably and pointedly focused. He never loses sight of the question of a *conditio humana* existing beyond all determination by human choices. Nor does he allow the question of whether "faith and reason" can adequately characterize the *conditio humana* to drop from view. He understands the *conditio humana* to implicate a morality genuinely given with it, and which calls forth a Christian ethos aiming to preserve the *conditio humana* in practice and in so doing witnessing to the world. He highlights one question as decisive: In what way do those entrapped in the "fatal history" of bioethics encounter a different story and—within this story—a different understanding of the *conditio humana* and the specifically configured ethics of practical reason it entails?

Engelhardt's discussion of bioethics is framed by an elaborate genealogy, by which he intends to demonstrate that today's secular bioethics represents a debased form of an initially Christian bioethics. The "Christian" character of this initial bioethical formulation is itself, however, presented as the outcome of problematic or even catastrophically fatal premises. The faulty assumption of the proponents of "Christian bioethics" is taken to have eventually come to the surface in the development of an openly secular bioethics. It is this initial assumption by Christian bioethicists that Engelhardt intends to show to be false by way of his critique of the secular bioethics it devolved into.

The genealogical history offered by Engelhardt is presented as a straight description, invoking facts and delineating processes presented as obvious and commonly agreed upon. Yet Engelhardt's presentation presupposes the appropriateness of an analytical framework resting on a range of theologically far-reaching terms such as "secular," "world," "reason," and "culture," to name a few. These are all concepts deserving theological scrutiny in order to ascertain whether they adequately grasp the salient aspects of human life with God.[14] McKenny has compared Engelhardt's genealogy with Hegel's history of reason: "Like Hegel, Engelhardt's argument traces the fate of reason in history to its culmination in immanence. But unlike Hegel, Engelhardt's narrative does not endorse this actualization of reason in history, and the moral content he seeks is not found in the immanent sphere of custom."[15] McKenny's proposal that Engelhardt's positive perspective remains bound to a (universal) Hegelian view of history is highly suggestive. Engelhardt apparently grants Hegel's conclusion that the ultimately unavoidable outcome of world history will be a liberal state allowing for unrestricted Christian worship as it safeguards freedom of religion.[16]

---

14. For the meaning of "secular" see Rowan Williams, *Faith in the Public Square* (London: Bloomsbury, 2012).

15. McKenny, "Desire for the Transcendent," 109.

16. H. Tristram Engelhardt, Jr., "*Sittlichkeit* and Post-modernity: An Hegelian Reconsideration of the State," in *Hegel Reconsidered: Beyond Metaphysics and the*

Thus, to our questions about Engelhardt's definitions of the terms "world," "history," and "Christianity" as a historical phenomenon, we also have to add a new question: What is the aim of Christian hope? What is Christian hope about if it is not bound to the expectation of a different world or history to the ones imagined by those who do not accept that God's story in Jesus Christ is in fact the true story of the cosmos? There is a difference in kind between (utopian) views that yearn for a different world (perhaps a morally fully developed world community) and the Christian hope to be in living contact with God's presence in continuation of God's story. Philosophically described, this is the difference between philosophies of history, with their distant conceptual roots in Christian traditions, and a Christian eschatology of hope bound to God's story as it was confirmed in Jesus Christ and has been witnessed by Christians (see Chapter 1). Philosophies of history are discourses about "history" as it can be grasped and narrated by historiographical techniques, while Christian hope is organized by Christian narrative in which God's story is understood as having a critical relation to "history" and "world"— with all the practical implications entailed in this critical counter-story.

Engelhardt's work is especially attentive to the specifically Western dispute between philosophies of history and Christian eschatology, and how these two approaches to the phenomena of historical occurrence generate paradigmatically different approaches to Christian ethics. These two approaches are linked to equally profound differences between Christian and post-Christian epistemologies (as he labels them) and their rival understandings of nature and human nature. Engelhardt's genealogy narrates this difference as being between a rational (Christian) and an irrational (post-Christian) epistemology. An epistemology, independent from the Christian ethos and its own rationality is presumed to be deficient. Engelhardt does not appear to consider the idea that these two epistemologies might spring from two rival rationalities.[17]

On McKenny's reading, Engelhardt's history of Western Christianity departs from Hegel in telling a story not of cultural ascent but decline, and here he is both formally and materially dependent on the account of Alasdair MacIntyre.[18] Christianity has decayed into what we know today as the cosmopolitan morality of Western culture, with the putrefaction being especially evident in the discipline of bioethics. Genealogies proceed by disclosing constitutive elements of a "culture,"[19] with morality often being assumed to be the most dominant and determining element of any culture. Engelhardt's is one of several genealogies that conclude by

Authoritarian State, ed. Engelhardt and Terry P. Pinkard (Dordrecht: Kluwer Academic, 1994), 211–24.

17. Cf. Habermas, *The Future of Human Nature*.

18. McKenny, "Desire for the Transcendent," 107–33. A. C. MacIntyre, *Three Rival Versions of Moral Enquiry: Encyclopedia, Genealogy, and Tradition* (Notre Dame: University of Notre Dame Press, 1990).

19. For critical reflections on the notion of "culture" as a static entity, see Williams, *Faith in the Public Square*.

showing how a particular state of affairs has been bequeathed by Christian faith and thought. Yet in each case such genealogies carve out a place for an alternative Christian tradition that has not been swallowed by all those transformations and secularizing processes and so should be understood as the true Christian tradition. Readers are left to decide which of these alternative traditions really proves not only to be comparatively closest to that "true" Christian tradition (a title Engelhardt claims for the tradition of Eastern Orthodoxy) but which also witnesses to a determinative and narratively organized story of God with the creation—the kind of witness that I have suggested is central—that would otherwise be obliterated in the historical change and decline of the church.

Friedrich Nietzsche's "history" of Christianity is one of the founding examples of the genre of genealogy. Even his history—rightly understood—allows that there is a true tradition which has been lost. Nietzsche's *Genealogy of Morals* (1887) analyzes the function and grammar of what he describes as the socially dominant morality. In the fundamental grammar of the modern West, Nietzsche spots the essence of Christendom. The content of this moral grammar is a specific set of obligations that Christians take to be imposed on all human beings. This obligation is grounded in "god," whose whole story, including the salvation achieved by Jesus Christ, is, Nietzsche claims, a response to a human desire for "justification" before God, a desire that is engraved into a "conscience"—again another Christian invention. The "god" of Nietzsche's genealogy, we have to agree, is not the "God" of the covenant with his people, nor is it the "God" who has reconciled His world in Jesus Christ for His glory and His coming kingdom. Nietzsche's genealogy traces the career of a merely moral "god." The moral "god" cannot be the active God who is the agent of His very own story with His creatures. The moral "god" is merely a guarantor and justifying authority of morality (and truth) as a conceptual system. Nietzsche rightly reminds Christians that their ethics should not be focused on moral justification. What his reminder bequeaths, however, is the question of how Christian ethics actually does relate to "God." Is there a different story with God and an equivalent ethos corresponding to an ethos of the type to which Engelhardt has directed our attention?

This moralistic, justifying god is dead, as Nietzsche's Zarathustra proclaims. His dying was not the result of disinterest, emancipation, or because secular substitutes outbid what he could offer. This god was killed, and not by radical critics and enlighteners like Nietzsche. Rather, Nietzsche suggests, the moralistic god was killed by the very grammar of moral obligation and justification itself. The human urge to codify God's relationship to humanity in terms of moral obligation was from the very start destined to be eventually decoded and dissolved. The work of a genealogy of morals is to reveal this dramatic process. Moral obligation, as a system, had been filled up with human ideas of good and evil rather than shaped and given content by God's own story with humanity. What Nietzsche's genealogy provokes, however, are questions about what moral obligation could be for if not satisfying the need for a way to justify and proclaim human acts good. Nietzsche's critique demands that we squarely face the question of how every notion of practical reason implicates certain actions as morally justified or not.

His attack affects any ethos or concept of practical reason that sets as its standard the desire for discursive rational justification and meaning. Engelhardt's account seems untouched by Nietzsche's critique and thus his constructive proposal ends up unable to negotiate the boundary between a corrupt because self-justificatory human ethics and an eternal (and essentially nonethical) divine ethos.

Reformation theology challenged mainstream Christianity on exactly the issue of discursive rational justification. The reformers charged the dominant forms of theology with affirming "god" as the source of justification and meaning. Hence the intense focus of Reformation theology on the topic of justification: its central aim was to replace the grammar of "justification" (including primarily moral justification) by the grammar of God's merciful judgment and justice that accords with God's own action with people. The search for justification or "meaning" could be given up in order to participate in God's actual enacted justice. God's justice means (in keeping with biblical language) God's faithfulness to His people—not to let them be given over to other powers nor to entrapment in their own trespasses. God's justice guarantees that His story will continue. God's justice to His people is again realized in Jesus Christ. To believe in God means to participate in that justice. This logic, notwithstanding the ways it has been misunderstood and corrupted, runs contrary to all games of human self-justification. Justification can be granted only by a living, present God, by "God in time," by God who is present to God's people in the governing of their hearts by the Holy Spirit. Engelhardt's work opens a range of avenues to explore the ways in which such a logic of Reformation theology can serve as a critical guide for fostering a Christian ethos in the field of "bioethics" in its contestation with secular calls for transformation. To engage in such explorative theology will require testing the extent to which Engelhardt's deployment of genealogical method synchronizes with that logic on the substance of Christian ethics as it criticizes or contradicts other ethical approaches. In so readily provoking such contests, as Engelhardt has suggested, bioethics proves to be a paradigmatic hot spot in the modern contestation of basic questions of faith, reason, and morality.

Two Approaches to a Common World?

With his astute last rites over the moral "god," Nietzsche was not suggesting that the pernicious nature of "moral" justification disappears. There will always be rational ways to justify one's actions and their effects on other people.[20] Such (self-) justification must appeal to a common moral ground, whether embedded in widely shared practical reason or explicitly shared ideals—and never merely by constructing one's own justifying grounds.[21] The practice of justification by

---

20. Cf. Rainer Forst, *Das Recht auf Rechtfertigung: Elemente einer konstruktivistischen Theorie der Gerechtigkeit* (Frankfurt: Suhrkamp, 2007).

21. Cf. Stanley Hauerwas, *With the Grain of the Universe: The Church's Witness and Natural Theology* (Grand Rapids: Brazos Press, 2001), 14–41.

way of practical reasoning must therefore be understood as focused on the ethical contours necessary for peaceful living together. That an act appears justified in public can neither be guaranteed nor be enforced by the liberal "state" or a supposedly preexistent universal human morality. Justification of one's action is always an explicit practice that can succeed or fail and must constantly be repeated by making appeal to moral beliefs of the community that never stand still. Nor is the practice of moral justification ever a mere procedure without content. It must always make its appeal before a common reality, a common "world" generated or realized in this practice.

Given that a common "world" or moral context is necessary for peaceful coexistence, the priority of the "right" over the "good" has been discussed in some depth by both John Rawls[22] and Engelhardt. The issue at this point is why human beings need not only—within the grammar of practical reason—justification in order to live in peace together but also "truth," that what counts as peace must be related to the truth of what might legitimately hold claim to be a "good life." Is peace just what human beings agree on, or is there even a good life conceivable as judged from the standpoint of beyond human evaluation, justification, and judgment, a "good life" constitutive for the *conditio humana*? Engelhardt's decision to rely exclusively on practical reason as the domain of the ethics of the secular public brings before us the pivotal question of whether it is even possible to reflect on this "good life" within the horizon—and limits—of practical reason.

The reality is that all talk of the "ethical" good or "ethos" has to be seen in its indissoluble connection to moral justification—that is, as positioned by the context and limits of practical reason. To justify one's action demands some form of affirmation of the overlapping content of the "right" and the "good" within the inescapable sphere of the political living together. It is not necessary for every action to be defensible by appeal to shared views of "the right" and "the good," except on topics that are indispensable for a peaceful political coexistence. An ethic of practical reason is necessary for all people, consisting in a recognition of the need for moral justification and consensus for sustaining all particular and therefore morally content-rich political coexistence. This common thick moral world of coexistence is not to be confined to a liberal "state." Rather, in its very moral content-richness it must be understood as contrasting with, or even opposing, the morally neutral and therefore permissive modern liberal state. In this sense "peaceable" political community is grounded in communities of thick moral justification, not the liberal state.[23] Today all political theories of justice

---

22. John Rawls, *A Theory of Justice* (Cambridge: Belknap Press of Harvard University Press, 1971), Part 3.

23. Stanley Hauerwas, "Not all Peace is Peace: Why Christians Cannot Make Peace with Engelhardt's Peace," in *Reading Engelhardt: Essays on the Thought of H. Tristram Engelhardt, Jr.*, ed. Brendan Minogue, Gabriel Palmer-Fernández, and James E. Reagan (Dordrecht: Kluwer, 1997), 31–44.

must wrestle with the sequelae to the death of the moral "god" by conceptually clarifying the procedures and practices of justification by which public discourse is kept strictly within the contours of practical reason. Christians, however, face such questions as those who confess that there is no other "god" than the Father of Jesus Christ, who has His own Law set within the context of His story with His people and all human beings.

Christian ethics must therefore negotiate two distinct perspectives. One is the "moral" perspective intrinsic to peaceful public living together. Christians cannot escape negotiating the given content-full political ethos of their time and place, including what is assumed to be the "good life." And they must do so as they look for the appearance and recognition of a genuinely multidimensional good life. They seek the ethos that accords with the exploration of "God's will, the good, the pleasant and the perfect" (Rom. 12:2).

The good life that Christians discover in this path is one that has to be witnessed to the "world," the common "moral world" of peaceful living together in which actions are considered justified in perhaps very different ways. Philosophers may well absolutely criticize the claim that the "good life" can be realized in any actual society, as did Theodor Adorno in a famous pronouncement: "There is no right life (good life) amidst a false one."[24] But to Paul, the genuinely good life is good precisely because it is a life of witness to those who lack a meaningful "history" or "moral world," given their enmeshment in the wisdom of this age.

Within the Christian ethos, the "good" life and "good works" make their appearance as a living and working within God's story, begun in His creative works and continued in His work of reconciliation. For the Christian all reflections on the "good" and its presence in the world are referred to this story; there is no freestanding "good," no independent point of view from which to evaluate "the good." Nor are God's commandments the "freestanding" moral code attacked by Nietzsche. They are not given to Israel by a moral "god," but by the God Who has chosen Israel to be His people and who has upheld and continued this story with Jesus Christ.

The task of Christian ethics is to ask about what this promised life with God actually entails on the ground. This is the constitutive task of the Christian ethos as it negotiates life amidst the "content-full morality" of its age—in order to discern what it implies for its witness within secular morality and its reflections on the *conditio humana*.[25]

---

24. "Es gibt kein richtiges Leben im falschen," Theodor W. Adorno, *Minima Moralia: Reflexionen aus dem beschädigten Leben* (Frankfurt: Suhrkamp, 1994), 42. See Habermas' commentary, *The Future of Human Nature*, 1–15, in which he translates the German *richtiges Leben* as "good life."

25. See also the debate in *Bioethics Critically Reconsidered: Having Second Thoughts*, ed. H. Tristram Engelhardt, Jr. (Dordrecht: Springer, 2012).

How Christian Hope Relates to the "World" Even in Modern Times

Christians, we have noticed, are provoked by Nietzsche to forgo trying to justify their account of the good life through the discursive reasoning that demands they present the "meaning" of their life in terms of the "meaning" of a secular history which they do not claim as their own true story. Christian hope is not reducible to what is considered rational or reasonable in a given place and time, and this is the problem that inevitably must be faced by "modern" Christians. There is no meaning in history that could bear or provoke this hope. Christian hope is rooted solely in God's story and God's promise to continue that story. Where Christians pray, "Thy kingdom come, thy will be done," worshipping Christians are contradicting all hopes rooted in "history." The "god" of this "history" is as dead as the moral "god," and has been killed along with it, observes Karl Löwith.

> We are neither ancient ancients nor ancient Christians, but moderns—that is, a more or less inconsistent compound of both traditions. The Greek historians wrote pragmatic history centered around a great political event; the Church Fathers developed from Hebrew prophecy and Christian eschatology a theology of history focused on the supra-historical events of creation, incarnation, and consummation; the moderns elaborate a philosophy of history by secularizing theological principles and applying them to an ever increasing number of empirical facts. It seems as if the two great conceptions of antiquity and Christianity, cyclic motion and eschatological direction, have exhausted the basic approaches to the understanding of history.[26]

Löwith's genealogical account of the secularization of the concept of "history" shorn of the content-rich grammar of Christian hope challenges Christians no less dramatically than Nietzsche's *Genealogy of Morals* and Engelhardt's genealogy of Western Christianity. Each of these stories challenges Christians to prove whether their hope is really in satisfying the demands of a moral code, or establishing itself on the "right side of history" or is organized according to some account of "proper" practical reasoning instead of depending upon being embedded in the living God's story with the world. The Christian ethos is only genuinely Christian it being oriented by God's story as it unfolds from creation to consummation, grounded in God's promise and affirmation in Jesus Christ.

This is why Christians cannot be "modern" in terms of an interpretation of "history" that provides the context of meaning and understanding. And as Löwith notes, we are also not "ancient Christians" but moderns to the extent that we pretend that we can explain ourselves through a historical account that locates our identity, giving it meaning. Löwith's backward-looking historical perspective seems to cut off any chance for genuine Christian "hope"—within the modern historicist frame of reference. We moderns appear determined by this "history" and

---

26. Löwith, *Meaning in History*, 19.

the "meaning" it gives our lives—that is, the supposed progress to a better world, the secular way of a hope, originating in a Christian eschatology, but deprived of its very content and grammar. "Ancient" Christians in contrast, according to Löwith, had a different form of hope that was not focused on achieving a better world according to historical progress or any other human judgments or desires.

Is then Christian hope in its relation to the present "world" obsolete, since "moderns" cannot forgo at least a meaning in history and trust in progress and development, because they—whether they are Christian or not—find their identities hopelessly married to this kind of justification? There must be an alternative to the historical disposition of the modern "world" and a "world" which is beyond or independent from the processes of secularization. The latter alternative would allow the modern "world" to remain "secular"—that is, to admit it having been shaped by earlier Christian traditions and corresponding to them. This is the "world" of "Western Christianity," as Engelhardt describes it. Engelhardt appears to grant this modern bifurcation: to be modern is to be historical, to be a real Christian, "timeless." Engelhardt laments that this timeless Christendom has been lost in modern descriptions of Christian-secular or post-Christian secular times.

The question, then, is how this secular or post-secular "world" appears within the perspective of real Christian hope—that is, within the perspective of God's story that Christians are part of and witnesses to—and how the *conditio humana* appears within the perspective of this hope. This is the essential task of Christian ethics: to explore the "world" and its phenomena as they are definitely determined by the story of Jesus Christ. The task is to determine how the "world" is determined by the real world, the real reality, as Dietrich Bonhoeffer often put it.[27] Its explorations follow the contours of God's story with all the phenomena determined by this story—the phenomena of "death" and "dying," of "suffering," and all the phenomena associated with human bodily life. How are these phenomena, constitutive for the *conditio humana*, determined by the life and resurrection of Jesus Christ and the hope grounded therein for resurrection? How is medical care determined by this hope?[28] This is one of the leading questions within any ethical reflection on our dependence on medical care and its ethical configuration, related, as it is to the ethos of physicians and medical professionals, as Engelhardt grasps:

> Traditional Christianity provides bioethics a language out of step with a culture of self-determination and pride. It sees matters of suffering, dying, and death without a central focus on considerations of rights, dignity, and self-satisfaction. Instead, the focus is on how life in the body of Christ teaches us to live and die. At stake is a goal beyond freedom, dignity, and virtue: union with the transcendent

---

27. See Chapter 2.
28. See *Hoffnung und Verantwortung Herausforderungen für die Medizin*, ed. Andreas Frewer, Florian Bruns, and Wolfgang Rascher (Würzburg: Königshausen & Neumann, 2010).

God through taking on Christ's divinity, as He took on our humanity. The culture of traditional Christian belief focuses on life regained through the humiliation of death on the Cross.[29]

"Life regained through the humiliation of death on the Cross": this is the story, with its striking reference to "taking on Christ's divinity," that contradicts the grammar of our public moral space, anchored as it is in notions of human freedom, autonomy, dignity, all couched in terms of the generic moral "God."

Configurations of Practical Reason and Public Rationality

Practical reason is much richer in content than abstract moral rules, in encompassing all the shared judgments and discernments by which a common social "world" is sustained. Hence there can be no sharp distinction between activities of practical reason designed to justifying the acts and habits of people who have to live together, and a substantive ethos of Christian public witness cannot be separated.[30] It is not difficult to imagine a filled-out and content-full common "world" that exists wholly within practical reason. But to imagine such a culture presupposes, as Jürgen Habermas has argued, a "third standpoint" between an abstract universal practical reason and a particular substantiated and realized "ethos"—which Habermas calls a "comprehensive worldview." In the course of a discussion with John Rawls, Habermas has wondered whether "Rawls can account for the possibility of an overlapping consensus without tacitly assuming such a third perspective from which "we," the citizens, can publicly examine in common what is in the equal interest of everybody."[31] To say that citizens are autonomous, and autonomously exercise practical reason cannot in the end escape the normative implications of their shared practical reason. Thus there

> seems to be no way around the explanation of the moral point of view in terms of a procedure that claims to be context-independent. . . . A procedure that operationalizes the moral point of view of impartial judgment is neutral with respect to arbitrary constellations of values but not with respect to practical reason itself.[32]

In modern political theory autonomy has been treated as a purely formal assertion shorn of particularity. Habermas is highlighting that if the logic of autonomy is to

---

29. Engelhardt, *The Foundations of Christian Bioethics*, 332.

30. On judging so understood see Hanna Arendt, *Lectures on Kant's Political Philosophy* (Chicago: University of Chicago Press, 1989).

31. Jürgen Habermas, "'Reasonable' Versus 'True,' or the Morality of Worldviews," in *Habermas and Rawls: Disputing the Political*, ed. James Gordon Finlayson and Fabian Freyenhagen (Oxford: Taylor and Francis, 2011), 101–2.

32. Habermas, "'Reasonable' Versus 'True,'" 112.

be applied not to isolated individuals but to moral persons as citizens of a given polity, such an account will only be workable if those individuals are understood to share much more than the formal capacity for self-determination or abstract moral rules. Nor do moral rules offer suitable "middle-ground" for political compromises. The negotiation of political compromise takes place in the political sphere of coexistence. If we grant Habermas's observations on this point, significant questions emerge about Engelhardt's account. How can Christians participate in a political sphere conceived in this thicker way, contributing ethical impulses and direction that grow from their own distinctive ethos? How might Christians understand the relation of the ethos to which they witness to the political ethos of the practical reason that dominates in their political context?

In his speech "Faith, Reason, and the University,"[33] Joseph Ratzinger made an emphatic plea for intercultural and interreligious dialogue as distinguished from the more familiar Roman Catholic tradition of appealing to a general (immediate) reference to "natural law" as a universal common ground for justification. His plea appears rooted in the confidence that the "truth" of Christian faith will be confirmed as it eventually but inevitably converges with reason.[34] Faith and reason are necessarily related because reason and faith need each other, irreducibly. "There can be no doubt that the two main partners in this mutual relatedness are the Christian faith and Western secular rationality; one can and must affirm this, without thereby succumbing to a false Eurocentrism."[35]

Ratzinger is proposing a route that differs from Habermas's "third perspective" in presupposing the (encompassing) convergence of faith and reason from the side of Christian faith. Habermas, in contrast, seeks a "discourse" by which an articulated common rational ground could be discovered that is in the end beyond "faith" in the historical instantiations we now know, even if it is (necessarily) rooted in a type of general faith that this new rational ground can be found. Thus for Habermas the practice of discourse—within that third perspective—is positioned as the limited, specific type of political practice that is needed for peaceful living together, peaceful according to an articulated peace, as a particularized "bond of peace" (Eph. 4:3). This practical coexistence does not demand that only fully morally and ethically formed political communities contribute to the discussion. Any comprehensive worldview, according to Habermas, may participate in this discourse for a limited purpose, without confining itself to the conventions of practical reason should it, for instance, be dismissive of religious worldviews and

---

33. Pope Benedict XVI, "Faith, Reason and the University." This is the title of his speech at the University of Regensburg, 2006 in Schall, James V.; *Benedict: The Regensburg Lecture* (South Bend: St. Augustine's Press, 2007), 130–48. Benedict has also been in dialogue with Jürgen Habermas: Habermas and Benedict XVI, *Dialectics of Secularization*.

34. H. Tristram Engelhardt, Jr., "Bioethics in the Post-modern World: Belief in Secularity," in *Duties to Others*, ed. Courtney S. Campbell and B. Andrew Lustig (Dordrecht: Kluwer Academic, 1994), 235–45.

35. Habermas and Benedict XVI, *Dialectics of Secularization*, 78, 79.

their associated moral understandings. In Habermas's view, both those who follow "faith" and those who follow "reason" must consider what their most important contribution might be to peaceful living together.

Exploratively Seeking Good Works as Christian Witness

Engelhardt is aware of the need for such a third perspective, given the inability of the modern state to generate or sustain morally united community.

> The state . . . cannot provide a content-full morality in which all can share. It provides instead a public thing, a *res publica*, through which common resources can be employed and individuals protected. The guiding thread is not a content-full secular morality, but a process that acts with common authority. The result is a secular state tolerant in principle because of the limits of secular morality and secular moral authority.[36]

Why should "the state" provide a "content-full morality" in which "all can share"? If one subscribed to the Hegelian narrative, one might expect this, given that his Christian perspective secularized the concept of a realized "kingdom of God" in history, in which state, community, morality, and reason coincide within the institution of law. Habermas's observations, however, provoke us to ask: Why could not the *res publica* nevertheless be partly "content-full" even if this content is limited to what is needed for a peaceful political coexistence?

The heart of this question concerns how the limits of practical reason that configure the *res publica* are not to be defined only negatively but gain positive content through the witness of a Christian ethos. Such a proposal will be plausible only once we see how this ethos might concretely contribute to the *res publica* by articulating its own ethos in terms that are intelligible in the context of a community's particular forms of practical reason. This would mean that Christians would participate in a practice of cooperation for the *res publica* as a "good work," a limited but nevertheless real work of establishing a "bond of peace" (Eph. 4:3) consisting of articulated substantial elements of "good life." Such a witness goes beyond a purely formal affirmation of toleration by materially supporting an ethically substantial peaceful living together.[37]

This cannot and must not imply accommodating Christian truth to a different logic. Christian faith witnesses by pointing to ways in which the common "world" might become more humane, understood on the basis of its distinctive vision of the *conditio humana*. It is precisely here that Engelhardt rests content too early in his criticisms of modern liberal politics. He affirms an empty procedural account

---

36. Engelhardt, "*Sittlichkeit* and Post-modernity," 241.

37. Nigel Biggar's description of a Christian "behaving in public" is useful here, especially his emphasis on seeking "narrative integrity." See Biggar, *Behaving in Public: How to Do Christian Ethics* (Grand Rapids: Eerdmans, 2011).

of the justice that can be achieved by the state. He thus abandons the idea that the insights and practical trajectories growing from the ethos of the witnessing community can indeed lend some ethical content to modern governance. This is the work of Christian witness.

Obvious examples of points at which Christian witness can make such a material contribution spring to mind. There remain articulated ways of living among Christians that contradict widespread moral assumptions about the language and practice around euthanasia, reproductive cloning, eugenics, and many other ideas that harmfully impinge on the *conditio humana* and its corresponding ethos. How could a peaceful living together be possible if one finds oneself unable to seek an articulated consensus about what will happen in each of these moments in which fundamental questions about the *conditio humana* are decided? Habermas has argued, to take one example, that cloning of human beings subverts the consensus that is currently assumed in democratic societies—that human beings are categorically equal because they are of absolutely equal origin. We must not allow human "creators" of human beings lest we risk dissolving the categorical equality of all human beings. Conceptually speaking, the notion of the equality of human beings is structured by a creator–creature distinction.[38] To speak up in support of such elements of a truly human ethos is essential for any civic society—and it is obvious that this needs the witness of people who are living out that ethos.

This understanding of an explicitly performed and witnessed ethos should be considered equivalent to a timeless "good work" in not being entrapped and so prevented from acting because of the given conditions or historical constellations in which it necessarily takes place. In *Foundations of Christian Bioethics* Engelhardt too recognizes the importance in medical care of something like good works as I have described it. We read, for example, "Instead, we must recognize with the Christians of the first centuries that we must care for pregnant women who need support, adopt children who would otherwise be killed, provide care for the dying such that self-murder does not become a temptation, and lovingly pray for those who murder."[39]

There are innumerable well-determined "good works" of this sort demanded and realized within medical care, including by professionals who are committed to an equivalent medical ethos. The Christian ethos goes beyond an ethos exclusively focused on therapeutic tasks in its openness to ethically reflected notions of therapy—in distinction, for instance to being positioned as purveyors of services or products. This hermeneutic work on the medical field is paralleled in the economic domain in which we find innumerable "good works" on various levels and alternative practices of entrepreneurship.[40] We must not assume that doing good works will be guaranteed to change the common language of a political community, although it may not be excluded (why should it?) that the witness of

---

38. Kampowski, *A Greater Freedom*, 156–7.
39. Engelhardt, *The Foundations of Christian Bioethics*, 395.
40. See Chapter 5.

Christian good works may catalyze substantive alterations to ways that medical care will come to be practiced in a given community.

Good works witness a *logos*, a word addressed to this world. As such, good works, like Christian hope, are timeless. As we read in Eph. 2:10: "For we are what he has made us, created in Christ Jesus for good works, which God prepared beforehand to be our way of life." This way of life belongs to the new "citizens of the saints" and the "members of the household of God" (Eph. 2:19). True peace, then, will not be substantiated by a permissive society or a liberal state, but only by good works. Good works do not necessarily guarantee that "the right" and "the good" will fully converge, but "good works" addressed to others—and not (only) rationally mediated—certainly can represent or give body to "the right."

The medical field is and will remain for the foreseeable future a vast field of conflict and contradiction, as Engelhardt describes it. It will be significant for medical professionals to find the orientation from which they can resist trajectories that they find counter to their ethos. There is, just as pressingly, a need for political and institutional solutions not least in order to maintain the tension between professional ethos and various medical ethics boards so that the witness of a different ethos—even if controversial—is guaranteed. This is why we must not forget the collective version of "good works": institutions. Engelhardt also highlights the importance of Christian medical institutions which aim to embody the Christian ethos. As of yet there are no constitutional barriers against religiously run institutions like hospitals, universities, schools, and allied health institutions which aim to preserve the medical ethos in its distinctive grammar. The state, yes, may grant them permission to practice and yet it is severely limited in its power to control them since it depends on these institutionalized counterparts to preserve the basic functioning of civic society. The parallel here is with the legal system that also can never ensure the vital and complex ground for a substantial peaceful—civic—living together. Ernst-Wolfgang Böckenförde pointedly summarizes what is at stake in the existence of institutions:

> The liberal secular state lives on premises that it cannot itself guarantee. On the one hand, it can subsist only if the freedom it consents to its citizens is regulated from within, inside the moral substance of individuals and of a homogeneous society. On the other hand, it is not able to guarantee these forces of inner regulation by itself without renouncing its liberalism.[41]

All political community depends on the sphere of good works that are not considered to be private but rather constitutive in being the indispensable context for the existence of any substantial public sphere.

---

41. Ernst-Wolfgang Böckenförde, *Staat, Gesellschaft, Freiheit: Studien zur Staatstheorie und zum Verfassungsrecht* (Frankfurt: Suhrkamp, 1976), 60; cf. Habermas and Benedict XVI, *Dialectics of Secularization*.

The Good Work of Understanding and Judging:
Discovering a Common World

In the work of living together human beings cannot avoid judging and in a manner that allows the reasons for those judgments to be shared. This is why the making of joint judgments discloses distinctions as to what we take to be real. Christian witness cannot avoid engagement in this fine-grained and necessarily particular activity of explicitly disclosing the "common world" through the practice of making concrete judgments.[42] In practice, what counts for a good judgment is set within the practices and protocols of institutions which are sustained by and also teach "the ways of judgment."[43] These institutionalized ways of judgment by which a common world is articulated may themselves exist within a more or less peaceful, liberal, and tolerant "society." What is clear, however, is that the permissions afforded by a liberal society will not be sufficient to build up this thicker form of a political coexistence, especially if we take into account the points at which this society touches on our "human condition," as for example elements of our bodily life—birth, death, bodily suffering and health— that so deeply shape our living together. How does our view of the substance and dimensions of our "common world" alter if seen within the perspective of the *conditio humana* as determined by God's story? This story includes the whole world and us human beings but also aspects that are decidedly not part of the narrative of secular modernity, namely, resurrection and the reconciliation of the whole cosmos.

Such a question swings the door wide open for epistemological and hermeneutical cooperation with biosciences insofar as they share the task of disclosing the *conditio humana* in its content-full givenness and appearance in a cosmic perspective. We must ask, of course, how best to describe that noetic task again as a practice which communicates that articulated and disclosed world to any other common "world." Judging is basically mediated by distinctions recognized as disclosing that common world on these frontlines where God's story meets this "world."[44] Judgments within the Christian ethos follow a theological grammar given with God's story, such as the distinction between God and "gods," between God and human beings,[45] between hope and desire, between advent and future, and numerous other similar fundamental distinctions.

The practice of judging again has to be seen as a good work addressed to public opinion with its characteristic patterns and languages. This is another iteration

---

42. See Chapter 3.

43. Oliver O'Donovan, *The Ways of Judgment* (Grand Rapids: Eerdmans, 2005). See also "The Ways of Discernment" in Chapter 3 of this volume.

44. This is to be seen in contradiction to a "modernity," which pretends to grasp the world by distinctions, yet produces hybrids instead. For that argument, see Bruno Latour, *We Have Never Been Modern* (Cambridge, MA: Harvard University Press, 1993).

45. Cf. Habermas, *The Future of Human Nature*.

of the work of faith seeking understanding. Faith in its very content has "to seek understanding"—that is, to articulate and to explore its own knowledge—a "noetic" faith as Paul has indicated (Rom. 12:2). This lived exploration is different in kind from faith as the rational exposition of beliefs, because, as Hauerwas observes, "understanding" is not a practice of rational (self-) assurance or (self-) justification, but exploration and witness of the content of faith as it is addressed to the world."[46]

Faith seeking understanding has, however, been conceived in at least two different ways—and this again is significant for its eschatological meaning.[47] On the one hand, some have proposed that faith seeks understanding in order to comprehend the content of faith that can be squared with rational evidence. A categorically different approach to faith's seeking of understanding takes "understanding" not as the procedure of assuring faith within our common "world" but as an exploration of God's promises in order to discern God's will—that is, what God's story with His world and with us human beings is about in the way Jesus did when he prayed in Gethsemane, "My Father, if this cannot pass unless I drink it, your will be done" (Mt. 26:42). Jesus was ready to explore His father's will by letting Him realize His will according to His story with His people.

Karl Barth's reading of Anselm's *fides quaerens intellectum* encapsulates the theological and epistemological implications of this second approach. Anselm, Barth says, is concerned

> to meditate upon a particular article of the Christian Credo by itself, that is to investigate the meaning of what it contains that he may place it in its relation to all the other articles or to the one next to it, comparing and connecting it with them and allowing them to illumine it. All this he does with the intention of himself conceiving by reflection the hidden law of the object of faith about which this article speaks, that thereby he may show it forth and so be able to know the thing believed: the noetic *ratio* becomes the discovery of the ontic *ratio* in so far as it follows after it; in which case the remaining articles of the *Credo* point the way along which the ontic precedes the noetic *ratio*, along which the noetic *ratio* has to follow to discover it.[48]

The "noetic" *ratio* as it is described here—the understanding (*intelligere*)—follows the "ontic" *ratio*; it follows the actual reality given with God's story. This noetic *ratio* tracks along with God's story in order to reflect on the logic displayed in its given content.

---

46. Hauerwas, *With the Grain of the Universe*.
47. See Chapter 3.
48. Karl Barth, *Anselm: Fides Quaerens Intellectum: Anselm's Proof of the Existence of God in the Context of his Theological Scheme* (London: SCM Press, 1960), 53.

Witnessing Another World to the World

We have seen that Engelhardt's genealogy rests on particular judgments about the history of Christianity and about the shape of the "common world" assumed in secular liberalism. What might it look like live out a different hope, the hope that God's world as it appears in God's reconciliation with the world (cosmos) through Jesus Christ will become really present within this "world-time" to which Paul points?

> All this is from God, who reconciled us to himself through Christ, and has given us the ministry of reconciliation; that is, in Christ God was reconciling the world [cosmos] to himself, not counting their trespasses against them, and entrusting the message of reconciliation to us. So we are ambassadors for Christ, since God is making his appeal through us; we entreat you on behalf of Christ, be reconciled to God. (2 Cor. 5:18–20)

According to this message Christians are to follow the "logos of reconciliation." This reconciliation includes the cosmos, Paul also insists: "For the creation was subjected to futility, not of its own will but by the will of the one who subjected it, in hope that the creation itself will be set free from its bondage to decay and will obtain the freedom of the glory of the children of God" (Rom. 8:20–21).

Following Paul on this point means turning the common question around, to ask how the "secular world" appears within the story of God's reconciled world (cosmos). Which "world" are we talking about? On the one hand, the secular world is—according to Paul—the present world-time (Greek *aion*, in the Latin *saeculum*, usually translated "world") whose patterns Christians should not adopt (Rom. 12:2). This is the basis for the Pauline injunction that Christians may not assimilate to a Christianity that is "conformed" to this "world-time" (*aion*). But a new reconciled world has been initiated, a new cosmos within God's story and its new time, as affirmed in Jesus Christ. To come into understanding will mean living into this promise, the *logos* addressed to this world-time. Christians bear witness to God's reconciliation in that any judgments they make must be judgments of the "ambassadors for Christ," witnesses of God's story.

Dietrich Bonhoeffer emphasized this disposition of Christian witness to the present world in a particularly pointed manner. "The New Testament is concerned only with the realization [*Wirklichwerden*] of the Christ-reality in the contemporary world that it already embraces, owns, and inhabits. There are not two competing realms standing side by side and battling over the borderline, as if this question of boundaries was always the decisive one," as he puts it in his *Ethics*. "Rather, the whole reality of the world has already been drawn into and is held together in Christ. History moves only from this center and toward this center.[49] The task of the Christian is to witness to the story of the cosmos reconciled to the world

---

49. DBWE 6, 58.

or "world-time" in which it finds itself. The *logos* of an already reconciled world (cosmos) is already present, addressing Christians and non-Christians alike with the call not to live their lives by the rules of a "world-time" destined to disappear.

How the New World Becomes Present: The Encounter of Worship and Bioethics

If "understanding" means "exploring the new world" within this "world-time" the criterion for Christian judgment is tied to the *adventus* of this new world. Engelhardt is right on this crucial point, that Christian faith has its actualized form as worship. It is through worship that Christians exploratively bear witness to God's world within the "world." As Paul puts it, "I appeal to you therefore, brothers and sisters, by the mercies of God, to present your bodies as a living sacrifice, holy and acceptable to God, which is your spiritual worship" (Rom. 12:1). "Spiritual" here translates *logike*, which is translated in other versions as "reasonable." Both translations are debatable. It is better to read *logike* as "in accordance to the logos, the Word." This translation highlights the central importance of worship being the sacrifice of the *somata*, which may also be translated into "lives" and "bodily existence." In worship people let their bodily lives be absorbed by, come into tune with, this *logike*. Christian morality is not a matter of principles, but of partaking of this living bodily ethos of a worshipping community.[50]

Essential aspects of the Christian ethos in the New Testament converge with Engelhardt's emphasis on the importance of Christian worship that includes the Christian ethos.[51] It is on this basis that we may affirm John Howard Yoder's decisive insight that there is

> a kind of mediation, a "bridging-over" . . . from the faith community to the other social structures. This kind of "mediation" is not a mental or verbal operation of translation or conceptual bridging, but rather the concrete historical presence, among their neighbors, of believers who for Jesus' sake do ordinary social things differently. They fraternize trans-ethnically; they share their bread; they forgive one another. These activities are visible; they are not opaque rituals. They lend themselves to being observed, imitated, and extrapolated.[52]

This is the witness of an ethos filled out in practices and producing good works. According to the New Testament, Christian worship is the primal site of witness. It is in this context that human beings may engage in practices whose mere existence already bears witness to the "world" that there is a different way of life that is oriented by an alternative reality. There is no world-historical reason

---

50. See John Howard Yoder, *Body Politics: Five Practices of the Christian Community Before the Watching World* (Scottdale: Herald Press, 2001).
51. For a further unfolding, see especially Bernd Wannenwetsch, *Political Worship: Ethics for Christian Citizens* (Oxford: Oxford University Press, 2004).
52. Yoder, *Body Politics*, 75.

for the endurance of the Christian form of "body politics" and its implicit announcement of the obsolescence of the common "world." Forgiving, baptizing, breaking bread are all practices that embody "a new mode of group relationships," organized around listening and teaching according to the "unity in Christ."[53] The Christian ethos so described is an ethos of creaturely life, an ethos of the new creation as it appears within the present world-time. Creaturely life within God's story is a living with God, in cooperation with God and transformed by the Spirit. Its witness takes the form of corresponding stories of how this living within God's story has concretely played out in transformations of the life-form (*morphe*) of believers. This means to become "holy." To be "holy" means to live within God's story, receiving and suffering God's very own will.[54] This witness of holiness will present a contrast to other (quite) different ways of thinking and arguing. In so doing it exposes a "faith seeking understanding" in its exploration of God's will.

The concreteness of Christian worship in its whole range and depth, including genuine Christian practices and good works, brings into view what is specifically Christian in relation to "bioethics." "Bioethics" appears as a crucial aspect of the Christian witness to today's world in touching so directly on the *conditio humana* as it is determined by God's story. Christian witness pivotally concerns bioethics, because God's story encompasses the phenomena of "body," "soul," "understanding," "mind," and "spirit." Any pulling apart of body from mind, body from soul, or body from spirit contradicts God's story in Jesus Christ with its constant emphasis on healing, bodily resurrection, bodily communication, and body politics. This is not because of an anthropological notion of "wholeness" or "unity of body and soul, body and spirit," but because of a human existence within the context of God's story, because of God's realization of bodily life in Jesus Christ; therefore, the phenomena of human life will be seen in a different logic.[55] The human "body" (*soma*) is involved in God's story because this story is essentially concerned with God's creatures in their bodily existence.

The growing awareness of the phenomenon of "biopolitics"—introduced pivotally by Michel Foucault[56]—highlights the increasing breadth and depth of contemporary attempts to govern the human body, body- and biotechniques.

---

53. Ibid.

54. Cf. Brian Brock and Stephanie Brock, "Being Disabled in the New World of Genetic Testing: A Snapshot of Shifting Landscapes," in *Theology, Disability, and the New Genetics: Why Science Needs the Church*, ed. John Swinton and Brian Brock (London: T&T Clark, 2007), 29–43.

55. For a deeper theological analysis, see Bernd Wannenwetsch, "Owning Our Bodies? The Politics of Self-Possession and the Body of Christ (Hobbes, Locke and Paul)," *Studies in Christian Ethics* 26 (2013): 50–65.

56. Michel Foucault, *The Birth of Biopolitics*, trans. Graham Burchell (Basingstoke: Palgrave Macmillan, 2008).

The question is how, or from what angle Christian ethics is to be involved in the debate largely being carried on by bioethicists. The critical approach proposed by Engelhardt concentrates on the difference between all rational descriptions of the body and human life and a categorically different Christian notion of human bodily existence in its determination by real Christian worship, as Corinna Delkeskamp-Hayes has noticed.

> In reconnecting our contemporary reflections in moral theory and ontology with the moral and metaphysical commitments that lie at the roots of Western culture, Engelhardt re-opens the question concerning man's place in the cosmos. He thus secures, once again, the ground on which one could even ask the question whether or not one should pursue that genuinely (non-reduced) Christian quest for ultimate Truth into which Engelhardt invites his readers.[57]

I have been suggesting a slightly different question: What should we reckon to be the "ground" of any notion of the *conditio humana* in the face of the urgent provocation of bioethical debates around biotechnology and biopolitical techniques? Can there be any other ground for a real understanding of the *conditio humana* independent of that "reality" (Bonhoeffer) determined by God's story in Jesus Christ? This is a grounding that can never be adequately replaced by a political consensus however it might be generated in a liberal society. Whether or not the judgments to which Christian ethical life bears witness find a place in the overlapping consensus of modern pluralist states, does not the demand remain unchanged for Christians to justify their actions making appeal to the terms of accepted practical reason while continuing to convey the message of a content-full ethos addressed to our political living together (including in legal forms[58])? Will there not always be at least a "good work" of witnessing through the enacted Christian ethos to the range of Christian worship and its significance for the world as a bearer of the good news of God's story?

The truth is that were there no Christian worship there would be no message, only the affirmation of a more or less unique Christian view or position. Engelhardt's reminder of the importance of Christian worship thus opens up the genuine task of Christian ethics in the vast field of bioethics. Bioethics is the focus of this task insofar as Christian ethics is not rooted in "ideas," "worldviews," or "anthropologies," but explores God's story with the world and His people, the transfiguration of human bodily life, its "holiness," including the renewal of human understanding.

---

57. Corinna Delkeskamp-Hayes, "Morality in a Postmodern, Post-Christian World: Engelhardt's Diagnosis and Therapy," in *At the Roots of Christian Bioethics: Critical Essays on the Thought of H. Tristram Engelhardt, Jr.*, ed. Ana Smith Iltis and Mark J. Cherry (Salem: M&M Scrivener Press, 2010), 59.

58. Cf. Williams, *Faith in the Public Square*.

Hopeful Good Works in the Medical Domain—And in Negotiation

In this chapter I have critically engaged Tristram Engelhardt and his insistence that it is impossible to assume that any secular bioethics could carry the core insights of an explicitly Christian bioethics. I have suggested he undermines his own case by relying on concepts such as "reason" and "culture" that remain within the secular logic that is the target of his critique. He thus runs head-on into an epistemological problem in assuming that there is a sharp disjuncture between Christian and secular/general epistemologies. Close attention to the practical rationality in which techniques of genetic alteration of the human genome are embedded has suggested why the secular/general rationality of modern medicine must in fact take its orientation from some extra-scientific rationality.

The Reformation traditions point us to what is, theologically speaking, the most important difference between the rationality of Christian faith and secular/general rationality: secular rationality seeks to establish the conditions for "justified" or "meaningful" action. To be deemed moral, human beings must conform to the rules set out by this rationality. In a properly theological account, however, human good works rest on the affirmation that God is the one who does justice and makes meaning. This is to understand good human actions as those actions serving God's own faithfulness and justice-making. As they negotiate the boundary between these two rationalities (medicine understood to be operating within the orbit of secular/general rationality) Christians engage in a political negotiation with the world. While affirming the validity of secular rationality, they nevertheless embody an ethos that constantly traverses the boundary of this rationality by enacting, and thus bearing witness to, a peaceable living within God's will and acts.

The hope that orients Christian action in the bioethical sphere catalyzes this exploration of the boundary between these two rationalities and their very different epistemologies. The differences that flow from these two epistemologies are amply displayed in the ways we perceive death, dying, and suffering. Like Engelhardt, I have explained why God's story, rather than the story of "history" or "progress," must determine a truly Christian assessment of these moments in human beings' lives.

I have also followed Engelhardt in affirming that modern political philosophies that rest their account of justice on the idea of an "overlapping consensus" are insufficient frameworks for reaching common public judgments in the context of ethically diverse and fragmented modern societies. In doing so, however, I have again suggested that Engelhardt rests content too early in his criticisms of modern liberal politics in his embrace of an empty procedural account of the justice that can be achieved by the state. This is too modest. Insights and practical trajectories growing from the ethos of the witnessing community can indeed lend some ethical content to modern governance.

This, I have suggested, is the essence of the "good work" of the Christian political community: to foster "bonds of peace" in modern states as they negotiate bioethical questions. By implication, debates about policies around euthanasia, reproductive cloning, and eugenics seem especially apt arenas for this witness. The solution to the problem of the integrity of the Christian medical professional is therefore not, as Engelhardt proposes, to demand a morally content-less public domain but to insist that the good works of Christians, including those of medical practitioners, can also be affirmed as contexts in which God's making of justice and peace can invade, overturn, and even absorb all sorts of content-rich practices and ideologies that may be held by the majority in a given polity. No liberal political system can survive if it does not, in fact, presume its rejuvenation by such generative practices. With this line of reasoning we are brought back to the epistemological problem.

It is through the concrete judgments of Christians that the way of knowing that is bound to God's story with humans enters the public story. Christians ought not aspire to shape society by claiming to possess the one "real" truth or to present theological knowledge as a foundation for all other knowledge, so positioning theology as the queen of the sciences. God's mercy and justice enter the world in the good works that articulate judgments in practical domains that may be embraced and emulated even by those who deny the ontology that orients the Christian ethos. It is in this way that Christian witness to God's rule is concretized in the life of mixed societies. At this central point I am in full agreement with Engelhardt's insistence that the "new world" of God's works emerges most determinatively in Christian worship. When we give our bodies over into the body politic of the church, changes happen that challenge and reshape the contrasting ethos of the societies in which Christians live.

Chapter 8

A Theological-Critical Hermeneutics of Life Engaging Genetic Science

Understanding Human Life: A Common and Public Ethical Task

Ours is a time of exponential growth in understanding the complexity of the interrelations between our minds, our bodies, and the material universe. At the same time (as Chapter 7 explored) ours is also a time of acute awareness of the paradoxes that attend the power of human beings to alter nature as this now begins to extend, through biomedical research, into the part of nature that is our selves. We are beings in the middle: increasingly aware of, and admiring of, the richness of nature, whose complexity becomes daily more apparent even as our awe grows at the capacity of our minds and the human spirit to understand and even direct developments at the most minute levels of life.[1] In such a situation, it behooves us to become more reflectively aware of what sort of exploration we are embarking on today in the biomedical domain. In this chapter I will clarify the idea that the epigeneticist Walter Doerfler and I have found most useful in our search for an interdisciplinary approach to this common task. We use the label *conditio humana* to highlight the complex indeterminacy of the human as well as clarifying what we are saying when we commit ourselves to interdisciplinary research.

In this chapter I will foreground the Latin term *conditio humana*. I do so because it usefully flanks several linguistic pitfalls on its way to setting the limits for a methodologically coherent procedure that can guide attempts to define the characteristics of human life. The crucial pitfall to be avoided is the collapse of the human into a definition that makes human beings yet another part of "nature."[2] Such a procedure allows us to ask about, rather than assert or assume the content of the *conditio humana*, by asking, for instance: In what sense is human identity describable or determinable at the level of molecular biology? Does it make sense

---

1. Walter Doerfler, "*Conditio humana* as Viewed by a Geneticist," in *Theology, Disability, and the New Genetics: Why Science Needs the Church*, ed. John Swinton and Brian Brock (London: T&T Clark, 2007), 117–31, citation from 118.
2. Keller, *Making Sense of Life*.

to say that the realities of human life that can now be seen by the new technologies of biomedical science tell us something about what it means to be human? Or are they rather only the raw materials out of which the "real" human will one day emerge? This is an example of the way in which—by placing an emphasis on the questions that lie between academic disciplines—we can put questions about human identity to biological science in a manner that does not close down the more fundamental questions that are typically skirted in contemporary biomedical ethics discourses. We share the premise that the work of trying to understand "nature" is simultaneously investigating the spiritual or intellectual conditions for understanding the *conditio humana*—whether we are aware of this or not—as many in both bioscience and biomedical ethics are not.

To ask about the *conditio humana* is ultimately a meta-inquiry into the aims and procedures of our biomedical explorations. For what purpose and on what grounds do we study the *conditio humana* in one way or another? My starting assumption is that, broadly speaking, the task of this sort of explorative account of our human condition is to become aware of the complexity of its inner configuration, and so the distinct coherence of human embodied wholeness. All the new approaches and instruments, at whatever level they view the human being, should be utilized in order to generate all sorts of descriptions and visualizations that might be relevant to ethical reflections on our human existence.

Theological ethics is the work of attending to the critical features and contexts of our human life so that human beings don't get lost and morally disoriented in their complexity. The implication of this presumption is that ethics is not to get bogged down in limited domains of rational thought (as it has often done in relation to so called "problem cases") but must focus its effort on articulating the implications of a lived ethos of human life. The labor of articulating those ethical implications includes becoming aware of the configurations of interpretative ethical praxis that are already being lived out in a specific domain. This is work that cannot be accomplished outside of a dialogical exchange between various languages and perspectives. Thus, the work of theological ethics in practice must begin by engaging in the hermeneutical work of understanding the ethical and the scientific languages involved, as well as the concepts and metaphors used to describe human life in a given domain. These concepts and metaphors deeply shape what can, or will, be understood as the ethical issues arising in a given domain. This work of critically examining our own ethical language and presumptions is hermeneutically complicated because it implicates our own interpretative practice. Thus to engage it means doing preparatory work on coming to terms with our own hermeneutic presumptions and interpretative models before we are able to engage in substantive judgment of the adequacy and implications of the models and practices we are attempting to interrogate.[3]

---

3. See Evelyn Fox Keller, *Making Sense of Life: Explaining Biological Development with Models, Metaphors, and Machines* (Cambridge, MA: Harvard University Press, 2003). Christoph Rehmann-Sutter presents one significant example in his critical work on the

The aim of this critical work is to assess the theological and philosophical adequacy of the languages and concepts we are using to understand a given phenomenon. The criterion in this assessment is this: In what sense does a given language or description open a path of insight, and offer the distinctions necessary for people to recognize the contours of human life and the human condition, so that it is present to them as a tangible and meaning-saturated reality? This is the sort of question that will not be answered by allowing ethical discussions to remain confined within common contemporary patterns of ethical thinking about biomedicine, focused as they most often are on ethical or moral dilemmas in the field of medical practice and not venturing further afield to examine the multiple contexts to which the questions under discussion also belong. To be serious, ethical reflection has to be properly located in its genuine context, and when we are talking about human life, the proper context must be one that looks to understand the human lives that we recognize, live, and will be forced to try to understand as long as we live.

In Chapter 2 I offered a reading of Bonhoeffer's account of Christian ethics as a reflection on, and exploration of, the reality God has determined to be good for human living. This divinely given and complete reality is one that we may not see in a given case, but is promised to become present to us as long as we do not obscure, distort, or restrict it by our ways and modes of grasping it. The task is to recognize the reality to which we human beings belong, which is graciously held out to us for us to live into the fullness of human life. From the perspective of sinners, this seems like an "alternative" reality—but Bonhoeffer insists that this is in fact the "real" reality that God has created and determined as it appears in Jesus Christ, God's way of sharing this reality with creatures. God's story of the world is a reality that reveals what we normally take to be real as the "alternative." Christian witness in every domain and amidst every ethical conflict has the remit not to distance itself from the alternative reality generated by each generation of this fallen aeon, but to carefully and critically engage it in order to highlight within it the paths of redeemed creatureliness.

Theological ethics understood in this way is a necessarily public affair, given its insistence on asking how publicly shared language is enclosed in God's word that has been entrusted to us. Theological ethics is necessarily public communication because its material is the universal human reality (as discussed in Chapters 4 and 7). Biotechnological research, as a human activity, insistently highlights the urgent necessity that both the church and members of secular society improve their mutual language skills. A theological interpretation of the human condition entails elaborating contemporary ways of speaking that accord with God's word in a dialogical and critical connection with scientific languages, especially with

---

program metaphor used to describe the function of the DNA. See Christoph Rehmann-Sutter, "Genetics, Embodiment and Identity," in *On Human Nature: Anthropological, Biological, and Philosophical Foundations*, ed. Armin Grunwald, Mathias Gutmann, and Eva M. Neumann-Held (Berlin: Springer, 2002), 23–50.

molecular biology and its interpretations of our human biological condition. It is thus an ineradicably hermeneutic process. Theology and bioscience do have a common field of description and interpretation, the human condition in its bodily appearance, and they share the question of how to describe and understand this condition to the extent that it is susceptible to human understanding. It is not only theologians who are trying not to be entrapped in false descriptions of the world. Scientists too are acutely aware of the distorting effects of ideological conceptions of the human condition and of interpretations implicit in scientific descriptions. They also know that these distorting views—which they too hold—cannot be rooted out by claiming a neutral position beyond them, but only by attending to the phenomena under investigation with a highly reflective and critical understanding.

The approach I am describing allows ethical inquiry to step out of the narrow remit of solving problems and dilemmas we have produced, such as what we can do or not do with human embryos according to the algebra of calculating the limits that morality or definitions of responsibility will allow us to go. Ethics, I am suggesting, is rather primarily work in the linguistic domain, a critical engagement with our dominant patterns of moral discourse in order hermeneutically to transform them by relating them to their real context as part of our human condition, as just described. Theological hermeneutics is enabled to recognize this more expansive domain of human discourse as the proper context for ethical discussion of our human reality because it affirms that the contours of human life are determined, preserved, and saved by God's work. Such a theological approach will lead us very deep into the hermeneutics of scientific approaches to human life as they communicate with all other contemporary ways of conceptualizing human life. As we enter into this hermeneutic work, we do so in awareness that there are virulent interpretations of human life that negatively impact on our human life and living together. It is these destructive and obscurantist descriptions of human life that we are trying to break down with this critical hermeneutics of human life in its social context. We deploy a hermeneutics that reaches the goals of the more familiar ethical approaches with their focus on questions of moral limits, or equal rights and mutual respect—by opposing and going beyond them.

The Common Task of Science, Hermeneutics, and Ethics: The Conditio Humana

For three years the molecular biologist Walter Doerfler and I have been engaged in a lecture series at the University of Erlangen under the title "Understanding the *conditio humana*—scientific and ethical approaches."[4] In this context,

---

4. The procedure followed in this jointly taught lecture course is recounted in Brian Brock, Walter Doerfler, and Hans G. Ulrich, "Genetics, Conversation and Conversion: A Discourse at the Interface of Molecular Biology and Christian Ethics," in *Theology, Disability, and the New Genetics*, 146–60. See also Doerfler, "*Conditio humana* as Viewed by a Geneticist."

"ethics" means the task of describing the *conditio humana* in order to find out what is addressed to us human beings as obligatory. Both molecular biology and theological ethics share the concern to bring their own ethical questions about the consequences of deploying techniques which touch so directly and sweepingly on our human existence. We engage in this work amidst intensive debates about the advisability of techniques related to gene-therapy, body-enhancement, data-governance, health-governance, reproduction technologies, and genetic counseling. Debates in almost all of these fields are framed as searches for limits, the limits of our human nature in terms of its identity and the moral obligations related to it, as well as the limits of our obligation to preserve it.[5] To see all these domains as best understood by looking for the (outer) limits of allowable behavior expresses a definite judgment about what the relevant context of the discussion is, and what moral approach to these contexts is best deployed.[6] For the reasons already outlined, however, these ethical debates do not evade the deeper debate about how to think well about altering human nature: How are we to distinguish between human nature as something that can be empirically described, identified, or treated? In what sense are the scientific, philosophical, and ethical approaches we deploy in this inquiry themselves simply expressions of this human nature?[7]

Taken together these debates have thoroughly unsettled many of the traditional ways of thinking about human nature and in so doing brought about a widespread clarity that some basic concepts, definitions and theories as gene, genome, genetic development, genetic heredity, genetics, and epi-genetics have already been undergoing radical change and development. The consequence of these intellectual shifts has produced an intellectual opening in many fields, making it necessary to discuss what is going on in these processes of discovery in a concerted way.[8] New approaches are emerging that converge with the theological focus I have just set out by foregrounding the methodological and linguistic work done by metaphors

---

5. See Grunwald et al., eds., *On Human Nature*.

6. These limit-seeking approaches are surveyed by Christoph Rehmann-Sutter, "Limits of Bioethics," in *Bioethics in Cultural Contexts: Reflections on Methods and Finitude*, ed. Marcus Düwell, Christoph Rehmann-Sutter, and Dietmar Mieth (Springer: Dordrecht 2006), 59, 71–2. For the relation between "religious" and "secular" ethics, the task of ethics, and a theological understanding of "limits" see Bernd Wannenwetsch, "Loving the Limit: Dietrich Bonhoeffer's Hermeneutics of Human Creatureliness and Its Challenge for an Ethics of Medical Care," in *Bonhoeffer and the Biosciences: An Initial Exploration*, ed. Ralf K. Wüstenberg, Stefan Heuser, and Esther Hornung (Frankfurt am Main: Peter Lang, 2010), 89–108.

7. See Evelyn Fox Keller, *Making Sense of Life: Explaining Biological Development with Models, Metaphors, and Machines* (Cambridge, MA: Harvard University Press, 2003); for the question of self-reference, see Christoph Rehmann-Sutter, "Genetics, Embodiment and Identity."

8. See Keller, *Making Sense of Life*.

in the descriptive and interpretative task. Christoph Rehmann-Sutter, for instance, defines ethical work in this field as

> a reflective and evaluative communicative practice that takes place in and is interwoven with other practices. It collaborates with different approaches and methods that can be integrated, even if tensions remain. But morality—the topics and issues that ethics evaluates and reflects on—is broader than the scope of ethical methods. It is the social and political context of ethical issues that provide them with a definite meaning, and which need to be investigated by other sciences as well, some hermeneutical and others empirical. Ethics relies upon their work. Ethics can help to facilitate communication across borders: across the divide between science and the humanities, and between subcultures and religious traditions. But it can contribute better by helping to understand and interpret the concerns of different people than by deducing rational solutions to the issues from moral principles.[9]

For Rehmann-Sutter (and me), ethics is a hermeneutical task, another way of approaching the "data," "facts," and "texts" provided by molecular biology—one that, incidentally, is fostering some of the most genuinely interdisciplinary work going on in the contemporary university and hospital.

Ethics seen from this perspective and encountering this intellectually open situation cannot make its central focus the search for moral or ethical limits.[10] Instead it seeks after the extensibility, possibilities, and specific characteristics of knowledge. It raises questions with far-reaching critical force about the limits of knowledge and procedures of research. Only on the basis of this work can ethical or moral reflections on "limits" be undertaken, and it should be pursued as a reflection on the knowledge that has so far been revealed to flow from these new research procedures and the biological data on which it is based. Such work will include critical questions about the genesis or the genealogies of knowledge, the models, metaphors and semantics of its presentation and its "production."

Within the ambit of this critical work of understanding the *conditio humana*—which is, as we have said, an irreducibly common work of ethical reflection—discussion must constantly return to clarify what "we" actually understand of molecular biology, and what that knowledge itself relates to outside of the narrow domain of the scientific lab. The common task is understanding together. Our shared hermeneutical task is to understand the "Of what?" "Related to what?" and the "For what?" Because asking such questions is a work of discovering an understanding that is shared, it needs to be ensconced in a public institutional

---

9. Rehmann-Sutter, *Limits of Bioethics*, 76. See also 71–5.
10. Brian Brock, *Christian Ethics in a Christian* (Grand Rapids: Eerdmans, 2010), 187–90.

level,[11] especially those levels where there is a need for discourse between ethics and science.[12]

Seeking the Conditio Humana *Together*

Walter Doerfler and I have found that the best way to gain initial purchase on our common project of seeking a new understanding of the *conditio humana* in the wake of the biotechnological revolution is to ask what we mean when we say we are engaged in interdisciplinary work. It is here that we first discovered the utility of the Latin concept *conditio humana*: it largely avoids the most misleading or insufficient understandings of this unique subject. The concept of the *conditio humana* allows us to consider the possibility that the subject under investigation is much bigger than the narrowly biological work of determining the conditions of living or surviving that go with the human biological body. Thus the term *conditio humana* is one that invites us to consider all of the characteristics of human life that give it sense or meaning, as Evelyn Fox Keller has discussed.[13] The term does include the question of the identity of human beings as it is describable or determinable at the level of molecular biology. Yet it also intentionally opens discussion of more complex and deeper understandings of what we may then identify as the contours of our human existence as it is embodied and as it can be viewed and reconstructed at the level of molecular biology.

In other words, we ask about the whole of the human being when we raise the question of the human condition as one that is lived as embodied. Human bodies are situated in a highly complex context of living, experience, description, and interpretation. To look at our bodies in this way may even widen our perspective on the traditional model of the book of nature in its relation to other unexpectedly

---

11. See, e.g., http://www.genenames.org/PUS/index.html.

12. The website in the previous note indexes information about genes and "diseases" and includes this very telling comment about the practical difficulties that call forth interdisciplinary engagement (footnote 8):

> Most of the genetic disorders featured on this web site are the direct result of a mutation in one gene. However, one of the most difficult problems ahead is to find out how genes contribute to diseases that have a complex pattern of inheritance, such as in the cases of diabetes, asthma, cancer and mental illness. In all these cases, no one gene has the yes/no power to say whether a person has a disease or not. It is likely that more than one mutation is required before the disease is manifest, and a number of genes may each make a subtle contribution to a person's susceptibility to a disease; genes may also affect how a person reacts to environmental factors. Unraveling these networks of events will undoubtedly be a challenge for some time to come, and will be amply assisted by the availability of the sequence of the human genome.

13. Keller, *Making Sense of Life*.

relevant books in which we discover the bodiliness of the *conditio humana* to be inscribed.[14] This hermeneutical approach to ethics rests on assumptions about the existence of different languages in the created realm. The language of nature and the language of the Word of God stand alongside one another, laying upon us the hermeneutical task of interpretation and translation. One of the paradigmatic encapsulations of this point in the biblical traditions is found in Psalm 19 and the long and rich history of interpretation that it stimulated.

> The heavens are telling the glory of God;
>   and the firmament proclaims his handiwork.
> Day to day pours forth speech,
>   and night to night declares knowledge.
> There is no speech, nor are there words;
>   their voice is not heard;
> yet their voice goes out through all the earth,
>   and their words to the end of the world.
> In them he has set a tent for the sun,
> which comes forth like a bridegroom leaving his chamber,
>   and like a strong man runs its course with joy.
> Its rising is from the end of the heavens,
>   and its circuit to the end of them;
>   and there is nothing hid from its heat.
> The law of the LORD is perfect,
>   reviving the soul;
> the testimony of the LORD is sure, making wise the simple. (Ps. 19:1-7, RSV)

Here we see the meeting of the two languages of creation: the language spoken by the heavens and the language of the law as it is written in the book of books. On this basis we are in general agreement with the remark of Rehmann-Sutter that:

> The impact of genetics on our understanding of the human body is even stronger than on our understanding of the human mind. As long as we do not separate the body from what we consider to be ourselves; as long as we resist the Cartesian flight into a philosophy of two substances, identifying ourselves with the spiritual part and treating the material part as *res extensa* in the objective world of nature; as long as we distrust such split-off theories of the self, the genetic explanation of our embodiment can be recognized as a central part of our discourse on identity.[15]

---

14. See Hans Blumenberg, *Die Lesbarkeit der Welt* (Frankfurt: Suhrkamp, 1979).

15. Rehmann-Sutter, *Genetics, Embodiment, and Identity*, 43. See also Rehmann-Sutter, *Limits of Bioethics*, 74f. Rehmann-Sutter links this assertion with a suggestion that ethicists should also draw on social-scientific research in order to be more clear about the "given" moral and ethical situation in which this moral debate is being had. "Empirical social

It is impossible to separate the spiritual and imaginative mind from its neurobiological substrate, and in this sense, biology is "the precondition for any philosophical endeavor."[16]

Here, however, it is critical not to forget Blaise Pascal's prescient warning:

> What makes our inability to know things absolute is that they are simple in themselves, while we are composed of two opposing natures of different kinds, soul and body. For it is impossible for the part of us which reasons to be anything but spiritual, and even if it were claimed that we are simply corporeal, that would still more preclude us from knowing things, since there is nothing so inconceivable as the idea that matter knows itself. We cannot possibly know how it could know itself.[17]

---

research into ethical issues and normative reflection in ethics are naturally related to each other. . . . Together they will produce a richer description and lead to a more informed reflection about the issues concerned. This is a plea for an integrative interdisciplinary approach to bioethics" (74–5).

16. "The relation between theories of genetics and ideas of human identity or nature is an interpretative one. The criteria for a critical evaluation of positive interpretations should be discussed by a genetic hermeneutics, which could be developed systematically as a subfield of the philosophy of biology" (Rehmann-Sutter, *Genetics, Embodiment, and Identity*, 43). See also Doerfler, "Conditio humana as Viewed by a Geneticist," 117–19.

17. Blaise Pascal, *Pensées*, trans. A. J. Krailsheimer (London: Penguin, 1966), Aphorisms 72, 94. The continuation of this passage is worth quoting, not least for its display of the implications of the break between all ancient teleological cosmologies of motion that is characteristic of modern thought in distinction from the ancient world into which Christianity was born:

Thus, if we are simply material, we can know nothing at all, and, if we are composed of mind and matter, we cannot have perfect knowledge of things which are simply spiritual or corporeal.

That is why nearly all philosophers confuse their ideas of things, and speak spiritually of corporeal things and corporeally of spiritual ones, for they boldly assert that bodies tend to fall, that they aspire towards their centre, that they flee from destruction, that they fear a void, that they have inclination, sympathies, antipathies, all things pertaining only to things spiritual. And when they speak of minds, they consider them as being in a place, and attribute to them movement from one place to another, which are things pertaining only to bodies.

Instead of receiving ideas of these things in their purity, we colour them with our qualities and stamp our own composite being on all the simple things we contemplate.

Who would not think, to see us compounding everything of mind and matter, that such a mixture is perfectly intelligible to us? Yet this is the thing we understand least; man is to himself the greatest prodigy in nature, for he cannot conceive what body is, and still less what mind is, and least of all how a body could be joined to a mind. This is his supreme difficulty, and yet it is is his very being. *The way in which minds are attached to bodies*

This warning does not contradict our awareness of the many new challenges concerning the complex interrelations of mind and body on different levels, including the level that Pascal indicates, namely, the level at which we human beings are part of that "natural" context which we are exploring. We are part of, but also addressees of nature, which offers itself to us for exploration, recognition and admiration. Even more importantly, to dive wholly into this exploration is to become acutely aware of its infinitude. The infinitude of the human being turns out to be the most fundamental insight of all, that our human condition is one that hangs in an oddly suspended middle between finite and infinite realms of knowledge and experience. Through science we are becoming even more aware of the concrete limits of our human bodily existence, learning, for instance, about the telomeres that determine when we shall die. At the same time the scope of our powers to engage in this research reveals with new clarity the openness of our embodied human spirit, sustained by our brains, to reach out into the infinite deeps of nature.[18]

As we search to understand the spiritual or intellectual conditions for understanding the *conditio humana* we are thus simultaneously trying to understand "nature." All understanding will have to be reflexive in the sense of having to consider how we as human beings "making" the present are in reality reshaping the reality to which we belong to in the very process of our exploration of the mechanics of the human body.[19] Long before the rise of anything like today's power to alter human life, Pascal recognized the infinite task implied in "making" present or rendering it "viewable."

To put the matter in this way is to include from the outset the question of what our explorations are for and to what they are directed. What is the purpose of our studying the *conditio humana* in one way rather than another? Such a question draws attention to the overarching task as an explorative one. Developing any account of our human condition in its embodied wholeness will be discovered in no other way, and precisely because the task is so complex and multifaceted it will not escape the constant need to be discovered ever anew in its complexity, relations, and coherence.[20] To define the task in this way never escapes its remit as a descriptive account, one that is in principle interested in all the new approaches and instruments at any level of possible description and visualization that appear to be relevant for ethical reflections on our human existence.

---

is beyond man's understanding, and yet this is what man is. [Augustine, *The City of God* XXI.10]. (ibid.)

18. Doerfler, "*Conditio humana* as Viewed by a Geneticist," 118.

19. On the question of self-reference, see Rehmann-Sutter, *Genetics, Embodiment and Identity.*

20. Ibid., 40.

Description and Visualization

The "endlessness" of explorations of the *conditio humana* can be more precisely stated. What we see is determined by how we look, and when we are looking at ourselves, our tools are constantly evolving. Molecular biology presents us with an immensely dense and complex description and visualization—but of what?[21] It is the "what" that is ultimately the central topic under discussion, and it is not necessarily the case that it becomes more clear the more the description develops. The reality is that what we see cannot be extricated from what we "want" to see.[22] What we "want" to see will be to a large extent determined by the heuristic we deploy by which we see anything at all as well as the models through which we visualize our embodiment.

But is the choice of investigative method and speculative models truly a free choice? Evelyn Fox Keller has argued that one of the key advantages of scientific research is the indefiniteness of its subject.[23] The very indefiniteness of living phenomena protects scientific research from the temptation to narrow its perspective and so preemptively limit what might come to be discovered. Scientific descriptions are continuously subjected to reevaluation and change as new findings emerge. This openness, and what we may consider as an infinite process of bringing about new elements of observation and calculation, makes scientific descriptions hermeneutically stimulating for understanding of the *conditio humana*. Any detail may once again catalyze new horizons of understanding. There is a parallel here to the development of historical narratives, in that the emergence of new data demands revision of the overall narrative of what is understood to have happened.[24]

Parallel other scientific areas, what we are looking for here are what Clifford Geertz calls "thick descriptions" of our embodied human condition.[25] To call this work descriptive is not to suggest that this mode of proceeding is not reflective of its linguistic, conceptual, and theoretical implications and presuppositions, because a central part of its task will be to become aware of the normative elements of the scientific methods involved. Calling this sort of ethics descriptive associates its work with empirical description or (even) explanation of its ongoing development. Description is an essential part of a hermeneutical approach as long as we realize that it uses and develops media such as language or visual representations in order to convey awareness and understanding, implicit and explicit, of our embodied human existence. Hermeneutical approaches can be called explicit when we draw on elaborated theories, models, or metaphors for our descriptions. They may be called "implicit" as far as we continue to rely on descriptions and visualization that

---

21. See Rehmann-Sutter on the "visual regime": *Limits of Bioethics*, 70.
22. Rehmann-Sutter, *Genetics, Embodiment and Identity*, 38.
23. Keller, *Making Sense of Life*.
24. For other parallel points see ibid., 39f.
25. Clifford Geertz, *The Interpretation of Cultures: Selected Essays* (New York: Basic Books, 1973), 6. For the concept of description, see Rehmann-Sutter, *Genetics, Embodiment and Identity*, 42.

have not yet been critically examined—admitting that even reflective examination will never fully transform descriptions and visualizations into "pure" descriptive accounts purged of all interpretive elements.

Naturalism?

The foregoing will have suggested the impossibility of the claim that the ethical act in relation to the human being is somehow to be responsible to "nature." A hermeneutic approach suggests a healthy caution toward arguments for naturalistic approaches in ethics. These approaches are united in presuming that there is a stable natural fundament from which ethics can take its independent orientation, apart from the self-presentation of science and its generation of facts by way of scientific methods and its process of conveying these facts to others through various methods of presentation and visualization. The factual results of scientific research are always susceptible to critical reevaluation since all possible scientific claims may be disproved by subsequent findings. In science, this process of disproving and revisiting what is understood to be a fact is understood as positive, and even enriching of ethical reflection. Examples of this process abound, as Thomas Kuhn most famously argued in *The Structure of Scientific Revolutions*, and in the biosciences this process has been most recently been highlighted by debates about epigenetic processes changing—sometimes radically—the advice given to prospective parents by genetic counselors.[26]

Here the descriptive-hermeneutical approach in ethics is especially important, because naturalistic accounts of ethics are locked into readings of the field of molecular biology and philosophy or ethics in order to discover the "limits" and ends given in nature. Naturalist approaches do offer various accounts of the limits that they seek, as well as where these limits are needed. Some seek moral limits of intervention into "human nature," not only with respect to therapeutic interventions or other forms of alteration of what we today call human nature but also seeking to limit scientific investigations into some features of the material world itself on the grounds that the very investigation is an objectification of human nature.

Beyond Moral Questions, to Seek the Good: Exploring Nature's Goodness

I have emphasized that the moral and ethical issues raised by biotechnology cannot be satisfactorily negotiated by an ethics of limits. Nor is this the only available moral perspective, despite its contemporary dominance, though to ask about these alternatives has to happen in an even higher level of metaethical abstraction.

---

26. See Eva M. Neumann-Held, "Erzwingen die biologischen Wissenschaften ein neues Menschenbild?" in *Natur—Technik—Kultur: Philosophie im interdisziplinären Dialog*, ed. Brigitte Falkenburg (Paderborn: Mentis, 2007), 143–62.

Nevertheless, there remain good reasons for some ethicists' preference for insisting on distinguishing between ethical and moral approaches.[27] For them the moral discourse engages questions around definitions of right and wrong, good and evil. An ethical approach, in contrast, explores the meaning of human existence with the aim of revealing the configuration and content of the *conditio humana*. The latter approach has a normative implication to the extent that it convincingly presents a vision of the *conditio humana* implicitly claiming to hold to this vision without betraying it. Such an approach assumes that the human condition has a describable identity to which no meaningful alternative can be posited, since the force of the description is to highlight the sense in which a description is normative because humankind cannot exist other than in the terms set by this condition.[28] Whatever may be gleaned from these philosophical reflections, the theological point is first and foremost encapsulated in the hopeful confession that our human condition is determined by the address that comes to us from its material givenness, because this givenness is the material substrate that has from its beginning been determined for God's salvation. The story of human embodied life has not yet come to an end.

At this point Dietrich Bonhoeffer's reflections on the givenness of the "natural" in distinction to the "un-natural" come back into view.[29] If we are to use the category of "the natural," says Bonhoeffer, it only makes sense if we understand it as "what is given."

> A decisive consequence follows from this. The natural can never be a construct of some part or some authority in the fallen world. Neither the individual nor any community or institution in the preserved world can set and decide what is natural. It has already been set and decided, and in such a way that the individual, the communities, and the institutions receive their respective share in it. What is natural cannot be determined by an arbitrary construct [*Setzung*]; instead, every arbitrary construct of this kind, whether by an individual, a community, or an institution, will inevitably be shattered and will destroy itself against the natural that already exists. Injury and violation of the natural avenge themselves on the violator.[30]

Bonhoeffer can make such a strong assertion because he holds that the materiality of the creaturely world is the form through which God's protection and of preservation of life is mediated. This is why all recognition of the natural by

---

27. Jürgen Habermas, *The Future of Human Nature* (Cambridge: Polity Press, 2003), 3–4. For my account of this distinction see the discussion in Chapter 4, "Political ἔθος—Political ἦθος."

28. For the concept of identity see Rehmann-Sutter, *Genetics, Embodiment and Identity*, 47.

29. DBWE 6, 171–85.

30. Ibid., 177–8.

"reason" can be understood as an affirmation of the "basic will" to understand why life perdures. There is no hint here that this basic will to know is a divine remnant in human beings, uninjured by the fall into sin, and thus capable of autonomously affirming the divine order. This basic will is as embedded within and immersed in the fallen and yet preserved world as human reason. Yet the will remains for some human beings, with or without faith, who concern themselves exclusively with the content of the natural and affirming the goodness of life as a protective reality. Those who really see what the continuance and functioning of life mean to humanity know that it is the given stability of natural life that guards against the unnatural. In the end, it is life itself that tends toward the natural and ever again turns against the unnatural to break it down. Here lies the ultimate basis of health and healing, both of body and of soul. Life, whether of the individual or of the community, is its own doctor. It has been given a self-righting capacity by which it fends off the unnatural as life-destroying.[31]

Bonhoeffer sees in this feature of life that the givenness of life is significant, not in transcendental or ethical terms, but because of the "content" of its own distinct existence. It is we human beings who have to become aware of this richness of content of life, including the mechanics that sustain this very visible logic of preservation. The self-righting capacity of life is constitutive of the "identity" of the natural. To explore "the natural" thus means to explore it in orientation to its basic character as a living being; otherwise we will not be able to find its essential content and will become lost in our explorations, given the fantastic, almost infinite, complexity of life. If we do not focus intensely on the natural givenness of life, the already determinate shape that life has, we will end up in a vitalistic reduction of life to the level of a biological machine or biological material with no destination but its own reproduction. "Natural life is formed life," Bonhoeffer points out, which means that its processes cannot be self-referential even though they do perpetuate their own equilibrium.[32] This equilibrium itself, however, is not its own goal; rather, "this form places life at the service of other lives and of the world; it makes life in a limited sense a means to an end."[33]

The form of the givenness of life matters, as does the destination of that life as indicated by its form.[34] To affirm this is to admit that the study of natural life does not generate morally neutral knowledge about life and its functions. Such neutral knowledge is impossible since science declares itself from the outset to be concerned with forms of life that it does not make but wants to understand.

---

31. Ibid., 175f.

32. DBWE 6, 178. See Hans G. Ulrich, "The Form of Ethical Life," in *The Oxford Handbook of Dietrich Bonhoeffer*, ed. Philip G. Ziegler and Michael Mawson (Oxford: Oxford University Press, 2019), 289–305.

33. Ibid.

34. Here we might well draw on other philosophies and concepts, such as the Aristotelian concept of life, which Rehmann-Sutter has shown to have some affinity to a certain program-models of living entities.

Any dilution of this point undermines the practice of science itself, since the subject being studied is obscured by demoting life, for instance, to the level of one perhaps especially interesting type of chemical reaction (in a class with acid rain) or physical process (in a class with the surface tension of water). The only way out of such classificatory absurdities is to admit that we are studying life that is formed, which has its own definite given appearance. This is the remit by which better and worse investigative methods may be distinguished, assuming that they understand human cognition and recognition as categorially different from the work of producing or constructing a different kind of reality.

The theological reflection involved in the study of life pursued along these lines does not seek to ferret out and make plain some hidden "meaning" or a "spirit" animating life. It is rather an enacted affirmation that the givenness of life can only be recognized to the extent that we follow its own given contours and live in accord with them. Once we have said this, we can ask the subsequent questions about which theories or theoretical models will best allow us to understand this formed life. The right model for this work will be one that fosters the kind of cognition and recognition that includes understanding, but of a specific type: the understanding of "life" in its formed givenness. This is the basis from which fruitful debates about the suitability of different heuristic models for understanding life may emerge, such as the program-model or system models being discussed today among scientists.

The Ethical Task

In this discussion of appropriate and inappropriate models for investigating life, the theologian must keep ethical reflection from drifting away from the central question: "What is good?" and "What is the given good?" which we have to discover and to explore. We may call it "explorative ethics." This question resists any presumption that scientific work can show or invent something better than this given good. To discover and to explore the given good is also a bar to certain ethical approaches, such as those that evaluate our human condition according to specific norms of what is considered good, perfect or normal, in distinction to bad, not normal, or not perfect—so seeking to "normalize" all life.[35] There are points of convergence here between Aristotelian and theological impulses in being committed to affirm the goodness that is already in the embodied human condition in the complex and rich form that is visible in every actual human life. Such an approach differs from attempts to generate moral norms out of the fact of our human finitude or "natural limits"—and approaches of this sort dominate bioethical and bio-philosophical discourses—in not taking its orientation from the absolute "outer" limits of life but on the complexity of its "inner" processes,

---

35. See Jackie Leach Scully, "Admitting All Variations? Postmodernism and Genetic Normality," in *Ethics of the Body: Postconventional Challenges*, ed. Margrit Shildrick and Roxanne Mykitiuk (Cambridge, MA: MIT, 2005), 49-68.

which are given to us in order to be understood, in order to be explored for good.[36] It is by looking at this "inner" complexity and contour of life that we discover that exploring the "given" and to "reveal the good" are interwoven.

Aristotelian and Christian ethical traditions can be said to converge in the sense that both can admit the truth of the biblical understanding of a given creation. Creation is good according to God's judgment: "And God saw everything that he had made, and behold, it was very good" (Gen. 1:31). Human beings are to explore what is good about creation of which they find themselves to be part.[37] Thus the task of Christian ethics is to redirect human attention to this work of exploring the goodness of created bodies and the natural world. The embodied form that life takes must not be subjected to norms or models expressing human judgments about how life might be made better or more useful. At the level of scientific exploration, this affirmation is more sweeping and directive than it might appear, since the exploration of the given creation or "nature" is directly connected to and interwoven with scientific methods that working researchers deploy to test or visualize the characteristic processes and structures of living organisms. Some experimental methods can legitimately be said, precisely as they and visualize and reproduce the minute mechanisms of life, to be making rather than simply observing the most fundamental components of life.[38]

Implications for Human Genome Exploration

Scientists themselves recognize that their tradition of research is beholden to the task of describing the givenness of life as just described, or at least it should be about this goal, the goal of providing a view of and insight into the conditions and functions of our human condition in its embodiment, offering a micro-perspective on the processes of biological development and system-related functions. Within the orbit of this shared presumption about the goal of research, a lively discussion is ongoing about the model or theoretical concept most capable of comprehending these basic processes as well as interpreting and presenting its data, observations, and concepts in a manner that can be integrated into an overarching understanding of our human condition as a whole—at least of complex functions like the heredity of diseases or the characteristics of our individual identity as shaped by, for instance, the epigenetic triggering of additions.

To date there have been long-running scientific discussions about how to understand the relation between genetic information and its operation as functioning genes (which comprise less than two percent of the genome), discussions that are now so well known that they have reached the level of popular

---

36. As Pascal has suggested.
37. See DBWE 6, 247: "The question about the good can no longer be separated from the question of life, of history." Bonhoeffer stresses that life cannot be separated from its "context," which has to be seen as its "history."
38. See Keller's insightful description in *Making Sense of Life*.

discourse. Similar but less well known questions remain hotly debated today among scientists about how and why genes are turned on and off by epigenetic signals.[39] There have also been intensive investigations into whether the development of a living organism has to be understood in terms of a "program" that controls all the functions of living cells, as well as whether this control includes all or only some gene expressions and biological processes in a living organism. Other scientists, finding the computer metaphor problematic, have proposed a more dynamic model of developing organisms, referred to as the Process Molecular Gene Concept.[40] Such disputes between proponents of different interpretative models of genetic functioning have sweeping consequences, for example, on how the genome is understood as relating to diseases.[41]

Such debates over interpretative models displays the territory in which molecular biology and theological ethics must work to discern what is given, and what is good. Such a discussion not only needs to deal with the general questions emerging from debates about interpretative models but must also discuss the relevance of the many material details that different models bring to light which may be of great significance for coming to some consensus about how the whole is to be understood. In moments of rapidly growing and changing scientific knowledge, it is always possible that a seemingly marginal new fact could carry the insight that could change the whole set of knowledge and theories. By wading into the thick of scientific discussions that seek appropriate new paradigms for understanding, the ethicist does not superimpose some ethical schema on top of the scientific work, choosing instead to begin from an affirmation of how scientific knowledge is built, and how its structures of knowledge develop.[42]

Debates about how to understand human life and its (genetic) mechanisms is in a high ferment in the field of biology today. These debates will gradually or suddenly lead to a new understanding of our human condition in terms of its embodiment. Not only will a newly formed and solidified idea of the biological nature of the *conditio humana* emerge, but it will do so by changing our understanding of this concept in general.[43] We have, in other words, been forced by biological science to revisit what we mean when we say "human nature."[44] As far as I can see, however,

---

39. *Cycles of Contingency: Developmental Systems and Evolution*, ed. Susan Oyama, Paul E. Griffiths, and Russell D. Gray (Cambridge, MA: MIT, 2001).

40. See also Neumann-Held, "Erzwingen die biologischen Wissenschaften ein neues Menschenbild?"

41. For example, see Scully, "Admitting All Variations?"

42. Thomas S. Kuhn's description of the practicalities of paradigm shifts in *The Structure of Scientific Revolutions* remains very helpful in discussions of the sort being described here.

43. Some philosophers have already begun to ask what this ferment suggests about anthropological conceptions such as Helmuth Plessner, *Die Stufen des Organischen und der Mensch*, Gesammelte Schriften vol. 4 (Baden-Baden: Nomos Verlag, 2003 [1938]), chap. 7. See Krüger, "Die condition humaine des Abendlandes."

44. Grunwald et al., eds., *On Human Nature*.

the philosophers and theologians involved in this discussion have not found their way to engage direct interchanges between scientific approaches and discoveries on the one side and philosophy or theology on the other side. Nor have discussions of a revised account of human nature generated any convincing new picture.

Thus, a question remains unanswered: Which of the new scientific discoveries will initiate a new understanding of the human condition, and which key questions or topics in anthropology will be affected by these changes? This is more difficult and open set of unknowns, as we do not yet even know how wide and how deep the debates over general interpretive frameworks in biological science will need to range in order to understand what we mean when we say "genetics" or "epi-genetics." We are in a field that at this moment has accepted the shift from older models of some specific biological processes, but in others there remain open questions, debated models, and unexplained biological functions. We must negotiate a variegated field in which some knowledge has been revised, some is only beginning to be understood enough to know what we do not know, and some in which we know enough to have substantive debates about what is going on.

In such a situation we can only attempt to ask the right questions, in dialogue with practitioners of multiple disciplines:[45]

- What are the critical features of life that can tell us something about the origin of the human species? What features of life as we know it will help us to understand the sense in which the human species is unified?[46]
- What biological features do we need to grasp in order to understand our human embodiment globally as a system with its own given inner configuration and parameters and its patterned relations with its outer environment and other organisms? What does this new knowledge mean for how we conceive the state of "embodiment"?
- What still needs to be understood in order to have a functioning understanding of the development of human individuals?
- What are the critical aspects we need to know to understand the implications of disease being "inheritable"?[47]
- What do we still need to understand about the biological reasons for, and ethical implications of, the stability or fragility of our human condition?
- In what senses can we talk of mutations or deletions, abnormality and normality?
- How developed is the systemic view of biological functioning?
- What genetic information resides between genes and in special epigenetic signals?

---

45. See Brock et al., "Genetics, Conversation and Conversion."
46. See G. Subramanian et al., "Implications of the Human Genome for Understanding Human Biology and Medicine," *JAMA* 286 (2001): 2296–307.
47. See Scully, "*Admitting All Variations?*"

With these more theoretical questions come associated questions that relate more directly to medical practice:

- What remains to be learned about how doctors should diagnose and predict disease?
- What are the consequences of the ferment in biological science for genetic counseling?[48] What do we need still to know about the changes that have already been accepted in the science about what we mean by the terms "therapy" or "enhancement"?

There are innumerable discoveries under way today that shed new light on, or even give answers to, these kinds of questions. But all these new perspectives rest on complex new descriptions and concepts of the gene, the genome, or epi-genetics, that are hotly discussed live fields of research. The meaning these developments give to the key terms in the debate inevitably generates new descriptions of the complex processes of heredity, of disease, as well as descriptions of the processes by which the phenotype comes into existence. All these questions implicate unresolved questions in the space between what has been called genetics and what is now called epi-genetics, the inquiry that investigates the complexity and context-relatedness of biological development in its most encompassing sense.

We are talking about a highly complex and highly mobile domain of human activity. We will get nowhere if we are not prepared to engage with the specific details of what is being studied and the debates surrounding how to describe what is being studied. It is useful to illustrate how specific biological details can trigger fundamental changes in complex scientific models with obvious ethical implications. For instance, genetic research can reveal the baselessness of racial theories. One set of researchers has pointed out that there is a complex and problematic social and political history of deployments of genetic science, and conclude: "At various times in the past, many societies, including our own, adopted theories of race and genetics as the justification for political oppression against vulnerable groups. . . . In such a discussion, we would offer that an analysis of the genome reveals a fundamental unity for all human beings."[49] Here a scientific discovery has almost immediately yielded a fundamental insight into our human nature. We can "see" at the level of molecular biology that human being is a unitary phenomenon, and thus at the biological level, by definition, to be a human being is to be equal.

The alternative notion, polygenism, proposes that there is more than one single human race as it is reflected in the story of God's creation and Adam. Polygenism has recurrently surfaced in scientific and political discussions over the last centuries, but, as Hannah Arendt has argued, to imagine multiple origins of multiple kinds of

---

48. See Genetic Alliance, www.geneticalliance.org.

49. Subramanian et al., "Implications of the Human Genome for Understanding Human Biology and Medicine," 2305.

human beings is to embrace a fundamentally different understanding of politics. Were any biological "fact" to establish polygenism as an incontrovertible feature of human life, it would be difficult to stem readings that imagine a basic hostile rivalry between different groups of people, as some political theories suppose, while also lending support to racist ideologies. Arendt writes:

> Hobbes affords the best possible theoretical foundation for those naturalistic ideologies which hold nations to be tribes, separated from each other by nature, without any connection whatever, unconscious of the solidarity of mankind and having in common only the instinct for self-preservation which man shares with the animal world. If the idea of humanity, of which the most conclusive symbol is the common origin of the human species, is no longer valid, then nothing is more plausible than a theory according to which brown, yellow, or black races are descended from some other species of apes than the white race, and that all together are predestined by nature to war against each other until they have disappeared from the face of the earth.[50]

This is only one of the many ways that the "facts" of molecular biology can be seen to shape our understanding of the *conditio humana* without collapsing in naturalistic or natural law ethics. Given features of life as it has been given exist, and they need to be investigated and described, meaning that they require the judgment that recognizes and interprets them in their goodness.

Further Topics: Changing Ethical Approaches and Questions

As we have discussed the question of "identity" as the focus of ethical and scientific description we have to be aware of other similar fundamental core issues.

Intervention

One of the oddities of our cultural moment is the striking gap between public and even ethical debates in the scholarly literature about gene-therapy or body-enhancement and other sorts of "manipulative" interventions from the actual state of the science with its complex descriptive models and experimental techniques. In the multiyear series of lectures Walter Doerfler and I undertook in Erlangen, one of the most striking things I learned was that scientists still face fundamental difficulties in understanding and manipulating genes, exchanging them or switching them on and off, despite the assumption in popular discourse that these things can now be done as a matter of course. As Doerfler described how epigenetic science works, his account repeatedly returning to the point that

---

50. Hannah Arendt, *Imperialism: Part Two of the Origins of Totalitarianism* (San Diego: Harcourt Brace, 1968), 37. See also the critique of "polygenism," 57–8.

we cannot yet understand what we "see." It is important to put "see" in scare quotes in this discussion, because nothing is seen directly, as all the relevant mechanisms function and the molecular, atomic or even subatomic levels and are only present to our perception through complex—and contested—representative models and techniques. Different methods can be deployed to visualize the patterns of methylization that appear to turn "genes" off and on. But what are the implications of the different means of visualization, which look at different levels of the mechanism being observed. What follows from these different pictures of the same process? This is just one of many examples of how what we know points only to the need for further progress in understanding, and this very need implies within it the possibility that a barrier may in fact exist that will hamper developments in the future any targeted intervention in the process.

It is remarkable how inexorably thinking deeply about such issues raises fundamental ethical questions. On the one hand, there is some evidence that the possibilities of visualization of, and insight into, the minute but all important processes of life are a standing invitation for us human beings to investigate them so that we genuinely understand who we are, and how our bodies work. It is good for us to touch and become aware of the full complexity and richness of our lives, whatever else might follow from this knowledge. We should become aware of this complexity, not because it begs for us to intervene or to change it, but simply because the visibility of embodied life is one of the intrinsic aspects of the specific *conditio humana* that is given to us. Even if we do not go so far as to deploy a Hegelian idea of ourselves as beings at the pinnacle of a reality that is coming to know itself ever more clearly and rationally, there are theological reasons to think that this deepening of understanding of our created nature is theologically justified. Simply having a body, a human body, issues an invitation and indeed an address to us to consider the given reality in all its richness and complexity. As Blaise Pascal pointed out, such study only makes us more acutely aware of our own place in this world:

What is a man in the infinite?

But, to show him another prodigy equally astounding, let him look into the tiniest things he knows. Let a mite show him in its minute body incomparably more minute parts, legs with joints, veins in its legs, blood in the veins, humors in the blood, drops in the humors, vapors in the drops: let him divide these things further until he has exhausted his powers of imagination, and let the last thing he comes down to now be the subject of our discourse. He will perhaps think that this is the ultimate minuteness in nature.

I want to show him a new abyss. I want to depict to him not only the visible universe, but all the conceivable immensity of nature enclosed in this miniature atom. Let him see there an infinity of universes, each with its firmament, its planets, its earth, in the same proportion as in the visible world, and on that earth animals, and finally mites, in which he will find again the same results as in the first; and finding the same thing yet again in the others without end or respite, he will be lost in such wonders, as astounding in their minuteness as the others in their amplitude. For who will not marvel that our body, a moment ago imperceptible in a universe, itself imperceptible in the bosom of the whole, should now be a colossus, a world, or rather a whole, compared to the nothingness beyond our reach? Anyone who considers himself in this way will be terrified at himself, and, seeing his mass, as given him by nature, supporting him between these two abysses of infinity and nothingness, will tremble at these marvels. I believe that with his curiosity changing into wonder he will be more disposed to contemplate them in silence than investigate them with presumption.

For, after all, what is man in nature? A nothing compared to the infinite, a whole compared to the nothing, a middle point between all and nothing.[51]

Pascal was enough of a scientist to understand the process of scientific investigation that includes the sort of molecular approach to nature that we are pursuing today. He does so with a clear awareness of the implications that we do so from an anthropological perspective. When at this point we follow the biblical logic, the study of the material world functions as an invitation to us human beings to find our place. The place of human being is first of all the place of praise and witness, and out of this place to praise and bear witness to God for this wonderful creation. This task is the "destination," the "home" for us human beings. What is our existence for except to praise God, as it is reflected in Psalm 8? It belongs to our human condition. Such praise cannot but be attracted to any kind of science that allows reality to become present in all its facets and dimensions.[52]

What scientific study reveals to us by means of its powers of visualization is a creation worthy of praise. The complexity of creation can come to us in many ways, given and mediated by various means and also by scientific description. What is visible to us can be shared with others. In asserting this we reiterate the point of Bonhoeffer (and others[53]) that life has its own content of which we must become aware—the only alternative is to invent songs of praise about the dexterity of our hands in making idols that we believe (wrongly) to be so much more impressive than what already exists. To sing such songs is an embodied embrace of a nihilism that could not but shape our minds and scientific practices.[54]

---

51. Pascal, *Pensées*, Aph. 72, 89–90.

52. See Stanley Hauerwas, *With the Grain of the Universe: The Church's Witness and Natural Theology* (Grand Rapids: Brazos Press, 2002), 205–15, on "the necessity of witness" and the relation of "witness" and scientific rationality. This witness includes the practices which are in accordance to God's reality.

53. We find many similar thoughts in Luther's commentaries on Genesis and the Psalms.

54. See Brian Brock, *Singing the Ethos of God: On the Place of Scripture in Ethics* (Eerdmans: Grand Rapids, 2007), 173–7.

Dissolving Moral Problems

There is one further set of points that are important to consider if we ask in what sense we human beings are invited or even charged to do all this research, to make ourselves aware of "reality" by rendering visible what can be seen of our creaturely realm. Moral insights can, and do, emerge when widely held moral certainties are dissolved or changed by scientific discoveries. To take one example, most discussions about the ethics of intervening in the human genome (including by means of genetic counseling) have focused on parsing these decisions according to a code of moral right and wrong.[55] There is now, however, a growing body of scientific evidence that many of the most vigorously debated biotechnological interventions are ones that simply cannot be accomplished, biologically speaking. In other words, it makes no sense to have a moral discussion about the moral legitimacy of an intervention that will never happen.

In cases where moral debates have drifted free of reality scientific research becomes a context in which morally doubtful ideas and agendas come under examination and criticism. For all we know, increasing scientific understanding may show that some interventions into genetic processes and pathways that people continue to find morally illicit may in due course also come to be seen as in principle (theoretically) not viable. Here again we see the power of the barriers thrown up by the given contours of existing life that differ in kind from "moral limits." The barriers and resistances that come with the given configuration of life may in the same way trigger new heuristics for alternative ways of understanding our morality. When Copernicus posited that the sun was not the center of the universe, he (abetted by the subsequent scientific instrumentation of Galileo[56]) destroyed the plausibility of certain (ancient) ways of doing theology at the same time as fresh theological impulses were unleashed that invigorate theology to this day.[57]

There are many points where moral debates would be sharpened and clarified by being in more direct contact with scientific research. Nor does this need to be done in a way that subordinates ethics to "nature" in a problematic way. Ethics gains from being in an interpretative relationship with those engaged with biological "reality." Such engagements are ones that promise substantial gains for our ethical descriptions of our human condition. There is no substitute for an ethics that recognizes the *conditio humana* in its complex fullness.

---

55. These discussions would be considered ethical as defined previously in the discussions of the "moral" and "ethical" levels of the debate.

56. Mario Biagioli, *Galileo, Courtier: The Practice of Science in the Culture of Absolutism* (Chicago: University of Chicago Press, 1993).

57. Jacob Taubes, "Theology and Political Theory," in *From Cult to Culture: Fragments Toward a Critique of Historical Reason*, ed. Charlotte Elsheva Fonrobert and Amir Engel (Stanford: Stanford University Press, 2010), 222–32.

Pathways to Common Research into the Conditio Humana

This chapter has suggested some senses in which "understanding the *conditio humana*" may be broken down into discrete pathways that converge in a work of a common research. It is not sufficient to begin by assuming a simple division of labor between scientific research into "given" facts on the one hand and interpretations (whether moral or scientific) on the other. What is needed is a complex collaboration to describe the *conditio humana*, or rather, what we need is an explicit and explicitly collaborative approach, rather than an implicit, disjointed, or privately decided approaches. Such collaborative work of description highlights the necessity of a hermeneutical approach to the ethics of life. We need a hermeneutical approach because life has its own given micro- and macro-structures, which the sciences are presenting to us in many new ways. Only a hermeneutical approach can engage with the ongoing process of discovery in the biological sciences, and so learn the possible importance of any detail for understanding biology and its continuous critique of our moral assumptions. Such an approach can be called theological because it is oriented toward discovering the good—in the sense of the good work as an acknowledgment of the goodness of creation—that is embodied in our human nature and becomes present to us human beings through our investigative work. To become aware of the goodness of creation is the ethical task (a good work) within this collaboration. The theologian will engage this process prepared to critically examine all interpretations of the *conditio humana* that obscure "formed nature" within the context of God's reality, as Bonhoeffer called it, which can never be corralled by our models and metaphors but addresses to us as something to be understood and praised as God's good creation.

Chapter 9

GOD'S TRANSFIGURING PRESENCE

NEWLY CREATED IN THE PRESENCE OF DISABLED PEOPLE

Where can I go from your spirit? Or where can I flee from your presence?
(Ps. 139:7)

This verse from Psalm 139 sounds paradoxical to modern ears, as the prayers of Christians today are often preoccupied with the question "where is God?" or call out for God to make an appearance or intervention in one's life. The concern of Psalm 139, in contrast, is with the overwhelming presence of God in His Spirit and His face-to-face presence. "Where can I flee from your presence" as some translations have it, which would be literally translated as "where can I flee from your face?" The one who prays inescapably encounters God face to face, unmediated by interpretive grids, pious practices, or moral habits. To pray Psalm 139 is to come to acute awareness of what it means to be a creature surrounded—almost claustrophobically—by God's presence. This chapter draws this volume to its pinnacle by listening to the witness of the disabled and those who live with them in order to draw attention to this overwhelming divine presence. Here again the question of the reality of human life emerges with particular force: When coming face to face with more significantly disabled human beings, will we find them unsettling our understanding of the human and in this way exposing the truth that we do not know who we really are?

Something very like this overwhelming experience of God's presence seems to continually crop up in the witness of those who live with disabled people. Hans Reinders's intensive study of the notion of God's providence helpfully points us in the right direction by asking us to consider why and in what sense people with intellectual disabilities experience "God's presence."[1] He demonstrates a theologically dense account of divine presence proves especially fitted to articulate the sort of experiences that often arise when people become involved in the lives of disabled people.

---

1. Hans S. Reinders, *Disability, Providence, and Ethics: Bridging Gaps, Transforming Lives* (Waco: Baylor University Press, 2014).

I would like to suggest that the common denominator we find constantly recurring in first-person narratives about the presence of God to and with disabled people is people's self-articulated realization that they have experienced a different, new reality appearing in the presence of the life of a disabled person. My contribution to the discussion in this chapter is to ask how the language of "God's presence" helps us to understand this new reality and to more precisely articulate its meaning and message.

The aim of such an attempt to describe the phenomenon of divine presence among the life of disabled people is to describe it in a manner that makes its message more easily apprehended. It can therefore be understood as one final attempt to articulate how God's drawing near reveals the human condition as set within God's present reality.[2] The drama of the ethical life as understood within this theological perspective plays out as modern humanity becomes disillusioned with the various alternative humanisms on offer and begins to glimpse the promise of their destruction and reconfiguration within a realist understanding of divine action which actively contradicts the nihilism that preys on human life. Our question in this chapter concerns the role that the witness of the disabled and those who encounter God with them might be understood to play in guiding others into this reality, by listening to them, and even allowing us to participate in it or share it. In the experience of the severely disabled, I am suggesting, the central questions for Christian ethics emerge with great clarity: Where is any human being really at home? How should human beings name the life-world that is most determinative for human flourishing? And how do they become tangibly aware of that life-world in its antecedent givenness? Do we live as creatures who seem even to be aware of the life-giving context in which we can truly be human beings?

Reinders's reflections orbit around the unique transformations that have taken place in the lives of people who have become involved in the lives of disabled people. Their way of life changes, their ideas about the phenomenon of the human changes as well as their perception and understanding more generally. This is especially evident for those who engage in extended contact with the lives of those with intellectual disabilities. He recounts a wide range of transformations in the lives of those who have encountered people with disabilities, changes in practices, viewpoints, minds, and hearts. Those who encounter people with

---

2. This chapter thus extends and concretizes the account presented in Chapter 1 as the "Messianic Contours of Evangelical Ethics." Though it will not be the focus of this chapter, my treatment is tacitly engaged with a range of instructive and biblically sensitive elaborations of the Messianic character of God's action such as that of Jürgen Moltmann, *The Way of Jesus Christ* (London: SCM Press, 1990), and Giorgio Agamben, *The Time That Remains: A Commentary on the Letter to the Romans*, trans. Patricia Dailey (Stanford: Stanford University Press, 2010). The philosophical issues at stake here arise from developments in biblical studies, which has seen language of transformation give way to increasing use of the language of transfiguration; see Peter Stuhlmacher, *Biblical Theology of the New Testament* (Grand Rapids: Eerdmans, 2018).

learning disabilities often learn to follow the "spirit of discernment," as Reinders describes the transformation.³ By describing the changes that happen to people in the presence of disabled lives, Reinders assumes that he is inviting us into a particular grammar which we, the listeners and readers of these stories, are called upon to understand and then to respond to in word and/or action.

Reinders's stories all emphasize a particular journey of learning traveled by people who have let themselves be drawn into the lives of people with intellectual disabilities, living together with them, sharing their time with them, learning from them, and learning together with them. Living together with intellectually disabled people is presented as a particular experience of learning and transformation that also makes visible in a new way particular characteristics of human life—such as asymmetric dependence, loneliness, indispensable friendship, patience, and sharing of time, listening and the importance of celebrating life, and throughout them all, experiences of love and hope. In this broad but recognizably similar set of experiences that arise among disabled people and their assistants, friends or parents, are allowed to witness and participate in a different reality. This alternative reality is one that is clearly evident to those who are present and participating in it.

The rub, for many readers of this literature, however, is the seeming impossibility of their being involved in such a hands-on and daily way in the lives of people with significant disabilities. This is why Stanley Hauerwas has insisted that theologians not write *about* disability.⁴ Such witnesses and their stories are too easily "used" or "instrumentalized" for our own purposes. Nevertheless, they powerfully communicate a message and a reality that otherwise would not be accessible to us, a message which has to be understood and received as a call for transformation addressed to anyone who is ready to listen. These stories challenge us, the recipients of the witness, to consider how we might be able to *follow* or *translate* what is so attractively revealed in these stories into a form that meets our own perhaps very different contexts which also are in need of a similarly profound transformation.

Reinders has unfolded the doctrine of providence to explicate the phenomenon of intellectual disability, and various contemporary theologians have attempted to capture what is going on in transformative relationship with the intellectually disabled by appeal to other theological loci. Brian Brock, for instance, has approached these themes by describing what happens to the Christian community when it receives disabled people as constitutive of Christ's body as it becomes present in worship.⁵ That the message of these witnesses can be linked to several

---

3. Reinders, *Disability, Providence, and Ethics*, 148.
4. See Stanley Hauerwas, "On the Ethics of Writing on the Ethics of Care of the Mentally Handicapped," in *Critical Reflections on Stanley Hauerwas' Theology of Disability: Disabling Society, Enabling Theology*, ed. John Swinton (Binghamton: Haworth Pastoral Press, 2004), 13–26.
5. Brian Brock, *Wondrously Wounded: Theology, Disability, and the Body of Christ* (Waco, TX: Baylor University Press, 2019).

doctrinal themes already reveals that such witnesses point to the whole of God's story with His people, with all of His creatures, and the whole of God's economy.

Theological reflection can also help to disclose in these eye-opening encounters promising anticipations and Messianic pre-appearances of the new—eschatological—reality. This is an experience not without pain and sacrifice, the experience of a "wound of knowledge" as Rowan Williams puts it, an experience Brock narrates as a being "wondrously wounded."[6] Notice the way in which Brock pinpoints the theological crux of his story with Adam, his son, in their joint life with the Christian community:

> Some Christians today have begun to appreciate how much the gifts of the Spirit in those who carry the label "disabled" exceed their all too visible neediness, dependence, and vulnerability. They dare to hope for a church that longs to receive the spiritual gifts that people like Adam bring into its body, despite their inability verbally to articulate their joy and pain. Christians dare hope that the challenge of lives like his will not be erased or hidden away for the impiety of challenging us all to slow down, to notice our reliance on others, to become aware of bodily communication, to love and become interreliant. Christians praise the God of annunciation and mercy for sending such gadflies to sting us awake.[7]

What is described here are the dynamics of the process of transformation. When this transformation is viewed against its origin in God's story, this transformation with all its pain, conflict, and pressure can be understood as the event of transfiguration. Experiences of love and hope are as essential in this process as are the tangible experiences of vulnerability, dependence, and desire for healing and comfort that inevitably accompany it. The convergence of such experiences is highly revealing of the human condition. The complexity and scope of these witnesses to being transformed by God's presence in life with people with intellectual disabilities may legitimately be read as vicarious experiences for all human beings since in them it is the one God's presence that is experienced.

This, at least, is what is suggested when we compare what those who witness to such transformative encounters to the examples of being transformed in the presence of God depicted in biblical stories. Again we return to Paul's promising enjoinder in Rom. 12:1-2, that Christian people be ready to "become transformed" through a "renewal of the mind," the renewal of awareness and understanding (Greek: *nous*). In the context of the main theme of this chapter it is important

---

6. Rowan Williams, *The Wound of Knowledge: Christian Spirituality from the New Testament to St. John of the Cross* (London: Darton, Longman & Todd, 1979); Brock, *Wondrously Wounded*.

7. Brock, *Wondrously Wounded*, 161.

to highlight that the Greek word *metamorphosis*[8] may be literally translated as "transfiguration." Transfiguration includes the handing over of the *somata*, the bodily formed substance of human life, including its bodily appearance to be created new, to become a "new creation" (*nova creatura*, 2 Cor. 5:17). Paul calls this event "spiritual worship," as some translations render the Greek *logike latreia*. Paul calls the members of the worshiping community to become "transfigured" by the renewal of their minds in order to "discern what God's will is about: the good, the pleasant, and the fulfilled," which is promised to us and which we become enabled to probe and to realize.

As it lives together, this worshipping community must hold itself ready "to become transfigured by the renewal of perception and understanding" in distinction to a life in conformity with the "patterns" of perception and understanding of this "world-age." We need not become preoccupied with the work of naming and categorizing these patterns of understanding, be it pre-modern, modern, post-modern, or whatever it may look like in a given time and place. What matters is that Christians learn to experience and to name the experience of transitioning from these widespread patterns of thinking[9] into a new, different age. This experience is the prime marker of coming to participating in the concrete dawning of the Messianic-eschatological arrival. The dawn of God's new age is promised to appear within their worship, their way of living and their daily practices, led by God's Spirit. This dawning is not just as a "Messianic idea" but a given reality that happens to us, appearing as a concrete offer into a lived life practiced within an embodied tradition of worship.[10]

The only necessity that this Messianic dawning happen is God's merciful faithfulness to continue God's story with his people. As God is so faithful it becomes necessary that there be these dramatic transitions in human lives, through which God assures the continuance of his story with his people. This including us, since all human beings are called into this unique story (Rom. 9:24). These are the sui generis dynamics of God's presence, through his Spirit, in Messianic times. That God's Spirit continues to invade our human world and transform it is intrinsic to the divine faithfulness, since God's Spirit is bound to God's word (*logos*) as heard in worship, in which God's Spirit encounters our human awareness and understanding (*nous*). It is this inner Messianic grammar of God's story to which Paul directs his Roman readers, and which appears luminously in the stories recorded by Reinders about the experience of God's transforming

---

8. I am only touching on the complex meaning, various translations and the philosophical context that surround the use of this term: Catherine Malabou, *The Heidegger Change: On the Fantastic in Philosophy*, trans. and ed. Peter Skafish (Albany: State University of New York Press, 2011), esp. 5–8.

9. "Transition" is a key word in Messianic theologies as in Jürgen Moltmann, *The Way of Jesus Christ* (London: SCM Press, 1990).

10. Gershom Scholem, *The Messianic Idea in Judaism and Other Essays on Jewish Spirituality* (New York: Schocken Books, 1971).

presence. Reinders has collected stories of witnesses to having been patiently yet passionately ready to be "transformed," "transfigured," and "translocated" into God's story. Whatever an individual must recognize or realize in order to become part of the one story that is God's will has its ground in the divinely given hope to be extracted from the many conflicting and divergent narratives that comprise the "history" of the world.

Translocation

Transformation or, in its more pointedly literal reading as "transfiguration," is in Paul's theological logic a matter of discovering one's self in an alternative new reality, that over time comes to be understood as the actual "reality" for human beings, beyond what is mediated by those patterns of perception and understanding that are characteristic of this "world-age," such as status consciousness and the desire to win competitively over others. This true reality seems most often to be realized through encounters with people whose views, judgments, and language somehow do not obscure God's spiritual presence. Objectively described, we have said that God's presence in the Spirit prompts people to discover their lives as a unique facet of God's very own story. What we can now add is that this can only happen as the story they once told of themselves, utilizing the vocabulary of their own culture and time, is displaced. The moral import of language displacement is visible in a pale version in the capacity of the norms of political correctness to highlight injustices. That the citizens of modern liberal societies feel that people with disabilities are subject to injustice is indicated by the constant churn of less offensive names that are felt to be appropriate to apply to them. But in a theological sense the much more difficult problem is the necessity of finding a language and grammar that is adequate to do justice to the rounded and unique lives of all the people within the story of transformation. As Stanley Hauerwas has highlighted, this more truthful language is one that can only be discovered within the variegated practices of living and worshipping together.[11] The reality disclosed by God in the lives of disabled people will not appear in abstraction from this context of life together that is the essential matrix of transformation. God's story only ever appears in the particular lives of unique people, as authentically witnessed by the people involved in it.

"Where can I go from your Spirit"? The psalmist is baffled by the thought that there could be a "place" somewhere outside God's presence. The semantics of the biblical narrative all circle around the assumption that human reconciliation and redemption is to occur through realizing the context of living to which God's own testimony points. The centrality of the divine presence in human redemption is emphasized by the positioning of the Torah in the Old Testament as the

---

11. See also Rowan Williams, "The Spiritual and the Religious: Is the Territory Changing?" in *Faith in the Public Square* (London: Bloomsbury, 2012), 85–96.

embodiment of God's reality given precisely to revive, to "turn"[12] the "soul" (Ps. 19:8) toward God's story and reality. This is not the return of platonic anamnesis—of the soul to its true self—nor is it an incremental departure from certain aspects of reality that diverge from what one takes to be one's true home. It is a wholesale translocation into another unique reality. Rowan Williams puts this Old Testament assumption about relocation in Christological terms, as a relocation into "the space occupied by Jesus Christ in his eternal relationship with the Father, a relocation which is enabled by his sacrificial death and his rising from the grave and ascension into heaven."[13] This is the meaning of Paul's Messianic message to the Corinthians: "Therefore, if anyone is in Christ, he is a new creation; old things have passed away; behold, all things have become new" (2 Cor. 5:17).

To be "in Christ" means to be translocated into God's story with Christ.[14] "There is neither Jew nor Greek, there is neither slave nor free, there is no male and female, for you are all one in Christ Jesus. And if you are Christ's, then you are Abraham's offspring, heirs according to promise" (Gal. 3:28-29). Here there is clearly also no abled and disabled. In Christ there are only unique individuals, each uniquely significant within God's story. To encounter transfiguration in Christ brings an entirely new formation to the question of disability: How often do we become aware of the unique significance of someone we encounter within the openness afforded to them in Christ? How often is their unique place in God's story obscured by the given patterns of perception and understanding of our age?

This question has been thematized in disability theology over the last decade or so in investigations of the reality that those who live with disabled people often discover in them an ability for friendship that comes as surprise to the expectations of human beings embedded in the characteristic thought-patterns of our age. In God's story with all his people, the poor, the weak, and the sick are no longer forced to secure their own sustenance or to justify or defend the form of bodily existence that they have been given. Instead they are drawn into that new reality where all encounter one another in new ways that seem best described as friendships. These are concrete examples from a contemporary context of people being exposed, passively, to God's story as it is realized in publicly visible ways, and so providing us with thought-provoking examples of transformation that other people may follow, step by step.

It is here that Reinders's new reading of the doctrine of providence is important and illuminating. He describes providence as, "the active presence of God, mediated by the Spirit, to guide us in learning to see the new life that is around us, and is there to be seen."[15] The work of the Spirit who conveys God's care for

12. Literal translation of the Hebrew (מְשִׁיבַת נָפֶשׁ).
13. Williams, "The Spiritual and the Religious," 92.
14. See the highly intensive and insightful discussion of this theme in *"In Christ" in Paul: Explorations in Paul's Theology of Union and Participation*, ed. Michael J. Thate, Kevin J. Vanhoozer, and Constantine R. Campbell (Tübingen: Mohr Siebeck, 2014).
15. Reinders, *Disability, Providence, and Ethics*, 190.

creatures cannot be willed, but it can be perceived and followed. "Providence" in this sense is God's gracious contradiction to all vain attempts to envision one's future by prolonging previous experiences or expectations into an imagined future, or to construct a meaning in "history" out of the contingent collection of past experiences. We will not be able to verify God's providence by coming up with a definitive narrative of our life and its "history" nor by grasping some hidden divine plan, but by that different story granted by God's presence here and now, by God's very own dedication to human life within His story and its Messianic appearance.[16]

The appearance of God's story is most easily seen in healing. The Messianic praxis of healing appears to be God's quite adventurous public way to encounter His people and to contradict their beliefs in other controlling powers or fates. This is, to use Karl Barth's phrase, God's humanity.[17] The unity and thrust of God's whole story are offered to us to see in Jesus Christ. In this revelation in God's healing of humanity we also see a theology that moves against and contradicts the empty and therefore perhaps threatening specter of other transformations, as we see, for instance, in "the Heidegger Change" (Catherine Malabou).[18] Hans Jonas saw almost immediately that theologians should resist Heidegger, as he argued in his famous speech "Heidegger and Theology":

> the theologian should resist the attempt to treat his message as a matter of historic fate, and thus as part of a comprehensive becoming, and thus as one element among others in a tradition, and as itself something divisible, assimilable in part and left in part, ready for the pickings of the unbeliever.[19]

The essence of the theological task is not to reveal an ineluctable fate, but to explore God's story according to the *fides quaerens intellectum*.[20] A God who acts is a God whose enactments are what need to be understood. It can only be a sign of having given up with the work of grappling with the drama of life with a living God when theologians end up defending fideistic positions or in the attitude of

---

16. Karl Barth focused his Christology on this particular turning point within the doctrine of God. On this important topic see Darren O. Sumner, *Karl Barth and the Incarnation: Christology and the Humility of God* (London: Bloomsbury T&T Clark, 2016).

17. Karl Barth, *The Humanity of God* (Louisville, Kentucky: Westminster/John Knox Press, 1999).

18. Malabou, *The Heidegger Change*.

19. Hans Jonas, "Heidegger and Theology," *Review of Metaphysics* 18, no. 2 (1964): 207–33, 215.

20. Karl Barth, *Anselm, Fides Quaerens Intellectum: Anselm's Proof of the Existence of God in the Context of His Theological Scheme* (Eugene: Pickwick Press, 2009). See in contrast Heidegger's definition of theology: Martin Heidegger, "Phenomenology and Theology (1927)" in *Pathmarks*, ed. William McNeill (Cambridge: Cambridge University Press, 1998), 39–62.

trying to think God as "primal" or "essential,"[21] instead of listening to the witness of God's word and actions.

Real Stories

"Where can I go from your spirit"? There is no way to escape God's encountering presence; no way to strike out on one's own, on the strength of one's own perspective and means of understanding to forge a meaningful story outside of God's domain of influence and action. Were this possible it could only be had at the cost of losing the only story that offers hope in the sense of a hopeful message that is addressed to our lived experience. More than that: it could only be at the cost of losing reality.

Walter Benjamin's reflections on the "Storyteller" explore this understanding the hope carried by a (the) true story.[22] "The art of storytelling is coming to an end," Benjamin observes, explaining that "one reason for this phenomenon is obvious: experience has fallen in value. And it looks as if it is continuing to fall into bottomlessness."[23] Benjamin is reflecting on the sense in which, through a story, a storyteller conveys the experience of some distant reality exclusively accessible to hearers through the witness of the storyteller. It is the eyewitness nature of a storyteller that makes what the story conveys different in kind from mere information or explanation. It is in this way that we should understand Hans Reinders's retelling of Amy Julia Becker's story[24] as a comment on the story told by a witness that highlights the step-by-step process of how she is slowly released from attempts to "explain" the birth of a baby who was diagnosed with Down syndrome. Becker slowly relinquishes the "Why has this happened?" and "Whose fault was it that this happened?" questions in a manner very like the narrative arc traced by Jesus' answer to the question asked by the Pharisees in John 9, who ask if a man is blind because of his parents' sin.

Such narratives invite us to discover a spiritual way of narrating life in its experienced and suffered reality, as opposed to novelistically inventing an artful meaning for our lives. At this point in the argument this chapter is fleshing out the argument of Chapter 8 in a personal key: just as the scientist is bound not to create but to *discover* biological life, learning to tell our *own* story is not a process of invention but of fine-grained description of what has happened to us, however artfully and creatively this is done. In distinction to the novelist, the storyteller speaks of passions and transformations already experienced, so giving full-blooded first-person testimony to the reality of what has already been experienced.

---

21. Jonas, "Heidegger and Theology," 212.

22. Walter Benjamin, "The Storyteller: Reflections on the Works of Nicolai Lescov," in *Illuminations*, ed. Hannah Arendt, trans. Harry Zorn (New York: Harcourt, Brace & World, 1968), 83–107.

23. Benjamin, "The Storyteller," 83–4.

24. Amy Julia Becker, *A Good and Perfect Gift: Faith, Expectations, and a Little Girl Named Penny* (Bloomington: Bethany House Publishers, 2011).

Such witness is absolutely central in orienting us to God's presence in God's Spirit, and therefore also for Jesus' promise that we can rely on God's Spirit. It is this experience that is also aptly described as a translocation into a new self. Reinders discovers the use of the language of a "new self" to be the common denominator among the various witnesses to transformation that he examines in his book.

> They are changed into a new self that enables them to negotiate the gap between the "before" and "after" by trusting the reality of friendship and love. The fountain of all that is good has not dried up; it continues to pour out friendship and love to those who are open to it. These are people who have learned how to die as an old self, which they managed to do because they found new eyes to see. Only to the extent that they are transformed into a new self, people succeed in moving beyond the initial experience of disability as a tragedy. Providence is the active presence of God, mediated by the Spirit, to guide us in learning to see the new life that is around us, and is there to be seen.[25]

How is someone changed into a "new self"? This is largely unthematized subject of many if not all of the stories that people tell about living with people with intellectual disabilities. The hidden point of unity of these stories is the grammar of life as a following of God's providence "mediated by the Spirit." To follow God's providence means to let one's life and self-understanding become transformed into a different story. So, we may say with Hans Joachim Iwand: "Faith has to do with the substance of our being, our very life and death. In faith, 'it is not I who live'! In faith, the life of a new person lives in the 'me' whom I shall become."[26] We have in this formulation a succinct encapsulation of the biblical grammar of the paradoxical appearance of the transfigured self.[27]

If providence is God's active working to sustain creation, it follows that the purpose of this activity is identified in Christ's name, Immanuel: "God with us." God is with us as the Christ who is present in the gift of the Spirit that God the Father sent upon him, and that he has promised to his friends. God's provision for those who are open to receive his gift is the gift of the Spirit, the Paraclete, who will accompany them as comforter and guide. Those who receive the gift of the Spirit will find themselves changed. Or as Amy Julia Becker puts it, they have received being changed.

---

25. Reinders, *Disability, Providence, and Ethics*, 189.
26. Hans Joachim Iwand, *The Righteousness of Faith According to Luther*, ed. Virgil F. Thompson, Randi H. Lundell, and Gregory A. Walter (Eugene, Or.: Wipf & Stock, 2008), 78–9. Iwand then cites Luther: "Therefore faith must be taught correctly so that it is clear that through it a new person is shaped and in it a new person comes into being that cannot be separated from Christ, but clings to Him steadfastly as if to say "I am like Christ . . ."." (LW 26, 168–9).
27. See also Clark J. Elliston, *Dietrich Bonhoeffer and the Ethical Self: Christology, Ethics, and Formation* (Minneapolis: Fortress, 2016).

Guided by the light of this Spirit, these different witnesses testify to having learned to see differently in a spirit of self-giving love. That is what the Holy Spirit does. It communicates the love of Christ to human beings so that they will love one another. The Spirit has poured this love into their hearts. These things are inseparable, as Paul says to his fellow Christians in Rome.[28]

Spirit of Discernment: Spirit of Love

It is striking how often stories as Amy Julia Becker's narrate the experience of learning in terms of the discovery of distinctions that are associated with the notion of God's presence. For instance, Becker discovers the distinction between an explanation—in which a newborn disabled child is spoken of as a tragedy—and understanding—which she discovers when her daughter Penny begins to appear to her as a beacon of hope and love. The discoveries that these very different appraisals of Penny provoke cut across the whole horizon of how people around her perceive Penny. Instead of allowing her daughter to be entrapped by what is visible from the hermeneutics of common patterns of understanding, Becker discerns that Penny exposes an aspect of human reality that is normally obscured. In Penny's life Becker sees for the first time that passivity and vulnerability are not accidental but essential aspects of the life of human beings as they appear in God's story.

"They learn to see differently," observes Hans Reinders, because they have received the "spirit of discernment." Discernment is one of the central biblical concepts linked to the type of understanding that can perceive the reality that is exposed in the presence of God. "When the apostle Paul speaks of what the Spirit does, he consistently speaks of love, agape. That is how one recognizes the gift that the Spirit is. The Spirit communicates God's love to human beings so that they will love one another."[29] Here the language of Spirit and love are both being deployed to point to the absolute passivity we experience in the face-to-face encounter with the other. Before another face, we too may say with the psalmist, "Where can I flee from your presence?"—understanding that the "your" here can mean God, my child's presence and/or my neighbor's face. The other can only become genuinely present to us if the Spirit is given that turns one's eyes away from self-absorption, from fears and expectations.

Guided by God's presence we are opened to a story that we discover ourselves to be sharing with the person we face. Within the process of translocation, this is how the biblical grammar defines love, as Martin Buber has observed.

> Jesus' feeling for the possessed man is different from his feeling for the beloved disciple; but the love is one. Feelings one "has"; love occurs. Feelings dwell in man, but man dwells in his love. . . . Love is a cosmic force. For those who stand

---

28. Quoted in Reinders, *Disability, Providence, and Ethics*, 189.
29. Reinders, *Disability, Providence, and Ethics*, 162.

in it and behold in it, men emerge from their entanglement in business; and the good and the evil, the clever and the foolish, the beautiful and the ugly, one after another become actual and you for them; that is, liberated, emerging into a unique confrontation. Exclusiveness comes into being miraculously again and again—and now one can act, help, heal, educate, raise, redeem.[30]

"Man dwells in his love." Buber marks out love as the locale in which people are drawn beyond themselves through unique personal encounters. Love is not somehow available, it "occurs," it is experienced passively and with suffering. Love is first received. Love generates real "stories," experiences of a new reality, such as the one on display in Amy Julia Becker's story.

Martin Buber and Emmanuel Lévinas are well-known for having explored the grammar of the biblical language of love in these terms and in rich detail.[31] I refer to their work at this point to emphasize how love as they describe it requires the language of change and translocation to be intelligible, and that the destination of this translocation is into a new story and reality in which one can find a place for a true life.[32] These dynamics are all paradigmatically present in the encounter with God's love, whose characteristic features are that God has submitted Godself to a particular story with Israel, his beloved people and then in Jesus Christ has, in love, invited all of us human beings into this story, and with we human beings and all creatures.[33]

John the Evangelist's summary of his gospel encapsulates this story: "For God so loved the world, that he gave his only Son, that whoever believes in him should not perish but have eternal life" (Jn 3:16). God has wholly involved Godself with the story of human beings. In doing so, God has ensured that the human story does not run into the sand but is instead translocated into that hopeful living with God on luminous display in Jesus. The message of John's Gospel is that God has promised human beings that they can experience God's story face to face in its reality, through spiritual love. What makes the reality opened up in Jesus different from the reality it displaces is its message of real hope, of the firm and tangible reality of hope. Reinders elegantly draws out how the stories told by people about being transformed by living with people with disabilities are invariably accounts

---

30. Martin Buber, *I and Thou* (New York: Charles Scribner's Sons, 1970), 66.

31. For Lévinas, see Bernhard Casper, "Geisel für den anderen—Vielleicht nur ein harter Name für Liebe: Emmanuel Lévinas und seine Hermeneutik diachronen "Da"-Seins (Freiburg im Breisgau: Alber, 2020); Corey Beals, *Lévinas and the Wisdom of Love: The Question of Invisibility* (Waco: Baylor University Press, 2007), 43–54.

32. I go here beyond, but along the path opened by Adorno's statement in his aphorism on "asylum for the homeless": "There is no right life within the wrong one" (*Minima Moralia*, Aphorism 18).

33. Hermann Spieckermann, "God's Steadfast Love: Toward a New Conception of Old Testament Theology," *Biblica* 81, no. 3 (2000): 305–27; Hans G. Ulrich, *Wie Geschöpfe leben: Konturen evangelischer Ethik* (Berlin: LIT, 2007).

of a change from hopelessness to hope.³⁴ These witnesses have been translocated from a hopeless history into God's story, carried by God's promise not to abandon his people and to continue his story with them. It is in this way that the grammar of God's reality as it is witnessed in Psalm 139 converges with the witness of people living with intellectually disabled people, whose communication may be so faint as to be almost unintelligible. Yet it is these very relationships in which Messianic time makes its appearance in the invitation to learn to live *together* and in *hope*.

To receive this Messianic dawning, however, does demand a change of direction away from ones' own intentions. This is repentance. The necessity of the repentant turn is especially obvious for those of us fully at home in the hegemonic patterns of thought and behavior that so broadly and subtly disparage disabled lives. Following the biblical semantic, the renewal of our mental disposition (Rom. 12:2) must be understood as a partaking of the new creation as it is promised to God's creatures and the whole creation. The creation of a new mind includes the creation of new forms of awareness, of recognizing what was not recognized before, and so of the reality created by God and determined to remain within God's story with his creatures. Each of us has this promise in common with every human being. It is not our bodies or our minds but this promise that makes us all equal preserving our uniqueness. It does so in pointing to God's story with all his creatures, in which everyone has a unique part to play, as the Hebrew text of Ps. 139:14 makes abundantly clear: "You have made me fearfully and singled me out." The unique significance of every human being exceeds infinitely any attributed or desired identity. More than that, every human being encounters in his or her given bodily existence what it means to be "holy," as a member of the sanctified community.³⁵ To belong to the community of the church universal is to know one's self as living in exposure to God's will and working instead of simply "existing" in a universal and so faceless history of being.

The Transfiguration of Bodily Existence

A temptation here that must be avoided is to allow the promised renewal of the mind (Rom. 12:2) to divert into a rationalist focusing of ethics on the "mind" and on "the renewal of our mind." This would, however, be to overlook the inner logic of the point I am pressing, which is not a call for an intellectual change nor a contribution to a still needed general enlightenment, though these might well be byproducts of the translocation I am emphasizing. In the original New Testament Greek, "mind" (*nous*) has a much larger semantic range than the English, and

---

34. Reinders, *Disability, Providence, and Ethics*, 189.

35. This definition of being holy has very different contours from the concept of a "homo sacer" who is subjected to human power and violence. See Giorgio Agamben, *Homo Sacer: Sovereign Power and Bare Life* (Stanford: Stanford University Press, 2017).

indicates the awareness, recognition, and understanding that is needed if Christians are to "explore" and "prove" what God wills according to His story with us.

This new awareness is something that must be given with grounded Christian hope. It is part of the promised becoming newly created, as it happened at the beginning of God's new world and continues to happen all around us, as narrated in John 9. Set within this divine work of new creation, it is more clear that the transformation of the mind should be understood as the transformation of our whole existence in its present bodily form. While the most common English translation of the Greek *metamorphousthe* (μεταμορφοῦσθε) is "transformation," metamorphosis[36] is more penetratingly translated as "transfiguration," understood as a theologically inflected replacement of the form of our life. The term "transfiguration" highlights the scope of the metamorphosis being undergone, in indicating that human beings are literally receiving a new "figure." They are receiving the figure that they need and which is fitting for the role they will play in God's story.

The logic of human transfiguration is emphasized in the transfiguration of Jesus' (Lk. 9:28-36) over whom God declares, "This is my Son, my Chosen One; listen to him!" In this declaration, God unveils his real story with Jesus. It is an event that is continuous with all the events of Jesus' Messianic appearance,[37] but which emphasizes that there will be an ongoing transition from transformation to transfiguration within the Messianic time. This transfiguration will culminate at the end of time, when God's elected children become "configured" (συμμόρφ ους) "to the image of his son" (Rom. 8:29). The message of transfiguration and metamorphosis is one that applies to every human being, even to Jesus Christ: "who will transform our lowly body that it may be conformed to His glorious body" (Phil. 3:21). This pronouncement draws attention to the eschatological transparency and significance of all the phenomena and stories of transformation and change in the life of people as they encounter Jesus in his Messianic epiphany and in continuation his eschatological coming. This Messianic epiphany unites the wide range of phenomenological disclosures of God's story, each of which can now be seen as an anticipation of the new creation.

What is crucial to note is that this Messianic transition includes an enacted "new creation" by making specific instances of transformation transparent as eschatological transfigurations. The dramatic of transfiguration is by definition

---

36. For the biblical context of this discussion, see *Metamorphoses: Resurrection, Body, and Transformative Practices in Early Christianity*, ed. Turid Karlsen Seim and Jorunn Økland, Ekstasis v. 1 (Berlin: De Gruyter, 2009).

37. This is the precise very point where the notion of Jesus' Messianic appearance in historically graspable contours and, therefore, for the notion of a salvation-history where God's story and "history" dramatically meet. For the exegetical elaboration of this point see especially the work of Martin Hengel and its discussion in Michael F. Bird, Martin Hengel, and Jason Maston, *Earliest Christian History: History, Literature, and Theology* (Tübingen: Mohr Siebeck, 2012).

not indexed to the limits of a given human "existence" thrown into an indefinite history. Nor is transfiguration another name for passages through normal stages of development or change. Transfiguration is solely a matter of the transition from an old being to the new creation.[38] In this logic the transformation of our human mind appears as fundamentally a transfiguration into new awareness of the eternal kingdom, as told of the disciples on the road to Emmaus whose, "eyes were opened and they knew Him" (Lk. 24:31).

This is the real message of witnesses of transfiguration: the life we encounter in others must be taken seriously in the contours and shapes it really has. Life is not an abstract energy; it can only appear as human life in a fully determined form. We become aware of this form by our "mind" (*nous*) as the locus of our readiness for understanding, awareness, and recognition of the other human encountering us. When we talk about human beings, we are speaking about an entity becoming present in an encounter with us. There is no third person observer's position we can occupy in order to perceive the other "truly." To be transfigured is to be brought into a new mode of encounter within a new reality with which we can participate as it encounters us in its embracing presence. It is a reality with its own *sui generis* features. To be drawn into this new reality will necessarily flow out into a reorientation of how the personal, bodily, given existence moves through any social world in its saturation by historical narratives. The ethos of this true human is inescapably bodily, because the other person always appears in formed givenness, seamlessly capable of being faced, related to and being committed to other people.

Why, though, and in what sense his human being inescapably "bodily"? Here the Aristotelian concept *ethos* again offers help, as long as we recall that there are two different notions of *ethos*.[39] The Greek word *ethos* (ἔθος) indicates the rules and laws that are obligatory for everybody, the so-called "tyranny of normality."[40] In distinction from this universal given law as it is articulated in categorical imperatives or given with an absolutely binding responsibility, *aethos* (ἦθος) points toward what each human being seeks, that context good for their living, for dwelling in peace and justice together with other people, and so feeling that they are home. Ethics—as reflection on our ethos (*aethos*)—is an invitation to recognize who we human beings actually are, and who we must become in order to live together, or at least to act together in a common political reality and a common "world" (Hannah Arendt). It is this second understanding of ethics that converges with the aim of the biblical imagery of metamorphosis. Both concepts raise the question that may be called the fundamental, rock bottom question of

---

38. On the insistence of that distinction, see especially Grant Macaskill, *Living in Union with Christ: Paul's Gospel and Christian Moral Identity* (Grand Rapids: Baker Academic, 2019).

39. See the discussion in Chapter 4, "Political ἔθος—Political ἦθος."

40. Stanley Hauerwas, *Suffering Presence* (Notre Dame: University of Notre Dame Press, 1986), 211.

human life: Where are we at home, what is the reality we are truly part of? What is the reality within which we really encounter one another and live together in peace and justice?

We turn now to ask directly: What is the aim of the change that recurs at the heart of so many accounts of being transformed through living together with disabled people? It is a change that is not presented as simply a matter of the wellbeing of the individual ("well, it was good for me!"), since what is described is couched as an experience of encounter with a new reality. This we may understand according to Romans 12 as a metamorphosis, as a transfiguration, because it is so clearly presented as a transition into a "new" reality that has appeared and claimed the speaker. This is a change, that goes beyond attempts to find given patterns or models in order to master change and become "change agents." These are changes that did not begin by a quest to overcome differences between human beings and their obviously divergent ways of living. This is a change that does not emerge, generically, when people "struggle of recognition."[41] Similarly, this is not a change that emerges from finding a better descriptive nomenclature or explanations. All of these descriptions of change may have been at play, as well as many more. But none of these imminent theories of change will shed light on transfiguration unless we view them as theories which do critical work and so let come into focus that new reality in which we are discovering ourselves to be wondrously re-created in God's story.

Witnesses who confess that the "spirit of discernment" (Hans Reinders) has been given to them have received it by allowing themselves to become involved in that transfiguring change characteristic of Messianic times. This spirit of discernment signifies a new ethical praxis, that is, the praxis to explore and probe the new ethos (*aethos*) where human beings find themselves in a new story beyond the logic of inclusion or exclusion and beyond other dominating patterns of this "world-age." This means that the ethical praxis of the Christian cannot be primarily a matter of securing equal rights for all nor setting out definitions of the "good life" for all human beings. Its central concern is, rather, with discerning the presence of that new common reality.

We will lose the track of this thought if we do not immediately specify that, in theological terms, when we speak of sharing bodily life we are not talking about the generic traits that all human beings share, nor about one aspect or another of a common "nature," even if in daily life we use this kind of language in order to resist other disintegrating concepts. Fundamentally, what counts as ethical praxis for the Christian is that which participates in God's story as it appears in real time amidst the world of human creatures. In an ethics so defined the central concern of ethical thinking is how we will participate in God's story sharing this bodily existence in a manner that coheres within a newly appearing context of living, a new ethos (*aethos*). This becoming real is a translocation, our witnesses tell us, into

---

41. Axel Honneth, *The Struggle for Recognition: The Moral Grammar of Social Conflicts* (Cambridge, UK: Polity Press, 2005).

a capacious space that perfectly fits our unique stature as human beings. It is this witness that I have been calling an opening of reality to us, an opening initiated by God in order to fulfill God's promise to continue His story.[42]

The core of Christian ethics is thus the exploration of the new reality of a human ethos (*aethos*), created by God's will to live with us, to have us live together, and that this living together be continuously preserved. It is in this Christian account that the Greek terminology of ethos (*aethos*) appears in its essential meaning. The ethos (*aethos*) of the Christian is a capacious space for living, in which we can take up residence and be sheltered within forms of living that suit our bodily being. The space suited to human life is not, therefore, simply the "body," its limits, capacities, and extensions, which we must of course negotiate and live with, but lies beyond our personal bodies, in that *aethos* that allows our personal bodily life to flourish in participation, encounter, and relationship.

The psalmists poignantly express their yearning for this ethos (*aethos*), and the promise of God to give it.

> There are many who say, "O that we might see some good!" Lift up the light of thy countenance upon us, O LORD! Thou hast put more joy in my heart than they have when their grain and wine abound. In peace I will both lie down and sleep; for thou alone, O LORD, makest me dwell in safety." (Ps. 4:7-9, RSV)

"Dwell in safety": Here is God's promise to give people that new context of living. It is this promise from outside of all human willing and making that prompts Christians to survey the lives and stories around us to see where the promise is being realized, lived, and brought to articulacy in our discourses. From the vantage point of this new reality none are judged perfect or imperfect, ordered or disordered, able or disabled, as living a valuable or worthless life. The whole project of evaluating human life is exploded by God's evident commitment to all human lives. Again we discover all such evaluative schemes as instances of the patterns and "schemata" of this world-age that fall away in this new form of life ("be not conformed to them," Rom. 12:2). The aim of the new life can be encapsulated in three iterations of a single question, which Christian ethics pursues with single-minded focus: How is God present with us? How does God continue to share his life with us? And how is God's ongoing story with us providing us the reality in which we can truly live?

Such a definition of the ethos (*aetos*) of Christian life answers the insightful challenge of Friedrich Nietzsche to modern Christianity. All Christianity is false, he insisted, that defers or deflects the question about the life we actually lead in favor of questions about being justified and confirmed by God or the reality of evil that point beyond the lived life.[43] So understood, the Christian ethos is nothing other

---

42. Hauerwas, *Suffering Presence*.

43. Friedrich Nietzsche, *On the Genealogy of Morality* (Cambridge: Cambridge University Press, 1994 [1887]).

than bodily worship carried on in every domain of live, in which Christians reach toward the encounter with God's active presence and in so doing find themselves constituted as the body of Christ. Christian theology and theological ethics can dispense with the soloutionless task of explaining the problem of the existence of evil in a world made by a good God, or of describing God's attributes and will, in favor of learning what it means to understand and describe our own bodies and lives as part of God's story. This is to embrace as good news the theological reality that as limited creatures we can never occupy the meta-position of the observer of our lives: we, as limited, weighty, bodily beings, are para-located with many other bodies within God's story.

The apostle Paul is concerned to point people toward a form of life he has experienced that is characteristic of transfigured human life in its bodily presence. He writes in Rom. 12:1 that transfiguration is something that happens to people within their whole bodily substantiated existence (*soma*). Paul's appeal to "present your bodies (*somata*) as a living sacrifice, holy and acceptable to God, which is your spiritual worship" indicates the practice through which new creation takes place. The term "bodies," *somata* (σώματα), indicates our personal existence as existing in a body that we did not create, with all its vulnerabilities— our bodily given existence as we actually experience it. To present your bodies means literally to para-locate your bodily life, to let it be given over into God's disposal to play its part in God's story rather than reserving it for your own purposes. Framed as an imperative: share your bodily life with God's story in its Messianic appearance. From here on the term "existence" becomes in its obsolete in its literal meaning, because we can no longer meaningfully understand human beings as "existing." "Existing" is the empty, vague, and generic language that arises when we view the determinative environment of humans as the "world" and history, as (according to Heidegger's narrative) a "Dasein" thrown into a fatal history without a definite story out of which some meaning must be made, or purpose for life constructed.

This presenting of our bodily substantiated existence as sacrifice (against self-affirmation and against the affirmation of a fulfilled human life) is what Paul calls worship (*logike*, λογικὴν λατρείαν), a praxeological alignment with the *logos* of God. A bodily substantiation of the logos as worship is an expression of alignment with God's story and its grammar as it is given in God's word. We encounter here the central focus of biblical ethics: sharing our bodily life with God and our neighbor. We share life with God and the neighbor not beyond, but precisely *as a form of our bodily existence* as it appears within the worshipping community.

The Messianic pre-appearance of the coming kingdom in the worshipping community concretely cancels all abstract evocations of a common world. It embodies a going-beyond communion or solidarity that is decreed but not enacted. Where worship exists, furthermore, all claims that there is one universal reality that all reasonable people should recognize as a common "world" are exposed as false. Transfiguration may be said to be an eschatological alteration of the characteristic patterns of recognizing our bodily life, for example, as weak and strong, self-reliant or dependent, resistant or vulnerable by way of the Messianic renewal of our mind in God's story with us. The medium of this transfiguration is God's creation of a new "mental (noetic) disposition" toward God's reality.

The new disposition can be actively awaited, Paul suggests in Rom. 8:26: "the Spirit helps us in our weakness; for we do not know how to pray as we ought, but the Spirit himself intercedes for us with sighs too deep for words" (RSV). We need God's Spirit, Christ's Spirit in order to worship in prayer precisely because what we hope for is not knowledge of God's being or anonymous transcendence, but to encounter God in God's actions This spirit, to reiterate, must not be understood as distinct from or even opposed to our bodily life. Rather it is that "Spirit" which has been breathed into the earthly body—according to Genesis 2, so that it became a "living soul," a living breathing existence encountering God.[44] It is precisely the bodily presence of a living soul endowed with God's Spirit that is apprehended afresh through Christ's Spirit in the experience of God's new creation, which includes the renewal of our mind. This new creation defines human existence—defines, which means it determines the *fines,* the contouring limits of human existence within God's story.[45] "The Spirit Himself bears witness with our spirit that we are children of God, and if children, then heirs—heirs of God and joint heirs with Christ, if indeed we suffer with Him, that we may also be glorified together" (Rom. 8:16-17). This narrative succinctly summarizes God's story in its Messianic continuity as it continues by way of Christ's heirs and their ongoing bodily substantiated worship in Messianic times.

Resources: Biblical Semantics and Witnesses

This brief look at the biblical tradition and its semantics of ethical "learning" can be understood as a description of what determines the human form of life as it is drawn into God's story. The human form of life is not addressed as given with subjective agency resting in its own existential being thrown into any kind of world, fate, or "history," but as subjected to God's story with it and its exposed Messianic reality. The biblical tradition provokes us to ask how this "ethos" (*aethos*) we are called to live in is still in need of transformation and determined for transfiguration—and how this can happen. I am proposing that at the heart of biblical ethics lies a specific bodily (*somatic*) ethos (*aethos*) determined for transition to transfiguration; it characterizes a lively yet passive event of learning, an experience that we both suffer and are called to actively recognize. "Learning" means to again and again be brought into line with God's story as he is continually re-initiating it and which he promises to bring to its fulfillment. The originary locus of this ongoing encountering experience is that worship where God is present. Worship happens as an event when the reality is present which renders God's people (passively) God's heirs. The Jewish tradition of God's people as a bodily

---

44. DBWE 3, 78.
45. We find this mode of a definition of "human beings" in Martin Luther's *Disputatio de homine* (1536) (32nd thesis), LW 34, 133–44.

entity parallels in substantial respects the Christian ethos (*aethos*) so described,[46] not least because both communities affirm that they are preserved by the Torah. Neither tradition focuses its intellectual efforts on defining the constitution of a moral agent who is made ethical by conforming to an absolute ethos (*ethos*).

The exploration of the Christian ethos is catalyzed and provoked by witness. The textual form taken by scripture offers a clue that this might well be the aim of writing letters, as did St. Paul, and not unlike the work of writing books such as that of Hans Reinders, Brian Brock, or John Swinton.[47] These witnessing forms of writing appear designed to provoke or challenge our awareness and touch the habits of our hearts, by concretizing the general claim that learning and exploring happens where people, as Paul expressed it, "prove" some way of living, where people are entrusting, subjecting their lives to what God's will has offered to them.[48] Only as they turning to live into what is given to them do they enter into a way that will provoke experiences that can be described and so provoke others to explore in a similar way their own context of experience. When we listen to the Christian theological tradition, with its descriptions, narratives, and concepts, we can learn to see how it "re-presents" human life in a manner designed to point hearers toward a life form that gives us new perception, that literally re-cognizes us. In perceiving this way of life, we too can experience and suffer it as our Christian life form in its contrast with and contradictions of the descriptions of the world that previously organized our "mind."

In other words, as 1 Pet. 3:15 suggests ("be ready always to give account of the hope present to you"), to talk about the Christian form of life is another way of exploring our hope for that new creation. We hope for the creation of a new mind and a new awareness. That we must still live in hope is to confess that we are in significant ways still hostage to distortions of our mind that limit our capacity to prove God's will. The renewal of our mind is essential if we are to give account of our hope instead of languishing in captivity to the patterns of this world-age, including the patterns of liberation, emancipation, and necessary revolution that place us back into the dynamics of the "will to power" detached from grounded hope in God's appearance. Christians have to account for their actions in terms of hope for the real advent of God in Jesus Christ.

Are, in fact, theological discourses about disability driven by the hope which became present in Jesus Christ? Or do they replicate well-known patterns of thinking, modern or postmodern, which obscure the Christian hope for God's redemption and His continuation of that story? This is the critical heuristic question for assessing disability theologies. It is also the hermeneutical key for

---

46. Michael Wyschogrod, *The Body of Faith: God and the People of Israel* (Northvale, NJ: Jason Aronson, 1996).

47. John Swinton, *Finding Jesus in the Storm: The Spiritual Lives of Christians with Mental Health Challenges* (Grand Rapids: Eerdmans, 2020).

48. Eph. 2:10: "For we are His workmanship, created in Christ Jesus for good works, which God prepared beforehand that we should walk in them."

any theological exploration of human existence and life. According to 1 Pet. 3:15, Christian hope understands its task as a theological exploration of human forms of existence as it appears within God's reality. We have seen how this heuristic key significantly effects theological reflections on disability, paralleling its critical importance for various other discourses like bioethics, as shown in Chapter 7.

A striking further example appears in Susan Parsons's discussion of some feminist theologies. She raises the question of whether some feminist theologies even attempt to "account for the hope" of redemption or whether they have chosen to follow in their "orthodoxies" such patterns of critical thinking and liberation which paradoxically affirm patterns that determine the main contours of the moral universe they aim to criticize. This type of conformity is, Parsons argues, not unconnected with their lack of "attention to the matter of nihilism," a nihilism characterized not at least by its loss of any horizon of a granted hope. For liberationist feminists, the only thing that can be hoped for will spring from human revolutionary actions. In such a discourse, Parsons suggests, a "renewed orthodoxy" is needed, an orthodoxy which "is a searching of mind that finds itself informed and challenged in the body of Christ to meet again and again in worship the coming of God to matter and the turning of the soul into love."[49]

To remain patiently awaiting God's coming in worship emerges as the prime focal point of the theological task of exploring the ethos (*aethos*) of transfiguration on display in the ministry of Jesus Christ. The promise of being created anew demands that we admit the necessity of critical engagement with all the forms of life that remain cut off, captured by the stasis of theory, constricted in the patterns of this world-age (Rom. 12:1). The problem is that this enclosure does and can only appear to us as "real life," making it impossible to perceive the new creation in its Messianically given reality, as Hans Reinders observes.

> There are within the tradition of Christian theology many strands of thinking about our humanity that make interior and self-referential matters central to their conception of being human. In that respect, my aim . . . is not so much . . . apologetic as it is to be self-critical: it is an attempt to investigate whether the Christian religion can find in itself the resources to develop a view that does not render the existence of profoundly disabled humans inherently problematic.[50]

In this chapter I am drawing this volume to a close by likewise looking for resources in the Christian tradition and its scriptures in which profoundly disabled people may be seen to be part of God's story. Like Reinders I too am also doing so by following accounts of the role played by the lively transformations people have

---

49. Susan Frank Parsons, "Accounting for Hope: Feminist Theology as Fundamental Theology," in *Challenging Women's Orthodoxies in the Context of Faith*, ed. Susan F. Parsons (Aldershot: Ashgate, 2000), 20.

50. Reinders, *Receiving the Gift of Friendship: Profound Disability, Theological Anthropology, and Ethics* (Grand Rapids: Eerdmans, 2008), 40.

undergone in their lives with people with disabilities, who have catalyzed their own renewal of life. My distinctive contribution to this discussion is to have asked the further question of *how* these stories might be said to provoke insights in readers and hearers that can help us in turn to better articulate the transformation of experience that lies at their heart. Where I differ from Reinders is in emphasizing that self-critical work cannot accomplish transformation, only the experiences of God's own presence and redemption. It is in this positive sense that the resources available in accounts of faith and disability are so potent and have such far-reaching heuristic power. This heuristic is especially inexhaustible as a way of understanding the dynamics of human bodily coexistence paradigmatically realized in the Eucharistic celebration of the body of Christ. My own harvest here will be a very limited and preliminary, and it awaits elaboration and articulation by others.

God's Reality and Story: Embodiment

God's story with us human beings presents itself as a new reality within this world-age. The abolition of all pain and suffering, of sickness and disability is an implication and indication that the new reality will be a genuinely new creation, not an alternative "world," but one that is new one in a thoroughly analogical sense. In the words of Rev. 21:1-5:

> Then I saw a new heaven and a new earth; for the first heaven and the first earth had passed away, and the sea was no more. And I saw the holy city, new Jerusalem, coming down out of heaven from God, prepared as a bride adorned for her husband; and I heard a loud voice from the throne saying, "Behold, the dwelling of God is with men. He will dwell with them, and they shall be his people, and God himself will be with them; he will wipe away every tear from their eyes, and death shall be no more, neither shall there be mourning nor crying nor pain any more, for the former things have passed away."

Thus, the story of God's willingness to coexist with his creatures, to dwell with them, culminates in an evidently "bodily" presence to us human beings, as already experienced in the bodily presence of the *logos* who shared his life with us, as emphasized in the prologue of John's Gospel. At the culmination of the story all human beings are members of the household of God and fellow citizens in His city: "So then you are no longer strangers and foreigners, but you are fellow citizens with the saints and members of the household of God."[51] This new communal and political way of living together as fellow citizens is the promise of transfiguration within that story.

---

51. Eph. 2:19. Luther translates: "So seid ihr nun nicht mehr Gäste und Fremdlinge, sondern Bürger mit der Heiligen und Gottes Hausgenossen."

The promise of the consummation of transfiguration is also a promise of our bodily life shared with other people, as theirs is shared with us. It now becomes clear, this is also where God's story begins, becomes realized, and ends. The immensely differentiated elaborations of utopian worldviews in the wake of Ernst Bloch's influential "principle of hope" appears against the backdrop of the eschatology offered in revelation as an attempt to find a final home and its concrete pre-appearance and as a countermovement to God's advent coming in Jesus Christ and His bodily presence in the Eucharist. It is here that the futuristic and utopian dynamic of the "principle of hope," the *futurum*, clashes with the *adventus* of God's story. This is the Messianic collision Walter Benjamin identified in Paul Klee's angel of history painting.[52] Here is the Messianic turning point within "history," the turning point of the limited transformation that happens in the progressive development of human life into eschatological transfiguration. The concern of the biblical narrative is with this Messianic-eschatological intervention of God's *adventus*, not simply about historical change. The renewal of our "mind" is not hope for historical change but for the appearance of the Messiah's redemptive reality.

Why Bodily Life?

When God created Adam and Eve, He created them from the soil, the earth, in a way fitted for life in the "garden" populated with a whole world of living creatures. The first couple was not far from animal life, being fully embedded and rooted in that earthly context and related to it in many ways (what we today call "nature").[53] Their existence as human beings was earth-bound, because they were bodily beings. Taking their being as creatures seriously entailed taking this bodily reality seriously before God, in relation to themselves and to other creatures. The sole way they could acknowledge that creation, and their own bodies as good was by receiving them and living in them in accord with the manifold earthly context in which human existence is embedded. Now it becomes clearer why bodily existence is not just about the body, but about the body's determined relations and their capacity to sustain the conditions of life, including taking seriously the spirit, breathed into this body. As Dietrich Bonhoeffer observes:

> The human body really does live only by God's spirit; that is what constitutes its essential being. God as such is glorified [*Gott verherrlicht sich*] in the body, that is, in the body that has the specific being of a human body. That is why where the original body in its created being has been destroyed, God enters it anew in Jesus Christ, and then, where this body too is broken, enters the forms of the sacrament of the body and blood. The body and blood of the Lord's Supper

---

52. See Susan A. Handelman, *Fragments of Redemption: Jewish Thought and Literary Theory in Benjamin, Scholem, and Lévinas* (Bloomington: Indiana University Press, 2010).

53. Benno Jacob, *The First Book of the Bible: Genesis* (Jersey City: KTAV, 1974).

are the new realities of creation promised to fallen Adam. Because Adam is created as body, Adam is also redeemed as body [and God comes to Adam as body], in Jesus Christ and in the sacrament.... Humankind created in this way is humankind as the image of God. It is the image of God not in spite of but precisely in its bodily nature. For in their bodily nature human beings are related to the earth and to other bodies; they are there for others and are dependent upon others. In their bodily existence human beings find their brothers and sisters and find the earth. As such creatures human beings of earth and spirit are "like" God, their Creator.[54]

Thus does Bonhoeffer formulate his insistence that to be given a body is to be placed into relation to other people. In this he is an heir of Martin Luther, who also characterized the human body as intrinsically related to others. Moreover, he understood the body as the instrument and medium for others, going as far as calling it their servant.

A man does not live for himself alone in his mortal body to work for it alone, but he lives also for all men on earth; rather, he lives only for others and not for himself. To this end he brings his body into subjection that he may the more sincerely and freely serve others, as Paul says in Rom. 14 [:7-8], "None of us lives to himself, and none of us dies to himself. If we live, we live to the Lord, and if we die, we die to the Lord." He cannot ever in this life be idle and without works toward his neighbors, for he will necessarily speak, deal with, and exchange views with men, as Christ also, being made in the likeness of men [Phil. 2:7], was found in form as a man and conversed with men, as Baruch 3 [:38] says.... Man, however, needs none of these things for his righteousness and salvation. Therefore he should be guided in all his works by this thought and contemplate this one thing alone, that he may serve and benefit others in all that he does, considering nothing except the need and the advantage of his neighbor. Accordingly, the Apostle commands us to work with our hands so that we may give to the needy, although he might have said that we should work to support ourselves. He says, however, "that he may be able to give to those in need" [Eph. 4:28].[55]

My body affects my neighbor in her bodily life and its need. The form of Christian life is bodily coexistence within a particular ethos (*aethos*), according to Paul's promising enjoinder "present your bodies (*somata*) as a living sacrifice, holy, and acceptable to God" (Rom. 12:2). Luther continues, "I will therefore give myself as a Christ to my neighbor, just as Christ offered himself to me; I will do nothing in this life except what I see is necessary, profitable, and salutary to my neighbor, since

---

54. DBWE 3, 79.
55. Martin Luther, "The Freedom of a Christian," in LW 31, 364–5.

through faith I have an abundance of all good things in Christ."[56] "Abundance of all good things": we are in a different universe to call for infinite responsibility to the other, one of the most influential themes deployed in moral philosophy to resist the enclosure of the other in dominant totalizing regimes.[57] By defending the ethical demand to satisfy the finite needs of the other we are not falling back from the frightening sweep of infinite responsibility. Instead, we are recognizing that human power is good in its limitation yet nevertheless abundantly endowed with good things and work by which others may indeed be served. The offering of good things to the neighbor is given with God's work, it is his new creation within the Spirit of God, Luther concludes:

> Therefore, if we recognize the great and precious things which are given us, as Paul says [Rom. 5:5], our hearts will be filled by the Holy Spirit with the love which makes us free, joyful, almighty workers and conquerors over all tribulations, servants of our neighbors, and yet lords of all. For those who do not recognize the gifts bestowed upon them through Christ, however, Christ has been born in vain; they go their way with their works and shall never come to taste or feel those things. Just as our neighbor is in need and lacks that in which we abound, so we were in need before God and lacked his mercy. Hence, as our heavenly Father has in Christ freely come to our aid, we also ought freely to help our neighbor through our body and its works, and each one should become as it were a Christ to the other that we may be Christs to one another and Christ may be the same in all, that is, that we may be truly Christians.[58]

"Becoming Christ to one another"[59] is highly dangerous language if it is displaced from the grammar of transfiguration. Transfiguration does not erase our given, bodily form. Instead, honoring it, Christ's new form is imprinted on its movement, its way of encountering others. Thus, far from questioning the givenness of bodily form, transformation makes luminous what that form has all along been created to be.

Luther theologically highlights the particularity of the bodily needs of human beings by describing people as "living souls." The Hebrew word he translates from the Greek of the New Testament as "soul," is semantically rooted in the Old

---

56. LW 31, 367.

57. Here it would be appropriate to discuss Lévinas's insistence on the infinite responsibility for the other in its primordial givenness as demanded his philosophical reading of Messianic eschatology. See: Silvia Richter, "Zur Verbindung Von Messianismus und Eschatologie im Denken Emmanuel Lévinas." *Zeitschrift für Religions- und Geistesgeschichte* 68, no. 1 (2016): 57–69; Martin Kavka, "Lévinas's Accounts of Messianism," in *The Oxford Handbook of Lévinas*, ed. Michael L. Morgan (Oxford: Oxford University Press, 2019), 360–82.

58. LW 31, 367–8.

59. Matt. 25: 31–40 also deserves comment here.

Testament metaphor of the throat—the bodily organ through which a creature receives what it needs for living: "My soul thirsts for God, for the living God. When shall I come and behold the face of God?" (Ps. 42:2, RSV). The soul is not one of the inner organs enclosed within the body but is the core feature of the body in being precisely configured for receiving what the body—the whole bodily existence—needs if it is to continue to live. Hence when Luther calls a human being a "soul" he uses it as a synecdoche for the whole human being in its essential neediness. Scripture is full of descriptions of that needy existence, especially the Psalms. Human need is not just a feature of their lives as it is for animals, because human need is positioned in scripture as a crucial medium in which human beings negotiate their coexistence with God. The specific sort of neediness of the bodily living soul is not properly called "religious," some religious yearning for rest and fulfillment or a religious desire for a different world beyond that earthly existence. On the contrary, what the soul awaits in the biblical semantic is an encounter with the real God, for God's presence and for participation in God's story in the midst of this world-age. This is the root existential need given with human bodily existence. In the words of Ps. 130:5-6, "I wait for the Lord, my soul waits, and in his word I hope; my soul waits for the Lord more than those who watch for the morning, more than those who watch for the morning." The "soul," the bodily living soul needs God's word. It yearns for the encounter with God. This yearning cannot be subsumed into a generic category of intimate "religious" relation of the human soul with its God because a specific God, and so a specific worship is meant here. As again highlighted in Ps. 23:3, "He restores my soul. He leads me in paths of righteousness for his name's sake" (RSV).[60] This literally means "He brings back" (Hebrew: *yeshobeb*) my soul to a place of living, He returns my soul to His "reality," in which human beings can find that form of living that sustains.

The foregoing makes it clear that all theologically meaningful talk about human beings must address the need that their bodily existence entails. This is more than simply a "reminder" that all human beings will find themselves depending on others as being "dependent rational animals."[61] It is an affirmation of God's interest in our existence *as bodies* because it is as bodies that we encounter other people. Our bodies are given to become a medium of God's presence with us. God does not remain apart from human affairs, but he wants to be our living God—bodily. Bodiliness appears to be given because of God's will to create an encountering other in some correspondence to Him. Encounter is given with bodiliness, the ontic figure in which every human being comes into existence. That the encounter with others and God is willed by God from eternity since He who is beyond being and non-being, not to be conceived ontologically, decided to create heaven and earth, and then human beings. To fulfill his promise to be with them God had to

---

60. Luther translates: "Er erquicket meine Seele; er führet mich auf rechter Straße um seines Namens willen" (Ps. 23:3).

61. Alasdair MacIntyre, *Dependent Rational Animals: Why Human Beings Need the Virtues* (Chicago: Open Court, 1999).

become human in Jesus Christ. The "incarnation" of the logos is realized in Jesus Christ, the real bodily figure of a human being drawn again into God's story—a new figure, the transfiguration of human existence, because God too was not entrapped in eternal self-enclosure but transcended a condition that we would be tempted to assume could not be escaped—being eternal and unchanging.

Sharing Bodily Existence and the Fulfillment of Bodily Life

Ethics—as reflection on the ethos (*aethos*) of human life—explores who we human beings really are, and who we become: what will be the real figure of our lives. Being and becoming transfigured are intermediated. This is why the human ethos (*aethos*) is inescapably bodily, intrinsically and inescapably related and committed to other people. The concern of ethics focuses on how we ought to share this bodily existence as those taught by God's sharing this bodily existence in Jesus Christ with us. In order to remain clear about the subject of Christian ethics, it is important to specify that, in theological terms, when we speak of sharing of bodily life, we are not talking merely about the generic traits that all human beings share, or about one or the other aspect of a common nature, but about that common human condition as it is given within God's story and the contours of living according to this reality.

This is the fundamental insight Hans Reinders weaves into his description of friendship as a gift that emerges from bodily relation.[62] Reinders seeks the paths of friendship, asking how through friendship one becomes a human being. Somehow someone elects me or asks me, even urging me to be their friend, indicating a readiness to share some of their own bodily life with me.

Friendship as bodily sharing of life is not limited by capacity or social presuppositions; it emerges unbidden, as a gift, as our bodily life touches and encounters other people. Again we discover pertinent biblical descriptions of that encounter and its practices within various forms of life sharing and body sharing. Psalm 82, to take one example, focuses on the doing of justice and injustice. It is clear from this psalm that justice entails faithfulness to the community one shares with someone else according to the ways God has been faithful to his community with us human beings. To the psalmist to be just is to live in passive awareness of the other, and in this way to remain involved in their life as it is, with all of its needs and pains. The unjust, by contrast, are characterized as people who do not "know" the other whom they therefore don't understand (85:5). Both sorts of knowledge arise in the matrix provided by real awareness through bodily communication.

The Hebrew word for "know," *yada*, means cognition/recognition, and is also used to describe making love as a particularly clear example of what it means to

---

62. Reinders, *Receiving the Gift of Friendship*. For a broader theological discussion, see *Freundschaft: Zur Aktualität eines traditionsreichen Begriffs*, ed. Marco Hofheinz, Frank Mathwig, and Matthias Zeindler (Zürich: TVZ Theologischer Verlag Zürich, 2014).

be aware of the other, and to listen to him or her.[63] Keeping this semantic context in mind ensures that our descriptions of the human condition always presuppose that to be human entails sharing in the bodily life that is the matrix of all human communication. God is concerned both with our individual bodies, and that they are configured with other bodies in life-giving forms of community. God acts to ensure that this comes about in order that the bodily reality of human life may be renewed—which is the concreteness of redemption.

We may even go so far as to say that the essence of biblical theology is the promise to release human beings from all the idols, figures, and pictures that lead attention away from the concreteness of the other. To tear down an idol is to free human beings to recognize the other in his or her bodily life. We see this claim in paradigmatic form in the prohibition of making God (as he is named in the Tetragrammaton YHWH) into a "bodily" picture, converting God into an idol that occupies our attention like the other idols.[64] God's presence is not something to be looked at, but must always be actually encountered in his word and perceived in his acts and ongoing story. God is the one who acts to release our bodily presence and attention from any distracting attraction to be present for the other. To live as a human is to live in the presence of this unmasking God. Thus we can say that God's Messianic presence is a translocating work in leading us beyond our idols of the human and into awareness of the other in their actual bodily presence and neediness.

Despite all of the assessment schemes that abound in every age with their promise to insulate us from vulnerability, there is no way and no reason to try to protect myself from becoming aware of the bodily presence of the other as it encounters and affects me. For in fact it is this attentive encounter alone that protects the other against being mobilized in my own projects. This ethos (*aethos*) of attentiveness given with the renewal of our mind (Rom. 12:2). The inescapable encounter with the face of the other as it is conceived in Lévinas's philosophical ethics is seen within the biblical tradition in its extended and substantiated appearance in Jesus' Messianic life. It is not in every face, but paradigmatically in Jesus' way of encountering people that the message is proclaimed that human beings hear and see: "The blind receive their sight, and the lame walk, the lepers are cleansed, and the deaf hear, the dead are raised up, and the poor have the gospel preached to them" (Mt. 11:5). This is the ethos (*aethos*) of Jesus' Messianic encounter in which the disciples participate. This is the Christian ethos in its eschatological advent within God's story. The disciples too are part of this story,

---

63. For this interpretation of the Hebrew words, see Martin Buber, *Good and Evil, Two Interpretations: I. Right and Wrong.* (Upper Saddle River: Prentice Hall, 1997), 560; and Buber, "The Election of Israel: A Biblical Inquiry," in *The Martin Buber Reader*, ed. Asher D. Biemann (New York: Palgrave Macmillan, 2002), 81. Buber also describes "thinking" as "bodily" mediated, "Dialogue," in *The Martin Buber Reader*, 200.

64. See the prophecy of Isa. 44:48.

the followers of Christ being the new figures of the Messianic time breaking into this world-age.

This account of the "space" of Messianic reality has several implications. For one, the biblical descriptions of God's presence often speak of His hands,[65] His voice, His ears, or His face. Such descriptions serve as provocations to us, for instance, that our human "hands" become present for the other, as servants of God's good will for them. It also draws attention to hands, voices, ears, and faces of the other as privileged points of bodily attention in which their "works" are perceptible on particular surfaces of their body.

This emphasis on bodily presence emphatically does not lead to any separation of body and mind. On the contrary, it points to an understanding of our human existence that emphasizes its mediated, external, and passive relations—which are "projected onto" bodies. Nor is this an artifact of a more "realistic" rather than "idealistic" view of the body and ethics. It is rather an attempt to take seriously God's will for human beings to be turned out of themselves and away from false gods by an existence that opposes and claims them, a *different* person. Bodily existence was not made to be enclosed within an incurved self, and in fact its very materiality and relational embeddedness resist all such gnostic escapism. Because we are bodily beings we are held within that Messianic throughout tensional status of real life in a world now destined to come to its promised end rather than an endlessly altered "material world." The desire to continually remake an endlessly plastic material world is the perpetually compelling temptation that has been labeled gnostic. Gnosticism is the proclamation that a new world exists, and human nature has been or will be fulfilled in another way than by awaiting that new creation witnessed Messianically in the midst of human suffering, experience, and desire.[66] The theological grammar of Messianic fulfillment will therefore always be distinguishable from any humanistic concept of the *conditio humana* and its "fulfillment" at precisely the point emphasized in scripture, the Messianic narrative with its semantics of participation in the "fulness" (*pleroma*) of God and Jesus Christ (Eph. 3:19).

Conceiving ethics as serving human translocation into God's story has the effect of emphasizing the bodily nature of human involvement in God's story. To

---

65. Oliver O'Donovan, "Die Hände Gottes," in *"Sagen, was Sache ist": Versuche explorativer Ethik*, ed. Gerard den Hertog, Stefan Heuser, Marco Hofheinz, and Bernd Wannenwetsch (Leipzig: Evangelische Verlagsanstalt, 2018), 177–93.

66. Here we are in tacit dialogue with the extensive discussion of Gnosticism within various philosophies as Eric Voegelin has diagnosed it, whatever our analysis of Voegelin's diagnosis. See Eric Voegelin, *Science, Politics and Gnosticism: Two Essays* (New York: Regnery Publishing, 2012). For a theological approach, see William Schweiker, "Theological Ethics and the Question of Humanism," *The Journal of Religion* 83, no. 4 (2003): 539–61. It should be noted that his conception of a "theological humanism" is illuminating, though his quest for a plausible "humanism" is finally a contradiction of the theological grammar of God's one particular story with God's human creatures.

"exist," therefore, doesn't mean (according to the omnipresent Heideggerian logic and the concept of "Dasein") to be thrown into an anonymous history of being, but to be promisingly exposed to God's own exposition in his story. By definition the bodily existence that one lives, whatever its capacities or skills, is the existence that God has a place for in his story with all His human creatures. It is along this path that we understand as paradigmatic Jesus message: "the Son of Man came to seek and to save the lost" (Lk. 19:10). Human beings are "lost" when they simply "exist." They are lost because no turn or change will bring them to their home, their place of flourishing. Where then can they turn?

Amidst the lost, God wills to continue God's story with God's creatures. This togetherness culminates in our participation in the bodily resurrection of Jesus Christ. The promise of resurrection as it is grounded in the resurrection of Jesus Christ is not God's response to a generic desire for eternal life but the announcement of God's will to live *with* us in the coming kingdom. The picture here could not contrast more with the dominant cultural narrative that human being is best understood in terms of the immense human struggle to overcome or to integrate death. "And can any of you by worrying add a single hour to your span of life?" (Mt. 6:27). "Worrying" translates the Greek word for the fundamental human concern about death as either to become controlled or to become meaningful for our human existence within the continuity of its own movement. The hope of resurrection includes, on the contrary, the translocation and transfiguration into God's story and coming reality, the new Jerusalem.

It was both Jesus' Messianic signature and an immense provocation to have resurrected Lazarus (Jn 11:43-44), though Jesus' Messianic mission in this act has not yet been fully appreciated in subsequent theological interpretation.[67] In resurrection salvation history breaks Messianically, apocalyptically into "history" in its most obvious form. The witness of Jesus' resurrecting epiphany is a stark confrontation of the metaphysics and phenomenology of being and time, life and death as David B. Hart pointedly observes:

> I find myself unable to credit the notion that there is any proper general definition of "metaphysics" that names an entire dimension of discourse that somehow proleptically precludes or distorts the genuine apocalyptic novelty, the *semper novum*, of God's manifestation of himself to us. And I can imagine no more disastrous alternative to metaphysical reasoning than the attempt to confine revelation within the severe limitations of phenomenological reasoning—most especially a phenomenology of saturation and intuitional excess that would

---

67. Martin Hengel has throughout his exegetical work shown the importance of the appearance of a different story, the salvation-history, within "history." See Roland Deines, "Pre-Existence, Incarnation and Messianic Self-Understanding in the Work of Martin Hengel," in *Earliest Christian History: History, Literature, and Theology*, ed. Martin Hengel, Michael F. Bird and Jason Maston (Tübingen: Mohr Siebeck, 2012), 75–16.

condemn theology forever to the false profundity of paradox, and the voice of theology to a monotonous register of perpetual surprise.[68]

In this chapter I have drawn out several aspects of a Christian ethos (*aethos*) of a bodily existence and coexistence as we find it within the biblical tradition. I have suggested that this ethos is one that may be recovered today as a resource for our understanding and practice of truly human life, paradigmatically within the context of our awareness of disability. The goal of the Christian ethos is that every human bodily existence gains a perspective on experience of real humanity that takes its point of orientation from God's story with us and what it reveals about the sharing of bodily life. God's promised humanity as encountered in Jesus Christ is external to the individual as is the bodily co-presence of the other and the story God has with him or her. The externality of humanity given to human being indicates why we must "become" human, transfigured according to God's story, and only in this way are we human beings independent from own powers and skills to shape, form, transform or transcend human life. Here we find ourselves relieved from the almost universal modern imperative to "change your life"[69] which always collapses into discussions of the techniques and methods we need if we are effectively to manipulate and "improve" our bodily presence.

The logic of Messianic humanity is different to the logic of all humanisms that propose that they have fundamentally understood the fulfillment of human life. This is especially true for those humanisms that lay claim to realize true being in human existence (and history) in its unique and fateful "ontological" importance. Such accounts see human as a medium, but a medium in which Being reveals its truth, so tracking Heidegger's philosophy of "being and time." Such philosophies assume that human existence lacks any other "reality" or story than its own, that human existence is finally a matter of human being comprehending and realizing in itself "being" in its true meaning and appearance. The problem here is that human existence is taken to manifest a reality that is itself unpolitical; that is, it is not situated within a (bodily constituted) context of a living together as it is not aware of any encountering other within a given common story. In contrast, Christian ethics as I have understood it suggests that the way to become a political entity and to realize "the political" is given for the worshipping community gathering in order to praise the Lord, to pray and to encounter God's word in opposition to any collective ensembles which claim to identity and establishing the logic and mechanisms of inclusion and exclusion.

The logic of inclusion and exclusion is one that inexorably levies a demand for conformity. The problem only becomes worse if we try to escape it by calling universal realities in which it is assumed everyone already participates. The only

---

68. See David Bentley Hart, *Theological Territories: A David Bentley Hart Digest* (Notre Dame: University of Notre Dame Press, 2020), 27.

69. Peter Sloterdijk, *You Must Change Your Life: On Anthropotechnics* (Malden: Polity, 2013).

reality in which everyone participates already is the reality of God's story. All human beings exist in this story of God's love for God's creatures and children so long as they refuse to insist on a human existence in its absolute (ontological) exposition and its "historic" fulfillment with God or without God. Only that promisingly destined existence as creatures, children, and disciples, only these transfigurations are in its political presence resistant against any "gnostic" realization of a fulfilled human existence and human condition within "history."

The difference between God's story and "history" as it given with God's presence in Jesus Christ is the prime marker that our time is Messianic, the time existing in the tension between this world-age which will pass away and God's coming kingdom. We need not seek a philosophical account of "world"-history and its fulfillment or its opposite a history of humanity as a story of successive pathologies. Neither is humanity a transient figure in a transcendent history of being. All of these (and more) are ways of escaping reality in its Messianic significance, and as such are in fact ways of conforming yet again to this world-age. They are species of a single conformity to our world-age in variously expressing a consistent gnostic yearning for a humanism capable of achieving the fulfillment of our human existence within the terms of the given phenomena, rather than realizing its epiphany in God's story.

Human existence will appear in its genuine fulfillment where people pray and listen to God's word. Human existence will appear in its genuine fulfillment where people are escaping their religious desires for a different world or for an alteration of human existence by becoming aware of God's encountering word and actions, God's realized promises, consolation, forgiveness, and commandment. This is the ethos (*aethos*) in which we human beings may find ourselves, together with all others, gathering in the specifically configured worship carried in Israel and the church, in which we are inescapably exposed to the other next to me. This worship is paradigmatically political, because there is no other interest or function of this bodily gathering than realizing that the church "is the congregation of the brethren in which Jesus Christ acts presently as the Lord in word and sacrament through the Holy Spirit" (Barmen Declaration). It is not the utopian place to be "at home," where no human being has ever yet been (Ernst Bloch[70]), nor is it the consummation of a universal human yearning to belong. It is that place which is constituted by the encounter with God in God's unique actions.

Discourses: Traps and Dilemmas

Having surveyed some of the available resources for perceiving human existence in its ethos (*aethos*), we may reengage the various contemporary discourses that articulate "who we are," and so position our habits and practices. We need to examine the points of convergence and divergence of these discourses with the ethos of shared bodily life articulated within the biblical and Christian tradition.

---

70. Ernst Bloch, *The Principle of Hope* (Cambridge: MIT Press, 1986).

For example, in the discourse on disability rights, Hans Reinders observes a "hierarchy of values" that "reflects a basic assumption about our human nature, namely, that selfhood and purposive agency are crucial to what makes our lives human in the first place."[71] Such an identification of the human being contradicts or stands in a paradoxical relationship to the awareness of our human existence in its participation in God's story and therefore to an anthropology focused on God's will to keep all human beings in that story. The issues at stake here became acute when we compare approaches that work from Jesus Christ's Messianic appearance with any approach that aims to strengthen the position of the weak within an already-given ethos, perhaps by defending their rights to exist in a range of ethical discourses, not least in the disability rights discourse.

To note this contradiction is to be provided with the critical opening into an ethical understanding of disability and illness that does not wind up making questionable affirmations or endorsing generic moral strategies. This is also a critical perspective that might be elaborated by tracing the ways in which the discourse of disability theology discourse is endangered by multiple traps or dilemmas in which it is inclined to become ensnared, precisely so that these pitfalls can be avoided.

One of these traps is to allow the division between an anthropology for the weak and one for the strong. The error of this approach is the assumption that the remit of anthropological speculation is to offer a description that comprehends the conditions of all possible human beings. An associated dilemma arises when we realize that this drive to construct an integrative or universal anthropological description of our *conditio humana* in terms of a common "nature" runs into difficulties with some disabilities. Sometimes this is dealt with in these approaches by letting "hard cases" drift out of sight, and other times by allowing the real differences between "disabled" and nondisabled lives fade into the background. Some, spotting these conceptual difficulties as traps, are tempted to describe them within further framing terms such as "normality," itself a term loaded with conceptual problems.

Despite these conceptual and linguistic traps, we go on using the word "disability" in common language as if it were possible to compare ability and disability. But when did we begin to think of talking about human beings in terms of abilities in the first place? Are we not already trapped in problematic ways of thinking once our anthropological imaginations have allowed the notion of ability to stand unchallenged? The pressing problem here is to name the context of discovery in which we are entrapped when we have already granted that some people are "able."

Yet another trap has long been recognized in disability theology and disability studies: it is very hard to avoid using those human beings we are talking about for our own purposes and in order to further our own intellectual agendas. Even if we manage to spot this trap aren't we still doing so in a more subtle way if we expect that we will encounter new insights or knowledge by attending to "the disabled,"

---

71. Reinders, *Receiving the Gift of Friendship*, 27.

listening to them or asking what they reveal to us, or more subtly, what is revealed to us through their existence? I have certainly skirted this trap by asking what might be revealed in a paradigmatic sense when we examine the role of needy people in Messianic time.

I will not pursue any further this tableau of critical pitfalls. What is important about highlighting the importance of doing this work is not to enjoin the construction of a complete typology of possible pitfalls but to provoke us to ask whether there might be any shared theological or philosophical logic that runs through various traps. The utility of such critical engagements with common discourses is that we gain insight as we do so into what our counter-discourses must grasp if they are to genuinely connect to people with disabilities.[72] People with disabilities can be seen as resistant to any attempt to integrate or include them into a given frame of reference as it is also given with any humanism and its normatively or expectantly set ideas. What should be sought instead is a practice of discovering and probing an explicit reality together with them, a reality where human beings genuinely come together in a new disposition that does not in a more subtle way ignore or integrate all disability into its account.

To discuss disability is a work of re-cognition of the reality in which we exist as we come together for conversation about what we actually are as we do so. The fundamental critical task is not to construct an anthropological or humanistic "idea of man" or "image of man." We have already been told "what is man" (Psalms 8) in the story of God's becoming a human being in Jesus Christ. In the Christological logic of the *homo novus* we encounter the only figure in which we can recognize who we are, because in Him we see our *conditio humana* as comprehensively defined by congruence with God's story. We cannot define what it means to be a human being outside of this story, as all attempts to do so will quickly become mired in the logics of exclusion and inclusion. Though never enclosing a full understanding of the *conditio humana*, we have been told a story that does comprehensively defines us.[73] In this story we hear that we human beings are the beloved children of God, God's special delight, with whom God wishes to dwell: to be our God, living with us and working in us.

To hear God's story is to begin to realize that God's encounter in the Messianic epiphany of Jesus Christ is finally a matter of God's making good on God's self-declared responsibility. Again we must not collapse this insight into the logic of a theodicy and its drive for explanation but must understand it as an encounter with God that opens a new beginning beyond the economy of justification. To follow this logic, then, means to look deep into my given situation for this encountering God and to hold onto God's presence. It is a liberation to discover here that I can abandon the search for a general meaning of my life. In his interviews with people

---

72. Bernd Wannenwetsch, "Angels with Clipped Wings: The Disabled as Key to the Recognition of Personhood," in *Theology, Disability, and the New Genetics*, ed. John Swinton and Brian Brock (London: T&T Clark, 2007), 182–200.

73. Luther, *Disputatio de homine* (1536), LW 34, theses 20–3.

facing mental health challenges John Swinton discovered their faith to be clear-sighted about this stance being the hermeneutical key of Christian faith:

> The interviewees perceived themselves as disciples of Jesus who were desperately trying to cling to him in the midst of complex and difficult circumstances. Their question was not simply: "Where can I find meaning in the midst of my brokenness?" but more to the real point: "Where and how can I find Jesus and hold on to God in the midst of this experience?" The question is simple; the answer is much more complex.[74]

God's Own Story, Fulfilled for Our Sake

God decided to create the "world" and us, God's human creatures, because God is not a selfish God but full of grace, mercy, and love. "For God so loved the world that he gave his only begotten Son, that whoever believes in Him should not perish but have everlasting life" (Jn 3:16). We cannot define God, but He has given Himself to be present within His story with the world. This then is the guarantee that God really remains God for us, refusing to be reduced to what we want him to be or what we can at best think of "God's" being. God risked cooption by human beings in exposing Himself bodily to His creatures rather than remaining untouchably separate from the world.

The decisive reality of God is that God has willed to share His lively being with us. In God's story with us no one is omitted, because God depends on individual human beings, that is, on real individual figures, to pursue God's will and so for God's will to become concretized in that particular way. God's story would run into the sand if the actors in it were to disappear. God's story *is*, in fact, a story about God's commitment to engagement with creaturely actors. This is why Christians affirm that *every* single human being in his/her particular condition confirms anew God's plan, and is neither a consequence or implication of what has gone before nor a tragic outcome of something that has gone wrong in natural or medical processes.[75] In this sense it is not going too far to we say that God is bodily present in the world of humans just as concretely and as vulnerably as God was when present in the body in Jesus Christ: "Bodily life is the final end of God's work."[76] So has Friedrich Christoph Oetinger's aptly summarized the final end of God's story in the new coexistence with God in the heavenly city as described in Revelation 20 and 21. We gaze here on fulfilled bodily existence,

---

74. John Swinton, *Finding Jesus in the Storm: The Spiritual Lives of Christians with Mental Health Challenges* (Grand Rapids: Eerdmans, 2020), 6.

75. Hannah Arendt, *The Human Condition*, 2nd edn. (Chicago: University of Chicago Press, 1958), 1768. See Karin Ulrich-Eschemann, *Vom Geborenwerden des Menschen: theologische und philosophische Erkundungen* (Münster: Lit Verlag, 2000).

76. Friedrich Christoph Oetinger, *Biblisches und emblematisches Wörterbuch* (Hildesheim: Georg Olms Verlagsbuchhandlung, 1969), 407.

not defined in terms of perfection but as a reaching of the end that has leant its figure to all the events of creation, the goal of the story of both God and God's human creatures (Eph. 3:19). To glimpse this goal facilitates our appreciation of its proleptic appearance within the course of creaturely life, as God shares His life with His creatures as it is worshipped in the Eucharist.[77] In those bodies that have been configured by God's bodily presence to become the Eucharist, we have all we need to understand the ethos appropriate to the church as a community that is intrinsically bodily mediated.[78]

We human beings depend on God's real presence insofar as we need the consolation of an encounter we can hold onto. What else could it mean to say that human beings need to hold on? When we say there is no precondition for participating in God's presence, we nevertheless associate His bodily presence with the consolation that is always given in bodily realities. To be consoled is to have something to hold on to, with which we literally collide, and this is what we are given in the bodiliness of God's encounter with us according to Ps. 23:4: "Yea, though I walk through the valley of the shadow of death, I will fear no evil; For You are with me; Your rod and Your staff, they comfort me" (NKJV).

The English word comfort or consolation is equivalent to the German word *Trost* and is cognate with the German word *Treue* (loyalty) and the English word trust. The Hebrew word "emet" means "truth" and "loyalty" and has a clear political dimension: "Speak each man the truth to his neighbor; Give judgment in your gates for truth, justice, and peace" (Zech. 8:16, NKJV). Trust is a specific form of confidence that does not rest on logical proofs and what can be expected within them (as, for instance, do explanations of the existence of evil in the world).[79] In the end, the task of theology is nothing more than a lifelong exploration of this particularly configured and focused trust. Where we human beings experience this trust, we recognize who we are and how we belong together. We come to know ourselves within the political context that arises from this common story of trust,

---

77. We may say that following God's story is the task of our common worship, with any relation between human beings being defined by that worship. Brent Waters, "Disability and the Quest of Perfection: A Moral and Theological Inquiry," in *Theology, Disability, and the New Genetics: Why Science Needs the Church*, ed. John Swinton and Brian Brock (London: Continuum, 2007), 201–13.

78. Stanley Hauerwas, "The Sanctified Body: Why Perfection Does Not Require a 'Self,'" in *Embodied Holiness: Toward a Corporate Theology of Spiritual Growth*, ed. Samuel M. Powell and Michael E. Lodahl (Downers Grove: InterVarsity Press, 1999), 19–38. For the biblical unfolding of this theme, see Brian Brock and Bernd Wannenwetsch, *The Malady of the Christian Body: A Theological Exposition of Paul's First Letter to the Corinthians*, vol. 1 (Eugene: Cascade Books, 2016) and Brian Brock and Bernd Wannenwetsch, *The Therapy of the Christian Body: A Theological Exposition of Paul's First Letter to the Corinthians*, vol. 2 (Eugene: Cascade Books, 2018).

79. For more details, see Hans G. Ulrich, *Wie Geschöpfe leben: Konturen evangelischer Ethik*, 2nd edn. (Münster: LIT, 2007).

within a story which ends in God's heavenly city. In this network of trust we appear as citizens within this world as we become present in the trust that is worship where we citizens gather according to the agenda, the liturgy of Christ's present lordship: "Now, therefore, you are no longer strangers and foreigners, but fellow citizens with the saints and members of the household of God" (Eph. 2:19, NKJV). We are not foreigners within God's city, but citizens of God's city as we appear in worship. Here we are neither conformed to this world-age nor fighting against it in gnostic opposition. In worship we live out a story that is not defined by any relation to this world-age but transfigures it by making it into new figures of the promised reality in its Messianic, eschatological, and wholly concrete appearance "between the times." Instead of being "existent," exposed to and pushed to and fro by an anonymous "history," across its times and intermediate periods, we find ourselves transfigured into participants in God's story in its Messianic appearance. To follow this hermeneutic key in our theological praxis means to remain faithfully in that worship of the *communio sanctorum* made of human beings, people exposed to God's transfiguration.

ULRICH PUBLICATION LIST

The Published Works of Hans G. Ulrich

1970

With Wolfgang Raddatz and Gerhard Sauter: "Verstehen." In *Praktisch-theologisches Handbuch*, edited by Gert Otto, 483–513. Hamburg: Furche Verlag.

1971

"Thesen zur Forschung und literarischen Produktion in der Theologie." *Evangelische Theologie* 31: 133–8.

1973

"Wissenschaftsethik." In *Wissenschaftstheoretische Kritik der Theologie: Die Theologie und die neuere wissenschaftstheoretische Diskussion: Materialien, Analysen, Entwürfe*, edited by Gerhard Sauter, Jürgen Courtin, and Hans-Wilfried Haase, 111–26. München: Kaiser.

1974

With Gerhard Sauter: "Einleitung." In *Philosophische Sprachprüfung der Theologie: Eine Einführung in den Dialog zwischen der analytischen Philosophie und der Theologie*, 7–16. Theologische Bücherei Systematische Theologie 54. München: Kaiser.

1975

"Grundlinien ethischer Diskussion." *Verkündigung und Forschung* 20: 53–99.

Anthropologie und Ethik bei Friedrich Nietzsche: Interpretationen zu Grundproblemen theologischer Ethik. Beiträge zur Evangelischen Theologie. München: Kaiser.

1978

With Hans Jörg Urban: "Einführung." In *Verbindliches Zeugnis der Kirche heute als ökumenische Aufgabe: Arbeitsbericht einer Studiengruppe des Deutschen*

Ökumenischen Studienausschusses, edited by Karl Kertelge et al., 3–7. Frankfurt am Main: Lembeck.

"Hat Religion eine kirchliche Zukunft?" *Verkündigung und Forschung* 23: 54–65.

1980

"Autarkie." In *Evangelisches Soziallexikon,* 7th edn., edited by Friedrich Karrenberg et al., 113–14. Stuttgart: Kreuz-Verlag.

"Manipulation." In *Evangelisches Soziallexikon,* 7th edn., edited by Friedrich Karrenberg et al., 862–4. Stuttgart: Kreuz-Verlag.

"Nihilismus." In *Evangelisches Soziallexikon,* 7th edn., edited by Friedrich Karrenberg et al., 953–4. Stuttgart: Kreuz-Verlag.

With Lothar Schreiner: "Wir sind herausgefordert." *In Christus und die Gurus: Asiatische religiöse Gruppen im Westen: Information und Orientierung,* edited by Lothar Schreiner and Michael Mildenberger, 12–21. Stuttgart: Kreuz-Verlag.

1982

"Entfremdung II: Theologisch-ethisch." In *Theologische Realenzyklopädie,* 9:673–80. Berlin: de Gruyter.

1983

"Erwartungen an da Reden von Gott: Verhindern Gottesbegriffe das Reden von Gottes Handeln?" *Evangelische Theologie,* 43: 36–52.

"Was ist theologische Wahrheitsfindung? Bemerkungen zu den Fragen von Heinrich Scholz an Karl Barth." *Evangelische Theologie,* 43: 350–70.

1984

"Öffentliche Verantwortung als Erwartung an Bildung und Beruf: Christlich-ethische Perspektiven." In *Gemeinsam für die Zukunft: Kirchen und Wirtschaft im Gespräch,* edited by Wolfgang Kramer and Michael Spangenberger. DIV-Sachbuchreihe 34. 483–510. Köln: DIV-Verlag, 1984.

1986

"Adiaphora." In *Evangelisches Kirchenlexikon (EKL): Internationale theologische Enzyklopädie,* edited by Erwin Fahlbusch, Jan M. Lochman, and John S. Mbiti, 1:41–3. Göttingen: Vandenhoeck & Ruprecht.

"Ethik 5: Aufgabe theologischer Ethik." In *Evangelisches Kirchenlexikon (EKL): Internationale theologische Enzyklopädie*, edited by Erwin Fahlbusch, Jan M. Lochman, and John S. Mbiti, 3:1148–55. Göttingen: Vandenhoeck & Ruprecht.

"Bekenntnis." In *Evangelisches Kirchenlexikon (EKL): Internationale theologische Enzyklopädie*, edited by Erwin Fahlbusch, Jan M. Lochman, and John S. Mbiti, 1:409–13. Göttingen: Vandenhoeck & Ruprecht.

"Eigentum." In *Evangelisches Kirchenlexikon (EKL): Internationale theologische Enzyklopädie*, edited by Erwin Fahlbusch, Jan M. Lochman, and John S. Mbiti, 3:992–1001. Göttingen: Vandenhoeck & Ruprecht.

"Ethik 4: Zur Geschichte der Christlichen Ethik." In *Evangelisches Kirchenlexikon (EKL): Internationale theologische Enzyklopädie*, edited by Erwin Fahlbusch, Jan M. Lochman, and John S. Mbiti, 3:1144–8. Göttingen: Vandenhoeck & Ruprecht.

"Das Zeugnis des Christen und die Politik: Zum Verständnis von Röm 13 bei Karl Steinbauer." In *Gott mehr gehorchen: Karl Steinbauer zum 80. Geburtstag*, edited by Friedrich Mildenberger and Manfred Seitz, 31–52. München: Claudius-Verlag.

"Hoffnung und Verantwortung." *Evangelische Theologie* 46: 26–37.

"Kennwort: Gebet." *Glaube und Lernen* 1: 13–20.

"Soziale Verantwortung im Entdeckungszusammenhang theologischer Erkenntnis und im Begründungszusammenhang Systematischer Theologie." *Christlicher Glaube und soziale Verantwortung: Beiträge zur siebten theologischen Konferenz zwischen Vertretern der Evangelischen Kirche in Deutschland und der Kirche von England*, edited by Klaus Kremkau, 69–89. Beihefte zur ökumenischen Rundschau 52. Frankfurt: Lembeck.

"Kirche in der Gegenwart des Geistes. Glaube und Lernen im Konfirmandenunterricht." In *Kirche in der Gegenwart des Geistes. Glaube und Lernen im Konfirmandenunterricht*, edited by Gottfried Adam et. al., 49–59. Arbeiten zum Konfirmandenunterricht 2. Hannover.

"Die Rolle des Zeithorizonts in ausgewählten Beispielen theologischer Ethik der Gegenwart." In *Ethik zwischen säkularer Apokalyptik und glaubensgestützer Hoffnung. Über die Handlungsrelevanz der Zukunftserwartung. Dokumentation*, editied by Hans May, 126–40. Loccumer Protokolle 62. Rehburg: Loccum.

1987

"Kennwort: Kirche glauben." *Glaube und Lernen* 2: 8–18.

"Wachstum und Gerechtigkeit: Ethisch-theologische Zugänge zur Wirtschaftsethik." *Glaube und Lernen* 2: 114–25.

"Technische und ethische Vernunft. Die Verantwortung der neuen Technologien in theologisch-ethischer Perspektive." In *Dokumentation einer Tagung des*

Niedersächsischen Kultusministers, der Konföderation Evangelischer Kirchen in Niedersachsen und des Katholischen Büros Niedersachsen: Neue Technologien und Schule. Der Niedersächsische Kultusminister 1, 27–58. Bad Salzdetfurth.

1988

Eschatologie und Ethik: Die theologische Theorie der Ethik in ihrer Beziehung auf die Rede von Gott seit Friedrich Schleiermacher. Beiträge zur Evangelischen Theologie 104. München: Kaiser.

"Ethik im Religionsunterricht: theologische und pädagogische Perspektiven." In *Grundlagen der evangelischen Religionspädagogik*, edited by Jörg Ohlemacher and Heinz Schmidt, 183–201. Göttingen: Vandenhoeck & Ruprecht.

"Kapitalismus." In *Theologische Realenzyklopädie*, 17:604–19. Berlin: de Gruyter.

"Konjunktur oder Aufbruch? Probleme und Tendenzen theologischer Ethik." *Evangelische Kommentare* 21: 199–202.

"Widerstand und Widerspruch: theologisch-ethische Überlegungen zur Erforschung des Widerstands." *Kirchliche Zeitgeschichte* 1: 124–9.

"Frieden als Thema einer Ethik des Politischen aus theologischer Sicht." In *Frieden als Thema in Elternhaus, Schule, Kirche und Bundeswehr*, 67–83. Loccumer Protokolle 12. Rehburg: Loccum.

"Kategorischer Imperativ." In *Wörterbuch des Christentums*, edited by Manfred Baumotte and Volker Drehsen, 596–7. Gütersloh: Mohn-Verlag.

"Praktische Philosophie." In *Wörterbuch des Christentums*, edited by Manfred Baumotte and Volker Drehsen, 989–90. Gütersloh: Mohn-Verlag.

"Struktur, Ordnung." In *Wörterbuch des Christentums*, edited by Manfred Baumotte and Volker Drehsen, 1191–2. Gütersloh: Mohn-Verlag.

1989

"Ethische Hilfestellungen in Entscheidungsfragen? Überlegungen und Perspektiven evangelischer Ethik: zugleich eine Auseinandersetzung mit Peter Singer." In *Pränatale Diagnostik: Eine Auseinandersetzung*, edited by Dietrich Berg, Patrick Boland, Rudolf Pfeiffer, and Hans-Bernhard Würmeling, 207–23. Braunschweig and Wiesbaden: Vieweg.

"Kennwort: In der Kirche neu anfangen." *Glaube und Lernen* 4: 8–16.

"Wege und Perspektiven ethischer Diskussion." *Verkündigung und Forschung* 34: 22–52.

"Das Zinsnehmen in der christlichen Ethik: historische und gegenwärtige Perspektiven." In *Der Zins in Recht, Wirtschaft und Ethik, Atzelsberger Gespräche*

1988, edited by Max Vollkommer, 53–73. Erlangen: Universitätsbund Erlangen-Nürnberg.

"Neuanfang in der Verkündigung? Kirche nach 1945 in theologischer Perspektive." *Kirchliche Zeitgeschichte* 2: 276–83.

1990

Editor, *Evangelische Ethik: Diskussionsbeiträge zu ihrer Grundlegung und ihren Aufgaben*. Theologische Bücherei 83. München: Kaiser.

"Evangelische Ethik: gegenwärtige Perspektiven." In *Evangelische Ethik: Diskussionsbeiträge zu ihrer Grundlegung und ihren Aufgaben*, edited by Hans. G. Ulrich, 382–411. München: Kaiser.

"Regeln im Reden von Gott: Ein Bericht." In *Implizite Axiome: Tiefenstrukturen des Denkens und Handelns*, edited by Wolfgang Huber, Ernst Petzold, and Theo Sundermeier, 151–74. München: Kaiser.

"Theologische Zugänge zur Wirtschaftsethik." In *Neuere Entwicklungen in der Wirtschafsethik und Wirtschaftsphilosophie*, edited by Peter Koslowski, 253–77. Studies in Economic Ethics and Philosophy. Berlin: Springer.

"Mit Kindern leben: Ethische Perspektiven." In *Bilden—Erziehen—Betreuen im Wandel. Schritte in die Zukunft mit unseren Kindern*. Symposion der Arbeitsgemeinschaft der Spitzenverbände der Freien Wohlfahrtspflege in Bayern, 59-69. Kronach.

1991

"Ökumenische Verständigung im Blick auf die Wissenschaft." In *Kirchen im Kontext unterschiedlicher Kulturen: Auf dem Weg in das dritte Jahrtausend*, edited by Karl Christian Felmy, Georg Kretschmar, Fairy von Lilienfeld, Trutz Rendtorff, and Claus-Jürgen Röpke, 165–76. Göttingen: Vandenhoeck & Ruprecht.

With Gerhard Besier: "Von der Aufgabe kirchlicher Zeitgeschichte: ein diskursiver Versuch." *Evangelische Theologie* 51: 169–182.

"Gottes Ökonomie und Wirtschaftsethik: Theologische Zugänge zur Wirtschaftsethik." In *Wirtschaft und Ethik*, edited by Hans G. Nutzinger, 37-60. Wiesbaden: Deutscher Universitätsverlag.

1992

"Die Ökonomie Gottes und das menschliche Wirtschaften: Zur theologischen Perspektive der Wirtschaftsethik." In *Theologie und Ökonomie: Symposion zum 100. Geburtstag von Emil Brunner*, edited by Hans Ruh, 80–117. Zürich: Theologischer Verlag.

"Nächste." In *Evangelisches Kirchenlexikon: Internationale theologische Enzyklopädie*, 3rd edn., 3:598-600. Göttingen: Vandenhoeck & Ruprecht.

"Wie mehrdeutig ist evangelische Ethik?" In *Protestantische Profile*. Sebalder Lenten sermons, 25-31. Nürnberg.

With Gerhard Ringshausen: "Zur Verständigung über Zeitgeschichte." *Kirchliche Zeitgeschichte* 5: 94-98.

1993

"Die Sehnsucht nach dem ganz Anderen und die Hoffnung für die Welt." *Das Baugerüst* 45, 238-240.

"Ethische Rechenschaft als Praxis der Freiheit: Bemerkungen zu 'Norm und Erfahrung' in der Ethik." *Zeitschrift für Evangelische Ethik* 37: 46-58.

Editor, *Freiheit im Leben mit Gott: Texte zur Tradition evangelischer Ethik*. Theologische Bücherei 86. München: Kaiser.

"Einführung: Die Freiheit der Kinder Gottes—Freiheit in der Geschöpflichkeit. Zur Tradition evangelischer Ethik." In *Freiheit im Leben mit Gott: Texte zur Tradition evangelischer Ethik*, edited by Hans G. Ulrich, 9-40. Theologische Bücherei 86. München: Kaiser.

"Theologische Ethik im englischsprachigen Kontext: Zur neueren Diskussion in Nordamerika." *Verkündigung und Forschung* 38, no. 1: 61-84.

"Kapitalismus." In *Lexikon der Wirtschaftsethik*, edited by Georges Enderle, 479-83. Freiburg: Herder.

"Solidarität." In *Lexikon der Wirtschaftsethik*, edited by Georges Enderle, 959-63. Freiburg: Herder.

"Utilitarismus." In *Lexikon der Wirtschaftsethik*, edited by Georges Enderle, 2276-78. Freiburg: Herder.

1994

"Die Sehnsucht nach dem ganz anderen und die Hoffnung für die Welt." *Brennpunkt Gemeinde* 47: 51-53.

"Das 'Gut' menschliche Arbeit: Wenn die Arbeit ausgeht: sozialethische Überlegungen." *Nachrichten der Evangelisch-Lutherischen Kirche in Bayern*, 49, no. 3:81-82.

"Neu leben lernen – den Tod zulassen." *Das Baugerüst* 46, 118-122.

"Theologische Ethik im englischsprachigen Kontext (II)." *Verkündigung und Forschung* 39, no. 2: 60-81.

Editor with Reinhard Hütter: Lindbeck, George A. *Christliche Lehre als Grammatik des Glaubens: Religion und Theologie im postliberalen Zeitalter*. Gütersloh: Kaiser.

"Katastrophenstimmung und Schöpfungsethik." In *Klima: Vorträge im Wintersemester 1992*, 165-77. Studium Generale Ruprecht-Karls-Universität Heidelberg 93. Heidelberg: Heidelberger Verlagsanstalt.

With Eberhard Finckh, Karl Heinz Neeb, Harald Popp, Manfred Seitz, and Hans Georg Weidinger: *Entsorgung radioaktiver Stoffe: Fakten, Probleme und verantwortungsbewusstes Handeln*. Erlanger Forschungen Reihe B, Naturwissenschaften und Medizin 24. Erlangen: Universitätsbibliothek.

"'Volk,' 'Nation,' Bürgersein: Bemerkungen zur politischen Bildung." In *Bausteine für eine christliche Ethik: Arbeitshilfe für den evangelischen Religionsunterricht an Gymnasien*, edited by Karl Friedrich Haag, 3-16. Bayern: Gymnasialpädagogischen Materialstelle der Evangelisch-Lutherischen Kirche.

"Was heißt 'ethische Kompetenz' in einer Ethik für Christen." In *Theologische Samenkörner: Dietrich Ritschl, dem Lehrenden, Gelehrten und Lernenden zum 65. Geburtstag*, edited by Reinhold Bernhardt, 237-47. Münster: LIT.

"Was heißt von Gott reden lernen? Zugleich Bemerkungen zum Verhältnis von Dogmatik und Ethik." In *Einfach von Gott reden: Ein theologischer Diskurs; Festschrift für Friedrich Mildenberger*, edited by Jürgen Roloff und Hans G. Ulrich, 172-98. Stuttgart: Kohlhammer.

"Wie 'Ethik' zu lernen ist." In *Verantwortlich leben*, volume 2: *Ergänzende Texte*, edited by Karl Friedrich Haag, 237-47. Arbeitshilfe für den evangelischen Religionsunterricht. Erlangen: Gymnasialpädagogische Materialstelle der Evangelisch-Lutherische Kirche in Bayern.

1995

"Christ und Politik (1)." In *Auf der Spur zum Leben. Christliche Texte für Zeitgenossen*, edited by Johanna Haberer and Helmut Winter, 62-3. München: Sonntagsblatt Edition.

"Erfahren in Gerechtigkeit: Über das Zusammentreffen von Rechtfertigung und Recht." In *Rechtfertigung und Erfahrung: für Gerhard Sauter zum 60. Geburtstag*, edited by Michael Beintker, Ernstpeter Maurer, Hinrich Stoevesandt, and Hans G. Ulrich, 362-84. Gütersloh: Kaiser.

"Hunger nach Realität: Theologie im Gespräch mit der Soziologie." *Nachrichten der Evangelisch-Lutherischen Kirche in Bayern*, 50, no. 17: 322-3.

"Heiliger Geist und Lebensform." In *Geist und Kirche: Festschrift für E. Lessing*, edited by Werner Brändle and Ralf Stolina, 55-78. Frankfurt am Main: Lang.

1996

"A Modern Understanding of Christian Ethics in the Perspective of Its own Tradition." In *Worship and Ethics: Lutherans and Anglicans in Dialogue*, edited by Oswald Bayer and Alan M. Suggate, 26–58. Theologische Bibliothek Töpelmann 70. Berlin: de Gruyter.

"Retrospect and Prospect." In *Worship and Ethics: Lutherans and Anglicans in Dialogue*, edited by Oswald Bayer and Alan M. Suggate, 285-93. Theologische Bibliothek Töpelmann 70. Berlin: de Gruyter.

1997

"Ein Wort: und zwei Sprachen? Überlegungen zur Praxis der Begegnung von Juden und Christen." In *Christen und Juden: Perspektiven einer Annäherung*, edited by Wolfgang Kraus, 67–88. Gütersloh: Kaiser.

"'Gentechnologie und Ethik' im Religionsunterricht." *Arbeitshilfe für den evangelischen Religionsunterricht an Gymnasien*. Gelbe Folge II, edited by Karl Friedrich Haag, 20–9. Erlangen: Gymnasialpädagogische Materialstelle der Evangelisch-Lutherische Kirche in Bayern.

"Gottes Gerechtigkeit und das Recht des Menschen." In *Solidarität ist unteilbar: Katholischer Kongreß 1996 in Hildesheim*, edited by Theodor Bolzenius and Heinz Terhorst, 385–408. Kevelaer: Verlag Butzon & Bercker.

"Israels bleibende Erwählung und die christliche Gemeinde: Systematisch-theologische Perspektiven." In *Christen und Juden: Perspektiven einer Annäherung*, edited by Wolfgang Kraus, 171–91. Gütersloh: Kaiser.

"'Meditation und Aktion': zur Tradition und Gegenwart einer Lebensform in christlicher Perspektive." In *Unverfügbare Gewißheit: Protestantische Wege zum Dialog mit den Religionen*, edited by Werner Brändle and Gerhard Wegner, 143–68. Hannover: Lutherisches Verlagshaus.

"Menschen als Text? Ethische Perspektiven zur Gentechnologie." In *Arbeitshilfe für den evangelischen Religionsunterricht an Gymnasien* 2, 3–19. Erlangen: Gymnasialpädagogische Materialstelle der Evangelisch-Lutherische Kirche in Bayern. Also in *Evangelium und Wissenschaft* 39 (2001): 4–21.

"Rationalität und kirchliche Lebenspraxis." In *Ethik, Vernunft und Rationalität (Ethics, Reason and Rationality): Beiträge zur 33. Jahrestagung der Societas Ethica*, edited by Alberto Bondolfi, 169–86. Münster: LIT.

1998

"An den Grenzen der Verständigung. Oder: was heißt es, den Anderen einzubeziehen?" In *Zwischen Universalismus und Relativismus*, edited by Horst Steinmann and Andreas G. Scherer, 221–39. Frankfurt am Main: Suhrkamp.

"Theologische Zugänge zum Menschenbild der Ökonomie." In *Homo oeconomicus: Der Mensch der Zukunft?* edited by Norbert Brieskorn and Johannes Wallacher, 147–64. Stuttgart: Kohlkammer.

1999

Beltz, Walter, Wolf Krötke and Hans G. Ulrich: "Gute Werke." In *Religion in Geschichte und Gegenwart*, 4th edn. Band 3: 1345-6. Tübingen: Mohr Siebeck. http://dx.doi.org/10.1163/2405-8262_rgg4_COM_09149.

With M. Heesch, M. Klöcker, W. M. Sprondel, V. Drehsen, E. Herms et al.: "Beruf III: Kirchengeschichtlich." In *Religion in Geschichte und Gegenwart*, 4th edn. Band 1: 1138-1341. Tübingen: Mohr Siebeck. http://dx.doi.org/10.1163/2405-8262_rgg4_COM_01823.

"Christliche Freiheit." In *Evangelischer Erwachsenenkatechismus*, 1999. Gütersloh: Gütersloher Verl.-Haus.

"Das Kapital: und seine Sozialpflicht." In *Wirtschaft und Sozialpolitik*, edited by Andreas Fritzsche and Manfred Kwiran, 13–35. München: Bernward bei Don Bosco.

"Jesus Christus gestern und heute und derselbe auch in Ewigkeit." In *Wer schreibt Geschichte? Die Jahrtausendwende als Anlaß zu theologischen Überlegungen*, edited by Karl-Friedrich Haag, 49–66. Arbeitshilfe für den evangelischen Religionsunterricht an Gymnasien 123. Erlangen: Gymnasialpädagogische Materialstelle der Evangelisch-Lutherische Kirche in Bayern.

"Metapher und Widerspruch." In *Metapher und Wirklichkeit: die Logik der Bildhaftigkeit der Rede von Gott, Mensch und Natur: Dietrich Ritschl zum 70. Geburtstag*, edited by Reinhold Bernhardt and Ulrike Link-Wieczorek, 196–206. Göttingen: Vandenhoeck & Ruprecht.

"Was ist eine 'gute' Technologie?" In *Geisteswissenschaften und Innovationen*, edited by Frieder Meyer-Krahmer and Siegried Lange, 217–28. Technik, Wirtschaft und Politik: Schriftenreihe des Fraunhofer-Instituts für Systemtechnik und Innovationsforschung (ISI) 35). Heidelberg: Physica-Verlag.

"Zwischen Utopie und Eschatologie." In *Wer schreibt Geschichte. Die Jahrtausendwende als Anlaß zu theologischen Überlegungen?* edited by Karl Friedrich Haag, 67–76. Erlangen: Gymnasialpädagogische Materialstelle der Evangelisch-Lutherische Kirche in Bayern.

2000

"Rechtfertigung und Ethik." *Berliner Theologische Zeitschrift* 17, no. 1: 48–64.

"Being and Becoming a Self in Ethical Perspective." In *Creating Identity*, edited by Hermann Häring, Mareen Junker-Kenny, and Dietmar Mieth, 121–30. London: SCM Press.

"Selbst-Sein – Selbst-werden in ethischer Perspektive." *Concilium* 36, no. 2: 239–48.

"'Soziale Bewegungen' und Differenzierungen in Gesellschaft und Kirche: Überlegungen zu ihrer ethischen Wahrnehmung." In *Kirche(n) und Gesellschaft*, edited by Andreas Fritzsche and Manfred Kwiran, 160–80. München: Bernward bei Don Bosco.

2001

"Altruismus." In *Evangelisches Soziallexikon*, 8th edn., edited by Martin Honecker et al., 35–8. Stuttgart: Kohlkammer.

"Embryonenforschung und Stammzellentherapie: zu den Folgen für Menschenbild und Krankheitsverständnis." In *Dokumentation Bioethik und Gentechnik* 26 (2001): 31–9.

"Freiheit." In *Evangelisches Soziallexikon*, edited by Martin Honecker et al., 505-11. Stuttgart: Kohlkammer.

"Menschliche Lebensform oder Leben aus dem Humanpool? Das Menschenbild der modernen Medizin im Wandel." In *Optionen für eine Medizin der Zukunft? Präimplantationsdiagnostik und Stammzellforschung*, edited by Volker Hörner and Katrin Patzer, 66–87. Speyrer Texte 6. Speyer: Evangelische Akademie der Pfalz.

"Menschen als Text. Ethische Perspektiven zur Gentechnologie." *Evangelium und Wissenschaft. Beiträge zum interdisziplinären Gespräch*, Berlin; Bensheim; Einhausen; Marburg: Karl-Heim-Gesellschaft H. 39: 4–20.

"Was heißt 'Ethos' in der Wirtschaft?" In *Ethos lernen: Ethos lehren*, edited by Andreas Fritzsche and Manfred Kwiran, 98–118. München: Bernward bei Don Bosco.

"Fides quaerens intellectum. Überlegungen zu einer explorativen Theologie." In *Theologie im Plural: Fundamentaltheologie—Hermeneutik—Kirche—Ökumene*, edited by Karl Grimmer, 61–76. Frankfurt am Main: Lembeck.

Series editor with Christopher Frey, Wolfgang Huber, Reinhard Hütter, and Hans Reinders: *Evangelium und Ethik*.

(Coauthor) Evangelische Kirche in Deutschland: *Einverständnis mit der Schöpfung* [2. Aufl.], Gütersloh: Gütersloher Verlagshaus.

2003

"Bildung woraufhin: Bildung woran? Theologische Anmerkungen zur Bildung in der Kompetenzgesellschaft." In *Nach Bildung fragen*, edited by Karl Friedrich Haag,

57-74. Arbeitshilfe für den evangelischen Religionsunterricht an Gymnasien/ Aktuelle Information 38. Erlangen: Gymnasialpädagogische Materialstelle der Evangelisch-Lutherische Kirche in Bayern.

"Das Leben als Design-Objekt: und das Recht zu leben." In *Reichtum und Unsterblichkeit – unser Traum von der Berechenbarkeit des Daseins: Chancen, Risiken und ethische Fragen der Biotechnologie*, edited by Burkhard Gmelin und Horst Weidinger, 55–74. Atzelsberger Gespräche der Nürnberger Medizinischen Gesellschaft e.V. Band 8. Nürnberg: Seubert.

"Ethische Konflikte bei der Präimplantationsdiagnostik." In *Medizin und Ethik: Aktuelle ethische Probleme in Therapie und Forschung*, edited by Jochen Vollmann, 31–59. Erlanger Forschungen, Sonderreihe Band 11. Erlangen: Univ.-Bibliothek.

"Fides Quaerens Intellectum: Überlegungen zu einer explorativen Theologie." In *Brauchbare Theologie? Überlegungen zur Bedeutung der Theologie im Religionsunterricht*, 53–8. Arbeitshilfe für den evangelischen Religionsunterricht an Gymnasien/Aktuelle Information 36. Erlangen: Gymnasialpädagogische Materialstelle der Evangelisch-Lutherische Kirche in Bayern.

"'Gott und Mensch in der Ethik': Zum Gegenstand ethischen Nachdenkens in evangelischer Perspektive." In *Nach Ethik fragen: Beiträge zur Werte-Diskussion, zu Fragen ethischer Orientierung und "Moralerziehung", zum "Gegenstand ethischen Nachdenkens,"* edited by Karl Friedrich Haag, 95–112. Arbeitshilfe für den evangelischen Religionsunterricht 127. Erlangen: Gymnasialpädagogische Materialstelle der Evangelisch-Lutherische Kirche in Bayern.

2004

"Güter oder Werte." In *Im Labyrinth der Ethik: Glauben—Handeln—Pluralismus*, edited by Günter Bader, Ulrich Eibach und Hartmut Kress, 294–306. Rheinbach: CMZ.

"Leben mit Gottes Wort—Zur Praxis christlicher Ethik." In *Beim Wort nehmen: die Schrift als Zentrum für kirchliches Reden und Gestalten: Friedrich Mildenberger zum 75. Geburtstag*, edited by Michael Krug, Ruth Lödel, und Johannes Rehm, 185-97. Stuttgart: Kohlkammer.

"Perspektiven für eine ökumenische Sozialethik: Grundpositionen evangelischer Sozialethik." *Catholica: Vierteljahresschrift für Ökumenische Theologie* 58: 175-98.

"Universalitätsanspruch und prophetischer Auftrag: kritische Korrektive christlicher Ethik. Zu Selbstverständnis und Perspektiven evangelisch-theologischer Ethik." In *Ethik im Konflikt der Überzeugungen*, edited by Andreas Lob-Hüdepohl, 119–36. Studien zur theologischen Ethik 105. Freiburg, Schweiz: Academic Press Fribourg.

"Wort und Ethik: Kennzeichen seelsorgerlicher Ethik." In *Wirksames Wort: Zum reformatorischen Wortverständnis und seiner Aufnahme in der Theologie Oswald*

Bayers, edited by Johannes von Lüpke and Johannes Schwanke, 79–94. Wuppertal: Foedus-Verlag.

2005

"On the Grammar of Lutheran Ethics." In *Lutheran Ethics at the Intersections of God's One World*, edited by Karen L. Bloomquist, 27–48. Geneva: Lutheran World Federation.

Wie Geschöpfe leben: Konturen evangelischer Ethik. Ethik im theologischen Diskurs 2. Münster: LIT, 2005.

"Zur politiktheoretischen Debatte über den Multikulturalismus und ihre Grenzen." In *Differenzen anders denken: Bausteine zu einer Kulturtheorie der Transdifferenz*, edited by Lars Allolio-Näcke, Britta Kalscheuer, and Arne Manzeschke, 205–18. Frankfurt, New York: Campus.

"Forschung für den Menschen: jenseits des Erlaubten?" In *Über die Grenzen von Forschung und Wissenschaft*, edited by Gunther Wanke and Jens Kulenkampff, 37–61. Erlanger Forschungen B/28. Erlangen: Erlanger Forschungen.

"Gottes Reich: der widerständige Trost seiner Verheißung." In *Grundlinien der Dogmatik. Gerhard Sauter zum 70. Geburtstag*, edited by Ernstpeter Maurer, 287–301. Rheinbach: CMZ-Verlag.

2006

"Der Ertrag lutherisch ethischer Prinzipien im Blick auf eine theologische Wirtschaftsethik." In *Was tun? Lutherische Ethik heute*, edited by Tim Unger, 210–39. Bekenntnis 38. Hannover: Lutherisches Verlagshaus.

"Fides Quaerens Intellectum: Reflections towards an Explorative Theology." Translated by Brian Brock. *International Journal of Systematic Theology* 8, no. 1: 42–54. https://doi.org/10.1111/j.1468-2400.2006.00182.x.

"Kirchlich-politisches Zeugnis vom Frieden Gottes: Friedensethik zwischen politischer Theologie und politischer Ethik ausgehend von John Howard Yoder, Stanley Hauerwas und Oliver O'Donovan." *Ökumenische Rundschau* 55, 149–70.

"Religion im Gehirn: Zum Diskurs zwischen Theologie, Religionswissenschaft und Neurowissenschaft." *Forum TTN* 16: 37–54.

"Lasst euch eure Lebensform verändern: durch ein neues Denken." *Themenheft: Woche für das Leben*, 11–14.

"Freiheit – Gewissen – Verantwortung: Schlüsselthemen ökumenischer Ethik." *Una Sancta: Zeitschrift für die ökumenische Bewegung* 61, no. 2: 90–102.

"Die Institutionalisierung der Ethik. Oder: Das säkularisierte Priestertum." In *Institutionalisierung und Ökonomie: Der Arzt und die Utopie der Gegenwart*, edited by Burkhard Gmelin and Horst Weidinger, 33–46. Interdisziplinäre Gespräche der Nürnberger Medizinischen Gesellschaft 10. Nürnberg: Seubert.

With Karin Ulrich-Eschemann: "Ethische Bezugsfelder religiöser Friedenserziehung." In *Handbuch Friedenserziehung. Interreligiös – interkulturell – interkonfessionell*, edited by Werner Haußmann et al., 176–81. Gütersloh: Gütersloher Verlagshaus.

2007

"Ist Gott zu erforschen?" In *Gott und die Wissenschaften*, edited by Hans Jürgen Luibl, Katharina Städtler, Christian Sudermann and Karin Ulrich-Eschemann, 45–59. Evangelische Hochschuldialoge 1. Berlin: LIT.

"'Political Ethics and International Order': Introductory Remarks to an International Ethical Discourse." *Studies in Christian Ethics* 20, no. 1: 5–12. https://doi.org/10.1177/0953946806075482.

Edited with Stefan Heuser: *Political Practices and International Order: Proceedings of the Annual Conference of the Societas Ethica, Oxford 2006*. Zürich: LIT, 2007.

Wie Geschöpfe leben: Konturen evangelischer Ethik. 2nd edn. Ethik im theologischen Diskurs 2. Münster: LIT.

Brian Brock, Walter Doerfler and Hans G. Ulrich. "Genetics, Conversation and Conversion: A Discourse at the Interface of Molecular Biology and Christian Ethics." In *Theology, Disability, and the New Genetics: Why Science Needs the Church*, edited by John Swinton and Brian Brock, 146–60. London: Continuum.

2008

"Jakobs Provokation Gottes: Zur Theologie der Geschichte in ihren ethischen Konturen." In *Ein Ringen mit dem Engel: Essays, Gedichte und Bilder zur Gestalt des Jakob*, edited by Richard Riess, 91–8. Göttingen: Vandenhoeck & Ruprecht.

Gerechtigkeit—als politische Praxis, In *Prekär. Gottes Gerechtigkeit und die Moral der Menschen ; im Gespräch mit Volker Eid*, edited by Klaus Bieberstein, Hanspeter Schmitt, 160-179. Luzern: Edition Exodus.

"The Need for the Public Appearance of Religion." In *Lidenskab og stringens: festskrift til Svend Andersen*, edited by Kees van Kooten Niekerk and Ulrik Becker Nissen, 383–93. Frederiksberg: Anis.

"Gerechtigkeit: als politische Praxis." In *Prekär: Gottes Gerechtigkeit und die Moral der Menschen: im Gespräch mit Volker Eid*, edited by Klaus Bieberstein and Hanspeter Schmitt, 160–70. Luzern: Edition Exodus.

2009

"Wie Geschöpfe leben—zur narrativen Exploration im geschöpflichen Leben: Aspekte einer Ethik des Erzählens." In *Ethik und Erzählung: theologische und philosophische Beiträge zur narrativen Ethik*, edited by Marco Hofheinz, Frank Mathwig and Matthias Zeindler, 303–28. Zürich: TVZ, Theologischer Verlag Zürich.

"Kirchengeschichte und Kulturgeschichte." *Kirchliche Zeitgeschichte* 22, no. 1: 243–71. https://www.jstor.org/stable/24713088.

"Ethik lernen mit dem Vaterunser: Das Gebet als paradigmatische Praxis einer Lebensform." In *Denkraum Katechismus: Festgabe für Oswald Bayer zum 70. Geburtstag*, edited by Johannes von Lüpke and Edgar Thaidigsmann, 435–48. Tübingen: Mohr Siebeck.

Edited with Johannes Rehm: *Menschenrecht auf Arbeit? sozialethische Perspektiven*. Stuttgart: Kohlhammer. Contributions by Heinz-J. Bontrup, Hanns Christof Brennecke, Christoph Butterwegge, Friedhelm Hengsbach, Franz Prast, Franz Segbers, Hans G. Ulrich, and Gerhard Wegner.

"Kritische Hoffnung lernen. Lehrreiche Erfahrungen im Arbeitsweltpraktikum für Theologiestudierende." In *Kirchliches Handeln in der Arbeitswelt. Grundlegung—Grenzüberschreitungen—Gestaltungsfelder*, 2nd edn., edited by Johannes Rehm, Roland Pelikan, and Philip Büttner, 87–95. Nürnberg: Mabase Verlag.

"Menschliche Arbeit und die Formen der Gerechtigkeit. Sozialethische Perspektiven." In *Menschenrecht auf Arbeit? sozialethische Perspektiven*, edited by Johannes Rehm and Hans G. Ulrich, 125–52. Stuttgart: Kohlhammer.

"Anthropologie der Endlichkeit: der Beitrag psychiatrischer Krankheit, speziell der Demenzerkrankungen, zu unserem Verständnis vom Menschen." In *Ethik und Erinnerung: zur Verantwortung der Psychiatrie in Vergangenheit und Gegenwart*, edited by Ekkehardt Kumbier, Stefan J. Teipel and Sabine C. Herpertz, 109–28. Lengerich: Pabst Science Publishers. https://rsf.uni-greifswald.de/storages/uni-greifswald/fakultaet/rsf/lehrstuehle/ls-sowada/Prof-Christoph-Sowada-Ethik-und-Erinnerung.pdf.

"On Finding Our Place: Christian Ethics in God's Reality." *European Journal of Theology* 18, no. 2: 137–44.

"'Stations on the Way to Freedom': The Presence of God: The Freedom of Disciples." In *Who Am I? Bonhoeffer's Theology Through His Poetry*, edited by Bernd Wannenwetsch, 147–74. London: T & T Clark.

2010

"Understanding the Conditio Humana: New Hermeneutical, Theoretical, and Practical Perspectives in the Field of Genome-Research." In *Bonhoeffer and the*

Biosciences: An Initial Exploration, edited by Ralf K. Wüstenberg, Stefan Heuser, and Esther Hornung, 147–68. International Bonhoeffer Interpretations 3. Frankfurt am Main: Peter Lang.

"Bonhoeffer's Work: Challenging the Ethical Approach in the Field of Bioethics for a Critical Hermeneutics of Life: Shared Insights from a Multiple Dialogue." In *Bonhoeffer and the Biosciences: An Initial Exploration*, edited by Ralf K. Wüstenberg, Stefan Heuser, and Esther Hornung, 169–74. International Bonhoeffer Interpretations 3. Frankfurt am Main: Peter Lang.

"'Nahe bei den Menschen—aufmerksam auf die Strukturen': Kirchliche Präsenz in der Arbeitswelt." In *Kirche und unternehmerisches Handeln: neue Perspektiven der Dialogarbeit*, edited by Johannes Rehm and Sigrid Reihs, 71–87. Stuttgart: W. Kohlhammer.

"Research on Human Life: New Demands for Moral and Ethical Discourses." In *Medicine at the Interface between Science and Ethics*, edited by Walter Doerfler, Hans G. Ulrich and Petra Böhm, 167–76. Nova Acta Leopoldina 381, 98. Halle (Saale): Deutsche Akademie der Naturforscher Leopoldina.

"Ethos (Moral-)Profile: ihre Generierung und Regenerierung im Kontext der Governanceethik." In *Behavioural business ethics: Psychologie, Neuroökonomik und Governanceethik*, ed. Josef Wieland, 199–232. Studien zur Governanceethik Band 8. Marburg: Metropolis Verlag.

With Urs Espeel: "Schuld, sühnende Praxis und ihre politische Präsenz." In *Der andere 11. September: Gesellschaft und Ethik nach dem Militärputsch in Chile*, edited by Cristian Alvarado Leyton, 224–52. Münster: Westfälisches Dampfboot.

"God's Commandments and Their Political Presence: Notes of a Tradition on the 'Ground' of Ethics." *Studies in Christian Ethics* 23, no. 1: 42–58. https://doi.org/10.1177/0953946809352999.

"Tradition und Reflexion." In *In Sprachspiele verstrickt, oder, Wie man der Fliege den Ausweg zeigt: Verflechtungen von Wissen und Können*, edited by Stefan Tolksdorf and Holm Tetens, 347–62. Berlin: De Gruyter.

"Ethische Konturen der Hoffnung und ihre Bedeutung für die Betreuung und Heilung von Kranken." In *Hoffnung und Verantwortung: Herausforderungen für die Medizin*, edited by Andreas Frewer, Florian Bruns and Wolfgang Rascher, 209–20. Jahrbuch Ethik in der Klinik 3. Würzburg: Königshausen & Neumann.

"Kirche der Freiheit, Kirche im Aufbruch: Reform als Klärungsprozess." *Kirchliche Zeitgeschichte* 23, no. 2: 482–519.

"'Sorget nicht …': Wirtschaften in Gottes Ökonomie: Unternehmensethik in theologischer Perspektive." In *Wirtschaft um des Menschen willen: Stichworte für eine erneuerte Soziale Marktwirtschaft*, edited by Johannes Rehm and Joachim Twisselmann, 178–98. Nürnberg: Mabase Verlag.

2011

"Bodily Life as Creaturely Life: The Ethical Coexistence of Human Beings with Disabilities and Its Fulfilment." *Journal of Religion, Disability & Health* 15, no. 1: 42–56. https://doi.org/10.1080/15228967.2011.539341.

"Biblische Tradition und ethische Praxis." In *Wie kommt die Bibel in die Ethik? Beiträge zu einer Grundfrage theologischer Ethik: für Prof. Dr. Wolfgang Lienemann*, edited by Marco Hofheinz, Frank Mathwig and Matthias Zeindler, 263–84. Zürich: Theologischer Verlag Zürich.

"Bitte erlauben Sie mir 'Schuld' zu sagen: Ein Begriff sucht Asyl." In *P&S: Magazin für Psychotherapie und Seelsorge*, no. 2: 33–7.

"Ethik lehren und lernen in den 'Kirchen des Südens.'" In *Kirche zwischen Theorie, Praxis und Ethik: Festschrift zum 80. Geburtstag von Karl-Wilhelm Dahm*, edited by Dieter Becker and Karl Wilhelm Dahm, 393–402. Empirie und kirchliche Praxis Band 11. Frankfurt am Main: AIM-Verlagshaus.

"Wortmeldung eines evangelischen Theologen." In *Aktuelle Probleme am Anfang des Lebens: Juden und Christen im Dialog mit Ethik, Recht und Medizin. Dokumentation einer gemeinsamen Fachtagung des Gesprächskreises "Juden und Christen" beim Zentralkomitee der Deutschen Katholiken (ZdK)*, edited by Hanspeter Heinz and Werner Trutwin. 59–67. München.

With Walter Beltz and Wolf Krötke: "Good Works." In *Religion Past and Present*. Leiden: Brill, 2011. https://referenceworks.brillonline.com/entries/religion-past-and-present/good-works-COM_09149#.

With Matthias Heesch, Michael Klöcker, Walter M. Sprondel, Volker Drehsen, and Eilert Herms. "Vocation." In *Religion Past and Present*. Leiden: Brill. https://referenceworks.brillonline.com/entries/religion-past-and-present/vocation-COM_01823#.

2012

"Explorative Ethik." In *Urteilen lernen: Grundlegung und Kontexte ethischer Urteilsbildung*, edited by Ingrid Schoberth, 41–59. Vandenhoeck & Ruprecht, 2012.

"Fehler machen: aber richtig! Praxis des Glaubens Teil 3: Der Biss in den Apfel: Von versagen und neu anfangen." *Sonntagsblatt*, no. 3.

"The Future of Ethics within the Reformation Heritage." *Studies in Christian Ethics* 25, no. 2: 174–80. https://doi.org/10.1177/0953946811435381.

2013

"Menschenrechte und die Praxis der Gerechtigkeit. Zur Diskussion um christliche Impulse für eine Ethik der Menschenrechte." In *Menschenrechte. Vier Vorträge*, edited by Karl Möseneder, 75–107. Erlanger Universitätstage Amberg 2012. Erlanger Forschungen, Reihe A, Geisteswissenschaften, 128. Erlangen.

"Karl Barths Darstellung Theologischer Ethik Forum Für Die Gegenwärtige Verständigung Über Ethik Im Englischsprachigen Kontext." *Theologische Literaturzeitung* 138, no. 3: 279–94. http://www.thlz.com/artikel/15906/?inhalt =heft%3D2013_3%23r6.

"Gottes Ebenbild und die Bedeutung von Menschenwürde in der christlichen Ethik." Romanian: "Chipul lui Dumnizeu si semnificatja demnitatii umane in etica crestina." In *"Was ist der Mensch?" "Ce este omul?" Theologische Anthropologie: ein lutherisch-orthodoxer Dialog. Antropologia teologica: un dialog ortodox-luteran*, edited by Metropolit Serafim, Hermann Schoenauer and Jürgen Henkel, 151–65 (166–81). Bonn: Schiller Verlag.

"Ethos als Zeugnis: Konturen christlichen Lebens mit Gott in der 'Welt' bei Stanley Hauerwas und Karl Barth." *Zeitschrift für dialektische Theologie* 29, no. 2: 50–73.

"Zur Dringlichkeit des Barth'schen Paradigmas theologischer Ethik heute." *Zeitschrift für Dialektische Theologie* 29, no. 2: 73–103.

2014

"Sinn und Geschmack für Gottes Willen." In *Urteilen lernen II. Ästhetische, politische und eschatologische Perspektiven im interdisziplinären Diskurs*, edited by Ingrid Schoberth, 41–68. Göttingen: Vandenhoeck & Ruprecht.

"Zur Wahrnehmung von Verantwortung: 'Verantwortung' in der gegenwärtigen evangelisch-theologischen Diskussion." In *Kein Mensch, der der Verantwortung entgehen könnte: Verantwortungsethik in theologischer, philosophischer und religionswissenschaftlicher Perspektive*, edited by Jürgen Boomgaarden and Martin Leiner, 27–66. Freiburg im Breisgau: Verlag Herder.

"Theologie als kritisches Zeugnis: Response zum Vortrag von Edgar Thaidigsmann und weitere Perspektiven zum Thema 'Versöhnung von Reformation und Moderne.'" In *Über das Zusammenleben in einer Welt: Grenzüberschreitende Anstöße Hans Joachim Iwands*, edited by Christian J. Neddens, Gerard Cornelius den Hertog, Michael Hüttenhoff und Wolfgang Kraus, 117–28. Gütersloh: Gütersloher Verlagshaus.

"Freundschaft: als sozialethische Kategorie?" In *Freundschaft: Zur Aktualität eines traditionsreichen Begriffs*, edited by Marco Hofheinz, Frank Mathwig and Matthias Zeindler, 209–43. Zürich: Theologischer Verlag Zürich.

"Ökumenische Ethik als kirchliche Ethik: Anmerkungen zu einem gemeinsamen Weg." In *Aus Liebe zu Gott: im Dienst an den Menschen: Spirituelle, pastorale und ökumenische Dimensionen der Moraltheologie: Festschrift für Herbert Schlögel*, edited by Gunter M. Prüller-Jagenteufel and Kerstin Schlögl-Flierl, 299–306. Münster: Aschendorff.

2015

Edited with Ulrich Duchrow: *Befreiung vom Mammon: Liberation from Mammon. Die Reformation radikalisieren. Radicalizing Reformation 2.* Münster: LIT.

"Mensch werden als Gottes Subjekt." In *Befreiung vom Mammon. Liberation from Mammon*, edited by Ulrich Duchrow and Hans G. Ulrich, 213–28. Münster: LIT.

"The Ways of Discernment." In *The Authority of the Gospel: Essays in Moral and Political Theology in Honor of Oliver O'Donovan*, edited by Robert Song and Brent Waters, 179–95. Grand Rapids, Mich.: Eerdmans.

"Theological Perspectives for a Human Economy at Its Limits and within Its Limits." In *Theology and Economics: A Christian Vision of the Common Good*, edited by Jeremy Kidwell and Sean Doherty, 165–82. New York: Palgrave Macmillan. https://doi.org/10.1057/9781137536518_12.

"God's Story and Bioethics: The Christian Witness to The Reconciled World." *Christian Bioethics* 21, no. 3: 303–33. https://doi.org/10.1093/cb/cbv011.

"Sich der kritischen Verständigung aussetzen: Zum Verhältnis von ethischer Theorie und ethischer Praxis." In *Theologische Sozialethik als Anleitung zur eigenständigen Urteilsbildung: Martin Honecker zum 80. Geburtstag*, edited by Jürgen Hübner, 69–82. Stuttgart: Kohlhammer.

2016

"The Messianic Contours of Evangelical Ethics." In *The Freedom of a Christian Ethicist: The Future of a Reformation Legacy*, edited by Brian Brock and Michael G. Mawson, 39–63. London: Bloomsbury.

"Menschenrechte und christliche Tradition: Evangelische Aspekte." In *Christentum und Menschenrechte in Europa*, edited by Vasilios N. Makrides, Jennifer Wasmuth and Stefan Kube, 183–90. Frankfurt: Peter Lang GmbH.

"Witness to God's Presence: Learning with Disabled People." In *Knowing, Being Known, and the Mystery of God: Essays in Honor of Professor Hans Reinders, Teacher, Friend, and Disciple*, edited by Bill Gaventa and Erik de Jongh, 71–80. Amsterdam: VU University Press.

Coeditor with Karen L. Bloomquist and Craig L. Nessan: *Radicalizing Reformation: Perspectives from North America. Die Reformation radikalisieren 6.* Wien: LIT, 2016.

"Tradition und Diskurstheorie." In *Interdisziplinäre Traditionstheorie: Motive und Dimensionen*, edited by Blahoslav Fajmon and Jaroslav Vokoun, 61–90. Studien zur Traditionstheorie 12. Wien: LIT

"Biogenetik und Traditionsbildung." In *Interdisziplinäre Traditionstheorie: Motive und Dimensionen*, edited by Blahoslav Fajmon and Jaroslav Vokoun, 195–214. Studien zur Traditionstheorie 12. Wien: LIT.

2017

"Die Befreiung von Schuld in Gottes Geschichte—und die Ethik der Vergebung." In *Schuld und Freiheit: Festgabe für Gerard Cornelis den Hertog*, edited by Arnold Huijgen, Cees-Jan Smits and Eberhard Lempp, 45–68. Dortmunder Beiträge zu Theologie und Religionspädagogik. Münster: LIT.

"Zur Hermeneutik der Bekenntnisse: Impulse von George A. Lindbecks *The Nature of Doctrine. Religion and Theology in a Postliberal Age* (1984)—*Christliche Lehre als Grammatik des Glaubens. Religion und Theologie im postliberalen Zeitalter* (1994)." In *Neuere reformierte Bekenntnisse im Fokus: Studien zu ihrer Entstehung und Geltung*, edited by Maren Bienert, Marco Hofheinz, and Carsten Jochum-Bortfeld, 131–57. Reformiert 2. Zürich: Theologischer Verlag Zürich.

"Ökumenischer Konsens in der Ethik—ein fälliges Zeugnis." In *Catholica* 71, no. 4: 261–77.

Coeditor with Andreas Frewer, Lutz Bergemann, and Caroline Hack: *Die kosmopolitische Klinik: Globalisierung und kultursensible Medizin*. Jahrbuch Ethik in der Klinik 10. Würzburg: Königshausen & Neumann.

Review: Razum, Oliver et al., *Global Health: Gesundheit und Gerechtigkeit*. In *Die kosmopolitische Klinik: Globalisierung und kultursensible Medizin*, edited by Andreas Frewer, Lutz Bergemann, Caroline Hack and Hans G. Ulrich, 349–57. Würzburg: Königshausen & Neumann.

Coeditor with Ulrich Duchrow, *Religionen für Gerechtigkeit in Palästina—Israel: Jenseits von Luthers Feindbildern*. Die Reformation radikalisieren Band 7. Berlin: LIT.

2018

"Entrusted for Creaturely Life within God's Story: The Ethos of Adoption in Theological Perspective." In *A Graceful Embrace: Theological Reflections on Adopting Children*, edited by John Swinton and Brian Brock, 69–86. Leiden: E.J. Brill.

"Mercy: The Messianic Practice." In *Mercy: Theories, Concepts, Practices*, edited by Hans Schaeffer, Gerard Cornelis den Hertog and Stefan Paas, 7–30. Ethik im theologischen Diskurs. Berlin: LIT.

"Social Practices of Peace—Against the Loss of Reality: The Christian Witness as a Critical Resource for Peace-making and Peacebuilding." In *The Present "Just Peace/Just War" Debate: Two Discussions or One?* edited by Ad de Bruijne and Gerard Cornelis den Hertog, 128–50. Beihefte zur Ökumenischen Rundschau 121. Leipzig: Evangelische Verlagsanstalt.

"Doch noch Utopie: der ethische Zugriff auf die Wirtschaft." In *Evangelische Wirtschaftsethik—wohin?* edited by Arne Manzeschke, 313–30. Berlin, Münster: LIT.

"Karl Barths Ethik: Rückblick und Ausblick." In *Karl Barths Theologie der Krise heute: Transfer-Versuche zum 50. Todestag*, edited by Werner Thiede, 157–72. Leipzig: Evangelische Verlagsanstalt.

"Vaterunser: 'Tischgebet' um den Fortgang von Gottes Geschichte mit uns." In *Der Sonntagsgottesdienst: Ein Gang durch die Liturgie*, edited by Peter Bubmann and Alexander Deeg, 216–21. Göttingen: Vandenhoeck & Ruprecht, 2018.

"'Alles braucht seine Zeit . . .': Stichworte und Leitfragen zum Ethiktag des Universitätsklinikums." In *Entschleunigung als Therapie? Zeit für Achtsamkeit in der Medizin*, edited by Andreas Frewer, Lutz Bergemann, and Caroline Hack, 19–33. Jahrbuch Ethik in der Klinik 11. Würzburg: Königshausen & Neumann.

"Verständigung, Verstehen, Urteilen im evangelischen Kontext am Beispiel der 'Bioethik.'" In *Ethik als Kunst der Lebensführung: Festschrift für Friedrich Heckmann* edited by Verena Begemann, Christiane Burbach, and Dieter Weber, 119–33. Stuttgart: Kohlhammer Verlag.

2019

"The Form of Ethical Life." In *The Oxford Handbook of Dietrich Bonhoeffer*, edited by Michael Mawson and Philip G. Ziegler, 289–305. Oxford: Oxford University Press.

"Tradieren von Ethik im Gottesdienst: Traditio activa—vita passiva." In *Die Tradierung von Ethik im Gottesdienst: Symposiumsbeiträge zu Ehren von Hans G. Ulrich*, edited by Marco Hofheinz, 267–300. Ethik im theologischen Diskurs 26. Berlin: LIT.

2020

"Tradition als Widerstand. Zu einer Ethik kritisch-messianischer Hoffnung." In *Traditionstheorie im Gespräch mit den Wissenschaften*, edited by Jaroslav Vokoun, 21–41. Studien zur Traditionstheorie 13. Berlin: LIT.

Wie Geschöpfe leben: Konturen evangelischer Ethik. 3rd edn. Ethik im theologischen Diskurs 2. Münster: LIT.

BIBLIOGRAPHY

Acemoglu, Daron and Robinson, James A., *Why Nations Fail: The Origins of Power, Prosperity and Poverty* (New York: Crown Publishers, 2012).
Adorno, Theodor W., *Minima Moralia: Reflexionen aus dem beschädigten Leben* (Frankfurt: Suhrkamp, 1994).
Adriaanse, Hendrik Johan, "Conditio humana," in *Religion Past and Present* (Leiden: Brill). http://dx.doi.org/10.1163/1877-5888_rpp_SIM_03187, accessed June 23, 2020.
Agamben, Giorgio, *Homo Sacer: Sovereign Power and Bare Life* (Stanford: Stanford University Press, 1998).
Agamben, Giorgio, *The Kingdom and the Glory: For a Theological Genealogy of Economy and Government*, Homo Sacer II, 2, trans. Lorenzo Chiesa and Matteo Mandarini (Stanford: Stanford University Press, 2011).
Agamben, Giorgio, *The Time that Remains: A Commentary on the Letter to the Romans*, trans. Patricia Dailey (Stanford: Stanford University Press, 2005).
Andeersen, Vagn, *Transformationen Gottes: Abwandlungen des Begriffs des Unbedingten in der Moderne* (Aarhus: Aarhus Universitetsforlag, 2008).
Arendt, Hannah, *The Human Condition*, 2nd edn. (Chicago: University of Chicago Press, 1958), 176–8.
Arendt, Hannah, "The Perplexities of the Rights of Man," in *The Origins of Totalitarianism (1951)* (New York: Harcourt, 1968), 290–302.
Arendt, Hannah, "Tradition and the Modern Age," in *Between Past and Future: Eight Exercises in Political Thought* (New York: Penguin Books, 1977), 17–40.
Arendt, Hannah, "Understanding and Politics," in *Essays in Understanding 1930–1954*, ed. Jerome Kohn (New York: Harcourt, Brace & Co., 1994), 307–27.
Arendt, Hannah, "Verstehen und Politik," in *Zwischen Vergangenheit und Zukunft*, ed. Ursula Ludz (München: Piper, 1994), 110–27.
Arendt, Hannah, Das Urteilen: *Texte zu Kants Politischer Philosophie* (Munich: Piper, 1985).
Arendt, Hannah, *Lectures on Kant's Political Philosophy* (Chicago: University of Chicago Press, 1989).
Arendt, Hannah, *The Origins of Totalitarianism* (Orlando: Harcourt, 1968).
Arendt, Hannah, *Thinking: Life of the Mind*, vol. 1 (London: Seeker & Warburg, 1978).
Arendt, Hannah, "Understanding and Politics," *Partisan Review* 20, no. 4 (1953): 377–92.
Austermann, Frank, *Von der Tora zum Nomos: Untersuchungen zur Übersetzungsweise und Interpretation im Septuaginta-Psalter* (Göttingen: Vandenhoeck & Ruprecht, 2003).
Babich, Babette E., ed., *Habermas, Nietzsche, and Critical Theory* (Amherst, NY: Humanity Books, 2004).
Bader, Günter, *Assertio. Drei fortlaufende Lektüren zu Skepsis, Narrheit und Sünde bei Erasmus und Luther* (Tübingen: Mohr Siebeck, 1985).
Barth, Friederike, *Die Wirklichkeit des Guten: Dietrich Bonhoeffers "Ethik" und ihr philosophischer Hintergrund* (Tübingen: Mohr Siebeck, 2012).

Barth, Karl, "Church and State," in Karl Barth, *Community, State, and Church*, ed. Will Herberg (Gloucester, MA: Peter Smith, 1968).
Barth, Karl, *Anselm: Fides quaerens intellectum: Anselm's Proof of the Existence of God in the Context of His Theological Scheme*, trans. Ian W. Robertson (London: SCM Press, 1960).
Barth, Karl, *Church and State*, trans. G. Ronald Howe (London: SCM Press, 1939).
Barth, Karl, *Ethics* (New York: Seabury Press, 1981).
Barth, Karl, *Gebete* (Munich: Chr. Kaiser, 1963).
Barth, Karl, Gesamtausgabe. Abt. II: *Das christliche Leben—Die Kirchliche Dogmatik IV/4, Fragmente aus dem Nachlass, Vorlesung 1959-1961* (Zürich: Theologischer Verlag, 1999).
Barth, Karl, *The Humanity of God* (Louisville, KY: Westminster/John Knox Press, 1999).
Bayer, Oswald, ed., *Worship and Ethics: Lutherans and Anglicans in Dialogue*, Theologische Bibliothek Töpelmann (Berlin, New York: Walter de Gruyter, 1996).
Bayer, Oswald, *Theologie* (München: Gütersloh, 1994).
Beals, Corey, *Lévinas and the Wisdom of Love: The Question of Invisibility* (Waco, TX: Baylor University Press, 2007), 43-54.
Becker, Amy Julia, *A Good and Perfect Gift: Faith, Expectations, and a Little Girl Named Penny* (Bloomington, MN: Bethany House Publishers, 2011).
Bellah, Robert N., *Habits of the Heart: Individualism and Commitment in American Life* (Berkley: University of California Press, 1985).
Benedict XVI, "Faith, Reason and the University. Memories and Reflections," in Schall, James V., *Benedict: The Regensburg Lecture* (South Bend, Ind.: St. Augustine's Press, 2007), 130-48.
Benjamin, Walter, "The Storyteller: Reflections on the Works of Nicolai Lescov," in *Illuminations*, ed. Hannah Arendt, trans. Harry Zorn (New York: Harcourt, Brace & World, 1968), 83-107.
Bennett, Jana, *Water is Thicker than Blood: An Augustinian Theology of Marriage and Singleness* (Oxford: Oxford University Press, 2008).
Bertau, Ingeborg, *Unterscheidung der Geister: Studien zur theologischen Semantik der gotischen Paulusbriefe* (Erlangen: Palm & Enke, 1987).
Besier, Gerhard and Sauter, Gerhard, *Wie Christen ihre Schuld bekennen* (Göttingen: Vandenhoeck & Ruprecht, 1985).
Biagioli, Mario, *Galileo Courtier: The Practice of Science in the Culture of Absolutism* (Chicago: University of Chicago Press, 1993).
Biggar, Nigel, "Karl Barth and Germain Grisez on the Human Good: An Ecumenical Rapprochement," in *The Revival of Natural Law*, ed. Biggar and Rufus Black (Aldershot: Ashgate, 2001), 164-83.
Biggar, Nigel, *Behaving in Public: How to Do Christian Ethics* (Grand Rapids: Eerdmans, 2011).
Biggar, Nigel, *The Hastening that Waits: Karl Barth's Ethics* (Oxford: Clarendon Press, 1995).
Bird, Michael F., Hengel, Martin, and Maston, Jason, *Earliest Christian History: History, Literature, and Theology. Essays from the Tyndale Fellowship in Honor of Martin Hengel* (Tübingen: Mohr Siebeck, 2012).
Blackburn, Vivienne, *Dietrich Bonhoeffer and Simone Weil: A Study in Christian Responsiveness* (Oxford; New York: Peter Lang, 2004), 93-104.

Bloch, Ernst, *Das Prinzip Hoffnung*, 3 vols. (Frankfurt am Main: Suhrkamp, 1954–59).
Bloch, Ernst, *The Principle of Hope*, trans. Neville Plaice, Stephen Plaice, and Paul Knight, 3 vols. (Cambridge: MIT Press, 1986).
Blond, Philip, "There is No Wealth but Life," in *Crisis and Recovery: Ethics, Economics and Justice*, ed. Rowan Williams and Larry Elliott (London: Palgrave Macmillan, 2010), 77–99.
Bloomquist, Karen L., ed., *Lutheran Ethics at the Intersections of God's One World* (Geneva: Lutheran World Federation, 2005).
Blumenberg, Hans, *Die Lesbarkeit der Welt* (Frankfurt: Suhrkamp, 1979).
Böckenförde, Ernst-Wolfgang, *Staat, Gesellschaft, Freiheit: Studien zur Staatstheorie und zum Verfassungsrecht* (Frankfurt: Suhrkamp, 1976).
Bockmuehl, Markus N. A., *Jewish Law in Gentile Churches: Halakhah and the Beginning of Christian Public Ethics* (Grand Rapids: Baker Academic, 2003).
Bonhoeffer, Dietrich, "Thy Kingdom Come: The Prayer of the Church for the Kingdom of God on Earth," in *A Testament to Freedom*, rev. edn., ed. Geffrey B. Kelly and F. Burton Nelson (San Francisco: HarperCollins, 1995), 92.
Bonhoeffer, Dietrich, "What is a Christian Ethic?" in *A Testament to Freedom: The Essential Writings of Dietrich Bonhoeffer*, rev. edn., ed. Geffrey B. Kelly and F. Burton Nelson (San Francisco: HarperCollins, 1995).
Bonhoeffer, Dietrich, *Letters and Papers from Prison*, ed. Eberhard Bethge, Enlarged edition (London: SCM Press, 1953).
Braun, Hermann, "Nietzsche Im Theologischen Diskurs," *Theologische Rundschau* 75, no. 1 (2010): 1–44.
Brennan, Patrick McKinley, *The Vocation of the Child* (Grand Rapids: Eerdmans, 2008).
Brock, Brian, *Christian Ethics in a Technological Age* (Grand Rapids: Eerdmans, 2010).
Brock, Brian, "Government, University and the Category of Religion," in *Religion as a Category of Governance and Sovereignty*, ed. Trevor Stack, Naomi R. Goldberg and Timothy Fitzgerald (Leiden: Brill, 2015), 228–47.
Brock, Brian, "Seeing through the Data Shadow: Communing with the Saints in a Surveillance Society," *Surveillance and Religion* 16, no. 4 (2018): 533–45.
Brock, Brian, *Singing the Ethos of God: On the Place of Scripture in Christian Ethics* (Grand Rapids: Eerdmans, 2007).
Brock, Brian, "Why the Estates? Hans Ulrich's Recovery of an Unpopular Notion," *Studies in Christian Ethics* 20, no. 2 (2007): 179–202.
Brock, Brian, *Wondrously Wounded: Theology, Disability, and the Body of Christ* (Waco, TX: Baylor University Press, 2019).
Brock, Brian and Brock, Stephanie, "Being Disabled in the New World of Genetic Testing: A Snapshot of Shifting Landscapes," in *Theology, Disability, And the New Genetics: Why Science Needs the Church*, ed. John Swinton and Brian Brock (London: T&T Clark, 2007), 29–43.
Brock, Brian, Doerfler, Walter and Ulrich, Hans G., "Genetics, Conversation and Conversation: A Discourse at the Interface of Molecular Biology and Christian Ethics," in *Theology, Disability, and the New Genetics: Why Science Needs the Church*, ed. John Swinton and Brian Brock (London: T&T Clark, 2007), 146–60.
Brock, Brian and Wannenwetsch, Bernd, *The Malady of the Christian Body: A Theological Exposition of Paul's First Letter to the Corinthians*, vol. 1 (Eugene, OR: Cascade Books, 2016).

Brock, Brian and Wannenwetsch, Bernd, *The Therapy of the Christian Body: A Theological Exposition of Paul's First Letter to the Corinthians*, vol. 2 (Eugene, OR: Cascade Books, 2018).

Bröckling, Ulrich, "Human Economy, Human Capital: A Critique of Biopolitical Economy," in *Governmentality: Current Issues and Future Challenges*, ed. Ulrich Bröckling, Susanne Krasmann, and Thomas Lemke (New York: Routledge, 2012), 247–68.

Brueggemann, Walter, "Vulnerable Children, Divine Passion, and Human Obligation," in *The Child in Christian Thought*, ed. Bunge, 399–422.

Brumlik, Micha, *Messianisches Licht und Menschenwürde: Politische Theorie aus Quellen jüdischer Tradition* (Baden-Baden: Nomos, 2013).

Bruni, Luigino and Zamagni, Stefano, *Civil Economy: Efficiency, Equity, Public Happiness* (Bern: Peter Lang, 2007).

Buber, Martin, "The Election of Israel: A Biblical Inquiry," in *The Martin Buber Reader*, ed. Asher D. Biemann (New York: Palgrave Macmillan, 2002).

Buber, Martin, *Between Man and Man*, trans. Ronald Gregor-Smith (New York: Routledge, 2002).

Buber, Martin, *Good and Evil, Two Interpretations: I. Right and Wrong* (Upper Saddle River, NJ: Prentice Hall, 1997).

Buber, Martin, *I and Thou* (New York: Charles Scribner's Sons, 1970).

Buber, Martin, *Right and Wrong: An Interpretation of Some Psalms* (London: SCM Press, 1952).

Buber, Martin and Rosenzweig, Franz, *Die Schrift und ihre Verdeutschung* (Heidelberg: Schneider, 1954).

Bubner, Rüdiger, *Dialektik als Topik. Bausteine zu einer lebensweltlichen Theorie der Rationalität* (Frankfurt/M.: Suhrkamp, 1990).

Bunge, Marcia J., ed., *The Child in Christian Thought* (Grand Rapids: Eerdmans, 2001).

Burke, Trevor J., *Adopted into God's Family: Exploring a Pauline Metaphor*, New Studies in Biblical Theology 22 (Downers Grove: InterVarsity Press, 2006).

Casper, Bernhard, "Geisel für den anderen—Vielleicht nur ein harter Name für Liebe": Emmanuel Lévinas und seine Hermeneutik diachronen "Da"-Seins. (Freiburg im Breisgau: Alber, 2020).

Clark, Adam C. and Mawson, Michael G., "Introduction: Ontology and Ethics in Bonhoeffer Scholarship," in *Ontology and Ethics: Bonhoeffer and Contemporary Scholarship*, ed. Adam C. Clark, Michael G. Mawson, and Clifford J. Green (Eugene: Pickwick Publications, 2013).

Clark, Adam C. and Mawson, Michael, G., eds., *Ontology and Ethics: Bonhoeffer and Contemporary Scholarship* (Eugene: Wipf & Stock Publishers, 2013).

Dabrock, Peter, "Responding to 'Wirklichkeit': Reclaiming Bonhoeffer's Approach to Theological Ethics between Mystery and Formation of the World," in *Mysteries in the Theology of Dietrich Bonhoeffer: A Copenhagen Bonhoeffer Symposium*, ed. Kirsten Busch Nielsen, Ulrik Nissen, and Christiane Tietz (Göttingen: Vandenhoeck & Ruprecht, 2007), 49–80.

Deibl, Jakob, *Menschwerdung und Schwächung: Annäherung an ein Gespräch mit Gianni Vattimo* (Vienna: Vienna University Press, 2013), 48–52.

Deines, Roland, "Pre-Existence, Incarnation and Messianic Self-Understanding in the Work of Martin Hengel," in *Earliest Christian History: History, Literature, and Theology. Essays from the Tyndale Fellowship in Honor of Martin Hengel*, ed. Martin Hengel, Michael F. Bird and Jason Maston (Tübingen: Mohr Siebeck, 2012), 75–116.

DeJonge, Michael P., "God's Being Is in Time: Bonhoeffer's Theological Appropriation of Heidegger," in *Dietrich Bonhoeffer Jahrbuch 5 / Yearbook 5*, ed. Clifford J. Green, Kirsten Busch Nielsen, and Christiane Tietz (Gütersloher Verlagshaus, 2012), 123–37.
DeJonge, Michael P., *Bonhoeffer's Reception of Luther* (Oxford: Oxford University Press, 2017).
Delkeskamp-Hayes, Corinna, "Morality in a Postmodern, Post-Christian World: Engelhardt's Diagnosis and Therapy," in *At the Roots of Christian Bioethics: Critical Essays on the Thought of H. Tristram Engelhardt, Jr.*, ed. Ana Smith Iltis and Mark J. Cherry (Salem, MA: M&M Scrivener Press, 2010), 59.
den Hertog, Gerard C., "Urteilen als Kernaufgabe des bürgerlichen Regiments: Ein Vergleich von Johannes Calvin und Oliver O'Donovan," in *Kirche, Theologie und Politik im reformierten Protestantismus: Vorträge der 8. Emder Tagung zur Geschichte des reformierten Protestantismus*, ed. Matthias Freudenberg and Georg Plasger (Neukirchen: Neukirchener Theologie, 2011), 37–50.
Derrida, Jacques, *Adieu to Emmanuel Levinas* (Stanford: Stanford University Press, 1999).
Doerfler, Walter, "*Conditio humana* as Viewed by a Geneticist," in *Theology, Disability, and the New Genetics: Why Science Needs the Church*, ed. John Swinton and Brian Brock, (London: T&T Clark, 2007), 117–31.
Dramm, Sabine, *Dietrich Bonhoeffer: An Introduction to His Thought*, trans. Thomas Rice (Peabody, MA: Hendrickson, 2007).
Duina, Francesco, *Institutions and the Economy* (Cambridge: Polity Press, 2011)
Dumas, Andre, *Dietrich Bonhoeffer: Theologian of Reality* (London: SCM Press, 1971).
Elliston, Clark J., *Dietrich Bonhoeffer and the Ethical Self: Christology, Ethics, and Formation* (Minneapolis, MN: Augsburg Fortress, Publishers, 2016).
Engelhardt, Tristram H., ed., *Bioethics Critically Reconsidered: Having Second Thoughts* (Dordrecht: Springer, 2012).
Engelhardt, Tristram H., "Bioethics in the Post-modern World: Belief in Secularity," in *Duties to Others*, ed. Courtney S. Campbell and B. Andrew Lustig (Dordrecht: Kluwer Academic, 1994), 235–45.
Engelhardt, Tristram H., *Foundations of Christian Bioethics* (Lisse, Netherlands: Swets & Zeitlinger, 2000).
Engelhardt, Tristram H., "*Sittlichkeit* and Post-modernity: A Hegelian Reconsideration of the State," in *Hegel Reconsidered: Beyond Metaphysics and the Authoritarian State*, ed. Engelhardt and Terry P. Pinkard (Dordrecht: Kluwer Academic, 1994), 211–24.
Evangelisches Gottesdienstbuch: Agende für die Union Evangelischer Kirchen in der EKD (UEK) und für die Vereinigte Evangelisch-Lutherische Kirche Deutschlands (VELKD) (Leipzig: Luther-Verlag; Evangelische Verlagsanstalt, 2018, 2020).
Feil, Ernst, *Die Theologie Dietrich Bonhoeffers: Hermeneutik—Christologie Weltverständnis* (Berlin: LIT, 2006).
Feyerabend, Paul K., *Wider den Methodenzwang: Skizze einer anarchistischen Erkenntnistheorie* (Frankfurt am Main: Suhrkamp, 1976).
Fisher, Jaimey, *Disciplining Germany: Youth, Reeducation, and Reconstruction after the Second World War* (Detroit: Wayne State University Press, 2010), 129–55.
Forst, Rainer, *Das Recht auf Rechtfertigung: Elemente einer konstruktivistischen Theorie der Gerechtigkeit* (Frankfurt: Suhrkamp, 2007).
Foucault, Michel, *The Birth of Biopolitics*, trans. Graham Burchell (Basingstoke: Palgrave Macmillan, 2008).
Frewer, Andreas, Bruns, Florian and Rascher, Wolfgang, eds., *Hoffnung und Verantwortung Herausforderungen für die Medizin* (Würzburg: Königshausen & Neumann, 2010).

Frick, Peter, *Understanding Bonhoeffer* (Tübingen: Mohr Siebeck, 2017), 120–1.
Geertz, Clifford, *The Interpretation of Cultures: Selected Essays* (New York: Basic Books, 1973).
Gordon, Peter, *Rosenzweig and Heidegger: Between Judaism and German Philosophy* (Los Angeles: California University Press, 2003).
Green, Clifford, "Book Review: Interpreting Bonhoeffer: Reality or Phraseology?," *Journal of Religion* 55, no. 2 (1975): 270–5.
Gregor, Brian E., "Shame and the Other: Bonhoeffer and Levinas on Human Dignity and Ethical Responsibility," in *Ontology and Ethics: Bonhoeffer and Contemporary Scholarship*, ed. Adam C. Clark, Michael G. Mawson, and Clifford J. Green (Eugene: Pickwick Publications, 2013), 72–85.
Gregor, Brian E., "The Transcendence of the Person: Bonhoeffer as a Resource for Phenomenology of Religion and Ethics," in *Early Phenomenology: Metaphysics, Ethics, and the Philosophy of Religion*, ed. Brian Harding and Michael R. Kelly (London: Bloomsbury Academic, 2016), 181–212.
Greiner, Dorothea, *Segen und Segnen: Eine systematisch-theologische Grundlegung* (Stuttgart: Kohlhammer, 1998).
Groenewald, André J., "Interpreting the Theology of Barth in Light of Nietzsche's Dictum 'God Is Dead,'" *HTS Teologiese Studies/Theological Studies* 63, no. 4 (2007): 1429–45.
Grünwaldt, Klaus, Tietz, Christiane, and Hahn, Udo, eds., *Bonhoeffer und Luther: Zentrale Themen ihrer Theologie* (Hannover: Amt der VELKD, 2007).
Habermas, Jürgen, *Between Naturalism and Religion: Philosophical Essays* (Cambridge, MA: Polity Press, 2008).
Habermas, Jürgen, "Faith and Knowledge," in *The Future of Human Nature*, trans. William Rehg, Max Pensky, and Hella Beister (Cambridge: Polity Press, 2003), 101–15.
Habermas, Jürgen, *The Future of Human Nature* (Oxford: Blackwell, 2003).
Habermas, Jürgen, "'Reasonable' Versus 'True,' or the Morality of Worldviews," in *Habermas and Rawls: Disputing the Political*, ed. James Gordon Finlayson and Fabian Freyenhagen (Oxford: Taylor and Francis, 2011), 92–116.
Habermas, Jürgen, *The Structural Transformation of the Public Sphere: An Inquiry into a Category of Bourgeois Society* (Cambridge: Polity Press, 2002).
Habermas, Jürgen and Benedict XVI, *Dialectics of Secularization: On Reason and Religion* (San Francisco: Ignatius Press, 2007).
Habermas, Jürgen and Blazek, John R., "The Idea of the University: Learning Processes," *New German Critique* 41 (1987): 3–22.
Hall, Amy Laura, *Conceiving Parenthood: American Protestantism and the Spirit of Reproduction* (Grand Rapids: Eerdmans, 2008).
Hamilton, Nadine, *Dietrich Bonhoeffers Hermeneutik der Responsivität: ein Kapitel Schriftlehre im Anschluss an Schöpfung und Fall* (Göttingen: Vandenhoeck & Ruprecht, 2016), 312–16.
Handelman, Susan A., *Fragments of Redemption: Jewish Thought and Literary Theory in Benjamin, Scholem, and Levinas*, Jewish Literature and Culture (Bloomington: Indiana University Press, 2010).
Hart, David Bentley, *Theological Territories: A David Bentley Hart Digest* (Notre Dame, IN: University of Notre Dame Press, 2020).
Hauerwas, Stanley, *A Community of Character: Toward a Constructive Christian Social Ethic* (Notre Dame: University of Notre Dame Press, 1981).
Hauerwas, Stanley, "'The Friend': Reflections on Friendship and Freedom," in *Who Am I? Bonhoeffer's Theology Through his Poetry*, ed. Bernd Wannenwetsch (London: T&T Clark, 2009), 91–114.

Hauerwas, Stanley, "Dietrich Bonhoeffer—Ekklesiologie als Politik," in *Kirche, Ethik—Öffentlichkeit: Christliche Ethik in der Herausforderung* (Münster: LIT, 2002), 99–130.

Hauerwas, Stanley, "Not all Peace is Peace: Why Christians Cannot Make Peace with Engelhardt's Peace," in *Reading Engelhardt: Essays on the Thought of H. Tristram Engelhardt, Jr.*, ed. Brendan Minogue, Gabriel Palmer-Fernández, and James E. Reagan (Dordrecht: Kluwer, 1997), 31–44.

Hauerwas, Stanley, "On the Ethics of Writing on the Ethics of Care of the Mentally Handicapped," in *Critical Reflections on Stanley Hauerwas' Theology of Disability: Disabling Society, Enabling Theology*, ed. John Swinton (Binghamton: Haworth Pastoral Press, 2004), 13–26.

Hauerwas, Stanley, *Performing the Faith: Bonhoeffer and the Practice of Nonviolence* (Grand Rapids: Brazos Press, 2004).

Hauerwas, Stanley, "The Sanctified Body: Why Perfection Does Not Require a 'Self,'" in *Embodied Holiness: Toward a Corporate Theology of Spiritual Growth*, ed. Samuel M. Powell and Michael E. Lodahl (Downers Grove, IL: InterVarsity Press, 1999), 19–38.

Hauerwas, Stanley, *Suffering Presence* (Notre Dame: University of Notre Dame Press, 1986).

Hauerwas, Stanley, *With the Grain of the Universe: The Church's Witness and Natural Theology* (Grand Rapids: Brazos Press, 2001).

Haynes, Stephen R., *The Bonhoeffer Phenomenon: Portraits of a Protestant Saint* (Minneapolis: Fortress Press, 2004).

Heidegger, Martin, *Nietzsche*, vols 1 and 2, ed. and trans. David Farrell Krell (New York: HarperCollins, 1991).

Heidegger, Martin, "Phenomenology and Theology (1927)," in *Pathmarks*, ed. William McNeill (Cambridge: Cambridge University Press, 1998), 39–62.

Heidegger, Martin, *What is Called Thinking?* (New York: Perennial Library, 1968).

Hell, Julia, "Katechon: Carl Schmitt's Imperial Theology and the Ruins of the Future," *Germanic Review* 84, no. 4 (2009): 283–326.

Heuser, Stefan, "The Cost of Citizenship: Disciple and Citizen in Bonhoeffer's Political Ethics," *Studies in Christian Ethics* 18, no. 3 (2005): 49–69.

Heuser, Stefan, *Instrumente des Guten* (Erlangen: Habilitationsschrift, 2009).

Higginson, Richard, *Faith, Hope and the Global Economy: A Power for Good* (Nottingham: Inter-Varsity Press, 2012).

Hill, Emily Beth, *Marketing and Christian Proclamation in Theological Perspective* (Lanham, MD: Lexington/Fortress Academic, 2021).

Hofheinz, Marco, Mathwig, Frank, and Zeindler, Matthias, eds., *Freundschaft: Zur Aktualität eines traditionsreichen Begriffs* (Zürich: TVZ Theologischer Verlag Zürich, 2014).

Hogrebe, Wolfram, *Sehnsucht und Erkenntnis* (Erlangen/Jena: Zweigniederlassung der Unibuch Erlangen-Jena OHG, 1994).

Honneth, Axel, *The Pathologies of Individual Freedom: Hegel's Social Theory*, trans. Ladislaus Löb (Princeton: Princeton University Press, 2010).

Honneth, Axel, *The Struggle for Recognition: The Moral Grammar of Social Conflicts*. Reprinted (Cambridge: Polity Press, 2005).

Huber, Wolfgang, Petzold, Ernst, and Sundermeier, Theo, eds., *Implizite Axiome. Tiefenstrukturen des Denkens und Handelns* (München: Gütersloh, 1990).

Hubig, Christoph, ed., *Unterwegs zur Wissensgesellschaft. Grundlagen-Trends-Probleme* (Berlin: Sigma, 2000).

Hütter, Reinhard, *Suffering Divine Things: Theology as Church Practice*, trans. Douglas Stott (Grand Rapids: Eerdmans, 2000).

Iwand, Hans Joachim, *Kirche und Gesellschaft*, Nachgelassene Werke 1 (Gütersloh: Gütersloher Verlagshaus, 1998).
Iwand, Hans Joachim, *The Righteousness of Faith According to Luther*, ed. Virgil F. Thompson, trans. Randi H. Lundell, Introduction by Gregory A. Walter ed. (Eugene: Wipf & Stock, 2008).
Jackson, Timothy P., ed., *The Morality of Adoption: Social-psychological, Theological, and Legal Perspectives* (Grand Rapids: Eerdmans, 2005).
Jacob, Benno, *The First Book of the Bible: Genesis* (Jersey City, NJ: KTAV, 1974).
Jasper, Gotthard, *Paul Althaus (1888-1966): Professor, Prediger und Patriot in seiner Zeit* (Göttingen: Vandenhoeck & Ruprecht, 2013).
Johnston, Adrian, *Badiou, Žižek, and Political Transformation: The Cadence of Change* (Evanston: Northwestern University Press, 2009).
Jonas, Hans, *The Gnostic Religion: The Message of the Alien God and the Beginnings of Christianity*, 2nd rev. edn. (Boston: Beacon Press, 1958).
Jonas, Hans, "Heidegger and Theology," *The Review of Metaphysics* 18, no. 2 (1964): 207-33.
Jonas, Hans, *The Imperative of Responsibility: In Search of an Ethics for the Technological Age* (Chicago: University of Chicago Press, 1984).
Jüngel, Eberhard, *God as Mystery of the World. On the Foundation of the Theology of the Crucified One in the Dispute Between Theism and Atheism*, trans. Darrell L. Gruder (Edinburgh: T&T Clark, 1983).
Kampowski, Stephan, *A Greater Freedom: Biotechnology, Love, and Human Destiny: In Dialogue with Hans Jonas and Jürgen Habermas* (Eugene: Pickwick, 2013).
Kant, Immanuel, *Grounding for the Metaphysics of Morals*, trans. James W. Ellington, 3rd edn. (Indianapolis: Hackett, 1993).
Käsemann, Ernst, "The Beginnings of Christian Theology," in *New Testament Questions of Today*, trans. W. J. S. L. Montague (London: SCM Press 1969), 82-107.
Käsemann, Ernst, "On the Subject of Primitive Christian Apocalyptic," in *New Testament Questions of Today*, trans. W. J. Montague (London: SCM Press, 1969), 108-37.
Kavka, Martin, "Lévinas' Accounts of Messianism," in *The Oxford Handbook of Lévinas*, ed. Michael L. Morgan (Oxford: Oxford University Press, 2019), 360-82.
Keller, Evelyn Fox, *Making Sense of Life: Explaining Biological Development with Models, Metaphors, and Machines* (Cambridge, MA: Harvard University Press, 2003).
Kreck, Walter, *Die Zukunft des Gekommenen: Grundprobleme der Eschatologie* (München: Chr. Kaiser, 1961).
Krüger, Hans-Peter, "Die condition humaine des Abendlandes," *Deutsche Zeitschrift für Philosophie* 55, no. 4 (2007): 605-26.
Kuhn, Thomas S., *The Structure of Scientific Revolutions*, 3rd edn. (Chicago: University of Chicago Press, 1996).
Latour, Bruno, *We Have Never Been Modern* (Cambridge, MA: Harvard University Press, 1993).
Lienemann, Wolfgang, *Gerechtigkeit* (Göttingen: Vandenhoeck & Ruprecht, 1995).
Liess, Kathrin, Der Weg des Lebens: Psalm *16 und das Lebens- und Todesverständnis der Individualpsalmen*, Forschungen zum Alten Testament, Reihe 2, 5 (Tübingen: Mohr Siebeck, 2004).
Lindbeck, George A., *The Nature of Doctrine: Religion and Theology in a Postliberal Age* (Philadelphia: Westminster Press, 1984).
Link, Christian, *Die Spur des Namens: Wege zur Erkenntnis Gottes und zur Erfahrung der Schöpfung* (Neukirchen: Neukirchener, 1997).

Lorenz, Kuno, "Forschung," in *Enzyklopädie Philosophie und Wissenschaftstheorie*, vol. 1 (Mannheim: Metzler, 1980), 663–4.
Löwith, Karl, *From Hegel to Nietzsche: The Revolution in Nineteenth Century Thought*, trans. David E. Green (New York: Holt, Reinhart and Winston, 1964).
Löwith, Karl, *Heidegger: Denker in dürftiger Zeit* (Frankfurt on Main: S. Fischer, 1953).
Löwith, Karl, *Martin Heidegger and European Nihilism*, ed. Richard Wolin, trans. Gary Steiner (New York: Columbia University Press, 1995).
Löwith, Karl, *Meaning in History: The Theological Implications of the Philosophy of History* (Chicago: University of Chicago Press, 1949).
Löwith, Karl, *My Life in Germany Before and After 1933: A Report*, trans. Elizabeth King (London: Athalone Press, 1994).
Luhmann, Niklas, *Funktion der Religion* (Frankfurt: Suhrkamp, 1977).
Luhmann, Niklas, *Paradigm Lost: Über die ethische Reflexion der Moral* (Frankfurt am Main: Suhrkamp, 1990).
Luhmann, Niklas, *Rechtssoziologie* (Reinbek: Rowohlt, 1972), translated as, *A Sociological Theory of Law* (London: Routledge, 1985).
Luther, Martin, "On the Freedom of the Will (*De servo arbitrio*) 1525," in *Martin Luther, Ausgewählte Werke*, ed. H. H. Borcherdt and Georg Merz (München: Kaiser, 1962), 11–14.
Lyotard, Jean-Francois, *The Postmodern Condition: A Report on Knowledge*, trans. Geoff Bennington and Brian Massumi (Manchester: Manchester University Press, 1984).
Macaskill, Grant, *Living in Union with Christ: Paul's Gospel and Christian Moral Identity* (Grand Rapids: Baker Academic, 2019).
MacIntyre, Alasdair C., *Three Rival Versions of Moral Enquiry: Encyclopedia, Genealogy, and Tradition* (Notre Dame: University of Notre Dame Press, 1990).
MacIntyre, Alasdair C., *Dependent Rational Animals: Why Human Beings Need the Virtues* (Chicago: Open Court 1999).
Malabou, Catherine, *The Heidegger Change: On the Fantastic in Philosophy*, trans. and ed. Peter Skafish (Albany: State University of New York Press, 2011).
Manow, Philip, *Religion und Sozialstaat: Die konfessionellen Grundlagen europäischer Wohlfahrtsstaatsregime* (Frankfurt am Main: Campus-Verlag, 2008),
Marchart, Oliver Marchart, *Die politische Differenz: Zum Denken des Politischen bei Nancy, Lefort, Badiou, Laclau und Agamben* (Berlin: Suhrkamp, 2010), 224–5.
Marion, Jean-Luc, *God without Being: Hors-Texte* (Chicago: University of Chicago Press, 1995).
Martin, David, *On Secularization: Towards a Revised General Theory* (Aldershot: Ashgate, 2005).
Martyn, Louis J., "A Personal Word about Ernst Käsemann," in *Apocalyptic and the Future of Theology: With and Beyond J. Louis Martyn*, ed. Joshua B. Davis and Douglas Harink (Eugene: Cascade Books, 2012), xiii–xv.
Martyn, Louis J., *Galatians*, The Anchor Yale Bible (London: Yale University Press, 1997).
McKenny, Gerald P., *Biotechnology, Human Nature, and Christian Ethics* (New York: Cambridge University Press, 2018).
McKenny, Gerald P., "Desire for the Transcendent: Engelhardt and Christian Ethics," in *At the Roots of Christian Bioethics: Critical Essays on the Thought of H. Tristram Engelhardt, Jr.*, ed. Ana Smith Iltis and Mark J. Cherry (Salem, MA: M&M Scrivener Press, 2010).
McKenny, Gerald P., *To Relieve the Human Condition: Bioethics, Technology, and the Body* (Albany: State University of New York Press, 1997).

Meadows, Donella H. et al., *The Limits to Growth: A Report for the Club of Rome's Project on the Predicament of Mankind* (New York: Universe Books, 1972).

Meadows, Donella H., Meadows, Dennis L., and Randers, Jørgen, *The Limits to Growth: The 30-Year Update* (White River Junction, VT: Chelsea Green Publishers, 2004).

Meadows, Donella H., Meadows, Dennis L., and Randers, Jørgen, *Beyond the Limits* (White River Junction, VT: Chelsea Green Publishing, 1992).

Meeks, Douglas, *God the Economist: The Doctrine of God and Political Economy* (Minneapolis: Fortress Press, 1990).

Meeks, Douglas M., *God the Economist: The Doctrine of God and Political Economy* (Minneapolis, MN: Fortress Press; Simon Pulse edition, 2000).

Mendes-Flohr, Paul, "Gnostic Anxieties: Jewish Intellectuals and Weimar Neo-Marcionism," *Modern Theology* 35, no. 1 (2019): 71–80.

Mildenberger, Friedrich, *Biblische Dogmatik. Eine biblische Theologie in dogmatischer Perspektive*, 3 vols. (Stuttgart: Kohlhammer, 1991–93).

Miller, Patrick D., "Divine Command/Divine Law: A Biblical Perspective," *Studies in Christian Ethics* 23, no. 1 (February 1, 2010): 21–34.

Mittelstraß, Jürgen, *Die Häuser des Wissens. Wissenschaftstheoretische Studien* (Frankfurt/M.: Suhrkamp, 1998).

Moberly, Jennifer, *The Virtue of Bonhoeffer's Ethics: A Study of Dietrich Bonhoeffer's Ethics in Relation to Virtue Ethics* (Eugene: Pickwick Publications, 2013).

Moltmann, Jürgen, *The Way of Jesus Christ* (London: SCM Press, 1990).

Moltmann, Jürgen, *Theologie der Hoffnung: Untersuchungen zur Begründung und zu den Konsequenzen einer christlichen Eschatologie* (München: C. Kaiser, 1965).

Moltmann, Jürgen, *Theology of Hope: On the Ground and Implications of Christian Eschatology*, trans. James W. Leitch (New York: Harper & Row, 1967).

Müller, Jan-Werner, *A Dangerous Mind: Carl Schmitt in Post-War European Thought* (New Haven: Yale University Press, 2003).

Nedelsky, Jennifer and Beiner, Ronald, eds., *Judgment, Imagination, and Politics: Themes from Kant and Arendt* (Lanham: Rowan & Littlefield, 2001).

Neumann-Held, Eva M., "Erzwingen die biologischen Wissenschaften ein neues Menschenbild?" in *Natur—Technik—Kultur: Philosophie im interdisziplinären Dialog*, ed. Brigitte Falkenburg (Paderborn: Mentis, 2007), 143–62.

Nietzsche, Friedrich, *Erkenntnistheoretische Schriften* (Frankfurt am Main: Suhrkamp, 1968).

Nietzsche, Friedrich, *On the Genealogy of Morality* (Cambridge: Cambridge University Press, 1994).

Nietzsche, Friedrich, *On the Genealogy of Morals*, trans. Douglas Smith (Oxford: Oxford University Press, 1996).

Niklaus, Peter, "Karl Barth als Leser und Interpret Nietzsches," *Zeitschrift für Neuere Theologiegeschichte/Journal for the History of Modern Theology* 1, no. 2 (1994): 251–64.

Novak, David, "Karl Barth on Divine Command: A Jewish Response," in *Talking with Christians: Musings of a Jewish Theologian* (Grand Rapids: Eerdmans, 2005), 127–45.

Novak, David, *Covenantal Rights: A Study in Jewish Political Theory* (Princeton: Princeton University Press, 2000).

O'Regan, Cyril, "Balthasar and the Eclipse of Nietzsche," *Modern Theology* 35, no. 1 (2019): 103–21.

O'Donovan, Oliver, "Die Hände Gottes," in *"Sagen, was Sache ist": Versuche explorativer Ethik*, ed. Gerard den Hertog, Stefan Heuser, Marco Hofheinz, and Bernd Wannenwetsch (Leipzig: Evangelische Verlagsanstalt, 2018), 177–93.

O'Donovan, Oliver, "History and Politics in the Book of Revelation," in *Bonds of Imperfection: Christian Politics, Past and Present*, ed. Oliver O'Donovan and Joan Lockwood O'Donovan (Grand Rapids: Eerdmans, 2004), 25–47.
O'Donovan, Oliver, *The Ways of Judgment* (Grand Rapids: Eerdmans, 2005).
Oetinger, Friedrich Christoph, *Biblisches und emblematisches Wörterbuch* (Hildesheim: Georg Olms Verlagsbuchhandlung, 1969).
Ostrom, Elinor, *Understanding Institutional Diversity* (Princeton: Princeton University Press, 2009).
Ott, Heinrich, *Reality and Faith: The Theological Legacy of Dietrich Bonhoeffer* (Philadelphia: Fortress Press, 1972).
Oyama, Susan, Griffiths, Paul E., and Gray, Russell D., eds., *Cycles of Contingency: Developmental Systems and Evolution* (Cambridge, MA: MIT, 2001).
Parsons, Susan Frank, "Accounting for Hope: Feminist Theology as Fundamental Theology," in *Challenging Women's Orthodoxies in the Context of Faith*, ed. Susan F. Parsons (Aldershot: Ashgate, 2000), 1–20.
Pascal, Blaise, *Pensées*, trans. A. J. Krailsheimer (London: Penguin, 1966).
Pitkin, Barbara, "The Heritage of the Lord: Children in the Theology of John Calvin," in *The Child in Christian Thought*, ed. Bunge, 160–93.
Plant, Stephen J., "'In the Sphere of the Familiar': Heidegger and Bonhoeffer," in *Bonhoeffer's Intellectual Formation: Theology and Philosophy in His Thought*, ed. Peter Frick (Tübingen: Mohr Siebeck, 2008).
Plessner, Helmuth, *Die Stufen des Organischen und der Mensch*, Gesammelte Schriften vol. 4 (Baden-Baden: Nomos Verlag, 2003).
Prather, Scott, *Christ, Power and Mammon: Karl Barth and John Howard Yoder in Dialogue* (London: Bloomsbury T&T Clark, 2013).
Raddatz, Wolfgang, Sauter, Gerhard, and Ulrich, Hans G., "Verstehen," in *Praktisch Theologisches* Handbuch, ed. Gert Otto, 2nd edn. (Hamburg: Furche-Verlag 1975), 602–33.
Rasmussen, Larry L., *Dietrich Bonhoeffer: Reality and Resistance* (Louisville: Westminster John Knox Press, 2005).
Rasmussen, Larry L. and Bethge, Renate, *Dietrich Bonhoeffer: His Significance for North Americans* (Minneapolis: Fortress Press, 1990).
Rasmusson, Arne, *The Church as Polis: From Political Theology to Theological Politics as Exemplified by Jürgen Moltmann and Stanley Hauerwas* (Notre Dame: University of Notre Dame Press, 1995).
Rawls, John, *A Theory of Justice* (Cambridge, MA: Belknap Press of Harvard University Press, 1971).
Rasmusson, Arne, *Political Liberalism* (New York: Columbia University Press, 2005).
Rehmann-Sutter, Christoph, "Genetics, Embodiment and Identity," in *On Human Nature: Anthropological, Biological, and Philosophical Foundations*, ed. Armin Grunwald, Mathias Gutmann, and Eva M. Neumann-Held (Berlin: Springer, 2002), 23–50.
Rehmann-Sutter, Christoph, "Limits of Bioethics," in *Bioethics in Cultural Contexts: Reflections on Methods and Finitude*, ed. Marcus Düwell, Christoph Rehmann-Sutter, and Dietmar Mieth (Springer: Dordrecht 2006).
Reinders, Hans S., *Disability, Providence, and Ethics: Bridging Gaps, Transforming Lives* (Waco: Baylor University Press, 2014).
Reinders, Hans S., *The Future of the Disabled in Liberal Society: An Ethical Analysis* (Notre Dame: University of Notre Dame Press, 2000).

Reinders, Hans S., *Receiving the Gift of Friendship: Profound Disability, Theological Anthropology, and Ethics* (Grand Rapids: Eerdmans, 2008).
Richter, Silvia, "Zur Verbindung Von Messianismus und Eschatologie im Denken Emmanuel Lévinas," *Zeitschrift für Religions- und Geistesgeschichte* 68, no. 1 (2016): 57–69.
Ritschl, Dietrich, "Nachgedanken zum 'Story'-Konzept: Die Koagulation Wiedererzählter 'Stories' auf dem Weg zu differierenden theologischen Lehren," *Theologische Zeitschrift* 61 (2005): 78–91.
Ritschl, Dietrich, *Memory and Hope: An Inquiry Concerning the Presence of Christ* (New York: Macmillan, 1967).
Rosenzweig, Franz, "Das Formgeheimnis der biblischen Erzählung," in Franz Rosenzweig and Karl Thieme, *Die Schrift: Aufsätze, Übertragungen und Briefe* (Königstein: Jüdischer Verlag Athenaeum, 1984).
Rosenzweig, Franz, "The New Thinking," in *Franz Rosenzweig's "The New Thinking,"* ed. Alan Udoff and Barbara Galli (New York: Syracuse University Press, 1999).
Sauter, Gerhard, "Die Begründung theologischer Aussagen—wissenshaftstheoretisch gesehen," in *Erwartung und Erfahrung* (München: Gütersloh, 1972).
Rosenzweig, Franz, *Das verborgene Leben: Eine theologische Anthropologie* (Munich: Gütersloher Verlagshaus, 2011).
Rosenzweig, Franz, *What Dare We Hope? Reconsidering Eschatology* (Harrisburg: Trinity Press International, 1999).
Rosenzweig, Franz, *Zukunft und Verheissung: das Problem der Zukunft in der gegenwärtigen theologischen und philosophischen Diskussion* (Zürich: Theologischer Verlag, 1965).
Schmitz, Florian, *"Nachfolge": zur Theologie Dietrich Bonhoeffers* (Göttingen: Vandenhoeck & Ruprecht, 2013).
Schneider-Flume, Gunda, *Die politische Theologie Emanuel Hirschs* (Frankfurt: Peter Lang, 1971).
Scholem, Gershom, *The Messianic Idea in Judaism and Other Essays on Jewish Spirituality* (New York: Schocken Books, 1971).
Schweiker, William, "Theological Ethics and the Question of Humanism," *The Journal of Religion* 83, no. 4 (2003): 539–61.
Schwöbel, Christoph, *Die Religion des Zauberers: Theologisches in den großen Romanen Thomas Manns* (Tübingen: Mohr Siebeck, 2008).
Sedlacek, Tomas, *Economics of Good and Evil: The Quest for Economic Meaning from Gilgamesh to Wall Street* (Oxford: Oxford University Press, 2011).
Segbers, Franz, *Die Hausordnung der Tora: Biblische Impulse für eine theologische Wirtschaftsethik*, 3rd edn. (Darmstadt: Wissenschaftliche Buchgesellschaft, 2002).
Seim, Turid Karlsen and Økland, Jorunn, eds., *Metamorphoses: Resurrection, Body, and Transformative Practices in Early Christianity*. Ekstasis v. 1 (Berlin, New York: W. de Gruyter, 2009).
Skully, Jackie Leach, "Admitting All Variations? Postmodernism and Genetic Normality," in *Ethics of the Body: Postconventional Challenges*, ed. Margrit Shildrick and Roxanne Mykitiuk (Cambridge, MA: MIT, 2005), 49–68.
Sloterdijk, Peter, *You Must Change Your Life: On Anthropotechnics* (Oxford, Cambridge: Polity Press, 2013).
Smith, Ted A., *The New Measures: A Theological History of Democratic Practice* (Cambridge: Cambridge University Press, 2007).

Spieckermann, Hermann, "God's Steadfast Love: Toward a New Conception of Old Testament Theology," *Biblica* 81, no. 3 (2000): 305–27.
Sternberger, Dolf, Storz, Gerhard and Süskind, Wilhelm E., *Aus dem Wörterbuch des Unmenschen* (Hamburg: Claassen, 1957).
Stuhlmacher, Peter, *Biblical Theology of the New Testament* (Grand Rapids: William B. Eerdmans Publishing Company, 2018).
Subramanian, G. et al., "Implications of the Human Genome for Understanding Human Biology and Medicine," *JAMA* 286 (2001): 2296–307.
Sumner, Darren O., *Karl Barth and the Incarnation: Christology and the Humility of God* (London: Bloomsbury T&T Clark, 2016).
Swatos, William H. and Wellman, James K., eds., *The Power of Religious Publics: Staking Claims in American Society*, Religion in the Age of Transformation (Westport: Praeger, 1999).
Swinton, John, *Finding Jesus in the Storm: The Spiritual Lives of Christians with Mental Health Challenges* (Grand Rapids: Eerdmans, 2020).
Taubes, Jacob, "Theology and Political Theory," in *From Cult to Culture: Fragments Toward a Critique of Historical Reason*, ed. Charlotte Elsheva Fonrobert and Amir Engel (Stanford: Stanford University Press, 2010), 222–32.
Taylor, Charles, *Sources of the Self: The Making of the Modern Identity* (Cambridge: Harvard University Press, 1989).
Thaidigsmann, Edgar, "Das Urteil Gottes und der urteilende Mensch: Gerechtigkeit Gottes in Jesus Christus bei Hans Joachim Iwand," *Neue Zeitschrift Für Systematische Theologie Und Religionsphilosophie* 39, no. 3 (1997): 285–303.
Thate, Michael J., Vanhoozer, Kevin J., and Campbell, Constantine R., eds. *"In Christ" in Paul: Explorations in Paul's Theology of Union and Participation* (Tübingen: Mohr Siebeck, 2014).
"The Theological Declaration of Barmen," in *The Constitution of the Presbyterian Church (U.S.A.) Part I, Book of Confessions* (Louisville, KY: Office of the General Assembly, 1996), 309–12.
Tietz, Christiane, "Bonhoeffer on the Uses and Limits of Philosophy," in *Bonhoeffer and Continental Thought: Cruciform Philosophy*, ed. Brian E. Gregor and Jens Zimmermann (Bloomington: Indiana University Press, 2009), 31–45.
Tietz, Christiane, *Bonhoeffers Kritik der verkrümmten Vernunft: eine erkenntnistheoretische Untersuchung* (Tübingen: Mohr Siebeck, 1999), 129–31.
Track, Joachim, *Sprachkritische Untersuchungen zum christlichen Reden von Gott* (Göttingen: Vandenhoeck & Ruprecht, 1976).
Ulrich, Hans G., *Eschatologie und Ethik: die theologische Theorie der Ethik in ihrer Beziehung auf die Rede von Gott seit Friedrich Schleiermacher*, Beiträge zur evangelischen Theologie 104 (München: Kaiser, 1988).
Ulrich, Hans G., ed., *Evangelische Ethik: Diskussionsbeiträge zu ihrer Grundlegung und ihren Aufgaben* (Munich: Chr. Kaiser Verlag, 1990), 9–40.
Ulrich, Hans G., ed., *Freiheit im Leben mit Gott: Texte zur Tradition evangelischer Ethik*, (Gütersloh: Chr. Kaiser Verlag, Gütersloher Verlagshaus, 1993), 9–40.
Ulrich, Hans G., "The Form of Ethical Life," in *The Oxford Handbook of Dietrich Bonhoeffer*, ed. Philip G. Ziegler and Michael Mawson (Oxford: Oxford University Press, 2019), 289–305.
Ulrich, Hans G., "Gebet," in *Glaube und lernen* (Göttingen: Vanderhoeck & Ruprecht, 1986), 13–21.

Ulrich, Hans G., "Kapitalismus," in *Theologische Realenzyclopädie*, vol. 17 (Berlin: Walter de Gruyter, 1988), 604–19.
Ulrich, Hans G., "Metapher und Widerspruch," in *Metapher und Wirklichkeit. Die Logik der Bildhaftigkeit im Reden von Gott, Mensch and Natur; Dietrich Ritschl zum 70 Geburtstag*, ed. Reinhold Bernhardt (Göttingen: Vandenhoeck & Ruprecht, 1999).
Ulrich, Hans G., "Mercy: The Messianic Practice," in *Mercy*, ed. Gerard den Hertog, Stefan Paas and Hans Schaeffer (Münster: LIT Verlag, 2014), 7–30
Ulrich, Hans G., "On the Grammar of Lutheran Ethics," in *Lutheran Ethics at the Intersections of God's One World*, ed. Karen L. Blomquist (Geneva: Lutheran World Federation, 2005), 27–48.
Ulrich, Hans G., "Tradieren von Ethik im Gottesdienst: *Traditio activa—vita passiva*," in *Die Tradierung von Ethik im Gottesdienst: Symposiumsbeiträge zu Ehren von Ulrich, Hans G.*, ed. Marco Hofheinz with Kai-Ole Eberhardt (Berlin: Lit Verlag, 2019), 267–300.
Ulrich, Hans G., "'Volk,' 'Nation,' Bürgersein: Bemerkungen zur politischen Bildung," in *Bausteine für eine christliche Ethik: Arbeitshilfe für den evangelischen Religionsunterricht an Gymnasien*, ed. Karl Friedrich Haag (Bayern: Gymnasialpädagogischen Materialstelle der Evangelisch-Lutherischen Kirche, 1994) 3–16.
Ulrich, Hans G., *Wie Geschöpfe leben: Konturen evangelischer Ethik*, 2nd edn., Ethik im theologischen Diskurs 2 (Münster: LIT, 2007).
Ulrich, Hans G. and Heuser, Stefan, "Political Practices and International Order," in *Political Practices and International Order: Proceedings of the Annual Conference of the Societas Ethica, Oxford 2006*, ed. Stefan Heuser and Hans G. Ulrich (Berlin: Lit Verlag, 2007), 8–27.
Ulrich-Eschemann, Karin, *Biblische Geschichten und ethisches Lernen: Analysen—Beispiele—Perspektiven* (Frankfurt am Main: Lang, 1996).
Ulrich-Eschemann, Karin, *Christliche Verkündigung mit Israel: 20 Gottesdienste im Kirchenjahr* (Göttingen: Vandenhoeck & Ruprecht, 2012).
Ulrich-Eschemann, Karin, *Gerechte in der Bibel, Sünder in der Bibel: was steht geschrieben?* (Göttingen: Vandenhoeck & Ruprecht, 2008).
Ulrich-Eschemann, Karin, *Gutes predigen nach dem Vorbild Jesu: Gottesdienste zu Lebensthemen* (Göttingen: Vandenhoeck & Ruprecht, 2011).
Ulrich-Eschemann, Karin, "The Importance of Knowing Where you Come From," in *A Graceful Embrace: Theological Reflections on Adopting Children*, ed. John Swinton and Brian Brock (Leiden: Brill, 2018), 107–118.
Ulrich-Eschemann, Karin, *Leben, auch wenn wir sterben: Christliche Hoffnung lernen und lehren* (Göttingen: Vandenhoeck & Ruprecht, 2008).
Ulrich-Eschemann, Karin, *Lebensgestalt Familie—miteinander werden und leben: eine phänomenologisch-theologisch-ethische Betrachtung* (Münster: LIT, 2005).
Ulrich-Eschemann, Karin, *Vom Geborenwerden des Menschen: theologische und philosophische Erkundungen* (Münster: LIT, 2000).
Vattimo, Gianni, "Os mé: Zur Haltung des 'als ob nicht' bei Paulus und Heidegger," *Zwischen Verzückung und Verzweiflung* 2 (2001): 169–82.
Voegelin, Eric, *Science, Politics and Gnosticism: Two Essays* (New York: Regnery Publishing, 2012).
von Kellenbach, Katharina, *The Mark of Cain: Guilt and Denial in the Post-War Lives of Nazi Perpetrators* (Oxford: Oxford University Press, 2003).
von Rad, Gerhard, *Old Testament Theology* (New York: Harper, 1962–65).

von Rad, Gerhard, *Old Testament Theology*, vol. 1, *The Theology of Israel's Historical Traditions* (London: SCM Press, 1975), 371–5.
Von Rad, Gerhard, *Wisdom in Israel*, trans. James D. Martin (London: SCM Press, 1972).
Wannenwetsch, Bernd, "Angels with Clipped Wings: The Disabled as Key to the Recognition of Personhood," in *Theology, Disability, and the New Genetics*, ed. John Swinton and Brian Brock (London: T&T Clark, 2007), 182–200.
Wannenwetsch, Bernd, "The Desire of Desire: Idolatry in Late Capitalism," in *Idolatry: False Worship in the Bible, Early Judaism and Christianity*, ed. Stephen Barton (London: T&T Clark, 2007), 315–30.
Wannenwetsch, Bernd, "A Love Formed by Faith: Relating Theological Virtues in Augustine and Luther," in *The Authority of the Gospel: Explorations in Moral Theology in Honor of Oliver O'Donovan*, ed. Robert Song and Brent Waters (Grand Rapids: Eerdmans, 2015).
Wannenwetsch, Bernd, "Loving the Limit: Dietrich Bonhoeffer's Hermeneutics of Human Creatureliness and its Challenge for an Ethics of Medical Care," in *Bonhoeffer and the Biosciences: An Initial Exploration*, ed. Ralf K. Wüstenberg, Stefan Heuser, and Esther Hornung (Frankfurt am Main: Peter Lang, 2010), 89–108.
Wannenwetsch, Bernd, "Luther's Moral Theology," in *The Cambridge Companion to Martin Luther*, ed. Donald K. McKim (Cambridge: Cambridge University Press, 2003), 120–35.
Wannenwetsch, Bernd, "Owning Our Bodies? The Politics of Self-Possession and the Body of Christ (Hobbes, Locke and Paul)," *Studies in Christian Ethics* 26 (2013): 50–65.
Wannenwetsch, Bernd, "Representing the Absent in the City," in *God, Truth, and Witness: Engaging Stanley Hauerwas,* ed. L. Gregory Jones et al. (Grand Rapids: Brazos Press, 2005), 167–92.
Wannenwetsch, Bernd, "'Responsible Living' or 'Responsible Self'? Bonhoefferian Reflections on a Vexed Moral Notion," *Studies in Christian Ethics* 18, no. 3 (2005): 125–40.
Wannenwetsch, Bernd, "'Ruled by the Spirit': Hans Ulrich's Understanding of Political Existence," *Studies in Christian Ethics* 20, no. 2 (2007): 257–72.
Wannenwetsch, Bernd, *Political Worship: Ethics for Christian Citizens*, Oxford Studies in Theological Ethics (Oxford: Oxford University Press, 2004).
Waters, Brent, "Disability and the Quest of Perfection: A Moral and Theological Inquiry," in *Theology, Disability and the New Genetics: Why Science Needs the Church*, ed. John Swinton and Brian Brock (London: Continuum, 2007), 201–13.
Waters, Brent, *The Family in Christian Social and Political Thought* (Oxford: Oxford University Press 2007).
Watson, James, *The Double Helix: A Personal Account of the Discovery of the Structure of DNA* (New York: Scribner and Sons, 1998).
Webster, John, *Barth's Ethics of Reconciliation* (Cambridge: Cambridge University Press, 1995).
Wells, Samuel, *Transforming Fate into Destiny: The Theological Ethics of Stanley Hauerwas* (Carlisle: Paternoster Press, 1998).
Wieland Josef, ed., *Behavioral Business Ethics: Psychologie, Neuroökonomik und Governanceethik* (Marburg: Metropolis-Verlag, 2010).
Williams, Rowan, *Faith in the Public Square* (London: Bloomsbury, 2012).

Williams, Rowan, "The Spiritual and the Religious: Is the Territory Changing?" in *Faith in the Public Square* (London: Bloomsbury, 2012), 85–96.
Williams, Rowan, *The Wound of Knowledge: Christian Spirituality from the New Testament to St. John of the Cross* (London: Darton, Longman & Todd, 1979).
Williams, Rowan and Elliott, Larry, eds., *Crisis and Recovery: Ethics, Economics and Global Justice* (London: Palgrave Macmillan, 2010).
Wolf, Erik, *Recht des Nächsten, ein rechtstheologischer Entwurf*, 2 vols. (Frankfurt am Main: Klostermann, 1958).
Wolf, Ernst, "Königsherrschaft Christi," *Theologische Existenz Heute* 64 (1958): 60–1.
Wolf, Ernst, *Sozialethik: Theologische Grundlagen*, ed. Theodor Strohm, 3rd edn. (Göttingen: Vandenhoeck & Ruprecht, 1988).
Wolin, Richard, *Heidegger's Children: Hannah Arendt, Karl Löwith, Hans Jonas, and Herbert Marcuse* (Princeton: Princeton University Press, 2001).
Wood Jr., James E., "Public Religion Vis-a-Vis the Prophetic Role of Religion," in *The Power of Religious Publics*, 33–51.
Wüstenberg, Ralf K., *A Theology of Life: Dietrich Bonhoeffer's Religionless Christianity* (Grand Rapids: Eerdmans, 1998).
Wyschogrod, Michael, *The Body of Faith: God and the People of Israel* (Northvale, NJ: Jason Aronson, 1996).
Yoder, John Howard, *Body Politics: Five Practices of the Christian Community Before the Watching World* (Scottdale: Herald Press, 2001).
Zartaloudis, Thanos, *Giorgio Agamben: Power, Law and the Uses of Criticism* (New York: Routledge, 2010).
Zehnder, Markus Philipp, *Wegmetaphorik im Alten Testament: Eine semantische Untersuchung der alttestamentlichen und altorientalischen Weg-Lexeme mit besonderer Berücksichtigung ihrer metaphorischen Verwendung* (Berlin: de Gruyter, 1999).
Ziegler, Philip G., "'Completely within God's Doing': Soteriology as Meta-Ethics in the Theology of Dietrich Bonhoeffer," in *Christ, Church, and World: New Studies in Bonhoeffer's Theology and Ethics*, ed. Michael G. Mawson and Philip G. Ziegler (London: Bloomsbury T&T Clark, 2016), 101–17.
Ziegler, Philip G., "Dietrich Bonhoeffer—an Ethics of God's Apocalypse?," *Modern Theology* 23, no. 4 (2007): 579–94.
Zimmermann, Jens, *Dietrich Bonhoeffer's Christian Humanism* (Oxford: Oxford University Press, 2019).

INDEX

Acemoglu, Daron 156–7
actions, God's 32–4, 100–2
adoption 160–76
aethos 128–9, 244, 246, 247, 261
Agamben, Giorgio 40–2, 74, 144–51
Anselm of Canterbury 91–4, 199
anthropology 16
apocalyptic 27–50
Arendt, Hannah 50, 101–2, 111, 165–6, 225, 244
ars inveniendi 84–91

Barmen Declaration 27–30, 39, 43–4, 46, 261
Barth, Karl 7, 9, 15–16, 31, 34, 36, 41–3, 46, 88–94, 124, 168, 170–1, 173, 199, 237
Becker, Amy Julia 238–9
Bible. *See* Scripture
bioethics 11, 179–205
birth 49–50
Blond, Philip 157–8
body/bodies. *See* embodiment
Bonhoeffer, Dietrich 7, 9, 13, 16, 35, 38, 43–5, 51–81, 123, 153–4, 192, 200, 208, 218–9, 227, 252
Bonn, University of 8, 10
born. *See* birth
Brock, Brian 232–3
Buber, Martin 169–71, 240–1
business ethics 11, 140–59

children 160–74
    as God's heritage 167–74
church. *See* ecclesia
citizen/citizenship 118–22, 127
commandments, God's 111–39
community
    of saints 63–4
    worshipping 43–4, 124
conditio humana 21, 122–31, 167, 172, 182–90, 206–29

Confessing Church 5–6, 9–10, 16, 51
conformation 57–62
creation 17–18, 174–6
creature. *See* creation

death 52, 73, 80
deliverance 29–30, 35, 37, 39
description 216–7
determinate/determination 46–7
disabled/disability 230–66
discernment 96–108, 232, 245
discipleship 63–4
discipline 59, 61, 63, 73, 76, 79–80
discovery 91–3
Doerfler, Walter 11, 206–29

ecclesia 25–108, especially 77–8, 124
economy 140–59
education 170
embodiment 247, 251–66
Engelhardt, H. Tristram 179–205
eschatology 16–17, 23, 27–50, 172
estates 63, 129. *See also* institutions; mandates; orders; stations
ethics 220–1
    concrete 71–2
    evangelical 27–50
ethos 42–8, 60, 128–9, 158–9, 244, 246, 247, 261
evangelical 163 *See also* ethics, evangelical

faith 67–8, 89–91
fides quaerens intellectum 91–4, 199
forgiveness 102
form 51–81, 135
freedom 28–37
Friedrich Alexander University Erlangen-Nuremberg 10–11, 209
friendship 256

genealogy 143–5, 180, 184
genetics 206–29

Germany   1–16, 19–22
God, living   15. *See also* actions, God's; commandments, God's; *oikonomia*, God's; presence, God's; reality, God's; speech, God's; story, God's; Word, God's; works of God
good/goodness   217–25
Göttingen, University of   5–7
government   140–59
grammar   23, 27–37
ground of ethics   112, 137–9

Habermas, Jürgen   7, 104, 135–6, 183, 194–5
Hauerwas, Stanley   18, 43, 76, 232, 235
Heidegger, Martin   4, 13, 42, 54, 237
hermeneutic(s)   17, 72, 75, 102, 113, 128, 132, 134–5, 206–29
history   35, 185–8
Holy Spirit   29, 137–9
hope   191–200
human beings. *See conditio humana*
human nature. *See conditio humana*

indeterminate/indeterminacy   48–9
institutions   63, 123, 154. *See also* estates; mandates; orders; stations
intervention   225–7
Iwand, Hans Joachim   7, 9, 11, 43, 238

Jesus Christ   28–9, 33, 36, 41, 53, 56–62, 67, 80, 95, 166, 168, 236
John, Gospel of   67 n.57, 71, 106, 241, 243, 251, 259, 264
Jonas, Hans   4, 168, 237
judgment   97–105
justice   89–91, 97–8, 103, 121–2, 127, 164–5, 204–5

Kant, Immanuel/Kantian   13, 14 n.28, 101, 124, 162
kingdom(s)   75–7, 129, 149–50
knowledge   79

labor   153–4
law
    human   122–37
    natural   133–4

of the Spirit   137–8
Lévinas, Emmanuel   69–70, 241
life, ethical   51–81
limits   140–59, 211
Lord's Prayer. *See under* prayer
love   240–2
Löwith, Karl   3–4, 13, 35, 191
Luther, Martin   47, 124, 126–7, 132, 137–9, 145, 253–5
Lutheran/Lutheranism   21–2, 63, 68, 111–15, 129
    Lutheran-Reformed   112, 123
Lyotard, Jean-François   82

Malabou, Catherine   22 n.48, 234 n.8, 237
mandates   55, 72–8, 123, 154. *See also* estates; institutions; orders; stations
Matthew, Gospel of   46, 52, 67, 90, 106–7, 138, 154–5, 174, 181 n.7, 199, 257, 259
medical ethics. *See* bioethics
medicine   179–205
mercy   31, 50
Messianic   27–50, 150–5, 234, 237, 242–3, 260–1
modern   179–205

National Socialists   2, 5–6, 10, 14, 51, 58, 65, 78, 80–1
nature/naturalism   73–5, 217–9
Nazis. *See* National Socialists
Nietzsche, Friedrich   3, 6, 8, 16–17, 37, 95, 125, 144, 187–8

O'Donovan, Oliver   96–8, 100, 103, 107, 111
oeconomia   73–5, 177–266
oikonomia, God's   143–5
ontology, critical   54
orders   55. *See also* estates; institutions; mandates, stations
orphans   164–6

parents/parenting   173, 175
Parsons, Susan   250
participation   53–5
Pascal, Blaise   214–5, 226–7

pastors 11
Paul's letters 39–40, 149, 200. *See also* Romans 12:1–2
peace 204–5
Peterson, Erich 150–1
politia 75–7, 109–76
politics. *See politia*
prayer 43, 49, 52, 67
   Lord's Prayer 31, 52
preaching 45
presence, God's 1, 19, 34, 36, 38, 40–3, 45, 47, 52–3, 55–6, 62–3, 149–50, 230–66
promise 163, 167
Protestant 28–37, 45
providence 237
Psalms 31–2, 89, 102, 108, 145, 153, 157, 160, 164–5, 171, 213, 230, 246, 255
public 111–39

ratio. *See* reason
rationality. *See* reason
Ratzinger, Joseph 194
reality, God's 36–8, 53–6, 208, 251–66
reason 75, 84, 182–95, 199
Reformed. *See* Lutheran-Reformed *under* Lutheran/Lutheranism
Rehmann-Sutter, Christoph 211
reign. *See* kingdom, kingdoms
Reinders, Hans 230–5, 238, 240, 245, 250, 256, 262
religion 111–39
renewal of our minds 28–9, 257. *See also* Romans 12:1–2
renovation of our minds. *See* renewal of our minds
research, theological 82–96, 229
responsibility 69–71, 160–76
res publica 120–1
rights, human 164–7
Robinson, James A. 156–7
Romans 12:1–2 22, 28–9, 61–2, 78, 96, 106, 119, 181, 199, 233, 242, 245, 257

Sauter, Gerhard 7–9, 15–16
Schleiermacher, Friedrich 17, 87
Schmitt, Carl 150–1

science, scientific 82–3, 86–7, 229
scripture 30
secret 78–81
Sermon on the Mount, the (Mt. 5–7) 46, 52, 106–7, 138, 154–5, 174, 181 n.7, 259
society 115–22
soul 254–5
speech, God's 44–5
state, modern 195
state of exception 153
stations 63. *See also* estates, institutions, mandates, orders
story, God's 23, 49–50, 161, 170, 174–6, 179–205, 208, 251–66
suffering 63, 66–9, 73, 75–6, 78, 80–1
Swinton, John 263–4

teaching 170
theology, explorative 82–108
thought 56
time 23, 152–5, 243
Torah 98, 139, 166
Track, Joachim 83
transfiguring/transfiguration 22, 230–66
translocation 235–42

Ulrich-Eschemann, Karin 10
understanding 78–81, 98–100

von Rad, Gerhard 103–4, 108

Wannenwetsch, Bernd 137–8
Waters, Brent 161–2
way(s) 96–8
Williams, Rowan 146
wisdom 75, 103–8
witness 16, 180–1, 195–205, 231, 245, 248–51
Wittgenstein, Ludwig 4, 23, 90
Wolf, Ernst 5–6, 29, 123
Word, God's 15–16, 22, 37, 44–5, 90
works
   of God 161, 170
   good 47, 175, 181–2, 190, 195–9
world/worldliness 64, 130, 188–205, 234
worship 179, 201–5, 247. *See also* community, worshipping
   political 126, 128

www.ingramcontent.com/pod-product-compliance
Lightning Source LLC
Chambersburg PA
CBHW070750020526
44115CB00032B/1609